Overcoming Destructive Beliefs, Feelings, and Behaviors

ALBERT ELLIS

New Directions for
RATIONAL EMOTIVE BEHAVIOR THERAPY

Overcoming Destructive Beliefs, Feelings, and Behaviors

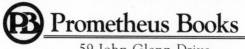
Prometheus Books

59 John Glenn Drive
Amherst, New York 14228-2197

Published 2001 by Prometheus Books

Inquiries should be addressed to
Prometheus Books
59 John Glenn Drive
Amherst, New York 14228–2197
VOICE: 716–691–0133, ext. 207
FAX: 716–564–2711
WWW.PROMETHEUSBOOKS.COM

05 04 03 02 01   5 4 3 2 1

Library of Congress Cataloging-in-Publication Data

Ellis, Albert.
    Overcoming destructive beliefs, feelings, and behaviors : new directions for rational emotive behavior therapy / Albert Ellis.
        p. cm.
    Includes bibliographical references and index.
    ISBN 1–57392–879–8 (cloth : alk. paper)
    1. Rational-emotive psychotherapy. I. Title.

RC489.R3 E455 2001
616'.89'14—dc21   00–068333

Printed in Canada on acid-free paper

For Janet L. Wolfe
Still my exceptionally helpful mate,
great collaborator,
and indispensable partner in directing the Albert Ellis Institute
for lo these thirty-seven years!

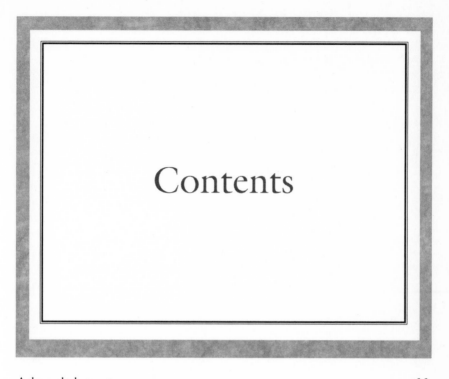

Contents

PART II: TREATING SPECIFIC EMOTIONAL AND BEHAVIORAL PROBLEMS AND SEVERE PERSONALITY DISORDERS WITH RATIONAL EMOTIVE BEHAVIOR THERAPY

Acknowledgments

My main acknowledgments for helping me learn the psychotherapy methods included in this book go, of course, to my individual and group therapy clients. They have incessantly collaborated with me in tentatively accepting my theories and practices and have experimentally used them in their own lives. Their valuable feedback on how Rational Emotive Behavior Therapy (REBT) has worked—and sometimes not worked—for them has been very important to me in formulating and revising its principles and techniques. I wish to thank them for courageously trying to implement my therapeutic suggestions and thereby aiding me in improving and adding to them.

Many of my colleagues at the Albert Ellis Institute in New York have discussed with me the theories described in this book and have helped me to develop them. These colleagues especially include Janet Wolfe, Catharine MacLaren, Kristene Doyle, and Michler Bishop, all of whom I gratefully thank. Patrice Ward and Tim Runion have been of enormous help in word-processing and editing the various revisions of this manuscript. Finally, Kevin Everett FitzMaurice, Shawn Blau, and Emmett Velten have read and critiqued sizeable portions of my manuscript and made most helpful suggestions on it.

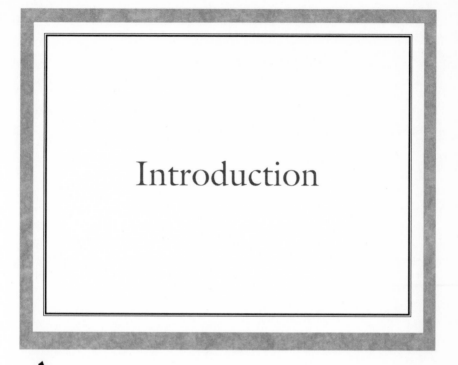

Introduction

Although Rational Emotive Behavior Therapy (REBT) basically upholds the same theory and practice that I originated in 1955, it has also changed considerably since that time. I have presented its important revisions in a series of articles published in psychological journals in the last several years, and it is about time that I summarized these articles and brought REBT fully into the twenty-first century. This is what I have done in this book.

Not only have I somewhat rewritten the articles in this book, but I have done so in the kind of writing that William James recommended a century ago and that has more recently been encouraged by Robert Zettle and William Glasser. This form of language, which can be called active language, favors verbs instead of nouns. As Zettle notes, we misuse many nouns in psychology instead of verbs and thereby create semifictional entities that Kevin Everett FitzMaurice (1997) calls "thought things." Thus we say, "My feelings upset me when panic overwhelms me when I am in closed spaces" instead of, "I upset myself by panicking when I am in closed spaces."

Glasser uses action language in his recent writings and deliberately uses verbs like "I depress" instead of "I suffer from depression." He then promotes the view that negative feelings do not occur or get maintained in their own right, but that we have a *choice* of creating or not creating them.

Agreeing with Zettle, FitzMaurice, Glasser, and other writers, I favor talking about human thinking, feeling, and behaving mainly in terms of verbs, to avoid creating thought-thinks that exist by themselves, out of our control. REBT says that we largely *can* control our emotional destiny. I emphasize this in some of the language I use in this book.

DISCLAIMER:

The information in this book is intended for instructional use only and not for self-diagnostic purposes. The theory of Rational Emotive Behavior Therapy and the practical application thereof is to be implemented by a qualified clinician or therapist. Readers who believe they are in need of psychological help are encouraged to seek the assistance of a qualified therapist specializing in REBT.

PART I

New Directions for Rational Emotive Behavior Therapy

1
Profound Therapy

HELPING PEOPLE TO
FEEL BETTER AND GET BETTER

T he goals of psychotherapy are twofold: to help clients disturb themselves less emotionally and to enable them to lead happier and more
fulfilling lives. When people seriously disturb themselves—that is, make
themselves severely panicking, depressing, or raging—and when they function poorly—that is, unduly inhibit themselves, withdraw, or act compulsively—they live less happily. Effective psychotherapy usually first tries to
reduce clients' disturbing but also teaches them the skills of leading a more
fulfilling, self-actualizing existence. Unless they achieve the first of these
goals, attaining the second one is, while not impossible, damned difficult!

If therapists focus on the first goal of therapy—to help clients minimize their
self-disturbing—they may find that helping them is more complicated than it at
first appears. As I pointed out in an article in 1972, helping clients to distress
themselves less has two important aspects: *feeling better* and *getting better*.
Feeling better is of course important because clients tend to make themselves
feel bad when they function poorly and they tend to function better when they
feel better. So their feeling better is almost crucial to successful therapy.

This chapter is adapted from "Profound Therapy: Helping People to Feel Better and Get
Better," in *The Evolution of Psychotherapy: The Fourth Conference*, ed. J. K. Zeig (Stamford,
Conn.: Zeig, Tucker, 2001). Used with permission.

Getting better is even more important. It consists of clients' (1) feeling better; (2) continuing to feel better; (3) experiencing fewer disturbing symptoms (e.g., depressing and needlessly inhibiting themselves); (4) making their distressing seldom recur; (5) knowing how to reduce it when they partly cause it; (6) using this knowledge effectively; (7) being less likely to disturb themselves when new adversities occur in their lives; (8) accepting the challenge of making themselves minimally undisturbing, even when unusually aversive events occur.

Getting better is different from feeling better and is usually much more difficult to achieve. There are many ways clients can feel better, both in and outside of therapy. Thus, on their own they can feel better by arranging interesting and enjoyable distractions, by meditation, by yoga and other kinds of relaxing, by socializing, by keeping busy, by exercising, and by using alcohol and drugs. With a therapist, they can be helped to feel better by receiving kindness, sympathy, cheeriness, optimism, acceptance, and support. There are thus almost innumerable ways, once clients disturb themselves, that they can help themselves feel better. Millions of people have used them over the centuries.

Catch-22: For the most part, these techniques of making oneself feel better work temporarily—for a few minutes, a few days, or a few months. Why? Because they are often forms of distracting: of focusing on the good instead of the bad things in life, of concentrating on anything *but* adversity, or of focusing so intently on solving a problem or playing a sport that people hardly have time to think of how poorly they are acting or may soon act.

Distracting thoughts and actions will often work very well—temporarily. They shunt aside the thinking that leads to clients' panicking and depressing and divert them from the "bad" things (against their desires and interests) that are happening, have happened, or most likely will happen. When people disturb themselves, they view these "bad" things as "awful" or "terrible" and think that they *absolutely must not* occur. It doesn't greatly matter whether their evaluation that an event is "bad" is accurate—whether most other people would see it as occurring and appraise it the way they do. They *view it* as "terrible" or "horrible" and contradictorily think that it *must not* be as bad as it is—so they greatly suffer.

Like other constructivists, I think that humans are innately problem-solvers, and have biologically or socially acquired tendencies to see and to change conditions that they consider "bad" or inimical to their basic interests. However, they are also innately predisposed to act sloppily and to fail to make several subtle distinctions between functional and dysfunctional behaving that would make them efficient constructivists. They therefore frequently wind up with inaccurate or self-destructive thinking, emoting, and behaving.

While human thinking is, as I shall contend, a prime source of cognitive-emotional dysfunctioning, I want to stress more than ever what I said in my first paper on REBT at the American Psychological Association annual convention in Chicago in 1956: thinking, emoting, and behaving are never pure, but accompany and holistically influence and integrate with each other. When we think, we also feel and behave; when we feel, we think and behave; and when we behave we think and feel. All three processes are practically never—at least for any length of time—disparate, but go together and include each other.

THE ABCS OF SELF-DISTURBING

In my early writings on REBT, I presented its ABC theory of self-disturbing. I noted that when people strongly desire to function productively and happily and when Adversities (A) interfere with their doing so, they have Beliefs (B) about their desires and about their Adversities that result in emotional and behavioral Consequences (C) that are either largely unhealthy and self-defeating or largely healthy and self-helping. I therefore said that A x B = C. I still retain this formulation, but realize that A, B, and C are more complicated than they first appear. First, they include aspects of and interact with each other; second, B, in particular, does not merely include the individual's Belief System but also includes integral aspects of his/her emotional and behavioral system.

Why? Because it just does. When we desire Adversities to improve, we think they preferably should be better and we act toward them in certain ways. Desire itself includes thinking, preferring, and behaving, not merely one of these processes. Again, thinking to a large extent includes feeling and behaving; and behaving includes thinking and feeling. In our culture, we (wrongly) view these aspects of our processing as disparate; but they practically never are (Ellis 1958, 1962).

In my recent formulations of the ABCs of human functioning, I therefore define B not merely as Believing—which, to be sure, it largely is—but as Believing-Emoting-Behaving, which I think is more accurate (Ellis 2000b, 2001). I point out that if people want to change their Irrational Bs, which lead to self-defeating Consequences, to Rational Bs, which lead to self-helping Consequences, they had better work on their Believing-Emoting-Behaving and not merely on their Believing. More specifically, they had better vigorously and forcefully (that is, emotively) change their dysfunctional Bs; and at the same time, they forcefully and persistently feel and act against them. Why? Because, once again, their Believing invariably includes their Emoting and their Behaving and is integrally related to these other aspects of their reacting to Adversities.

While holding that people think, feel, and behave dysfunctionally when they act neurotically, I am going to stress in this book their thinking or phi-losophizing as a crucial aspect of their dysfunctioning. I am particularly going to hold that when they *get* better rather than merely *feel* better, they especially emphasize the cognitive aspects of their Believing-Emoting-Behavings.

Let me consider people's feeling better rather than getting better. They often do so for two main reasons: First, they have a good relationship with their therapist, because s/he listens to them, seems interested in them, acts helpfully towards them, and gives them confidence that her/his form of therapy actually works. This shows them that they have consistent support and a true ally. They really like that. Second, they are presented with rela-tively easy and quick techniques for distracting themselves from their woes and thus acquire confidence that they will work. They are taught methods of cognitive distraction, relaxation, insight into "sources" of their problems, and other methods that show them that their therapist probably knows what will help them, and can present it in such a manner that they do not have to work too hard or too long to achieve emotional health. With these two methods, they acquire support and reassurance and relative ease about improving their condition. Of course, it is their *view* of these advantages that partly works for them rather than just their *feelings* about them. But I believe we can legitimately say that their feelings are emphasized, and that is largely why they feel better with therapy. When people are in the process of *getting* better and not just feeling better, I suggest that they (and their therapists) preferably emphasize some thinking and philosophizing aspects of their changing. Let me now consider some of people's major Irrational Believing-Emoting-Behavings (IBs) and show how they include important cognitive, emotive, and behavioral elements.

Musturbating. People have healthy, and often strong, desires, goals, and values that they raise to absolutistic musts, shoulds, demands, and necessi-ties. As Karen Horney noted, they frequently invent "the tyranny of the shoulds." "Because I strongly want to be achieving and winning significant others' approving, I *absolutely must* keep fulfilling these goals!" "Because I greatly *prefer* that people and conditions treat me considerately and fairly, they *absolutely must* do so!"

This kind of Believing-Emoting-Behaving consists of overgeneralizing, because it implies that at all times under all conditions clients must perform well and that other people and conditions must always be the way they want them to be. It is wish-fulfilling (or demand-fulfilling) because it insists that clients' strong desires are sacred and have to be fulfilled. Because they strongly prefer something to be a certain way, their very wish demands that it *must* be that way. This kind of demanding compulsively drives people toward or away from other activities that they think they must or *must not* do. It is therefore strongly emotive and behavioral.

Illogical overgeneralizing. People evaluate or rate their thinking, feeling, and behaving as "good" when it seems to help them and their social group, and as "bad" when it seems to harm them and their group. But they also overgeneralize and give global ratings to their selves, their personalities, and their essences. They illogically use what Alfred Korzybski (1933/1990) calls "The *is* of identity." "I *am* a *good person* when I do *good things*; and I *am* a *bad person* when I do *bad things.*"

This amounts to patent overgeneralizing, because the individual is making part of her behavior equal to the whole of her behavior—and even to her future behavior, which cannot be known. It is demand-fulfilling, since its main underlying goal may be to make the demander a totally good *person* who deserves to ascend to heaven in a golden chariot when she has merely done *some* personally or socially "good deeds." Unfortunately, it frequently rates the individual as totally bad or worthless when she has merely done a "bad" *deed*. Actionwise, this kind of overgeneralizing almost compels people to do "good" acting and to stay away from "bad" acting. In regard to thinking, feeling, and behaving, it puts people's entire *worth*, instead of their mere *performances*, on the line.

Awfulizing. People see certain events as bad or unfortunate for achieving their goals, and therefore healthily try to change them or make themselves somewhat happy in spite of them. But they also frequently view these happenings as *awful* and *terrible* and thereby create much *more* frustrating and painful feelings. When they awfulize, they tend to view frustrating conditions as totally bad, as bad as they could possibly be, and sometimes as more than bad. "This unfortunate condition (e.g., not getting something that I want) is *completely* bad, is the end of the world, is totally devastating, is the worst possible thing that could happen, and makes my life totally devoid of all possible pleasure!"

Awfulizing is also a form of generalizing. When they awfulize, people see something that has unfortunate qualities as *completely* bad and *not at all* beneficial; it is therefore a form of overgeneralizing. Humans take something that they wish were not happening and claim that therefore it absolutely *must not* happen and that it therefore is *horrible* if it does. It is a very "hot" cognition, as Robert Abelson indicates, and has a strong emotional quality. It practically compels people to escape and avoid "awful" conditions (and thus creates phobicizing) and to indulge in short-range hedonistic activities (such as compulsion and addiction).

Musturbating, illogical overgeneralizing, and awfulizing have been described by me (Ellis 1962, 1994, 1999, 2000b, 2001) and by many cognitive behavior therapists (Beck 1976; Burns 1999; Meichenbaum 1977). Additional dysfunctional beliefs have also been added over the years including such self-defeating irrationalities as focusing on the negative, perfectionizing, mind-reading, emotional reasoning, and either/or thinking.

I shall be contending in this paper that all of these philosophizings have explicit (conscious) or implicit (unconscious) cognitive, emotional, and behavioral elements. I therefore now call them, instead of Irrational Beliefs, Irrational Believing-Emoting-Behavings (IBs). However, because this terminology is long-winded and awkward, I shall often refer to these IBs as Irrational *Beliefs*, and hope that my readers will see that the italicized word *Beliefs* also has important emotional and behavioral aspects.

I have kept my original formulation that when people confront Adversities (A) and they experience dysfunctional emotional and behavioral Consequences (C) about these Adversities, they almost always have rational self-helping or Rational Beliefs (RBs) about these Adversities as well as self-defeating or Irrational *Beliefs* (IBs) about them. Therefore, A x B = C. This formula is the root of the theory and practice of REBT, as well as is fundamental to many other forms of cognitive-behavior therapy (CBT).

Helping Clients to Feel Better

One of my *main* points is that if, as a therapist, you want to help your clients merely to feel better rather than more thoroughly to get better, you have a choice of persuading them to use many cognitive, emotive, and behavioral techniques. Thus, if they are anxietizing or panicking, you can help them help themselves with several methods that stress cognizing, such as meditating. By intently focusing on a neutral form of thinking (such as, "om, om, om") or by focusing on observing but not evaluating their thinking, they can temporarily block their anxietizing. Or you can help them by using techniques that stress emotional-experiential processes. Thus, you can care for them, support them, and show them that you thoroughly respect them as persons and thereby encourage them to relate to you, an obviously accepting person. Or you can employ a method of therapy that stresses behavioral techniques, such as skill training in asserting themselves, which can distract them with activity, and also, perhaps, let them conditionally accept themselves because they are doing well at this training—are self-efficaciously performing it.

All these techniques stress a cognitive, emotive, or behavioral aspect, but they also include to some extent the other two aspects of human processing. Mainly, however, they help your clients to focus on other things than those that lead to their anxietizing, to feel good conditionally because you support them, and to feel good because they are doing better than they did before and can therefore (inaccurately) rate themselves as good rather than bad *people*.

These palliative techniques of helping people feel better rather than get better are quite useful because good feelings are pleasurable in their own right—certainly better than anxietizing or depressing!—and they may sometimes lead to more profound ways of getting better. Thus, some forms of meditating include philosophizing about the value of oneself and one's ability to enjoy life in spite of its many hassles. They therefore are not merely temporary and palliative, but may lead to a profound philosophical changing that includes important emotional elements (e.g., unconditional self-accepting) and behavioral elements (e.g., experimentally exposing oneself to "fearful" events until one thoroughly sees that they are by no means as "dangerous" as one first thought them to be).

HELPING CLIENTS TO GET BETTER

The problem is: How are you, if you are a therapist, to include in your armamentarium of techniques those that help your clients not only to *feel* better but also to more thoroughly *get* better? There is of course no absolute and certain answer to this question, since in individual cases any of the many cognitive, emotive, and behavioral techniques you may use with certain clients—and REBT has twenty or thirty techniques in each of these major categories that it frequently uses with some amount of success—may help them both to feel better *and* to get better. To begin, let me present a core method of therapy that is likely to lead to the kind of profound Believing-Emoting-Behaving outlook that helps clients get and stay better.

I shall start with unconditional self-acceptance (USA), an idea which I took from several existentialist thinkers, especially Paul Tillich (1953), from whom I believe Carl Rogers (1961), who was a student at Union Theological Seminary where Tillich taught, also adopted this technique. Practically all people accept themselves conditionally—particularly when they have productive and good relationship-producing thinking, feeling, and behavings. "I am succeeding at important tasks, performances, and relationships, and therefore I am a good, worthy person. But if I keep failing in these respects, I am a loser, an incompetent, and an unworthy individual."

Conditional self-acceptance (CSA) leads people to feel good about their self or their personhood in the short run, and often leads to self-efficacy that helps them function better. But it is inconsistent and shaky when raised to musturbatory and overgeneralizing extremes, as is often the case, since all humans are fallible and cannot perform well or relate well all of the time; and when they perform less adequately than they think they *should* and *must* perform, they anxietize and depress themselves. Moreover, the anxietizing and depressing that they feel when they strongly follow this self-competitive and other-competitive outlook interferes with their functioning, contributes to their performing less adequately, and often leads to more self-deprecating. What is also important, people's anxietizing and depressing are often so uncomfortable and handicapping that they devalue themselves, not merely their bad feelings, and they then create secondary symptoms (anxietizing and distressing) about their primary symptoms of anxietizing and depressing. To make their predicament still worse, they often have low frustration tolerating or discomfort anxietizing, and insist that it is not only bad to feel panicking, but that it is *awful* and *horrible*, meaning worse than it *should be*, totally bad, and so bad that they are unable to live happily at all.

Self-downing, or the feelings and behavings that go with lack of unconditional self-accepting, seem to afflict practically all humans at many times during their lives; and profound and persistent self-downing accompanies serious neuroticizing and particularly accompanies severe personality disorders and psychosis. Rating one's performances is healthy and productive. It preserves the human race and enables improved reacting to and dealing with Adversities. Virtually all humans at times accurately rate their performances as ineffectual. But then illogically, overgeneralizingly, they often rate *themselves* as incompetent, worthless individuals. Korzybski held that this self-rating tendency is innate—a function of their thinking and their language. I agree. But they also learn overgeneralized self-deprecating from their family, peers, and teachers: "You are a bad boy because you do bad things!" "You are an unlovable person where you fail to win significant people's approval." Finally, once they innately and by social learning become prone to self-downing, people practice it continually and strongly, and make it habitual. For all these reasons they have great difficulty in consistently interrupting and eliminating it and they remain victimizable by indulging in it all their lives.

How can you reduce your clients' self-deprecating and its accompanying feeling of utter worthlessness? Carl Rogers thought that therapists could do this by giving clients unconditional other-acceptance (UOA). If they thoroughly and completely accepted clients, in spite of their ineffective and sometimes socially immoral behaving, then these clients would presumably learn the value of their therapists doing so, model after the therapists themselves, and thus change their conditional to unconditional self-accepting. This sometimes happens; if you are a therapist, your clients will occasionally fully accept themselves when you unconditionally do so.

TEACHING CLIENTS UNCONDITIONAL SELF-ACCEPTING (USA)

I would say that unconditionally accepting your clients does a world of good, but rarely helps them to unconditionally accept themselves. Why? For the same reasons that conditional accepting seems useful in the first place.

People's innate and learned tendency is to quickly give themselves a good rating because they have performed well and a bad rating because they have performed badly. Perhaps this is because conditional self-accepting often leads to self-efficacy and thus helps preserve the human race and lets people give birth to progeny who also are predisposed to use it. Anyway, clients who are treated with Rogerian other-accepting therapy often turn it into conditional self-accepting. "Because Carl Rogers (or Albert Ellis) approves of me, I *therefore* am a *good person* and will continue to be one as long as he or other important people favor me." This is a really highly conditional accepting!

Back to the question: How can you help your clients (or friends) *un*conditionally accept themselves, whether or not they perform well and whether or not you or anyone else favors them? Quite a problem! The answer, I say, seems to be by clear directive teaching; and by persuading them to back up your *teaching* with experiential-feeling and by activity-oriented homework assignments. In other words, you can help clients change the thinking, emoting, and behaving that makes them accept themselves conditionally and rarely to accept themselves unconditionally.

First, let me describe some therapy methods of unconditional self-accepting (USA) that stress cognitive or philosophizing techniques. Mary, let us say, is a difficult customer who keeps accepting herself only when she performs well and is approved by significant others, and who seriously castigates herself and feels worthless when she does not achieve this kind of succeeding and relating. You, as her therapist (or friend), first give her unconditional other-accepting (UOA) and show her that you completely respect her as a person, a human individual, even though she keeps telling you about her stupid, incompetent, unloving, and perhaps immoral behaving. Your unconditionally accepting her may help her considerably, because it may show her that unconditional accepting of people who behave badly is at least possible.

Where do you go from here? First, you may employ several cognitive-oriented methods of showing Mary that she—and in fact, all people—can unconditionally accept herself. You explain what she is now doing—highly conditional self-accepting—and show her that it does not work in the long run. You show her that it leaves her always on the verge of anxietizing, which in turn creates self-inefficacy and a greater tendency to fail. You point out that she is obviously a fallible human and that therefore she cannot always succeed at important tasks, and that even if she succeeds more than others do, that won't necessarily make them approve of her the way she desires. In fact, it may lead them to become envious and less approving!

You use, in other words, what REBT calls realistic disputing of Mary's Irrational *Belief* (IB): that she *absolutely must* keep succeeding and being approved by others or else she is an inadequate, worthless individual. You show her that she often accepts other friends and relatives with their mistake-making, and can realistically accept herself with her own. No matter how well she performs and how greatly she is favored by significant others, she will always encounter people—scores of people—who do as well or better than she in these respects. By comparing herself with them, therefore, she will tend to see herself as an inferior person. Again, there are many individuals who succeed less than she does and who get less social approval, and yet they do not put themselves down as much as she does and often lead happy lives.

You also dispute Mary's self-downing logically. You show her that it cannot possibly follow that if she does poorly in some respect—say, at school or at work—she is an inept or inadequate *person*. If she thinks that failing makes her a complete failure, this is an illogical jump, because a complete failure would have to fail at everything and she surely does not do that. A complete failure would also be doomed to fail in the future—which cannot be proven.

You also dispute Mary's self-downing heuristically or practically. Where will it get her, you ask, if she continually puts her self, her entire being down for inept performances and for having poor relationships? The answer is: it will make her anxietizing and depressing. The disturbing feelings she then creates will make her less likely to succeed and to win approval of significant others. Her anxietizing and depressing will make her lead a more miserable life. The benefits of her insisting that she *absolutely must* keep succeeding are hardly worth the costs of achieving such benefits—the anxietizing she feels and the interfering with her achieving that she creates.

If you really want to help Mary reduce her self-damning and keep it minimal, preferably for the rest of her life, you had better use the cognitive-oriented technique of Disputing (D) that REBT and CBT employ. Notably, take her profound Irrational *Beliefs* (IBs) and show her that they are unrealistic and illogical, and that as long as she distinctly holds them, she has little chance of feeling the way she wants to feel and doing the things she wants to do. The most effective cognitive disputing methods to use probably fall under these three realistic, logical, and practical headings. Try to keep teaching, teaching, teaching Mary how to use them.

As you teach Mary how to use these cognitive-emphasizing methods to dispute her Irrational *Beliefs* (IBs) that accompany her self-deprecating, you also use these methods forcefully and vigorously, which gives them a distinctly emotional quality. Thus, you *strongly* show her that it is really impossible to give herself, including her future, a global rating, though it is very possible—and desirable—to rate her specific thinking, feeling, and behaving.

As you are doing this, you also show Mary how to use several emotional techniques of giving up her notions that she is a worthless individual. You can give her Rational Emotive Imagery (Maultsby 1971) where she imagines some of the stupidest and worst things she can do, allows herself to feel anxietizing and depressing, and then works on changing her feeling to the healthy negative feelings of disappointing and regretting about her *performing* but not about *herself* and her total being. You can encourage her to place her Irrational *Beliefs* on a tape cassette, to very powerfully and vigorously dispute them on this same tape, and then let friends who know about her self-downing problems listen to them, critique her disputing, and suggest how to make it more vigorous. Mary can also do role-plays in which other role-players severely put her down for her poor behavior and during which she teaches herself to stop reacting so seriously to them and to accept herself in spite of their strong criticizing. She can do reverse role-playing, where she gives one of her main Irrational *Beliefs* to a friend (such as "I *must not* act incompetently, for when I do I am a worthless person!") and has this friend hold and stubbornly hang on to it, while she tries to talk this role-playing friend out of her own convictions. She thereby gets practice in forceful disputing.

Mary can also do one of my famous shame-attacking exercises where she deliberately does something foolish or ridiculous in public—such as wearing outlandish clothes or telling someone that she just got out of the mental hospital—lets herself first feel very ashamed about people's negative reacting, and then makes herself less shameful (by disputing the notions that she is no good for meriting their criticizing) (Ellis 1973, 2000b). In encouraging Mary to do these emotion-oriented methods of combating her self-downing, you may again note (to yourself and to her) that they have definite thinking and behaving elements.

Third, you can use a number of REBT's (and other therapies') active behavioral techniques with Mary. Thus, you can have her do cognitive and emotive homework, as noted above, to repetitively practice her Disputing skills. You can encourage her to do a number of behavioral techniques, such as facing, rather than running away from, situations where she easily fails and self-deprecates. She can use principles of reinforcement to reward herself when she does her cognitive, emotional, and behaving homework, and she can sometimes penalize herself with some unpleasant activity when she fails to do it. She can make herself uncomfortably practice some anxietizing activity, such as remaining in a "risky" situation, until she becomes familiar with it, unfearing, and often enjoying. Again, as she does these behaving assignments, Mary can cognitively dispute the Irrational *Beliefs* that accompany her anxietizing or depressing about "dangerous" situations. She can vigorously and forcefully let herself experience the unhealthy feelings of "horror" and "terror" that she feels while risking them and work hard at changing these to healthy feelings of disappointment and regret.

Let me parenthetically say that if you have your own feelings, as a therapist, of anxietizing about Mary's dysfunctional thinking, feeling, and behaving, you can discover your own irrational musts and overgeneralizings, can get in touch with and change your own disturbing, and can face your own inaction if you see what it would be better to help Mary do but you still fail to confront her. If you self-deprecate about any aspect of your therapy with Mary, by all means acknowledge this, don't put yourself down for feeling it, and work against it yourself. You can then serve as a helpful model to Mary, and use this modeling—which is a cognitive-behavioral technique—to enable her to help herself (Ellis 2002).

While you are actively teaching Mary these cognitive, emotional, and behavioral methods, you can persistently show her how they all interrelate: how her thinking accompanies her feeling and behaving, how her feeling accompanies her thinking and behaving, and how her behaving accompanies her thinking and feeling. This will help her keep looking for all three elements of her self-distressing and also keep looking for the interrelationships among them.

My hypothesis is that if you help your clients, especially your seriously disturbed ones, to consciously philosophically, emotionally, and behaviorally achieve unconditional self-accepting, you can distinctly help them not only to feel better, but also get better. For practically all people strongly wish to perform well and to win significant others' approving. If they unconditionally accept themselves as "good" humans even when they are performing badly and relating poorly, they can minimize their anxietizing and depressing.

OTHER IMPORTANT THERAPY METHODS

I could now take other major Irrational *Beliefs* and show how you, as a therapist, can use other REBT methods of helping clients reconstruct these IBs and change them back to rational, self-helping preferrings. I describe them later in this book, but let me now indicate that these methods include some of the following important therapy procedures.

1. You, as a therapist, can become more acutely aware yourself of the natural tendency of all humans to slip into destructive *Beliefs*. The "nice neuroticizing individuals" often do it and the severely disturbing individuals do it more often. It is quite difficult to avoid doing it, to be aware that one is doing it, and to change and think differently even when one becomes aware of it.
2. You had better not only clearly see the prevalence of your clients' Irrational *Beliefs*, but unconditionally accept them with their frequent lapses into them. These lapses consist of unintelligent, foolish cognizings, emotings, and behavings, and it is easy, even for therapists, to put their *clients* down, rather than constructively criticizing their *performances*. For therapists, too, are human; and, as Korzybski (1933/1990) trenchantly observed, humans carelessly make themselves "unsane" by rating and evaluating themselves and others as

persons rather than evaluating what they do but *not* denigrating themselves for doing it. As a therapist, therefore, you had better work very hard and consistently at achieving and retaining UOA—unconditional other-accepting of your clients.

3. You had better actively, forcefully, and directively bring your clients' major cognizing errors to their attention and not merely wait for them to arrive at this kind of insight themselves. Some do it without therapy and some when their therapist is passive. But I would say relatively few!

4. You, as a therapist, had better see the unrealistic, illogical, and practical disadvantages of your clients indulging in their Irrational *Beliefs* and keep bringing to their attention the cost-benefit ratio of doing so. You can show them that dysfunctional behaving results quite frequently and intensively from their cognitive-emotive indulgences and that it is well worth their time and effort to reveal them and think, feel, and actively work against them.

5. You can show your clients that completely and irrevocably eliminating their dysfunctional Believing-Emoting-Behaving is probably impossible, since it is part of the human condition. But because your clients are constructivists, they can choose, with some hard work and practice, to reduce and minimize this all-too-human tendency.

6. You can show your clients how to reflect on their dysfunctioning by using specific means of improving and reorganizing their philosophizing. You can encourage them to use, more than they would naturally and easily do, several methods of disputing and revising their Irrational *Beliefs*. Clients can be taught, again, three main methods of disputing their IBs: (1) realistically dispute them to show that they do not hold water in the world of fact; (2) logically see that they are mistaken overgeneralizations; and (3) pragmatically realize that they very likely will lead to poor results for themselves and others.

Now that I have stressed the importance of you, as a therapist, showing your clients their Irrational *Beliefs* (IBs) that help make them and keep them self-disturbing, and the value of using several REBT methods of changing them to Rational *Beliefs* (RBs), let me theorize about a crucial element in your clients' getting better rather than merely feeling better. That element, I hypothesize, is their using conscious reflecting and philosophizing to help bring about ultimate automatic and unconscious changing.

In this respect, I cite the recent experiments of several psychologists on the power of unconscious processes of human thinking and behaving. Thus Bargh and Chartrand (1999), Gollwitzer (1999), and Kirsch (1999) have emphasized the importance of unconscious and automatic processes in human behavior but have also shown that what Gollwitzer (1999) calls "effective implementation intentions" help us form specific resolutions about where and how to get started in changing ourselves. If we specifically work at consciously committing ourselves to functional *Beliefs*, our automatic processes often take over and turn our conscious intending into unconscious behaving. This concept gives us a place for choice, will, and effort in constructively changing our conscious and unconscious self-defeating into self-helping functioning (Martin and Sugarman 2000).

Let me apply this idea to your clients getting better instead of merely feeling better in therapy. I say once again that getting better consists of clients recognizing their self-disturbing, reducing its symptoms (such as anxietizing about social relations), reducing related symptoms (such as other kinds of anxietizing), maintaining these healthy changes, using methods of reducing dysfunctioning again if and when they fall back to it, and finally—and perhaps most important—your clients prophylactically predicting and committing themselves to work at warding off new disturbing when some most unfortunate Adversities assail them. Along with all this, they can keep creating and striving for self-actualization and happiness-producing living. Let us assume that these goals are not utopian and are somewhat achievable.

As I have hypothesized in this chapter, if you, as a therapist, clearly recognize the *Beliefs* that lead to emotional dysfunctioning and teach clients how to acknowledge and strongly dispute these with active, persistent, cognitive, emotive, and behavioral methods, many clients will probably feel better, and a few will actually get better. But even those who temporarily get better are at risk of relapsing and having to take therapeutic steps over and over again.

ADDITIONAL METHODS OF HELPING CLIENTS TO GET BETTER

Can clients be helped to automatically and unconsciously stay better and rarely keep upsetting themselves about dire Adversities that occur in their lives? I say, yes—if they will commit themselves to "effective implementation intentions." This involves clients making the kinds of *Belief* changes I have expounded in this chapter *after* they are self-disturbing, but also involves committing themselves prophylactically to a profound self-helping philosophy (which includes feelings and actings) *before* they make themselves disturbing. Easily said, but how to do this? I suggest that clients be taught—yes, actively-directively taught—to reflect upon and do the following:

1. To be distinctly aware of the important role that their Irrational *Beliefs* contribute to their emotional dysfunctioning and possible improved functioning.

2. To recognize that they have the power to change their Irrational *Beliefs* (IBs) if they work persistently and strongly at doing so with several cognitive, emotive, and behavioral methods.

3. To realize that after a while of working at their Irrational *Beliefs*, they can turn from automatically and unconsciously dysfunctional ways of holding them to automatic and unconscious functional ways of thinking, feeling, and behaving. After a while! And after work and practice!

4. To see that they had better have strong *intentions* to change along with the *will* to change. Will *power*, as I have noted (Ellis 1999, 2000b, 2001; Ellis and Velten 1998), includes the intention, the decision, and the determination to change—and, particularly, the *action* required to do so. Will has no power without action.

5. To recognize that changing to get better as well as feel better usually involves deep, dedicated, conscious *commitment* to do so. The action required for their will *power* involves strong, persistent commitment to act and to keep acting until their changing becomes solid.

6. To see that intending, determining, and acting to change had better be taken in advance of changing, during changing, and after changing. Continuously and ongoingly!

7. To be taught that they had better work at using a cost-benefit ratio to determine whether to try to maintain or change some of their behaving and to keep calculating the personal and social advantages and disadvantages of doing so, particularly in regard to their harmful compulsing and avoiding.

8. To be shown that changing can be plotted and schemed in advance by their imagining that the worst things—like death of several family members or fatal disease to oneself—*can* happen, and by working on how they can think, feel, and do if they *did* happen. They had better imagine and plan to work through real adversities several times, until they automatically believe, feel, and prepare to act on any grim possibilities.

9. To take the *challenge* and *adventure* of creating and maintaining a profound attitude of unconditionally accepting themselves, other people, and world frustrations, no matter what occurs in life. They had better strongly, determinedly commit themselves to this challenge and adventure and make it an integral, unforgettable part of their living.

10. To acknowledge that their strong desires, preferences, and goals usually add to their life, health, and happiness, but that their escalating their desires into absolutistic and rigid musts, shoulds, demands, and necessities frequently leads them to malfunctioning.

11. To see that having an optimistic rather than a pessimistic view of themselves and their future is highly preferable, as long as they do not take this view to overoptimistic extremes (Seligman and Csikzmenthalyi 2000).

12. To see that they can think, feel, and function better if they have some central meanings, purposes, and values that they create in their lives and keep maintaining on an ongoing basis (Ellis and Harper 1961/1997; Frankl 1959).
13. To often see the stressors or Adversities of their lives humorously instead of too seriously and thereby create more functional Believing-Emoting-Behavings.
14. To give due regard to their individualistic and competitive goals and strivings, but clearly work for them within a social and societal context. Their personal and social functioning and happiness had better include helping others thrive with minimal pain and maximum happiness.

There are doubtless other ways than these in which you can help your clients (or friends) get better and stay better. But for most clients much of the time, I suggest that these are among the main ones that will work. If I am correct about this, then I again would suggest that although these methods integrally include emotional and behavioral factors, they are all highly cognitive and philosophical. For they call for you, as a therapist, to be conscious of them, to preferably use them yourself, and to persistently teach them to those of your clients who are willing to learn to use them.

Moreover, practically all these therapy suggestions include highly conscious, calculating awareness and determining. For example, point number seven, using a cost-benefit analysis to determine whether clients maintain or try to change some of their behaving, involves active considering, reflecting, and calculating. This can be helped by experiential and behavioral exercises, but it can rarely be done without conscious planning. The other therapeutic suggestions that I list also seem to require strong teaching and self-teaching by both you and your clients. But they emphasize cognizing, while including important emotional and behavioral elements.

After I had finished this chapter, I read fifteen articles in the January 2000 special issue of *American Psychologist* on positive psychology, edited by Martin Seligman and Mihalji Csikzmenthalyi (2000). In these articles many outstanding psychologists and researchers review recent studies to show what factors probably contribute significantly to positive psychology and the minimizing of cognitive-emotional-behavioral dysfunctioning. Naturally, I was interested in knowing how their findings are consistent with the fourteen main points I made about therapists teaching their clients to make themselves and keep themselves less self-disturbing. I was pleased to discover that these authorities on the psychology of human happiness largely agreed with my main therapeutic points.

Thus, they consistently agreed with my first three points: (1) that believing, emoting, and behaving all significantly and interactively contribute to positive human functioning; (2) that people are able, though with difficulty, to make themselves happier and healthier if they work persistently and strongly at doing so with several cognitive, emotive, and behavioral methods; and (3) that people who constructively work at their dysfunctional Believing-Emoting-Behavings can turn from experiencing automatic and unconscious dysfunctional ways to experiencing automatic functional ways of living. If these researchers and REBT are on the right track, people partly construct their own disturbing and can teach themselves to be less dysfunctional and happier.

My remaining points about people helping themselves emotively, cognitively, and behaviorally are also largely endorsed by the studies reported in the January 2000 issue of the *American Psychologist*. I have now suggested several aspects of therapy that will presumably help therapists actively teach their clients to feel better and, more importantly, get better. Naturally, I believe—and strongly and emotionally believe—that these hypotheses have some validity. Only considerable research will test them out. Let us see!

Shortly after I wrote this chapter, I read the Spring 2000 special issue of the *Journal of Social Issues*, edited by Ellen J. Langer and Mihnea Moldoveneau (2000) on "Mindfulness Theory and Social Issues." I saw that it included some important therapeutic ideas that I partly have neglected. Langer's concept of mindfulness, on which she has been doing considerable research since 1974, holds that people can choose to think either mindlessly or mindfully, and that when they choose the latter thought process they often achieve dramatic mental and physical changes.

Although I have strongly implied in my chapter that therapists who encourage and teach their clients to be more consciously mindful and reflective will particularly help them to get better as well as feel better, I have not stressed this point definitely enough. So now let me briefly address it.

Mindfulness, according to Ellen Langer and her collaborators, involves several highly cognitive aspects, but it also has emotional and behavioral involvements. As Langer and Moldoveanu say (2000, p. 2), it "is not a cold cognitive process. When one is actively drawing novel distinctions, the whole individual is involved."

More specifically, Langer and Moldoveanu define mindfulness in these terms:

1. "The process of drawing novel distinctions." (p. 1)
2. "Actively drawing these distinctions keeps us activated in the present." (pp. 1–2)
3. It leads to "enhanced awareness of multiple perspectives in problem solving." (p. 2)

4. It "introduces information about objects in a conditional way; using language like "I'd be" rather than the more traditional, absolute way ("it can only be"). (p. 3)

If you look closely at these definitions of mindfulness, you will see that they include several ideas that I stress in my chapter. Thus they highlight choosing to think unconventionally, to reorder one's past history and behavior in the present, to seek alternative methods of problem solving, and to stop overgeneralizing and musturbating. These are the very cognitive-emotive-behavioral processes that REBT emphasizes!

Nonetheless, Ellen Langer and her collaborators lead me to add another specific point to the fourteen recommendations to therapists in this chapter. So let me conclude with point no. 15: Therapists had better encourage and teach their clients to check their strong tendencies to automatically and habitually think, feel, and act. If clients mindfully and consciously contemplate and examine their self defeating and sociality-destroying dysfunctioning, they can appreciably contribute both to their feeling better *and* to their getting better.

SELF-HELP SUGGESTIONS

As I said in my introduction, the chapters included in this book originally were written for therapists and counselors. Some of my main books for the mental health profession, especially *Reason and Emotion in Psychotherapy* (Ellis 1962, 1994), have been very helpful to my clients and to other readers. So I shall go out of my way, at the end of each chapter of this book, to highlight how some of its main points can be specifically used for self-help purposes.

- You, like virtually all humans, probably have self-defeating or Irrational *Beliefs* (which also include Irrational Believing-Emoting-Behavings) that lead you to create dysfunctional feelings and actions. Be fully aware that you have them and that you have ability to change them to self-helping Rational *Beliefs*.
- You can change your musturbatory Irrational *Beliefs* into more rational preferential *Beliefs*—with some amount of work and practice!
- You have choice or will to change yourself, but your will *power* includes strong determination and, especially, *action*.
- To *feel better* and to *get better* requires your conscious and persistent *commitment* to do so.
- Seek pleasures and happiness today—and also tomorrow! Do cost-benefit calculations to determine if your gains, now and in the future, are too costly.
- If you can imagine some of the worst misfortunes that may occur in your

life and still make yourself sorry and frustrated but *not* panicking and depressing, you've really aided your emotional healthiness!

- Take the *challenge* and *adventure* of thinking, feeling, and acting so that you can unconditionally accept yourself, other people, and world frustrations, no matter what occurs in your life.
- See that your strong desires, preferences, goals and purposes usually add to your existence, but try not to escalate them into absolutistic and unachievable musts, shoulds, demands, and necessities.
- Take an optimistic rather than a pessimistic view of yourself and your future—as long as you do not take to unrealistic extremes.
- Try to create a vital meaning and absorbing interest in your life that you adapt from others or mainly construct for yourself. Dedicate yourself, but not rigidly, to developing and following your meaning.
- Lighten up! Take the major stressors of your life seriously but not too seriously.
- Strive, if you will, for personal, and even outstanding, achievement, but also for your community and social interests. Recognize and honor both society's contributions to your interests and your contribution to your society's interests.

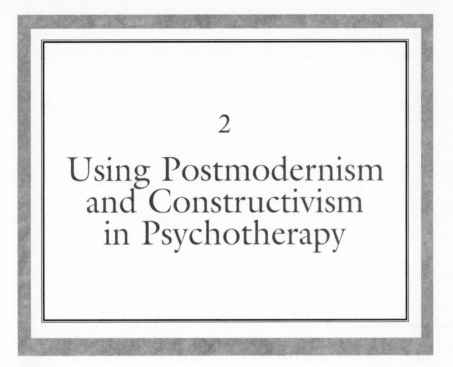

2

Using Postmodernism and Constructivism in Psychotherapy

E arl Ginter chaired a symposium at the American Counseling Association's World Conference in Pittsburgh, on April 22, 1996, "Ethical Issues in the Postmodern Era," in which Jeffrey Guterman and I appeared along with Sandra A. Rigazio-DiGilio, Don C. Locke, and Allen E. Ivy. This chapter consists of the main remarks that I made at this symposium. It continues my discussions and adds a more detailed description of the postmodern and constructivist aspects of Rational Emotive Behavior Therapy (REBT) and their application to some of the active-directive methods used in this form of counseling and psychotherapy.

POSTMODERNISM AND REBT

Although I was formerly in the logical positivist camp, I now consider myself largely a postmodernist and constructionist. Some of my main beliefs about humans and the world in which we live include the following:

This chapter is partly adapted from A. Ellis, "Postmodern Ethics for Active-Directive Couseling and Psychotherapy," *Journal of Mental Health Counseling* 19 (1997): 11–25. Used with permission.

1. Perhaps some kind of indubitable objective reality or thing in itself exists, but we seem to apprehend or know it only through our fallible, personal-social, different and changing, human perceptions. We do not have any absolute certainty about what reality is or what it will be—despite our often being strongly convinced that we do.

2. Our views of what is good or bad, what is right or wrong, what is moral or immoral are, as George Kelly (1955) pointed out, largely personal-social *constructions*. Kelly held that the identification of universal truths is an impossible task and that all ethical beliefs have a constructionist nature.

3. Although human personality has some important innate and fairly fixed elements, it also largely arises from relational and social influences and is much less individualistic than is commonly thought.

4. People are importantly influenced or conditioned by their cultural rearing. Their behaviors are amazingly multicultural and there is no conclusive evidence that their diverse cultures are *right* or *wrong*, *better* or *worse* than others (Ivey, Ivey, and Sinek-Morgan 1997).

5. Either/or concepts of goodness and badness often exist and are rigidly held, but they tend to be inaccurate, limited, and prejudiced. More open-minded perceptions of human and nonhuman reality tend to show that things and processes exist on a both/and and an and/also basis. Thus almost every human act or condition has its advantages *and* disadvantages. Even helpful acts have their bad aspects. Giving people money, approval, or therapy may encourage them to be psychologically weaker, more dependent, and less self-helping. Berating people may encourage them to become stronger, less dependent, and more self-helping. Because monolithic, either/or solutions to problems have their limitations, we had better consider the range of alternate, and/also solutions and test them out to see how well—and how badly—they work.

6. Unfortunately—or fortunately—all the solutions we strive to achieve for our problem depend on *choosing* our goals and purposes from which to work. Such goals and purposes are just about always arguable, never absolute. Even the near-universal human goal of survival is debatable, because for some of us stress individual and others stress group or social survival. And at least a few people choose suicide; and a few think that the annihilation of the whole human race—and perhaps of the whole universe—is preferable. So we can arrive here at a consensus but not any absolute agreement of what goals and purposes are better or worse.

These postmodernist views have recently been promulgated by a host of writers, especially Gergen (1995). They also have been applied to the field of mental health counseling and psychotherapy by many other writers, such as Ellis (1994), Guterman (1994), Kelly (1955), and Mahoney (1991). Postmodernism is an important and growing aspect of today's psychotherapy.

Rational Emotive Behavior Therapy (REBT), along with other cognitive behavior therapies, has been criticized as being rationalist and sensationalist by several writers (Guidano 1991; Guterman 1994; and Mahoney 1991). I have refuted this charge and tried to show that REBT is quite constructionist, and in some ways is actually *more* so than many of the other constructionist therapies (Ellis 1994, 1996). Among other reasons, it is particularly constructionist because of the following:

1. Kelly (1955), Guidano (1991), Mahoney (1991), and other constructionist therapists show that disturbed people generate deep cognitive structures and that they had better be helped to adopt alternate models of the self and the world so that their deep structures can work in a more flexible and adaptive manner. REBT more specifically holds that the rigid, absolutistic musts and necessities by which people usually upset themselves are not merely learned from their parents and culture, but also created by their own constructionist and partly biological tendencies.

2. Therefore, REBT holds that both clients and their therapists can work hard, preferably in a highly active-directive and persistent manner, to help bring about profound philosophic, highly emotive, and strongly behavioral changes. Discovering and disputing their automatic self-defeating thoughts, as most cognitive-behavioral therapies do, is not enough. In addition, they can be helped to see that they create dysfunctional core philosophies and that they can constructively change their thinking by thinking about their thinking, and by thinking about thinking about their thinking (Dryden 1999; Ellis 1994, 2000b, 2001; Ellis and Dryden 1997).

3. In dealing with people's basic problems about self-worth, REBT agrees with the constructionist and existentialist position of Martin Heidegger, Paul Tillich, and Carl Rogers that humans can define themselves as good and worthy simply because they choose to do so. But it also shows them how to construct a philosophically unfalsifiable position of choosing life goals and purposes and then rating and evaluating their thoughts, feelings, and actions as good when they fulfill, and as bad only when they fail to fulfill, their chosen purposes. In this REBT solution to the problem of unconditional self-acceptance (USA), people can choose to view their self or essence as too complex and multifaceted to be given *any* global rating. It exists and can be enjoyed without the rigidities and dangers or "either/or" evaluation.

4. Constructionists like Guidano (1991) emphasize people's tacit observations and reactions to life problems, and I have always agreed that unconscious and tacit processes create both self-disturbing and problem solving (Ellis 1962). But REBT also particularly emphasizes and abets people's innate and acquired constructive abilities to design, plan, invent, and carry through better solutions to life's problems and to self-actualiza-

tion. It shows clients how to make themselves aware of their unconscious intentions and plans to lead a happier, more constructionist life.

5. Mahoney, Guidano, and other constructionists often hold that because people are natural constructionists—with which I agree—active-directive cognitive-behavior therapy may interfere with their natural ability to change. But this is like saying that because people have natural abilities to problem-solve and help themselves, their parents and teachers should give them little if any instruction. REBT takes a both/and instead of an either/or position here, holds that clients do have considerable natural ability to make themselves both more and less disturbing, and teaches them how to help themselves minimize their disturbing. Moreover, while encouraging them to use their self-aiding tendencies—which obviously they are usually doing badly when they come to therapy—it tries to give them greater under-standing—and determination—to collaborate with the therapist to help themselves more. It also stresses therapist and client efficiency in their choice and practice of the multitude of therapeutic techniques now available.

6. Constructionist approaches often put down science, especially rational science, and in some ways this makes sense. Science has many advan-tages, such as a lack of dogma, but it is hardly sacrosanct. REBT holds with postmodernists that science has its limitations, especially because the objec-tive truths that it often claims to reveal are, at bottom, person-centered and include important subjective aspects.

Science, however, is important for psychotherapy. For if we can agree on what the main goals of counseling and therapy are—which is not as easy as it may at first seem—scientifically oriented observation, case history, and experimenta-tion may check our theory and show us how accurately our goals are achieved. So science has its usefulness, and REBT, along with other cognitive-behavior therapies, uses science and rationality and also other criteria to check its theories and to change them and its practices. Moderate constructivism includes rational scientific method while abjuring dogmatic scientism (Held 1995).

For the above reasons—and more that could be presented, REBT tries to be equally constructionist, and in some ways more constructionist, than many other therapies. Whether it actually succeeds in this respect only fur-ther study, including scientific and experimental study, will show.

The foregoing positions sound, to my prejudiced ears, like open-minded, flexible, and postmodern views. I favor them and try to follow them in my life and in my theory and practice of therapy, albeit with some difficulty. For although I am willing to live with answers and rules that I realize are not final, utterly consistent, and indubitably correct, I would like to have some degree of probability that the ethics I choose for my life and my therapy relationships are reasonably correct and beneficial. George Kelly thought that although we cannot be certain about the goodness or rightness of our morals, we can still have probabilistic faith that they are workable. I tend to agree with him.

The trouble with postmodern ethics, as many critics have pointed out, is that they can easily be taken to relativist and even anarchic extremes (Held 1995). Humans seem to require fairly clear-cut social rules when they live and work together, and counselors and therapists especially had better adopt and follow fairly strict ethical standards. Active-directive therapists like me are particularly vulnerable in this respect, because they tend to be more authoritative, more didactic, and more forceful than passive, quiescent therapists. Therefore, they are often accused of being more authoritarian, self-centered, and harmful than passive therapists. I do not quite agree with this allegation—and I could write a book about the enormous harm that is frequently done by passive therapists, who often keep clients in needless pain and solidly block what they can do to change themselves. But let me fully admit that directive therapy has its distinct dangers and show how I, partly from taking a postmodernist outlook, ethically deal with these dangers.

AN ACTIVE-DIRECTIVE APPROACH

Let us take one of the very important problems of therapy, and one that has distinct ethical considerations, and see how I use postmodern views to handle the situation. As a therapist, shall I mainly be a fairly passive listener, hear all sides of my clients' problems, explore with them the advantages of their doing this and not doing that, have faith in their own ability to make presumably good decisions for themselves, and patiently wait for them to do so? Or should I instead more actively-directively zero in on what I think are my clients' core self-disturbances, show them what they are specifically thinking, feeling, and doing to needlessly upset themselves, and directly challenge them and teach them how to think, feel, and behave more effectively?

Many schools of therapy—especially classical psychoanalysis, Rogerian person-centered, and cognitive-experiential therapy—largely favor the more passive approach, and many other schools—especially behavior therapy, cognitive-behavior therapy, problem solving, and Gestalt therapy—largely favor the more active-directive approach. Which one is more ethical and which shall I use?

As almost everyone in the field of therapy already knows, I favor the active-directive methods of REBT. I consider this to be ethical and efficient for several reasons:

1. Most clients, especially those with severe personality disorders, disturb themselves as a result of both biological and environmental reasons. They are innately prone to anxiety, depression, and rage, and they also learn dysfunc-

tional thoughts, feelings, and behaviors. They practice them so often that they have great difficulty changing even when they gain considerable insight into their origin and development. Therefore, they had better be taught how they are probably upsetting themselves and taught specific and general methods to change themselves (Ellis and Dryden 1997; Ellis and MacLaren 1998).

2. Clients are usually in pain when they come to therapy and active-directive methods, as research has shown, tend to be more effective in a brief period of time than are more passive methods (Hollon and Beck 1994; Lyons and Woods 1991; Silverman, McCarthy, and McGovern 1992).

3. Therapy is often expensive and it seems ethical to help clients benefit from it as quickly as feasible, which is what active-directive methods tend to do (Ellis 1996).

4. There is some evidence that the active-directive methods of cognitive-behavior therapy may lead to a more lasting change than do some more passive techniques (Alford and Beck 1997).

5. More passive therapists—such as classical analysts and Rogerian person-centered practitioners—have often seemed to be passive, but actually sneak in active methods, and may therefore not be as honest compared with active therapists who fully acknowledge their directiveness.

6. In REBT terms, passive techniques, such as relating warmly to clients instead of focusing on their specific dysfunctioning, may help them feel better but not get better. They often enjoy being endlessly listened to rather than urged to change, and they feel conditionally better because their therapist approves of them rather than becoming unconditionally self-accepting whether or not their therapist likes them (Ellis 1972, 1994).

7. Actively showing clients how to function better often helps them achieve a sense of self-efficacy, which may not amount to unconditional self-accepting (USA) but nonetheless may be quite therapeutic (Bandura 1997).

8. Active therapy may push clients to perform difficult beneficial tasks such as in vivo desensitization that are quite beneficial but that they would rarely perform on their own. Clients often change more when they first make themselves uncomfortable and then later become comfortable with their new behaviors. Active-directive therapy is likely to encourage them, more than passive therapy, to uncomfortably change.

For all these advantages of active-directive therapy, I had better acknowledge its possible disadvantages, including these:

1. It may be too directive and interrupt clients' innate proactive propensities to work on their own problems and to actualize themselves.

2. It may induce clients to use methods that the therapist strongly believes in but that have little efficacy. They may even be iatrogenic.

3. It may encourage clients to try suggested methods too quickly without giving them proper thought and preparation.

4. It may lead clients to adopt goals and values that the therapist sells them on and therefore not really to fulfill themselves.

5. Directive therapists may fairly easily go to authoritarian, one-sided, and even righteous extremes and may neglect important individual differences, multicultural influences, and other aspects of individual and group diversity.

6. Active-directive therapy may put too much power and responsibility on the therapist, disrupt a potentially collaborative and cooperative client-therapist relationship, and detract from the humanistic aspects of counseling.

Even though much published evidence shows that active-directive therapy is often quite advantageous and effective, we can question whether, at bottom, these results are really effective, good, deep, or lasting in a postmodernist fashion. These terms have multiple meanings, some of which directly contradict other meanings of the same term. Which of these meanings shall we accept as true?

My solution to this issue is to take an and/also rather than an either/or approach. Thus, in accordance with REBT theory, I usually zero in quite quickly on my clients' basic or core philosophies, especially on their dysfunctional or irrational *Beliefs*, show them how to differentiate these from their rational and functional preferences and how to use several cognitive, emotive, and behavioral methods to dispute and act against these beliefs. But I also show them some important other sides of their dysfunctional thinking, feeling, and behaving.

1. Even their highly irrational ideas—their absolutistic shoulds, oughts, or musts—have advantages and virtues. "I must perform well or I am worthless!" produces anxiety and avoidance, but it is also motivating, energizing, and brings some good results.

2. Even questionable ideas—such as the Pollyannaish beliefs, "Day by day in every way I'm getting better and better" or "No matter what I do kind Fate will take care of me"—may jolt one out of a depressed state and help one function better.

3. Strong negative feelings can be good and bad, helpful and unhelpful. When you do poorly, your strong feelings of disappointment and regret may push you to do better next time. But your strong feelings of horror and self-hatred may harm you immensely. Yes, but even your feelings of horror and self-hatred may sometimes help you give up compulsive smoking or drinking.

4. Rational ideas and behaviors are not always really rational—certainly

not always sensible and effective. Rationally and empirically believing that the universe is senseless and uncaring will help some people be self-reliant and energized, and help others to be depressed and hopeless. Accurately believing that no one in the world really cares for you will motivate some people to work at being more social and others to withdraw socially.

CAUTIONS AND LIMITATIONS

Despite the disadvantages of active-directive therapy, I strongly favor it over passive therapy. But to make reasonably sure that I do not take it to extremes I try to keep several safeguards in mind. What follows are some of my main—and I think postmodern-oriented—cautions.

Awareness of my technique's limitations. I do therapy on the basis of my sincere and strong faith in REBT—meaning, my belief that it probably works well with most of my clients much of the time but that it also has its distinct limitations. I tentatively endorse and follow it but keep looking for its flaws. I keep checking my own results, those of my colleagues and those I train, and those reported in the literature. I try to keep especially aware of its dangers and its inefficiencies. Thus, I keep looking for the limitations of my active-directiveness, pointing them out to my clients and encouraging them to be more active-directive in their own right.

Awareness of clients' different reactions to my techniques. I assume that REBT methods help most of my clients much of the time—but not all of them all of the time. Although I often see them as disturbing themselves stemming from similar dysfunctional or Irrational *Beliefs*, I also keep reminding myself that even clients with the same problems (e.g., severe states of depression) have vastly different biochemical reactions, temperaments, histories, family and cultural influences, socioeconomic conditions, therapeutic experiences, and so forth. Moreover, they react differently to me and my personality and preferences. Although I still start out with what I think are the best REBT methods for each of them—which usually means the ones I have successfully used with somewhat similar clients in the past—I remain quite ready to vary my methods considerably with each individual client. I even consider, when REBT does not seem to be working, using poor or "irrational" methods that REBT theory and practice usually opposes (Ellis 1996, 2000b, 2001). Thus, I act more active-directively with some clients and less so with others. With those that I am consistently directive, I at times deliberately make myself much less so, to see whether we achieve worse or better results.

Experimenting with various techniques. Aubrey Yates, a behavior therapist, once said that each session of therapy had better be an experiment—

and one that leads therapists to change their tactics as the results of that experiment are observed. I add: I had better observe and review each series of sessions, and the length of therapy as a whole, as an experiment. As I note the good and bad results—or what I think are the good and bad results—of my sessions with each individual client, I try to repeat successful REBT methods and modify my unsuccessful ones with this particular client. If my REBT methods do not seem to be working, I experiment with some non-REBT or even anti-REBT methods. If these do not seem to be effective, I refer the client to another REBT or non-REBT therapist. As usual, I keep experimenting with many active-directive methods and with some more passive ones as well.

Using multimodal methods. From the start, REBT has always used a number of cognitive, emotive, and behavioral methods with most clients; over the years it has added to them additional methods that seem to be effective (Ellis 1988, 1994, 1996; Kwee and Ellis 1997, 1998; Lazarus 1997). All of these methods have their disadvantages and limitations, particularly with some clients some of the time. I therefore try to keep these limitations in mind and to have available for regular or occasional use literally scores of REBT techniques, as well as many non-REBT techniques. I thereby remain open-minded and alternative-seeking in my therapy. Most methods of REBT are active-directive. But some, like the Socratic method of discovering and questioning Irrational *Beliefs*, are more passive. When directiveness fails, more passive methods are borrowed from psychoanalytic, person-centered, and other therapies.

Using therapeutic creativity. I originally used or adopted several REBT methods from other theorists and therapists, believing them to be effective implementers of REBT theory, which tentatively but still strongly holds several major propositions. I soon found that I could better adapt many of these methods to REBT—and to therapy in general—by slightly or considerably modifying them. And I also devised new methods, such as REBT's shame-attacking exercising and its very forceful and vigorous disputing of clients' Irrational *Beliefs*, which seem to add to and improve my original ones (Ellis 1988, 1994, 2000c; Walen, DiGiuseppe, and Dryden 1992). I—and, hopefully other REBT practitioners—remain open to using our therapeutic creativity to adapt and devise new methods with special clients and with regular ones. I mostly have created new active-directive methods, but I also designed the more passive method of exploring clients' early irrational beliefs, as well as the dysfunctional *beliefs* of others, to probe them indirectly to use in dealing with their own self-defeating ideas. I have also for many years encouraged clients to teach REBT to their friends and relatives and thereby indirectly learn it better themselves. I use a number of paradoxical methods with my clients, such as encouraging them to get at least three rejections a week, so that they indirectly see and believe that being rejected is not horrible or shameful.

Varying relationship methods. REBT theory holds that the majority of therapy clients can benefit from achieving unconditional self-accepting (USA)—that is, fully accepting themselves as good or deserving persons *whether or not* they perform well and *whether or not* significant other people approve of them. Consequently, I try to give all my clients what Carl Rogers called "unconditional positive regard," and I go beyond this and do my best to teach them how to give it to themselves. I recognize, however, that even USA has its limitations, because some people change their self-defeating and antisocial behavior only by damning themselves as well as their actions. I especially recognize that different methods of showing clients unconditional acceptance range from warmly loving or approving them to unemotionally accepting them with their revealed failings and hostilities. All these methods have their advantages and disadvantages, and all of them work well or badly with different clients. So I vary the specific ways I relate to clients and cautiously observe the results of my interactions with them. Occasionally, I even go along with their self-damning when, oddly enough, it seems to help them. So I *generally* give clients unconditional acceptance and actively teach them how to give it to themselves, but in many different individual and specific ways, including those that are indirect and passive.

Varying interpersonal methods. REBT, again on theoretical grounds, teaches clients the advantages of unconditional other acceptance (UOA)— or the Christian philosophy of accepting the sinner but not the sin (Ellis 1962, 1994; Ellis and Harper 1997; Ellis and MacLaren 1998; Ellis and Tafrate 1997; Nielsen, Johnson, and Ellis 2001). I do this with my clients because I believe that their anger, rage, and fighting frequently is self-destructive and also ruins relationships with others. One of the essences of psychotherapy, therefore, is helping people achieve both USA and UOA (Sampson 1989; Seligman 1991).

Nonetheless, clients' achieving unconditional self- and other-accepting may have some drawbacks, such as helping people to justify their own and other people's immoral behavior and thereby encouraging it. So I try to realize it is not exactly a panacea.

Moreover, therapists' ways of giving and teaching USA and UOA can easily be interpreted wrongly by their clients. Thus, when Carl Rogers showed clients unconditional positive regard, they often wrongly concluded that they were good persons because of his approval of them. But this is highly conditional self-acceptance. Similarly, if I accept my clients unconditionally when, say, they have stolen or cheated, they may wrongly conclude that I think that their behavior is not really evil and may therefore excuse it.

So, although I do my best to give my clients unconditional accepting and encourage them to give it to others, I closely watch their reception and interpretation of what I am doing. I solicit their feedback, watch their reactions with themselves, with me, and with others—and, once again, use a variety of relationship and interpersonal relating approaches to determine which ones actually seem to work. I actively give and teach self-accepting and forgiveness to others, but I also actively watch and try to counter its potential dangers.

Again, REBT has always actively used the therapeutic relationship to help clients become aware of their interpersonal cognitive, emotional, and behavioral interpersonal disturbing. But I keep reminding myself that if my clients involve themselves too closely with me that may increase their neurotic neediness and interfere with their outside relations with others. I also am skeptical of my assumption that the main ways my clients react to me—who may be a uniquely accepting person in their life—are the same ways that they react to others. So I often tone down their involvement with me, encourage their participation in one of my therapy groups, recommend suitable workshops, talks, and books, and teach them interpersonal skills specifically designed to help them in their outside life. I do not assume that their relationships with me are clearly transferred from their feelings and prejudices about their early family members—though occasionally that is so. I assume, rather, that they often have an idiosyncratic and personal relationship with me and I watch closely to see how it can be constructively used despite its possible dangers. When my actively relating to my clients seems to be iatrogenic, I try to deliberately ameliorate it with a more passive kind of interaction with them.

I also assume that what the psychoanalysts call transference often occurs, and that it has both advantages and disadvantages. To minimize its disadvantages, I go out of my way to interpret my and my clients' transference and countertransference "findings" as *probable* and *preferential* rather than absolutistic and musturbatory (Ellis, in press).

Skepticism about the infallibility of the therapist and the main therapeutic methods used. REBT encourages clients to have two almost contradictory beliefs. First, that they are able to understand how they largely disturb themselves, how they can reduce their disturbing and increase their individual and social fulfillment, and how they can use several REBT cognitive, emotive, and behavioral methods to try to actively work at doing what they theoretically can do. REBT thus tries to help clients to have an active, strong feeling of self-efficacy about changing themselves. Second, it keeps encouraging them realistically to see and accept their human fallibility and imperfection—to acknowledge that they now are, and in all probability will continue to be, highly error-prone, inconsistent, unreasonable, inefficacious individuals. Always? Yes. To a high degree? Yes.

Can clients, then, have confidence in their ability to grow and change—have a sense of self-efficacy in this regard—and still acknowledge and accept their quite human fallibility? Why not? People are fallible at all sports—and also have real confidence that they can usually play one of them well, and actually do so. They are highly fallible students—but feel efficacious, say, at test-taking and usually get decent marks. So it is almost certain that they are generally fallible. But at the same time, they are highly proficient in certain tasks, know they are proficient, and help themselves remain proficient by having a sense of self-efficacy about these tasks.

So I can safely actively-directively show my clients that they are generally fallible, and even often fallible about changing themselves. Nonetheless, they can, if they are willing to work at changing themselves, have what I call achievement-confidence and what Albert Bandura (1997) calls self-efficacy. Believing that *highly probably—not certainly—*they *can* change, they often do.

Therapists, too, can feel confidence that they are effective—despite their fully acknowledging their therapeutic (and general) fallibility. That is what happens as I do active-directive REBT. I am quite confident that I often will significantly help my clients, and usually help them more than if I used another main form of therapy. But I also know full well that I am a fallible human—quite fallible. I recognize that with each client I can and, at times, easily do REBT inefficiently—yes, even though I created it, have used it with many thousands of clients, and am the world's leading authority on it. Nonetheless, with this particular client, I may well have my prejudices, weaknesses, hostilities, frustration tolerances, ignorances, rigidities, stupidities, and so forth. Indeed I may!

While seeing a client, I therefore often do several things: (a) acknowledge my prejudices and weaknesses; (b) accept myself unconditionally with them; (c) try to ameliorate and compensate for them; (d) decide whether, in spite of my failings, I still probably am able to effectively help this client; (e) if I decide that I am able, I push myself on with a good degree of confidence or self-efficacy; (f) do my best to use REBT (and possibly other) methods with each client; (g) sometimes discuss my weaknesses with clients, to see if they are willing to continue to see me; (h) if so, I proceed actively, energetically with the therapy—mainly with a high degree of confidence but also with some doubts; (i) keep checking on my doubts and often changing my tactics with clients or refer some to another therapist.

Active-directive therapies, however, may dangerously neglect some aspects of constructionist therapy, such as ignoring less intrusive and more passive ways of collaboration between therapists and their clients. This chapter shows how I, as an active-directive practitioner of REBT, address some of its potential dangers and use postmodernist ethics and safeguards to retain its efficiency and reduce its risks. In particular, it stresses therapists' becoming aware of REBT's limitations and of clients' different reactions to its techniques; experimenting with various multimodal methods of REBT and non-REBT therapy; using therapeutic creativity; varying relationship and interpersonal approaches; and remaining highly skeptical about the therapist's and the therapeutic model's infallibility. These caveats and cautions will not make active-directive REBT—or any other form of therapy—entirely flexible and safe. But they may help considerably.

SELF-HELP SUGGESTIONS

- Postmodern philosophy stresses the point that truth with a capital T cannot be absolutely validated and favors the REBT importance of looking for your self-disturbing absolutistic shoulds, oughts, musts, and necessitizing, questioning and challenging them, and replacing them with flexible preferences and desires.
- Constructivism overlaps with postmodernism and holds that you have considerable power to construct self-helping thoughts, feelings, and actions as well as to construct self-defeating behaviors. You have the ability, if you use it, to *choose* healthy instead of unhealthy thinking, feeling, and acting. REBT is one of the main choice therapies that helps you create and maintain self-helping philosophies and relationships.
- Seeing what are your constructive life choices is not enough. You had better energetically and persistently act on them—in REBT terms, PYA—push your ass.
- Active-directive therapies like REBT often work well but also have some limitations and disadvantages. They may be *too* directive, authoritarian and therapist-centered for *you*. You're a unique individual who can *selectively* use REBT and other active-directive methods for your chosen purposes.
- Experiment with various therapy and self-help procedures to discover which ones work best for *you*. Be somewhat skeptical of all therapy theories and practices!
- Even "good" thinking, feeling, and acting has possible disadvantages and drawbacks. Again: try it and see!
- Persistent use of one or two therapy methods may help you considerably. But using a variety of thinking, feeling, and behaving techniques—which REBT amply provides—is more likely to deal with your particular problems. Investigate and explore!
- Your achieving a close and supportive relationship with a competent, likeable therapist can considerably help. But not too close! Doting on a therapist or having her or him too warmly attached to you can do more harm than good. Watch it!

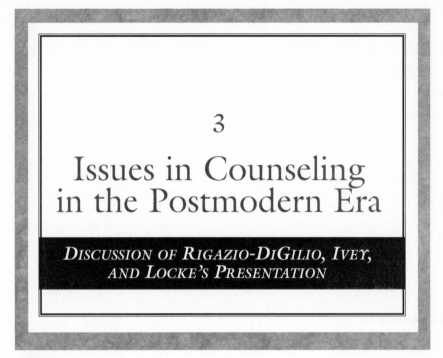

3

Issues in Counseling in the Postmodern Era

DISCUSSION OF RIGAZIO-DIGILIO, IVEY, AND LOCKE'S PRESENTATION

This chapter will mainly discuss Rigazio-DiGilio, Ivey, and Locke's (1997) article, "Continuing the Postmodern Dialogue: Enhancing and Contextualizing Multiple Voices," which I consider a very important contribution to our postmodern dialogue. Their article makes many trenchant points, with which I mostly agree, but with some of which I would like to offer caveats.

First, Rigazio-DiGilio et al. (1997, p. 234) state one of their primary theses as follows: "Theories of counseling that primarily address the thought and action processes of individuals (e.g., REBT, psychoanalysis, CBT, Gestalt Therapy, Reality Therapy) offer unique perspectives on mental health and how to achieve it, but omit action with and reflection on the wider social systems that may have contributed to or labeled the distress. Similarly, social constructivist models listen to the client's narrative."

Let's face it: These critics of various therapies are partly accurate and make an important point. On the other hand, they almost forget and only lightly mention Adler, who always stressed social interest and the contribu-

This chapter is partly adapted from "A Continuation of the Dialogue on Issues in Counseling in the Postmodern Era," *Journal of Mental Health Counseling* 22 (2000): 97–106. Used with permission.

tions to mental health. They also forget that Wilhelm Reich was a propagandist for a revised social and sexual system and that Carl Rogers repeatedly campaigned for international cooperation and peace.

In my early articles and books on REBT, I emphasized that people had better change their inner musts and demands, with which they upset themselves, about the social system. But at the same time, they had better fight against that unfair and irrational system. Thus, in books like *Sex Without Guilt* (Ellis 1958/1965), *The Intelligent Woman's Guide to Dating and Mating* (Ellis 1963/1979), and *Sex and the Liberated Man* (Ellis 1976), I took a firm stand against the social-sexual system that endorsed Puritanism, encouraged machismoism in men, downgraded women in many respects, and otherwise helped to cause many cultural and personal emotional evils. Along with other writers in the 1950s and 1960s, such as Bertrand Russell and Alfred Kinsey, I think I can say that I was one of the main instigators of the social-sex revolution of the 1960s.

Whether counselors should preferably strive for social action along with their functions as therapeutic practitioners is a complicated and debatable question—as is the question of whether scientists, including counselors, should strive for "objective truth" as well as take a social-political stand. Much can probably be said both for and against counselors assisting their clients. Rigazio-DiGilio et al. (1997, p. 236) advocate "chang[ing] their inner thoughts and meanings to assume new behaviors that have ameliorating effect within their own personal sphere while also interrupting constraining interactions that may exist in their wider sociocultural and sociopolitical context."

Personally, I favor counselors taking this kind of sociocultural and sociopolitical stand, as my history (since I became a therapist in 1943) has shown. But while I have always been a sociopolitical "liberal"—as, it seems to me Rigazio-DiGilio et al. likewise are—what of the many counselors who are arch conservatives or reactionaries? Yes, some indeed are. As such, they may choose *not* to interrupt constraining interactions that may exist in their clients' wider sociocultural and sociopolitical content. Instead, these reactionary counselors may choose—yes, choose—to aid, tighten, and even aggravate their clients' contextual constraining interactions. Thus, a counselor who is quite conservative (as I think not a few are) may encourage clients to bolster the antifemale, prochauvanistic, antisexual, child-, woman-, and ethnic-abusing content that is still prevalent in our Western society as well as in some Asian, African, and other regions (Ivey, Ivey, and Simek-Morgan 1977). Are we to rule that all these "reactionary" counselors are indubitably wrong? Some postmodern, relativist philosophies would especially say that neither liberal nor reactionary sociopolitical views are right or wrong in themselves. It is how you *view* them that constitutes their rightness. Personally, I believe with Richard Rorty that some pragmatic standards of what is "right" and "wrong" for a given society can be reasonably established. But I have a hard time—and so would Rigazio-DiGilio et al.—validating this view.

Let us assume that the advocacy of sociopolitical action as an integral part of therapy has dangers (especially in a democracy) but still assume that it has more advantages than disadvantages and is therefore to be implemented. Rigazio-DiGilio et al. also posit a theory of developmental counseling and therapy (DCT) and its extension, systematic cognitive-developmental theory (SCDT) that include four important points:

> In this theory four levels or orientations through which individuals, families, and wider social systems process information, including stress-inducing stimuli, are described: sensorimotor/elemental, concrete situational, formal/reflective, and dialectical/systemic . . . . These four informational styles . . . challenge traditional theories such as person-centered and REBT, because these tend to give attention to only parts of the more inclusive information-processing paradigm.

Let me clearly define what Rigazio-DiGilio et al. seem to mean by the four informational styles of counseling they include in their DCT and SCDT systems. By the *sensorimotor/elemental* level they seem to mean that counselors will deal with their clients' bodily, physical, and experiential information processes; by the *concrete situational* level they seem to mean the practical problems of living that therapists will help their clients to handle; by the *formal/reflective* level they seem to mean the cognitive processes that counselors will help their clients to understand and deal with; and by the *dialectic/systemic* level they seem to mean the attempts of counselors to encourage and help their clients change the stressful environmental events about which they tend to upset themselves.

Rigazio-DiGilio et al. (1997, p. 237) hold that if counselors and their clients have access to all four of these orientations, they "have more options for growth, adaptation, and change." I have no quarrel with this formulation and think that it is probably more comprehensive and therapeutically more efficient than most other theories. The authors wrongly state, however, that traditional theories such as REBT "tend to give more attention to only parts of the more inclusive information-processing paradigm." That is, REBT omits important aspects of Rigazio-DiGilio et al.'s four-point theory. They repeat a common misconception of REBT, since it actually emphasizes the formal/reflective processing of information in the creation and maintenance of emotional disturbance, but it by no means exclusively does so. In fact, in my first paper on REBT, presented at the American Psychological Association annual convention in Chicago on August 31, 1956, I emphasized the interaction of emotion (and of emotional disturbance) with other information-processing human elements. I specifically said:

> The human being may be said to possess four basic processes—perception, movement, thinking, and emotion—all of which are integrally interrelated. Thus, thinking—aside from consisting of bioelectrical charges in the brain cells, and in addition to comprising remembering, learning, problem solving, and similar psychological processes—also is, and to some extent has to be, sensory, motor, and emotional behavior. Instead, then, of saying, "Jones thinks about this puzzle," we should more accurately say, "Jones perceives-moves-feels-THINKS about this puzzle." Emotion, like thinking and the sensori-motor processes, we may define as an exceptionally complex state of human reaction that is integrally related to all the other perception and response processes. It is not one thing, but a combination and holistic integration of several seemingly diverse, yet actually closely related, phenomena (Ellis 1958, p. 35).

In addition to holistically integrating perception, cognition, emotion, and behavior and as I noted above, REBT from its start in January 1955 has been unusually multimodal in its methods of therapy. Along with several techniques of cognitive restructuring, it has advocated the use of more emotive-evocative-expressive and more action-oriented techniques than probably any other form of therapy. As I also noted above, it has often encouraged the Rigazio-DiGilio et al.'s (1997) fourth therapeutic process, dialectic/systemic processing.

To be sure, REBT has not emphasized dialectic/systematic counseling or counselors working to change the socio-political system as much as it is heavily encouraged in DCT and SCDT. Quite possibly, it and most other popular counseling procedures are relatively lax in this respect. The unique element of the Rigazio-DiGilio et al.'s article is their stress on this fourth process. REBT had better seriously consider emphasizing it more than it sometimes has done in the past and, thereby, learn from DCT and SCDT. But much can be said on the hazards as well as the advantages of stressing this aspect of counseling. It is nonetheless accurate, as Rigazio-DiGilio et al. (1997, p. 241) note: "Theories of counseling and practice that perpetuate the notion of individual and family dysfunction without giving equal attention to societal dysfunction and to the dysfunctional interactions that can occur between individuals, families, and societies (e.g., intentional and unintentional power differentials) may unwittingly reinforce the oppressive paradigm." All systems of counseling had better give serious thought to this hypothesis—as, in fact, few of them have to date done.

Rigazio-DiGilio et al. (1997, p. 235) particularly emphasize Freire's (1972) insistence on action and point out that DCT and SCDT put "an emphasis on action as well as treatment within multiple layers of reality." I heartily endorse this view. As they also indicate (p. 248), "Ellis was one of the first individually oriented theorists to stress the importance of *homework*. He is a leader in tying counseling to environmental conditions, because he expects his clients to enact behaviors at home and in the community." Indeed so! I created REBT as the pioneering form of cognitive-*behavioral* therapy in 1955 because I fully realized, at that time, that human thinking promotes changes in human action; but, at the same time, that human action promotes changes in human thinking. The two so-called separate processes are really quite interactional.

Moreover, therapists' *actions* often encourage clients' changes in cognitions and behavior. That is why I keep emphasizing that, unlike many counseling methods, REBT is both postmodern *and* active-directive. Rigazio-DiGilio et al. imply that therapists using DCT and SCDT are more active-directive than other kinds of therapists; but, except for their socially-directed activity, they do not specifically indicate how they are active in the counseling processes. They certainly appear to be far from Rogerian!

REBT AND THE FOUR STYLES OF DCT AND SCDT

Rigazio-DiGilio, Ivey, and Locke (1997, p. 246), as a primary ethical imperative, ask theorists and practitioners espousing a particular counseling perspective "to clearly specify the cells falling outside the parameters of their approaches, and the cells currently under development." Fair enough. But since they have some 225 cells in their multimodal cube, let me consider the four main styles of DCT and SCDT and see how REBT fares in regards to them:

1. *Sensorimotor/elemental.* REBT, with many clients (though not all), uses emotional imagery, forceful coping statements, experiential exercises, relaxation techniques, physical exercise, in vivo desensitization, shame-attacking exercise, deliberate heightening of states of feeling, and experimenting with sexual and other sensory-motor techniques of therapy. It frequently refers clients for psychotropic medication. It usually does not favor body manipulation such as Rolfing and Reichian methods, but may possibly be deficient in not experimenting with them more.

2. *Concrete/situational.* REBT has pioneered in homework assignments, assertion training, role modeling, conflict-management strategies, practical problem solving, cost-benefit analysis of behaviors, exposure to phobic situations, relapse prevention, and many other concrete/situational methods of therapy. I am not sure where Rigazio-DiGilio et al. would find it deficient in this respect.

3. *Formal/reflective.* REBT is famous for its cognitive restructuring, reframing, empirical and logical questioning, socratic dialogues, use of stories and metaphors, doing cost-benefit analysis of feelings and behaviors, and many other reflective techniques. It is often accused of over-emphasizing these aspects of therapy, but actually combines and integrates them with affective and behavioral methods.

4. *Dialectic/systemic.* REBT, along with showing clients how to achieve unconditional self-acceptance (USA), reminds them that they choose to live in a social group and had better heed the rules and mores of this group, and work for unconditional other-acceptance (UOA). It particularly interrupts and overcomes feelings of anger and rage and fosters peaceful cooperation (Ellis 1994; Ellis and Tafrate 1997). It also stresses feminist therapy (Ellis 1963/1979; Wolfe 1980; Wolfe and Naimark 1987) and anti-homophobia and sex-liberationist therapy (Ellis 1963/1979, 1976; Ellis and Blau 1998). It has also stressed marriage and family therapy since the 1950s (Ellis 1957/1975; Ellis and Crawford 2000). It is not as active in urging clients to improve the social context in which they live as Rigazio-DiGilio et al. might like it to be, but it is not exactly a slouch in this respect.

From what I have said so far, I hope it can be seen that I and REBT definitely favor the Rigazio-DiGilio et al. Development Counseling Theory. Of all the many systems of counseling that have been used, theirs seems to be the more comprehensive and potentially most effective. In some ways, I am definitely prejudiced in its favor since I believe that in many respects it overlaps with, and has often been preceded by, REBT theory and practice. But the authors describe it in unusual detail; that makes it a valuable addition to the counseling movement. I also agree with them that it has many postmodern aspects but that it warns against some of the extreme aspects of postmodernism and social constructionism that I have previously criticized. Development Counseling Theory is therefore not radical constructionism or postmodernism, but takes a more sensible middle-of-the-road postmodernist position.

THE TIME CONSTRAINTS OF DCT, SCDT, AND REBT

This present chapter is already long, but let me briefly mention one important point that may seriously interfere with the actual practice of comprehensive systems of counseling like DCT, SCDT, and also with REBT, as I have usually presented it. These systems take immense time and energy for counselors to learn and practice. If they are adequately shown to clients, as they preferably should be, these clients would also have to take a considerable number of therapy hours and an even greater number of homework time to thoroughly learn and follow their methods.

Thus, even if the main aspects of DCT and SCDT were actively-directly taught to clients (as REBT is usually taught) they would have to devote much thinking, emoting, and behaving time to following their therapeutic procedures. This may be especially true of clients' implementing, in thought and in action, the dialectic/systemic aspect of using DCT and SCDT, as

Rigazio-DiGilio et al. (1997, p. 238) advocate, "to seek solutions that incorporate resources from the self, the other, and the wider environment."

Now, of course there is nothing wrong with this. Clients energetically using what REBT calls PYA (push your ass) to really help themselves and others significantly change may well be what is required in practically all effective counseling. The fact remains, however—as many studies of therapy show—that the average client remains in counseling only a few sessions, usually no more than six. Moreover, today's socioeconomic forces, and particularly the influence of HMOs, seem destined to continue this paucity of treatment session. If so, how will the therapists using DCT and SCDT, as well as those using the many-faceted methods of REBT, have the time to encourage their clients to effectively learn and practice the methods of these comprehensive systems of counseling?

REBT, like some other forms of individual and group counseling, has developed brief therapy and self-help procedures that seem to be effective (Ellis 1996; Ellis and Harper 1997; Ellis and Velten 1998). Rigazio-DiGilio, Ivey, and Locke had better consider this important problem. Otherwise, counselors who are trained to use DCT and SCDT properly may have a hard time holding their clients long enough to make these systems of counseling effective. But, again, this chapter is long enough already, so I leave this important aspect of counseling for further discussion.

SELF-HELP SUGGESTIONS FOR READERS

- You always live in a social setting and therefore had better consider some degree of social activism—changing your personal environment and also to some extent working to change the restricting social system in which you live.
- Of course, you do not have to be a "liberal" social activist and you may be more "conservative" and willingly go along with the disadvantages—for you and for others—of the social system. But at least *consider* working to change the social system as well as changing yourself within the system. *Choose* to be—or not to be—somewhat socially active.
- Sandra Rigazio-DiGilio, Allen Ivey, and Don Locke first emphasize that you and your possible counselors had better work to change (1) your bodily, physical, and experiential conditions; (2) your practical problems of living; (3) your cognitive and philosophic ways of viewing yourself and others; (4) your stressful environments about which you tend to upset yourself. This is a fairly comprehensive approach to personality change and it is largely endorsed by REBT. Consider these four important aspects of changing your life and give some considerable thought and effort to doing so.
- If you choose to concentrate on one or two of these human change

processes, and perhaps later choose to work on the other ones, unguiltily try to do so. Don't forget, as is emphasized in this book, that your thoughts, emotions, and behaviors all interact with and influence each other. Your efforts to change even one of these major modalities will most likely lead to changes in the others. Try at least one, and preferably all, of these change methods, to see what works best for you.

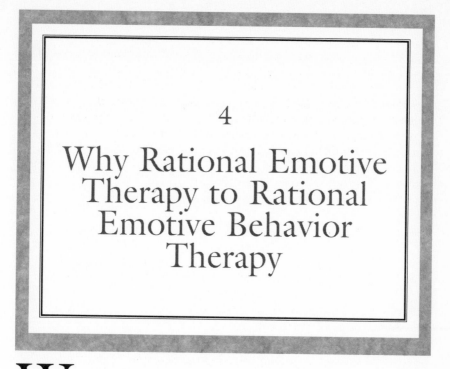

4

Why Rational Emotive Therapy to Rational Emotive Behavior Therapy

Why have I now decided, after almost forty years of creating and using rational-emotive therapy (RET), to change its name to rational emotive behavior therapy (REBT)? I now see that I was wrong to call it, for a few years, rational therapy (RT) and then, in 1961, to change it to RET.

Using the term *rational* itself was probably an error, because it means empirical and logical, and its use has been rightly criticized by some postmodern thinkers because we can have no absolute criterion of rationality. What is deemed rational by one person, group, or community can easily be considered irrational by others.

In REBT, "rational" has always meant cognition that is effective or self-helping, not merely cognition that is empirically and logically valid (Ellis 1994). If I were to rename RET today I might call it cognitive-emotive instead of rational-emotive therapy; but it is a little late for that change, because cognitive therapy and cognitive-behavior therapy are already well known, and REBT is somewhat different from these other therapies.

This chapter is partly adapted from "Changing Rational-Emotive Therapy (RET) to Rational Emotive Behavior Therapy," *Behavior Therapist* 16 (1993): 257–58, and "Why Rational-Emotive Therapy to Rational Emotive Behavior Therapy?" *Psychotherapy* 36 (1999): 154–59. Used with permission.

RET is a misleading name because it omits the highly behavioral aspect that rational-emotive therapy has favored. In *Reason and Emotion in Psychotherapy* (Ellis 1962), which is largely an extended version of several articles on REBT that I published in the 1950s, I make many references to its behavioral components, including these:

"The therapist encourages, persuades, cajoles, and occasionally even insists that the patient engage in some activity (such as doing something he is afraid of doing) which itself will serve as a forceful counter-propaganda agency against the nonsense he believes" (p. 95).

"The rational therapist . . . uncovers the most important elements of irrational thinking in his patient's experience and energetically urges this patient into more reasonable channels of behaving" (pp. 103–104).

"REBT insists on homework assignments, desensitizing and deconditioning actions, both within and without the therapeutic sessions, and on other forms of active work on the part of the patient" (p. 188).

"Vigorous verbal rethinking will usually lead to changed motor behavior; and forcefully repatterned sensory-motor activity will usually lead to changed ideation" (p. 205).

REBT "is, at one and the same time, highly rational-persuasive-interpretive-philosophical *and* distinctly emotional-directive-active-work-centered" (p. 330).

"Rational-emotive therapy is one of the relatively few techniques which include large amounts of actions, work, and 'homework' assignments of a so-called nonverbal nature" (p. 334).

REBT "is a highly active, *working* form of treatment—on the part of both the therapist and his or her patient" (p. 364).

I also wrote, in an article published in 1975, REBT theory states that "humans rarely change and keep disbelieving a profound self-defeating belief unless they often *act* against it" (Ellis 1975, p. 20).

Corsini (1979), among other writers, has made the same point. To help clients change their thinking he uses the "betting" technique and insists that if they actually do a "fearful" task that he asks them to do, their cognitions will change. He says, "Do this and your thoughts and feelings will change." They reply, "No, this will not happen." He says, "I'll bet you two dollars. Do it and if I am wrong, I will pay you and you will be the judge." He claims he has never lost one of these bets.

Actually, REBT has always been one of the most behaviorally oriented of the cognitive-behavior therapies. In addition to employing systemic desensitization and showing clients how to use imaginal methods of exposing themselves to phobias and anxiety-provoking situations, it favors in vivo desensitization or exposure. REBT often encourages people to deliberately stay in poor situations—for example, a poor marriage or a bad job—until they change their disturbed thoughts and feelings, and then decide whether to flee from these situations. Several of REBT's emotive-dramatic exercises—for example, its famous shame-attacking exercises—are also more behavioral than the procedures of other leading cognitive behavioral therapies.

As I showed in the previous chapter, REBT has always seen cognition, emotion, and behavior as holistically integrated, and therefore has always been, to use Arnold Lazarus's (1997) term, multimodal in its therapy techniques. Although it stresses the importance of clients' making profound philosophical changes, it often uses emotional-evocative and behavioral methods, as well as cognitive methods, to help them do so. Similarly, it uses all three modalities to help them make emotional and behavioral changes.

Actually, rational emotive behavior therapy uses a large number of cognitive, emotive, and behavioral methods, probably more than the other cognitive-behavior therapies. At the same time, it is unusually philosophic and stresses cognitive processes in human disturbance.

Thus, REBT theorizes that most clients have somewhat similar Irrational *Beliefs* (IBs), especially the three major absolutistic musts that frequently plague the human race: (a) "I must achieve outstandingly well in one or more important respects or I am an inadequate person!" (b) "Other people must treat me fairly and well or they are bad people!" (c) "Conditions must be favorable or else my life is rotten and I can't stand it!" When one, two, or three of these are strongly and consistently held, people tend to make themselves emotionally and behaviorally disturbed.

Men, women, and children, the theory of REBT holds, have biological tendencies to construct rational wishes and preferences, such as the desire to be productive and achieving and the desire to relate well to other people. But they also have the choice of holding and raising their preferences to absolutistic, rigid demands. People have an existential choice of whether to be relatively preferring or demanding, and consequently to act in a healthy, self-helping manner or in an unhealthy, self-defeating manner. Usually they constructively choose self-helping behaviors and thereby aid their survival and happiness by being proactive and self-actualizing. But they easily often fall into obsessive-compulsive *addictions* to their life-enhancing preferences, however, and make themselves self-sabotaging. Why? Because they find it difficult to distinguish consistently between strong desires, which are usually life-enhancing, and rigid demands, which are often destructive.

The human tendency to create self-sabotaging demands out of self-helping desires and preferences is exacerbated by a number of common biological and environmental factors, including these:

1. Some individuals are born as demanders. At certain times in their lives or across the whole life span, demanders think and feel that they must have what they *really* want, no matter what the cost.

2. Some individuals have, temporarily or permanently, physiological deficiencies that impair arranging an efficient cost-benefit ratio between preferences and their demands. For various biological or environmental reasons they have hormonal, neuro-chemical, sensory, or other defects that interfere with normal reasoning and checking processes. At times it is nearly impossible for such individuals to keep their desires from escalating into demands. For example, inherited or acquired brain anomalies may lead some people to compulsive alcohol or drug use.

3. Family, social, and cultural influences learned at a young age may strongly encourage people to engage in behaviors that, under different conditions would not lead to addiction. For example, in order to win the approval of peers, youths may "willingly" addict themselves to smoking, drinking, and criminal acts.

4. Human habituation processes that involve self-defeating behaviors that are difficult to break may seem to "force" continuation of the behavior even though it is destructive. For example, once an individual is habituated to smoking, procrastinating, or staying up too late at night, it is most difficult to stop continuing these harmful habits.

5. Traumatic events sometimes severely disrupt protective checking mechanisms that prevent turning desires into demands. If, for example, a youngster is fairly well controlled in taking care of herself physically or tending to her school routines, and she is traumatized by rape, incest, or physical abuse, she may stop her self-controlling habits and almost uncontrollably resort to disruptive behaviors.

For many biological and environmental reasons, then, people consistently or sporadically make their healthy desires and preferences into unhealthy, self-sabotaging necessities. They are prone to do so by their psychophysical makeup, and they are encouraged to do so by various kinds of social reinforcement or conditioning. Do they then have any real choice in how they think, feel, and behave; or do they, as B. F. Skinner implied, have very limited freedom and dignity?

REBT holds that they have considerable existential choice. Skinner himself was a humanist and believed, as he showed in *Walden Two*, that people had the ability to change their contingencies of reinforcement and create something of a utopia for themselves. In REBT we say that although it is indeed difficult for humans to stop demanding and go back to strong desiring, thereby making themselves less disturbed, they have the ability to do this constructively. Why? Because not only can they think, but unlike other animals, they can think about their thinking, and think about thinking about their thinking. This hardly makes us superhuman, but it gives us at least a modest degree of free will or choice.

Yes, people can choose to change their ways, though that is difficult, even when they are born and reared to be self-defeating. The reason is that they are able to see how demanding they frequently are and *choose* to do the hard work and practice that is usually required for change. Being innate constructivists, they can change their habitual destructive tendencies including some of their biological tendencies, even in the face of neurological deficiencies such as attention deficit disorder and learning disabilities. They can learn to improve them and become less deficient. They may have endogenous depression, which makes them prone to catastrophic and awfulizing thinking. But they can use REBT and other forms of cognitive-behavior therapy to improve their depressive thinking. They can take Ritalin, antidepressives, and other psychotropic medication, which partially rectify some of their neurological and other physiological deficiencies.

Practically all people fairly frequently raise their healthy preferences to unhealthy demands, and many of them have biochemical deficits that incline them to think, feel, and behave self-defeatingly—against their own interests and those of the social groups in which they reside. Still, they can *choose* to improve themselves emotionally as well as to grow and develop into a happy and self-actualizing state of existence.

REBT is no panacea for all human ills. It has its limitations and drawbacks, as have all kinds of psychotherapy. But it is realistic and less limited by using, as noted above, a large number of cognitive, emotive, and behavioral methods. The addition of new methods seems to be effective. REBT theory states that most people are conflicted by making their desires into demands. They become less disturbing when therapy helps them restructure their demands and turn them back into desires.

Other biological, conditioning, and habituation factors are also involved with and may wither, create, or intensify emotional disturbance. Also, lack of skill training is frequently involved in dysfunctional behavior. For example, if you want to succeed at tennis, you may raise your want to a dire need and anxietize and depress yourself when you do not succeed as you think you must. Because of your self-disturbing, you may fail to do well at tennis, making yourself more anxious and depressed. But playing tennis also depends on coordination and the physical ability to hit the ball well, good instruction and learning the rudiments of tennis, and practice. So your blaming yourself for not playing "well enough" may depend not only on your demand that you play quite well, but also on your physical prowess, the kind of instruction you have had, and how much time you actually play the game.

REBT has a somewhat unique theory and practice of what usually causes human disturbing and what can be done to alleviate it. The REBT therapist assumes that most clients have absolutistic shoulds and musts and that they can be helped by recognizing that imperatives lead to needless disturbance. With REBT they learn that they will feel and act better—by getting more of what they want and less of what they do not want—if they clearly acknowledge demands and change them into preferences.

Many clients have special kinds of disorders or may react idiosyncratically to therapy and therefore may not benefit from the usual procedures of REBT or cognitive-behavior therapy (CBT). They may be mentally deficient, psychotic, brain injured, or have neurobiological defects such as attention deficit disorder or special educational disabilities. Other clients may resist using various REBT or CBT techniques because they are temperamentally opposed to them, will not do required homework, are hostile to the therapist, get neurotic gains from their disturbances, are convinced that they are hopeless, do not want to risk getting better, or for a variety of other idiosyncratic reasons.

Similarly, therapists who try to use the methods of REBT and CBT and do so ineffectually may not truly understand them, may be temperamentally opposed to them, will not take sufficient time or energy to apply them, have hostile attitudes toward some of their clients, or may have various other reasons. As many research studies have shown, the success of therapy depends on many relationship factors between clients and therapists. Negative aspects of the relationship may interfere with REBT and CBT techniques that are usually effective but do not work for a particular client or therapist.

For these and other reasons, clients often spend large amounts of time and money in therapy with relatively poor results. Some clients, because of the nature of their temperament, fail to use the potentially best cognitive, emotive, or behavioral methods that their therapists recommend. Some clients favor one or a few techniques that may not be the best for them and even favor irrational or inelegant methods that rarely work.

What does this mean for therapists who wish to be effective for as many of their clients as possible? It means that they can specialize in a particular mode of treatment, such as that which is primarily cognitive, experiential, or behavioral, and that they can honestly believe in and vigorously practice their specialty. Therapists should be prepared, however, for clients to resist their "best" methods and require different and perhaps "inferior" ones. Therapists must recognize that they, too, will at times be averse to using the best methods of a system of therapy and will tend to use them ineffectually.

REBT offers several therapeutic methods that have worked well with most clients much of the time. The therapy also includes many other cognitive, emotive, and behavioral methods that may be useful for particular clients when its most popular methods are resisted by client, therapist, or both. REBT practitioners are free to experiment with a wide variety of techniques, some of which may seem irrational. It is useful to follow Paul's (1967, p. 117) well-known statement about gauging which therapy is effective by seeing "*what* treatment by *whom*, is most effective for *this* individual, under what set of circumstances." To make this goal achievable, REBT always has available, as noted, with some unique clients, a large number of therapeutic varied methods to work with. That is why it accurately merits the name, Rational Emotive Behavior Therapy. The most effective system of psychotherapy will probably always include many cognitive, emotive, and behavioral procedures. REBT definitely does, and will most likely continue, to include this comprehensive array of approaches to psychotherapy.

How can therapists at least partially overcome resistance in themselves and their clients? First, REBT practitioners can learn and practice how to find and dispute their clients' Irrational *Beliefs* (IBs), particularly their absolutistic shoulds, oughts, and musts. They can learn cognitive restructuring and also effectively teach their clients to persistently and forcefully practice it.

Second, REBT therapists can learn and practice a number of other cognitive, emotive, and behavioral methods that help clients surrender their irrational beliefs, such as rational emotive imagery (Maultsby 1971) and shame-attacking exercise (Ellis 1996, 1999, 2000c, 2001).

Third, they can employ many of these same cognitive, emotive, and behavioral techniques to help clients who resist giving up their Irrational *Beliefs* but who can still derive considerable benefits from therapy. Therapists can thereby help clients make inelegant but beneficial therapeutic changes.

Fourth, when all else fails, REBT therapists can use various techniques from other forms of therapy, including even some "irrational" techniques, to help clients who resist employing the "best" methods. To take an extreme case, if the client rigidly believes that only his allegiance to and collaboration with the Devil will help him overcome his phobias or panic states, and the therapist thinks that this is a very crazy idea but it looks like the only one that will reduce the client's suffering, the therapist can "rationally" encourage this irrational belief (2000a, 2001).

SELF-HELP SUGGESTIONS

- It is easy for you—or anyone—to think that REBT is almost purely rational or cognitive because it uniquely emphasizes thinking; and I made the mistake of originally calling it Rational Psychotherapy (RT) and Aaron Beck still calls his form of therapy Cognitive Therapy (CT). But we were partly wrong! Rational, in REBT, means self-helping and society-helping in all possible ways—cognitive, emotional, and behavioral. So I rightly changed its name in 1993 to Rational Emotive Behavior Therapy.
- Although nothing is absolutely or perfectly rational—meaning, humanly helpful—you can often check out the workability of anything you think, feel, or do by using empirical and logical checking to partially, not completely, see whether it gets you the results you want. So empiricism and

logic *help* your rationality but don't necessarily *make* you effective.

- REBT holds that your thinking *includes* feeling and behaving, your feeling *includes* your thinking and behaving, and your behaving *includes* your thinking and feeling. So it gives you a *choice* of many cognitive, emotional, and acting techniques to help you improve your dysfunctioning and also enhance your happiness. Experiment in trying them out!

- An important behavioral aspect of REBT is skill training. Even if you are psychologically tuned to improving your functioning, you often require special skills—such as speaking, writing, or relating—to effectively do so. If you are lacking in some of these important skills, push yourself to learn them with cognitive, emotional, and behavioral elements. Yearn, burn, and turn to learn!

- Psychotherapy and self-help techniques that are good for others may, or may *not*, be good for you. That is why REBT provides you with a good many rational (cognitive), emotional-evocative, and behavioral techniques to experiment with. Go to it!

- Although "rational," as noted above, usually or normally, means methods that are empirically (realistically) and logically (uncontradictorily) checkable, this is not *always* true. When "rational" techniques do not seem to work for you, it is "rational"—meaning, sensible—to try some "irrational" self-help methods. Don't be *rigidly* rational!

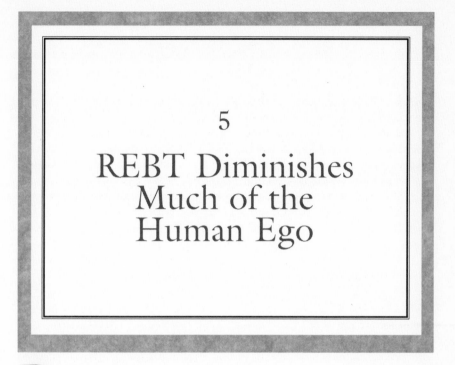

5

REBT Diminishes
Much of the
Human Ego

Rational Emotive Behavior Therapy includes the fundamental tenet of unconditional self-accepting (USA) which I adapted from Paul Tillich (1953) and other existentialists and from Alfred Korzybski (1933/1990) and the general semanticists. I included it in my first professional paper on REBT in 1956 (Ellis 1958) and, at greater length, in *Reason and Emotion in Psychotherapy* (Ellis 1962).

I soon learned that Robert Hartman, a professor of philosophy, actively taught that humans all had worth just because they were alive and human (Hartman 1967), became friendly with Hartman, and was invited to write a chapter of a book honoring his work. I enjoyed writing this chapter, "Psychotherapy and the Value of a Human Being" (Ellis 1972/1991), and came up with what I thought was an original solution to the problem of people rating themselves. They would be wiser to rate *only* their many behaviors but not *also* rate or evaluate their *selves*. Hartman agreed that that was an excellent solution to the human tendency of human self-rating and wrote me that if I were a Ph.D. student of philosophy, he would consider my chapter a valid dissertation and award me the doctorate on the basis of it.

This chapter is partly derived from *REBT Diminishes Much of the Human Ego*, rev. ed. (New York: Albert Ellis Institute, 1999). Used with permission.

Since my chapter on human worth was quite long, I wrote a summary of it for our clients at the Albert Ellis Institute, and I include the recently revised version of my pamphlet on it here. It is addressed to individual readers but also presents the REBT theory of unconditional self-accepting (USA) to the mental health profession.

Much of what we can call the human "ego" is vague and indeterminate and, when conceived of and given a global rating, interferes with survival and happiness. Certain aspects of "ego" seem to be vital and lead to beneficial results: for people do exist, or have aliveness, for a number of years, and they also have self-consciousness, or awareness of their existence. In this sense they have uniqueness, ongoingness, and "ego." What people call their "self" or "totality" or "personality," on the other hand, has a vague, almost indefinable quality. People may well have "good" or "bad" traits—characteristics that help or hinder them in their goals of survival or happiness—but they really have no "self" that "is" good or bad.

To increase their health and happiness, Rational Emotive Behavior Therapy (REBT) recommends that people would do better to resist the tendency to rate their "self" or "essence" and had better stick with rating only their deeds, traits, acts, characteristics, and performances. In some ways they can also evaluate the *effectiveness* of how they think, feel, and do. Once they choose their goals and purposes, they can rate their efficacy and efficiency in achieving these goals. And, as a number of experiments by Albert Bandura and his students have shown, their *belief* in their efficiency will often help make them more productive and achieving. But when people give a global, all-over rating to their "self" or "ego," they almost always create self-defeating, neurotic thoughts, feelings, and behaviors.

The vast majority of systems of psychotherapy seem intent on—indeed, almost obsessed with—upholding, bolstering, and strengthening people's "self-esteem." This includes such diverse systems as psychoanalysis, object relations, gestalt therapy, and even some of the main cognitive-behavioral therapies. Very few systems of personality take an opposing stand, as does Zen Buddhism, and try to help humans diminish or surrender some aspects of their egos; but these systems tend to have little popularity and to engender much dispute.

REBT (Rational Emotive Behavior Therapy) constitutes one of the very few modern therapeutic schools that has taken something of a stand against ego-rating, and continues to take an even stronger stand in this direction as it grows in its theory and its applications. This chapter outlines the up-to-date REBT position on ego-rating and explains why REBT helps people *diminish* their ego-rating propensities.

LEGITIMATE ASPECTS OF THE HUMAN EGO

REBT first tries to define the various aspects of the human ego and to endorse its "legitimate" aspects. It assumes that an individual's main goals or purposes include: (1) remaining alive and healthy and (2) enjoying oneself—experiencing a good deal of happiness and relatively little pain or dissatisfaction. We may, of course, argue with these goals; and not everyone accepts them as "good." But assuming that a person does value them, then he or she may have a valid "ego," "self," "self-consciousness," or "personality" which we may conceive of as something along the following lines:

1. "I exist; I have an ongoing aliveness that lasts perhaps eighty or more years and then apparently comes to an end, so that 'I' no longer exist."
2. "I exist separately, at least in part, from other humans, and can therefore conceive of myself as an individual in my 'own' right."
3. "I have different traits, at least in many of their details, from other humans, and consequently my 'I-ness' or my 'aliveness' has a certain kind of uniqueness. No other person in the world appears to have exactly the same traits as I have nor equals 'me' or constitutes the same entity as 'me'."
4. "I have the ability to keep existing, if I choose to do so, for a certain number of years—to have an ongoing existence, and to have some degree of consistent traits as I continue to exist. In that sense, I remain 'me' for a long time, even though my traits change in important respect."
5. "I have awareness or consciousness of my ongoingness, of my existence, of my behaviors and traits, and of various other aspects of my alivenss and experiencing. I can therefore say, 'I have self-consciousness'."
6. "I have some power to predict and plan for my future existence or ongoingness, and to change some of my traits and behaviors in accordance with my basic values and goals. My 'rational behavior,' as Myles Friedman has pointed out, to a large extent consists of my ability to predict and plan for my future."
7. "Because of my 'self-consciousness' and my ability to predict and plan for my future, I can to a considerable degree change my present and future traits (and hence 'existence'). In other words, I can at least partially control 'myself'."
8. "I similarly have the ability to remember, understand, and learn from my past and present experiences, and to use this remembering, understanding, and learning in the service of predicting and changing my future behavior."
9. "I can choose to discover what I like (enjoy) and dislike (disenjoy) and to try to arrange to experience more of what I like and less of what I dislike. I can also choose to survive or not to survive."
10. "I can choose to monitor or observe my thoughts, feelings, and actions to help myself survive and lead a more satisfying or more enjoyable existence."

11. "I can have confidence (believe that a high probability exists) that I can remain alive and make myself relatively happy and free from pain."

12. "I can choose to act as a *short-range* hedonist who mainly goes for the pleasures of the moment and gives little consideration to those of the future, or as a *long-range* hedonist who considers both the pleasures of the moment and of the future and who strives to achieve a fair degree of both."

13. "I can choose to see myself as having worth or value for pragmatic reasons—because I will then tend to act in my own interests, to go for pleasures rather than pain, to survive better, and to feel good."

14. "I can choose to accept myself unconditionally—whether or not I do well or get approved by others. I can thereby refuse to rate 'myself,' 'my totality,' 'my personhood' at all. Instead, I can rate my traits, deeds, acts, and performances—for the purposes of surviving and enjoying my life more, and *not* for the purposes of 'proving myself' or being 'egoistic' or showing that I have a 'better' or 'greater' value than others."

15. "My 'self' and my 'personality,' while in important ways individualistic and unique to me, are also very much part of my sociality and my culture. An unusually large part of 'me' and how 'I' think, feel, and behave is significantly influenced—and even created—by my social learning and my being tested in various groups. I am far from being *merely* an individual in my *own* right. My personhood includes socialhood. Moreover, I am rarely a hermit, but strongly *choose* to spend much of my life in family, school, work, neighborhood, community, and other *groups*. In numerous ways 'I' and 'me' are *also* a 'groupie'! 'My' individual ways of living, therefore, coalesce with 'social' rules of living. My 'self' is *both* a personal *and* a social product—and process! My unconditional self-acceptance (USA) had better intrinsically include unconditional other-acceptance (UOA). I can—and will!—accept other people, as well as myself, with *both* our virtues *and* our failings, with *both* our important accomplishments *and* our nonachievements, simply because we are alive and kicking, simply because we are human! My survival and happiness is well worth striving for and so is that of the rest of humanity."

These, it seems to me, are some "legitimate" aspects of ego-rating. Why legitimate? Because they seem to have some "reality"—that is, have some "facts" behind them. And because they appear to help people who subscribe to them to attain their usual basic values of surviving and feeling happy rather than miserable.

SELF-DEFEATING ASPECTS OF THE HUMAN "EGO" (SELF-RATING)

At the same time, people subscribe to some "illegitimate" aspects of the human "ego" or of self-rating, such as these:

1. "I exist not only as a unique person, but as a *special* person. I am a *better individual* than other people because of my outstanding traits."

2. "I have a superhuman rather than merely a human quality. I can do things that other people cannot possibly do and deserve to be deified for doing these things."

3. "If I do not have outstanding, special, or superhuman characteristics, I am subhuman. Whenever I do not perform notably, I deserve to be devil-ified and damned."

4. "The universe especially and signally cares about me. It has a personal interest in me and wants to see me do remarkably well and to feel happy."

5. "I *need* the universe to specially care about me. If it does not, I am a lowly individual, I cannot take care of myself, and must feel desperately miserable."

6. "Because I exist, I *absolutely* have to succeed in life and I *must* obtain love and approval by all the people that I find significant."

7. "Because I exist, I *must* survive and continue to have a happy existence."

8. "Because I exist, I *must* exist forever, and have *immortality.*"

9. "I *equal* my traits. If I have some significant bad traits, *I* totally rate as bad; and if I have some significant good ones, *I* rate as a good person."

10. "I particularly equal my character traits. If I treat others well and therefore have a 'good character,' I am a good person; and if I treat others badly and therefore have a 'bad character,' I have the essence of a bad person."

11. "In order to accept and respect myself, I must prove I have real worth—prove it by having competence, outstandingness, and the approval of others."

12. "To have a happy existence, I *must* have—absolutely *need*—the things I really want."

The self-rating aspects of ego, in other words, tend to do you in, to handicap you, to interfere with your satisfactions. They differ enormously from the self-individuating aspects of ego. The latter involve *how* or *how well* you exist. You remain alive as a distinct, different, unique individual because you have various traits and performances and because you enjoy their fruits. But you have "ego" in the sense of self-rating because you magically think in terms of upping or downing, deifying or devil-ifying yourself *for* how or how well you exist. Ironically, you probably think that rating yourself or your "ego" will *help* you live as a unique person and enjoy yourself. Well, it usually won't! For the most part it will let you survive, perhaps—but pretty miserably!

ADVANTAGES OF "EGO-ISM" OR SELF-RATING

Doesn't ego-ism, self-rating, or self-esteem have *any* advantages? It certainly does—and that is probably why it survives in spite of its disadvantages. What advantages does it have? It tends to motivate you to succeed and to win others' approval. It gives you an interesting, preoccupying *game* of constantly comparing your deeds and your "self" to those of other people. It often helps you impress others—which has a practical value, in many instances. It may help preserve your life—such as when you strive to make more money, for egoistic reasons, and thus aid your survival by means of this money.

Self-rating serves as a very easy and comfortable position to fall into—humans seem to have a biological tendency to engage in it. It can also give you enormous pleasure when you rate yourself as noble, great, or outstanding. It may motivate you to produce notable works of art, science, or invention. It can enable you to feel superior to others—at times, even to feel godlike.

Egoism obviously has real advantages. To give up self-rating completely would amount to quite a sacrifice. We cannot justifiably say that it brings no gains, or that it produces no social or individual good.

DISADVANTAGES OF "EGO-ISM" OR SELF-RATING

These are some of the more important reasons why rating yourself as either a good or a bad person has immense dangers and will frequently handicap you:

1. To work well, self-rating requires you to have extraordinary ability and talent, or virtual infallibility. For you then can elevate your ego only when you do well, and concomitantly depress it when you do poorly. What chance do you have of steadily or always doing well?

2. To have, in common parlance, a "strong" ego or "real" self-esteem really requires you to be above-average or outstanding. Only if you have special talent will you likely accept yourself and rate yourself highly. But obviously very few individuals can have unusual, geniuslike ability. And will you personally reach that uncommon level? I doubt it!

3. Even if you have enormous talents and abilities, to accept yourself or esteem yourself consistently, in an ego-rating way, you have to display them virtually all the time. Any significant lapse, and you immediately tend to down yourself. And then, when you down yourself, you tend to lapse more—a truly vicious circle!

4. When you insist on gaining "self-esteem," you basically do so in order to impress others with your great "value" or "worth" as a human. But the need to impress others and to win their approval, and thereby view your-

self as a "good person," leads to an obsession that tends to preempt a large part of your life. You seek status instead of seeking joy. And you seek universal acceptance—which you certainly have virtually no chance of ever getting!

5. Even when you impress others, and supposedly gain "worth" that way, you tend to realize that you do so partly by acting and falsifying your talents. You consequently look upon yourself as a phony. Ironically, then, first you down yourself for not impressing others; but then you also down yourself for phonily impressing them!

6. When you rate yourself and succeed at giving yourself a superior rating, you delude yourself into thinking you have superiority over others. You may indeed have some superior traits; but you devoutly feel that you become a truly superior person—or semigod. And that delusion gives you an artificial or false sense of "self-esteem."

7. When you insist on rating yourself as good or bad, you tend to focus on your defects, liabilities, and failings, for you feel certain that they make you into an R.P., or rotten person. By focusing on these defects, you accentuate them, often making them worse; interfere with changing them; and acquire a generalized negative view of yourself that frequently ends up in arrant self-deprecation.

8. When you rate your *self*, instead of only evaluating the effectiveness of your thoughts, feelings, and actions, you have the philosophy that you *must* prove yourself as good; and since there always exists a good chance that you will not, you tend to remain underlyingly or overtly anxious practically all the time. In addition, you may continually verge on depression, despair, and feelings of intense shame, guilt, and worthlessness.

9. When you preoccupyingly rate yourself, even if you succeed in earning a good rating, you do so at the expense of becoming obsessed with success, achievement, attainment, and outstandingness. But this kind of concentration on success deflects you from doing what *you* really desire to do and from the goal of trying to be happy: some of the most successful people actually remain quite miserable.

10. By the same token, in mightily striving for outstandingness, success, and superiority, you rarely stop to ask yourself, "What do I really want—and want for myself?" So you fail to find what you really enjoy in life.

11. Ostensibly, your focusing on achieving greatness and superiority over others and thereby winning a high self-rating serves to help you do better in life. Actually, it helps you focus on your so-called *worth* and *value* rather than on your competency and happiness; and consequently, you fail to achieve many things that you otherwise could. Because you *have* to prove your utter competence, you often tend to make yourself less competent—and sometimes withdraw from competition.

12. Although self-rating may occasionally help you pursue creative activities, it frequently has the opposite result. For example, you may

become so hung up on success and superiority that you uncreatively and obsessively-compulsively go for these goals rather than that of creative participation in art, music, science, invention, or other pursuits.

13. When you rate yourself you tend to become self-centered rather than problem-centered. Therefore, you do not try to solve many of the practical and important problems in life but largely focus on your own navel and the pseudoproblem of *proving* yourself instead of *finding* yourself.

14. Self-rating generally helps you feel abnormally self-conscious. Self-consciousness, or the knowledge that you have an ongoing quality and can enjoy or disenjoy yourself, can have great advantages. But extreme self-consciousness, or continually spying on yourself and rating yourself on how well you do takes this good trait to an obnoxious extreme and may interfere seriously with your happiness.

15. Self-rating encourages a great amount of prejudice. It consists of an overgeneralization: "Because one or more of my traits seem inadequate, I rate as a totally inadequate person." This means, in effect, that you feel prejudiced against *yourself* for some of your *behavior*. In doing this, you tend also to feel prejudiced against others for their poor behavior—or for what you consider their inferior traits. You thus can make yourself feel bigoted about blacks, Jews, Catholics, Italians, and various other groups which include some people you do not like.

16. Self-rating leads to necessitizing and compulsiveness. When you believe, "I must down myself when I have a crummy trait or set of performances," you usually also believe that "I absolutely *have* to have good traits or performances," and you feel compelled to act in certain "good" ways—even when you have little chance of consistently doing so.

WHY "EGO-ISM" AND SELF-RATING ARE ILLOGICAL

In these and other ways, attempting to have "ego-strength" or "self-esteem" leads to distinctly poor results: meaning, it interferes with your life and happiness. To make matters even worse, ego-ratings or self-ratings are unsound, in that accurate or "true" self-ratings or global ratings are virtually impossible to make. For a global or total rating of an individual involves the following kinds of contradictions and magical thinking:

1. As a person, you have almost innumerable traits—virtually all of which change from day to day or year to year. How can any single global rating of you, therefore, meaningfully apply to all of you—including your constantly changing traits?

2. You exist as an ongoing *process*—an individual who has a past, pre-

sent, and future. Any rating of your you-ness, therefore, would apply only to "you" at single points in time and hardly to your ongoingness.

3. To give a rating to "you" totally, we would have to rate all of your traits, deeds, acts, and performances, and somehow add or multiply them. But these characteristics are valued differently in different cultures and at different times. And *who* can therefore legitimately rate or weigh them, except in a given culture at a given time, and to a very limited degree?

4. If we did get legitimate ratings for every one of your past, present, and future traits, what kind of math would we employ to total them? Can we divide by the number of traits, and get a "valid" global rating? Could we use simple arithmetic? Algebraic ratings? Geometric ratings? Logarithmic ratings? What?

5. To rate "you" totally and accurately, we would have to know *all* your characteristics, or at least the "important" ones, and include them in our total. But how could we ever know them all? All your thoughts? Your emotions? Your "good" and "bad" deeds? Your accomplishments? Your psychological states?

6. To say that you have no value or are worthless involves several unprovable (and unfalsifiable) hypotheses: (1) that you have, innately, an essence of worthlessness; (2) that you never could possibly have any worth whatsoever; and (3) that you deserve damnation or eternal punishment for having the misfortune of worthlessness. Similarly, to say that you have great worth involves the unprovable hypothesis that (1) you just happen to have superior worth; (2) you will always have it, no matter what you do; and (3) you deserve deification or eternal reward for having this boon of great worth. No scientific methods of confirming or falsifying these hypotheses seem to exist.

7. When you posit global worth or worthlessness, you almost inevitably get yourself into circular thinking. If you *see* yourself as having intrinsic value, you will tend to *see* your traits as good, and will have a halo effect. Then you will falsely conclude that because you have these good characteristics, you have intrinsic value. Similarly, if you see yourself as having worthlessness, you will view your "good" traits as "bad," and "prove" your hypothesized lack of value.

8. You can pragmatically believe that "I am good because I exist." But this stands as a tautological, unprovable hypothesis, in the same class with the equally unprovable (and undisprovable) statement, "I am bad because I exist." *Assuming* that you have intrinsic value because you remain alive may help you feel happier than if you assume the opposite. But philosophically, it remains an untenable proposition. You might just as well say, "I have worth because God loves me," or "I have no value because God (or the Devil) hates me." The assumptions cause you to feel and act in certain ways; but they appear essentially unverifiable and unfalsifiable.

For reasons such as those just outlined, we may make the following conclusions: (1) You do seem to exist, or have aliveness, for a number of years, and you also appear to have consciousness, or awareness of your existence. In this sense, you have a human uniqueness, ongoingness, or, if you will, "ego." (2) But what you normally call your "self" or your "totality" or your "personality" has a vague, almost indefinable quality; and you cannot legitimately give it a global rating or report card. You may *have* good and bad traits or characteristics that help you or hinder you in your goals of survival and happiness and that enable you to live responsibly or irresponsibly with others, but you or your "self" really "are not" good or bad. (3) When you give yourself a global rating, or have "ego" in the usual sense of that term, you may help yourself in various ways; on the whole, however, you tend to do much more harm than good and preoccupy yourself with rather foolish, side-tracking goals. Much of what we call emotional "disturbance" or neurotic "symptoms" directly or indirectly results from globally rating yourself and other humans. (4) Therefore, you'd better resist the tendency to rate your "self" or your "essence" or your "totality" and had better stick with only rating your deeds, traits, acts, characteristics, and performances.

In other words, you had better reduce much of what we normally call your human "ego" and retain those parts of it which can help you experiment with life, choose what you tentatively think you want to do or avoid, and enjoy what you *discover* is "good" for you and for the social group in which you choose to live.

More positively, the two main solutions to the problem of self-rating consist of an elegant and an inelegant answer. The inelegant solution involves your making an arbitrary but practical definition or statement about yourself: "I accept myself as good or evaluate myself as good because I exist." This proposition, though unabsolute and arguable, will tend to provide you with feelings of self-acceptance or self-confidence and has many advantages and few disadvantages. It will almost always work, and it will preclude your having feelings of self-denigration or worthlessness as long as you hold it.

More elegantly, you can accept this proposition: "I do not have intrinsic worth or worthlessness, but merely aliveness. I'd better rate my traits and acts but not my totality or 'self.' I fully *accept* myself, in the sense that I know I have aliveness, and I *choose* to survive and live as happily as possible, and with minimum needless pain. I require only this knowledge and this choice—and no other kind of self-rating." In other words, you can decide only to rate or measure your *acts* and *performances*—your thoughts, feelings, and behaviors—by viewing them as "good" when they aid your goals and values and as "bad" when they sabotage your individual and social desires and preferences. But you can simultaneously decide not to rate your "self," "essence," or "totality" at all. Yes, at *all*!

Rational Emotive Behavior Therapy (REBT) recommends this second, more elegant solution, because it appears more honest, more practical, and leads to fewer philosophical difficulties than the inelegant one. But if you absolutely insist on a "self"-rating, we recommend that you rate yourself as "good" merely because you are alive. That kind of "egoism" will get you into very little trouble!

SELF-HELP SUGGESTIONS

This chapter was originally written for clients at the psychologic clinic of the Albert Ellis Institute and for readers all over the world. It therefore includes several important self-help suggestions that can be read in the chapter itself. For help with your personal problems, read it over and try to follow its main points on how you can achieve and maintain unconditional self-accepting (USA).

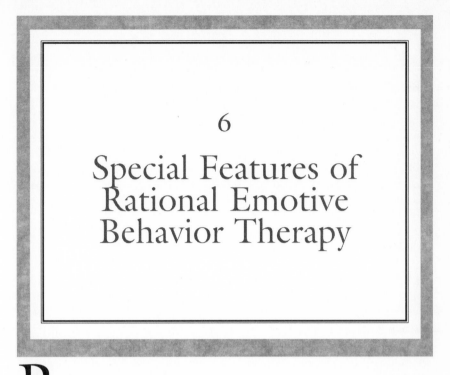

6

Special Features of Rational Emotive Behavior Therapy

Rational emotive behavior therapy (REBT) has several special features that distinguish it from the cognitive therapies of Aaron Beck, Maxie Maultsby, Donald Meichenbaum, George Kelly, and other proponents of cognitive-behavior therapy, as well as from other forms of psychotherapy. Let me describe some of the special features of REBT that are commonly followed by practitioners.

SOURCES OF PSYCHOLOGICAL DISTURBING

More than most other forms of psychotherapy, REBT realistically emphasizes the innate propensity of people to think and act dysfunctionally and holds that this biological tendency is one of the main reasons that people frequently resist change even when they presumably want to effect it. But REBT also highlights the innate tendency of humans to train themselves to choose or not to choose unproductive thoughts, feelings, and actions—and to keep changing them (Ellis 1976, 2000b, 2001).

This chapter was partly derived from "Special Features of Rational Emotive Behavior Therapy," in W. Dryden, R. DiGiuseppe, and M. Neenan, *A Primer on Rational Emotive Behavior Therapy* (Champaign, Ill.: Research Press, 2000). Used with permission.

In addition, REBT stresses the tendency of almost all humans to create secondary as well as primary disturbing symptoms. Thus, when people anxietize themselves, they frequently construct Irrational *Beliefs* about their anxietizing and therefore make themselves anxious or self-downing about that. When they depress themselves, they frequently depress themselves about their depressing. Although their primary distressing often has profound emotional, behavioral, and cognitive sources, their secondary self-distressing is perhaps even more cognitive because clients *observe* their primary dysfunctional feelings, negatively *think* about them, and awfulizingly *conclude* about their "horror."

ASSESSING SELF-DISTURBING

REBT tends to employ at times all the assessing procedures used by other cognitive-behavior therapies, but it can also be done with a minimum of these procedures in some instances. This is largely because REBT favors therapy itself as an important means of assessing and holds that, in many (but not all) cases, zeroing in on some of the client's Irrational *Beliefs* can be highly diagnostic and can indicate how and under what conditions the client is likely to react to psychotherapy. For example, clients who have great difficulty in acknowledging their Irrational *Beliefs*, in recognizing that such Beliefs contribute significantly to their upsetting themselves, and in forcefully and persistently disputing them (as they are shown how to do in REBT) will usually differ from other clients. Their ways of reacting to REBT will give their therapist important diagnostic and prognostic data.

REBT notably distinguishes between healthy and unhealthy feelings when people react to some unfortunate Adversities (As). It considers consequent feelings of sorrow, regret, frustration, and annoyance as healthy or self-helping; and it sees anxietizing, depressing, and raging as unhealthy or self-sabotaging. REBT practitioners therefore actively look for healthy and unhealthy feelings; and may show clients that it is appropriate to make themselves quite sorry or frustrated about a loss without also depressing or terrifying about it. In REBT terms, keenly sorrowing and regretting about a serious loss is not considered to be having an unhealthy emotional problem. Similarly, an REBT practitioner may not try to help clients become unconcerned about, say, losing a job or acquiring poor physical health, because lack of such concern may lead to poor results.

LOOKING FOR IRRATIONAL BELIEFS

Although virtually all systems of cognitive and cognitive-behavior therapy help clients look for Irrational *Beliefs,* self-defeating ideas, or dysfunctional cognitions, REBT takes a somewhat unique stand in this respect:

1. According to REBT, the main kinds of evaluative IBs that lead to disturbance are absolutistic and unconditional shoulds, oughts, musts, demands, commands, and expectations. More specifically, almost all people who are diagnosed as behaving "neurotically" (and especially those with personality disorders) absolutistically and dogmatically command that they themselves *must* do well and be approved by significant others, that others *have* to treat them considerately and fairly, and that conditions of living have *got to* be reasonably easy and enjoyable.

2. Emotional self-disturbing also results from Irrational *Beliefs* other than absolutistic evaluations (i.e., from awfulizing, I-can't-stand-it-izing, and from damning oneself and others). But these kinds of Irrational *Beliefs* seem, in most cases, to accompany explicit or implicit absolutistic musts and would rarely exist without them. Thus, when I irrationally hold, "The earth must be flat!" I then tend to conclude, logically but erroneously, (a) "It is *awful* if the earth is not as flat as it must be!" (b) "I *can't stand it* when the earth is not as flat as it has to be!" and (c) "I'm *no good* if I fail to see the earth as being as flat as it must be!"

3. In addition to absolutistic or "musturbatory" thinking, people often contribute to their disturbances with antiempirical or unrealistic inferences. For example, they tell themselves, "Because I failed a few times, I will always fail." They personalize, overgeneralize, resort to non sequiturs, and use always-and-never thinking about their strong desires. But they especially do so when they escalate these desires into absolutistic demands and musts. Irrational, unrealistic, and illogical inferring is itself an important aspect of human behavior and results in many poor outcomes. But unless it is tied to absolutistic musts and commands and to human evaluations, it does not usually lead to what we call emotional disturbance.

DISPUTING IRRATIONAL BELIEFS

REBT emphasizes the use of scientific method and of logico-empirical disputing to help people change the Irrational *Beliefs* that encourage self-disturbing. It often actively questions and challenges all kinds and levels of IBs, but it particularly challenges dogmatic musturbating and necessitizing and helps people change them to desiring and preferring. It favors science and the scientific method in several ways that many other therapies do not mention or favor:

1. It holds that people who consistently employ scientific, flexible, non-dogmatic, nonabsolutistic thinking about themselves and others tend to make themselves minimally disturbing and that dogma, inflexibility, and refusal to accept reality are the essence of much serious self-upsetting.

2. It teaches the scientific method of questioning and disputing irrational hypotheses to its clients and shows them how to apply it when the therapist is not present.

3. It accepts the religious beliefs and values of its clients and shows them how to live undisturbedly with religious, mystical, or superstitious ideas. But it questions devoutness and sacredizing—whether theological, political, economic, or social—and shows people how to combat rigid dogma and absolutism.

4. In some cases, it may use nonscientific and religious views that are antiempirical but that may help people ameliorate their disturbance and do them more good than harm (Ellis 2000a; Nielsen, Johnson, and Ellis 2001).

THERAPEUTIC RELATIONSHIP

REBT favors the building of a good rapport with clients, uses empathic listening and reflection of feeling, and particularly strong encouragement, to help clients look at themselves and change. At the same time, it acknowledges the dangers of building too warm or close a relationship between client and therapist. This is because many clients tend to have a dire need for everyone's, including the therapist's, approval; therefore, the therapist's favoring them may help accentuate this need.

REBT acknowledges that the therapist also may have a dire need for clients' approval and may consequently hold back from actively disputing the clients' Irrational *Beliefs* and from giving them difficult homework assignments. REBT therefore encourages therapists to look at their own motives for building overly warm relationships with clients. At the same time, REBT especially holds that the therapist should emphasize unconditional positive regard or unconditional accepting (UOA) for all clients—no matter how obnoxiously they may behave in or out of therapy. It encourages therapists to evaluate clients' acts, feelings, and thoughts, but not to rate them globally as humans, nor especially to denigrate their selves, beings, or essences in any way—yes, even when they act "stupidly," "wrongly," or "self-defeatingly."

REBT often tries to show clients that they are equal and active collaborators with the therapist in looking at and changing themselves. But it also sees the therapist as a highly active-directive teacher, who knows more about human personality and its self-disturbing tendencies than many clients and who therefore had often better take the lead in explaining, interpreting, and disputing clients' dysfunctional behaving as well as in aiding them to come up with better solutions to their practical problems of living.

MULTIMODAL AND COMPREHENSIVE USE OF TECHNIQUES

REBT has a distinct theory of human disturbance and of how it may efficiently be reduced. But its theory, as discussed earlier, is interactive and multimodal, and sees emotions, thoughts, and behaviors as transacting with and including one another. Hence REBT has always been multimodal in its uses of many therapeutic techniques: cognitive, emotive, and behavioral. Because it emphasizes the biological as well as social sources of human disturbance, it frequently recommends medication and physical techniques such as diet, exercise, yoga, and relaxation methods.

At the same time, REBT is highly selective in its techniques and only occasionally uses a method because it works temporarily and superficially (e.g., positive thinking). Instead, REBT looks at the long-range as well as the short-range effects of employing various methods, considers many techniques as more palliative than curative (e.g., cognitive distraction), and tries to emphasize those methods that lead to a profound philosophical and emotional change and that help clients' *getting* better in addition to their mainly *feeling* better (Ellis 1999, 2000a, 2001).

Almost all forms of psychotherapy try particularly to help clients with ego problems—particularly those clients who anxietize, depress, and deprecate themselves. REBT, while specializing in such problems, also looks for difficulties stemming from clients having trouble tolerating frustration. REBT calls this kind of self-upsetting *discomfort disturbance*. It assumes that most clients create important aspects of ego anxietizing and *also* some discomfort anxietizing. When one of these forms of self-distressing is prominent it looks for (but does not necessarily always find) the other. REBT uses some of its methods to combat ego-upsetting and some to combat discomfort-upsetting; and it looks for the interrelationship between these two partially distinct, but overlapping, kinds of problems. Thus, REBT shows clients how to accept themselves when they are doing poorly. But it also shows them how to give up their low frustration tolarence and their awfulizing that often accompanies it. When they think that it is awful to do the work involved in stopping their self-downing and refuse to take the effort to do so, it reveals their intolerance of frustration—"Therapy *shouldn't* be so hard for me to work at! It's too hard!" Rational emotive behavior therapists then show clients how to tackle their low frustration tolerance (LFT) and how to get back to *working* at their therapy.

EMOTIVE ASPECTS

In keeping with its comprehensive and multimodal character, REBT almost
invariably uses a number of emotive as well as cognitive and behavioral techniques. Its theory hypothesizes that disturbed people not only repeat, but
forcefully, vigorously, and emotionally repeat their self-defeating musturbatory convictions. Therefore they had better use some strong, dramatic,
evocative methods of changing themselves, and REBT specializes in seeing
that they do so. It encourages clients *forcefully to* dispute their Irrational
Beliefs and *actively* get in touch with and work on changing their feelings.
REBT practitioners, moreover, often *powerfully* show clients how they are
disturbing themselves and how they will remain dysfunctional unless they
vigorously strive for and actively commit themselves to self-change.

Toward this end, REBT usually favors a number of emotive methods,
including Rational Emotive Imagery, shame-attacking exercises, role
playing, strong self-statements, therapeutic encouragement, group support,
and various other affective techniques. But, as previously mentioned, it
employs these methods not only for their immediate benefits but also to
help clients make a profound and lasting affective-philosophical change.

HUMANISTIC ASPECTS OF REBT

Unlike some of the other cognitive behavior therapies, REBT takes a definite
humanistic-existential approach. It is not purely objective, scientific, or tech-
nique-centered; it adheres to the humanistic principles that are described in detail
in the next chapter. It particularly emphasizes the importance of will and choice
in human affairs, even though it acknowledges that some human behavior is partially determined by biological predispositions and by social learning.

REBT VIEW OF UNCONDITIONAL SELF-ACCEPTANCE AND UNCONDITIONAL OTHER-ACCEPTANCE

Two of the main goals of REBT are to help clients achieve unconditional
self-acceptance (USA) and unconditional other acceptance (UOA) and to
see that these are interrelated. If clients will fully accept themselves, they will
also tend to fully accept all other humans, and vice versa. They will then
enhance their individualistic self-direction and their social interest and interpersonal relationships. Carl Rogers gave his clients unconditional positive
regard and hoped that they would then model it for themselves. REBT practitioners go out of their way to give it but also actively teach their clients

how to achieve it personally and interpersonally. Self-accepting and other-accepting then become reciprocal. Details of the REBT view of USA and UOA are given in the previous chapter.

VIEW OF EFFICIENCY AND ELEGANCE IN PSYCHOTHERAPY

REBT, unlike some other types of psychotherapy, especially strives for efficiency and elegance in therapy. To this end, it attempts the following:

1. REBT aims not merely for symptom removal but also for a profound change in the basic philosophy that largely creates people's disturbing.
2. It tries to alleviate or remove most emotional and behavioral distressing long-lastingly, not just transiently, though it acknowledges that people have a tendency, from time to time, to retrogress and reinstitute ther dysfunctioning once they have originally minimized it.
3. REBT tries to help as many of its clients as feasible make profound philosophical changes that will deter them from creating new distressing in the future.
4. REBT shows clients how to quickly see what they do to create new or recurring emotional dysfunctioning and how they can promptly alleviate it. It motivates people to quickly undo their neuroticizing and to prevent its reoccurring.
5. REBT tries to develop methods of elegant psychotherapy that require relatively little therapeutic time and can be used for self-help homework after therapy sessions have ended. It tries to produce maximum results quickly and efficiently. But it also stresses the point that some clients may have to keep using therapeutic work and practice for years to come.
6. REBT tries to develop and promote psychoeducational methods that can help clients help themselves and that also can be applied to large numbers of people and not only to clients. It specializes in bibliotherapy, audiotherapy, videotherapy, talks, workshops, courses, and other media presentations that present some of the main REBT teachings to large groups of individuals. In this way it tries to help people prophylactically before they disturb themselves, as well as after they do.

BEHAVIORAL METHODS

REBT almost always uses behavioral techniques of therapy, but it particularly favors in vivo desensitization rather than purely imaginative forms of systemic desensitization, especially with difficult clients who resist other methods. More specifically, it holds that people rarely change their disturbance-creating philosophies unless they strongly and steadily *act* against them. It frequently urges clients to make themselves deliberately uncomfortable (e.g., in performing exercise or dieting) until they finally become comfortable and, perhaps, enjoying.

REBT uses behavioral reinforcement procedures in many instances but often uses them differently than do other schools of cognitive behavior therapy:

1. It is wary of using love or approval as a reinforcer because many people may thereby become more needy, less autonomous, and more dependent on others—including their therapist!

2. It tries to help people think through for themselves and decide on their own goals and purposes, and hence to become less suggestible and reinforceable by external influences.

3. It endeavors to help people do things (e.g., art and science) for the intrinsic enjoyment of doing them and not merely for the extrinsic rewards of, say, money or fame.

4. It encourages clients who are not easily reinforceable to use, instead of or in addition to rewards, stiff penalties when they want to change dysfunctional behaviors. But it tries to make very clear that penalties are not to be used as punishments that may encourage clients to feel undeserving or worthless.

MULTIPLICITY OF COGNITIVE METHODS

Although REBT favors disputing, skepticism, and the use of logical-empirical methods of science to help people to see and to surrender their basic Irrational *Beliefs*, it also employs many other cognitive methods of therapy to help people change their self-defeating thinking, emoting, and behaving:

1. It often uses positive self-statements or Rational *Beliefs* and encourages clients to write these down, think about them, and steadily and strongly repeat them to themselves. For example, if a client irrationally believes, "I must be loved by so-and-so in order to accept myself," an REBT practitioner can: (a) illustrate how to actively dispute this idea; (b) ask, "What alternate rational statements could you make to yourself instead of this irrational statement?"; and (c) have the client write down a list of rational coping statements (e.g., "I do not *need* what I *want* " or "It is highly desirable to be loved by so-and-so, but I can also live happily without that love"). As cognitive homework, the client keeps going over these statements, figuring out why they are accurate and helpful, and through this process, really—yes, really—believes them.

2. REBT uses many forms of cognitive distraction (e.g., relaxation methods, yoga, meditation, reading, creative writing, and socializing) to help clients interrupt their obsessions with self-defeating ideas and actions.

3. It often uses considerable philosophical discussion, including existential dialogues with clients.

4. It teaches people how to do practical problem solving, including how to go back to Adversities (As) and improve them.

5. It uses imaging techniques, including positive imagery (in which people are able to imagine themselves succeeding rather than failing at an important task) and negative imagery (as in Rational Emotive Imagery, in which clients imagine some of the worst things that could happen to them and make themselves feel healthily sorry and regretful instead of unhealthily panicked).

6. It employs modeling methods, through which clients are shown how to help themselves and how to do cognitive restructuring by observing others successfully doing so while dealing with Adversities.

In employing these cognitive methods, as well as in its emotive and behavioral techniques, REBT practitioners are rarely satisfied with symptom improvement, even when this is radical and startling. Their main goal is to try to help clients achieve a profound attitudinal or philosophical change—to internalize a new way of looking at themselves, at others, and at the world—so that they seldom seriously disturb themselves about anything that may happen and, when they do, quickly acknowledge their own contribution to their disturbance and work at undisturbing themselves. Therefore, REBT is not only a theory and practice of psychotherapy but a philosophy that holds that human disturbance is largely, although not completely, self-created and that most people are capable of uncreating their own disturbances and of stubbornly refusing to upset themselves severely about almost anything for the rest of their lives. REBT acknowledges that many clients will only partially accept and internalize this elegant attitude, but it strives to help as many as feasible to do so.

SELF-HELP SUGGESTIONS

- REBT emphasizes, more than most other forms of psychotherapy, that one of the quickest and most profound ways of changing your disturbing feelings and behaviors is to work hard at changing your thinking. But it also points out the interrelationship of thoughts, emotions, and actions and the fact that sometimes—no, not *always*—the best way to change your dysfunctional thinking is to work on your feelings and your behaviors.
- REBT therefore gives you a large number of cognitive, emotional, and behavioral methods of self-change, and encourages you to use several— sometimes many—of them. Instead of downplaying your feelings it

encourages you to feel, and strongly feel, healthy negative emotions—such as sorrow, regret, frustration, and displeasure—when something goes wrong in your life, instead of unhealthy, sabotaging feelings of panicking, depressing, and raging. Look for this difference and distinguish between your unhealthy and your healthy negative reactions to Adversities.

- Important hint: Your unhealthy negative feelings are almost always are accompanied by some Irrational *Belief* (IB) that explicitly or implicitly includes a pronounced *demand* or *must*. For example: "I *absolutely must* perform important tasks well!" "Other people absolutely *must* treat me fairly and considerately." "My life conditions *definitely have to be* comfortable or else I can't stand it!" When you're miserable and not merely sorrowful, regretful, or frustrated, find your musturbating *demands* and change them back to *preferences*. Then you will have *healthy* negative feelings.

- You change your IBs by actively Disputing them realistically, logically, and practically—as shown in this chapter and in other sections of this book.

- You can use several of REBT's emotive, humanistic, and behavioral methods—particularly unconditional self-accepting (USA), unconditional other-accepting (UOA), and high frustration tolerance (HFT)—which are also described in this chapter.

7

The Humanism of Rational Emotive Behavior Therapy

In his article "Humanistic Psychology," in Raymond Corsini's *Encyclopedia of Psychology*, M. Brewster Smith (1994) pointed out that secular humanism is "a neglected version of humanistic psychology," and showed that where Pascal and Kierkegaard defined the religious version of existentialism, Shakespeare, Montaigne, Nietzsche, Sartre, and other thinkers "proposed a mundane, Godless humanism, also existentialist in its concern with the responsibility entitled by human self-consciousness" (p. 158). Smith also contrasted the somewhat irreconcilable perspective of causal and interpretive understanding in psychological science and argued that "for the distinctly human world, interpretation and causal explanation must somehow be joined . . . . Indeed, the only satisfactory science of human experience and action must be one on which the hermeneutic interpretation plays a central part conjoined with causal explanation" (p. 158).

Quite a problem! Secular humanism is in many ways opposite to the religious, mystical, and spiritual humanism such as that which seems to prevail in the Association for Humanistic Psychology (AHP), as well as in the

This chapter is partly adapted from "The Humanism of Rational Emotive Behavior Therapy and Other Cognitive Behavior Therapies," *Journal of Humanistic Education and Development* 35 (1996): 60–88.

Division of Humanistic Psychology of the American Psychological Association. Secular humanism tries to be quite existential, social, phenomenological, and even postmodernistic. But it also does its best to be rigorously (not rigidly) empirical, naturalistic, relativistic, and scientific. On the other hand, transpersonal psychology, a dominant theme in recent AHP publications, claims to be scientific because it uses some of the methods of science, but actually is often dogmatic and absolutist (Ellis and Yeager 1989; Kurtz 1986). Let me focus on what secular humanism is and how it specifically is applied in rational emotive behavior therapy (REBT).

Secular humanists see men and women as unique individuals who almost always choose to live in a social group. They are individuals in their own personal right but also are—and had better be—social creatures who try to live together peacefully, fairly, and democratically. Even their discrete "personality," as Sampson (1989) noted, is also a social product. Secular humanists fully acknowledge people to be human—that is, very limited and fallible—and in no way either superhuman (*more than* human) or subhuman (*less than* human). They all seem to have both good and bad behaviors but, as Alfred Korzybski pointed out, they *are not* what they *do*.

The personalities of men and women are an ongoing, ever-changing, constructing and reconstructing *process*. Once they set up goals and purposes, which as humans they invariably seem to do, their acts and deeds are measurable or ratable but *they, themselves*, their *essence*, their *being* are too complex and changeable to be given any global rating or report card. We consequently have no accurate or meaningful way of deifying or damning them. They are not *good* or *bad*, they merely exist. If they *choose* to continue to exist and to enjoy their existence, then some of their behaviors are "good" because they aid their goals and some are "bad" because they sabotage these goals. People's goals and purposes cannot be assessed scientifically or objectively because, as individuals, they can choose from a wide variety of goals, none of which (except by arbitrary definition) can be assessed as unconditionally good or bad. But once they pick a certain goal (e.g., succeeding at work, love, or psychotherapy) it can often be scientifically or empirically determined whether (a) they actually achieve it, and (b) they achieve the results they wanted by achieving it.

Secular humanists, in other words, favor certain values such as human life and well-being, but do not claim that these values are absolutely good or bad.

Secular humanists acknowledge that humans have the *human* ability to imagine, fantasize, and strongly believe in all kinds of superhuman entities and powers such as gods, angels, spirits, and fairies. In fact, they often create *meaning* and *explanations* for anything they do not fully understand. Therefore, they often invent supernatural entities and forces as "explanations." But, along with Karl Popper, humanists contend that unless these spirits and forces are in some way empirically falsifiable, any imaginative person can invent an infinite number of them. Moreover, many of these fantasized creations are contradictory to other supernatural fantasies. *Belief* in supernatural spirits may of course help some people to overcome some of their emotional problems (such as anxetizing) or behavioral problems (such as addiction to alcohol). But devout belief in improbable gods and spirits often creates its own difficulties, such as dependency, dogma, bigotry, pollyannaism, and wars with nonbelievers.

Secular humanists are, almost by definition, relativists, skeptics, and nondogmatists. Though many of them used to be logical positivists, they now mostly realize that logical positivism in some respects is itself not falsifiable, so they have revised it. Although they do not tend to be radical or devout constructionists, they do tend to favor the more moderate kind of postmodernism which "recognizes ambiguities, indeterminacies, undertones and overtones, complexities, uncertainties, tensions, interactions, exchanges, equivocations" (Levin 1991, pp. 251–52). This kind of thinking is favored by today's secular humanism.

What is called "humanistic psychotherapy" tends to consist of (a) existential encounters between therapists and their clients, (b) experiential and body-oriented exercises, and (c) transpersonal therapy. The first two of these methods have often proven useful and even the third one has shown, at times, that it helps some people, though I suspect that on the whole it does more harm than good.

The one form of therapy that has been most neglected by many humanist therapists is cognitive-behavioral therapy, perhaps because its main proponents have largely been secular humanists. Thus, Alfred Adler was a pioneering cognitive therapist, as was George Kelly, and both of them were secular humanists. I started to do rational emotive behavior therapy (REBT), the first of the modern cognitive-behavior therapies, in 1955, and I followed a secular humanist model, which I largely derived from several philosophers, including Epictetus, Epicurus, John Dewey, George Santayana, Bertrand Russell, and Alfred Korzybski.

Today's cognitive behavior therapies were originally derived from REBT but are sometimes not existentialist and philosophic like REBT. REBT, as noted above, is quite humanistic, but abjures magical and mystical overtones and implications. Its secular humanistic origins lead to some of the following theories and practices.

CONSTRUCTIVISM AND PHENOMENALISM

Like Kelly's theory of personal constructs, REBT is highly constructivist. It holds that although humans largely learn their own goals, standards, and values from their family and their culture, they construct, yes, create, most of their emotional disturbances. For, unlike rats and guinea pigs, they take their strong desires and preferences, and they raise and propel them into Jehovian, absolutist *musts*, *shoulds*, and *demands*. Thus, when people want and prefer to succeed at school, work, or love, they frequently upset themselves by insisting, "At all times and under all conditions I must, *I have to* succeed!"

REBT holds that it is not things and events alone that upset us, but our *view* of these Activating Events or Adversities (As). As definitely influence us, but our IBs (Irrational Beliefs) about these As largely lead to disturbed Cs (Consequences), such as anxiety and depression. Therefore, to *undisturb* ourselves, we can proceed at D—to actively and forcefully Dispute our self-defeating, *musturbatory* Bs. The ABCDE Theory of emotional disturbance and how to change it is distinctly phenomenalistic.

The ABCs of REBT also stress the *meanings* and *interpretations* people give to events and to results rather than the events and results in themselves. Thus, being thwarted at point A may mean a horrible hassle to one person and mean an adventurous challenge to another. Also, anxietizing at point C may be viewed as awful and terrible by some individuals, who thereby create their own anxiety about anxiety and make themselves doubly or triply disturbed. But other people may view this same kind of anxiety as "damned inconvenient" and may make real efforts to understand and to cope with it. REBT tries to help people look at the meanings and interpretations they give to events and results and, especially, to their own possibilities of creating *new* meanings and interpretations. It doesn't focus mainly on people's gruesome past but on the possibilities they can create for the present and future.

REBT theorizes that people do not greatly fulfill themselves when they make themselves distinctly disturbed, so it first helps them to significantly reduce their disturbing. It favors hedonism and fulfillment and tries to help people become less disturbed and happier. However, because immediate gratification—like excessive drinking—may easily lead to harmful results, REBT favors long-range rather than short-range hedonism.

UNCONDITIONAL SELF-ACCEPTING AND OTHER-ACCEPTING

As particularly shown in chapter 7, REBT, like person-centered therapy, accepts people unconditionally, whether or not they perform well or are likeable. But it also actively teaches them how to unconditionally accept themselves (and others). It shows them they can choose to fully accept themselves, no matter what they do, simply because they choose to do so. It also shows them a more elegant philosophical solution in which they refuse to rate themselves and their totality at all, and rate only what they do and do not do (Dryden 1999a; Ellis 1973, 1994; Ellis and Harper 1997; Hauck 1991; Mills 1993).

FLEXIBILITY AND ALTERNATIVE-SEEKING

While helping people to give up their dogmatic, rigid shoulds and musts, REBT also shows them how to look for other alternative solutions and pleasures. As they work to change their absolutist demands, they see the wide world for what it is—a place with many possible knowledges and adventures. They learn and teach themselves that either/or rules are often unnecessary and that all kinds of possibilities ("both/and" or "and/also") can be made to occur (Ellis 1962, 1994; Ellis and Crawford 2000b; FitzMaurice 1994; Korzybski 1933/1990).

PROFOUND PHILOSOPHICAL CHANGE

Like the other cognitive-behavior therapies, REBT helps people to give up their unrealistic, anti-empirical attributions and inferences, such as, "Because he frowned, I am sure he thinks I acted badly, he hates me, and he knows I am a real loser!" It shows them how to dispute and challenge these misperceptions and false *Beliefs*. But it also looks beyond them to people's absolutist demands by which they often create their misperception, such as, "He absolutely must, and at all times, approve of me. And because he frowned this time—as he must not!—that proves that I acted badly, that he hates me, and that he knows I am a real loser!" Instead of getting only to people's disparate dysfunctional cognitions, REBT tries to help them get to their basic, core philosophies from which these spring, and to show them how to actively dispute them until they make a profound philosophic change. As they make this change, they may change their basic patterns of dysfunctional thinking and automatically and tacitly tend to think more rationally in the future.

INDIVIDUALITY AND SOCIALITY

Although REBT has been part of the human potential movement since the 1960s, REBT practitioners have tried to avoid its excesses by helping people see that they choose to live in a social group and that they are interdependent with this group. An essential part of people's lives is group living and their economic, ecological, political, and other happiness depends on the well-functioning of their community. While they had better not be too self-sacrificing and other-directed, they had also better not be too self-indulgent and self-centered. The principle of both/and, rather than either/or, is important. Active democratic participation in community affairs rather than self-centered isolation will usually aid oneself and one's social group. REBT tries to help each individual in a family, community, or other system understand and healthfully change himself or herself. But it also stresses the importance of improving and changing the system in which all humans interdependently live (Ellis 1962, 1994, 1999, 2000, 2001; Ellis and Dryden 1997; Ellis and MacLaren 1998).

THERAPEUTIC ENCOUNTER

REBT consists of a therapeutic encounter between the client and the therapist in the course of which the therapist may not personally like or want to befriend all clients but cares very much about helping them overcome their emotional-behavioral problems and lead happier lives. Like their clients, therapists and counselors are humans in their own right and are not blank screens, nor are they purely objective. They may therefore reveal a good deal of themselves to clients and have human relationships with them, but still take care to be responsible professionals and not get personally involved with their clients. REBT practitioners clearly show clients their shortcomings and disturbances, but always try to accept them as people, and never to condemn them for their poor behaviors.

EMOTIONAL AND BEHAVIORAL METHODS OF REBT

Humanistic psychotherapy, in the REBT view, is the study of the whole individual for the purpose of helping people live a happier, more self-actualizing and more creative existence. It accepts them with their human limitations; it particularly focuses on and uses their experiences and their values; it emphasizes their ability to create and direct their own destinies; and it views them as holistic, goal-directed individuals who are important in their own right, simply because they are alive, and who (together with their fellow humans) have the right to continue to exist and to enjoy and fulfill themselves. This concept of humanistic psychotherapy and counseling includes both an ethical and a scientific orientation.

Humanistic psychotherapy has often gone off into its own idiosyncratic realms and has been particularly preoccupied in recent years with experiential, nonverbal, and physical approaches to personality change. It has assumed that modern man has become too intellectualized, technologized, and unemotional, hence alienated and dehumanized. It has therefore tried, as a corrective experiential force, to make up for the lapses of classic behaviorism and orthodox psychoanalysis. In this respect it has made notable contributions to psychotherapy and to the actualizing of human potential.

However, humans do not live by emotional bread alone. They are remarkably complex, cognitive-emotive-behaving creatures. Of their main traits, their high-level ability to think about their thinking is probably the most unique and most "human" quality. If, therefore, people effectively work against their strong tendencies to dehumanize themselves, they had better, as Ellen Langer has shown, vigorously use some of the highest level thinking and metathinking of which they are innately capable, but which they easily neglect and avoid (Piatelli-Palmarini 1994).

In addition to having a strong cognitive emphasis (as shown in other chapters of this book) REBT uses a large variety of evocative-emotive and behavioral-motorial methods of helping troubled individuals change their irrational core philosophies and acquire more sensible, actualizing lives. Because it is exceptionally persuasive, educational, and active-directive, and because it straightforwardly challenges many of the sacred myths and superstitions that are so prevalent among humans, REBT is often viewed as being antihumanistic and mechanistic.

Not only are these accusations mistaken, but they miss an important point—that efficient therapies that stress the potentialities of cognitive and behavioral control over dysfunctional living are in many respects the most humanistic methods of personality change yet developed. They are unusually person-centered, creatively oriented, and encouraging the maximal actualization of human potential. Although experientially oriented psychologists such as Fritz Perls and Carl Rogers were outstanding humanists, so too were and are cognitive-oriented therapists such as Aaron Beck, Eric Berne, George Kelly, Arnold A. Lazarus, and Richard Lazarus.

THE HUMANISM OF REBT AND CBT

The cognitive therapies in general, and rational emotive behavior therapy in particular, are among the most humanistic of psychological treatment processes for a number of reasons:

1. *Cognitive-behavior therapies largely deal with beliefs, attitudes, and values, rather than mainly with stimuli and responses, as many other therapies do.* Psychoanalysis, for example, heavily emphasizes the activating events of people's lives, especially stimuli that impinge upon them during their early childhood. Classical behavior therapy is mainly preoccupied with their

responses or symptoms. But REBT quickly zeros in on and deals with people's most uniquely human behaviors, namely, their cognitions and beliefs.

2. *Cognitive-behavior therapies squarely put people in the center of the universe and give them a wide range of choice or existential freedom.* REBT holds that people's behavior, although to some degree determined and limited by their biological nature and history, is considerably less determined than the orthodox Freudians or behaviorists seem to think that it is.

3. *Cognitive-behavior therapies are deeply philosophic and reeducative, emphasizing the more elegant types of personality-restructuring solutions, as opposed to symptom-removal types of solutions to human problems.* REBT and CBT show clients (a) that self-acceptance is a tautological and definitional concept and may always be had for the asking by people who think logically; (b) that humans do not have to rate their self or personhood at all while still pragmatically rating their thoughts, feelings and actions; and (c) that much human disturbance is the result of absolutistic thinking and can be minimized by helping individuals to think and feel preferentially rather than musturbatorily. With REBT and CBT, troubled people can understand their fundamental difficulties in the course of relatively few sessions, and can also be taught a method of dealing with their problems that can serve them for the remainder of their life.

4. Most major problems of living involve people taking a two-sided, tolerant, and both/and attitude toward themselves, others, and the world. This kind of attitude is much more likely to be arrived at through comprehensive CBT and REBT interaction with an accepting therapist than it is through immersion in more one-sided types of therapy.

5. *The cognitive-emotive therapies help the individual strike a balance between short-range and long-range hedonism.* Thus, REBT deals with anxiety and depression stemming from self-rating issues, but also attacks self-defeating low frustration tolerance and short-range hedonism. It helps people to consider the pleasures of today and tomorrow in order to achieve long-range benefits.

6. *The cognitive-emotive therapies tend to be unusually accepting of human fallibility and to encourage maximum understanding of and tolerance for human frailty.* They show people how to realistically accept humans as humans (instead of as superhumans or subhumans) and how to desist from deifying and "devil-ifying" themselves and other people. In this particular sense, in its complete acceptance of people as being incredibly human and never anything but fallible and ungodlike, REBT and CBT strive for the epitome of humanistic psychology and psychotherapy.

Following the secular humanist tradition, REBT deifies nothing, holds no absolutes, and is quite comfortable with the world of probability, uncertainty, fallibility, and even disorder. It encourages people to desire and prefer many goals, but not to *demand*, to *need*, or to *dictate* anything. In this sense, and quite revolutionarily, it helps free humans of their own anxietizing, depressing, and raging, much of which stems from their aspirations to be grandiose and godlike. REBT truly accepts and fosters their humanness!

In view of human complexity, I can see no perfect solution to individual and world problems. Solving these problems now often seems to create the need for newer, often quite different, solutions later. So, is our task therefore hopeless? Not quite, for as the outstanding modern humanist George Kelly said, people easily are irrational and self-destructive, but they are also marvelously constructive, creative, experimental, and scientific. The process of helping them to be more constructive and less hostile to themselves and others is surely one of the most important humanistic goals. If people will be nonabsolutist, open-minded, scientific, and flexible, that seems to provide one possible answer. Let us experimentally, and humanistically, try it.

SELF-HELP SUGGESTIONS

- You have little choice of being human, so REBT recommends—but doesn't dictate—that you choose to be humanistic: that is, favor yourself individualistically *and* also favor humanity in general and the social group in which you reside.
- Consequently, it shows you how to give up striving to be infallible and superhuman *and* to unconditionally accept yourself as never being damnable or subhuman. You won't achieve either of these extremes!
- If you are humanistic, you do not subscribe to rigid dogmas, but almost by definition try to be flexible, somewhat relativistic and postmodern, and open-minded. Yes, *try*—although you may have strong innate and acquired tendencies to slip into dogmatism.
- Humanism says that you partly *construct* your goals and values and can also constructively *choose* to change them. Often, it's hard to change your self-defeating and society-defeating thinking, feeling, and behaving. But you can!
- You, like nearly all humans, have *many* possible choices, alternatives, goals, and fulfillments. You can experimentally and experientially *discover* what your better paths of living seem to be, try them out, and change them if they don't seem to be working. You are rarely *doomed* to stick to one set of pathways—unless you *think* you are. You have wide potentialities for self-actualizing and for work to help social-actualizing.
- REBT hypothesizes that because you are human, your self-helping and self-defeating emotions and actions include thinking, feeling, and behaving—all of which processes include and interact holistically with

each other. Therefore, to change your dysfunctioning, you'd better use a number of its cognitive, emotional, and activity methods and push yourself, as homework, to actualize them. No rest for the weary! Many possible REBT methods work. Try them!

- It would be nice if you had magical, superhuman, and easy ways to improve your emotional-behavioral problems. Lots of luck. Fortunately, you have many human—yes, pluralistic—ways of doing so. Use your flexible humanity!

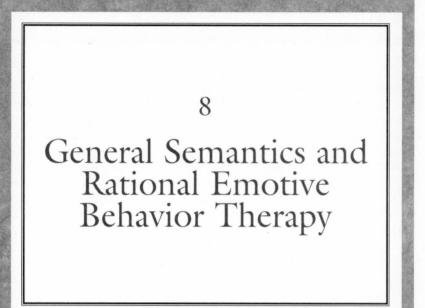

8

General Semantics and Rational Emotive Behavior Therapy

I never would have originated rational emotive behavior therapy (REBT) had I not been strongly influenced by philosophers rather than psychotherapists. For when I founded REBT in 1955, the field of therapy was almost completely run by clinicians, ranging from psychoanalysts to behaviorists, who firmly and rather dogmatically believed that people's early experiences, especially with their parents, made them or conditioned them to emotionally disturbing.

This theory, of course, has some degree of validity because all humans live in an environment. As Alfred Korzybski (1951) put it, a person is "an organism-as-a-whole-in-an-environment." People seem to be born teachable and self-teachable and therefore partly acquire their feelings from their experiences with others and with the objects they encounter in their early and later life. Also, because they are more gullible or influenceable when they are young, they may well—though not necessarily always—be more disturbable in their childhood and adolescence than when they are older.

This chapter was adapted from the 1991 Alfred Korzybski Memorial Lecture, sponsored by the Institute of General Semantics. It is partly adapted from P. D. Johnston, D. D. Bourland Jr., and J. Klein, *More E-Prime* (Concord, Calif.: International Society for General Semantics, 1994), pp. 213–40. Used with permission.

The ABC theory of REBT, which I largely derived from several ancient and modern philosophers, states that people have Goals and values (Gs), especially to stay alive and be happy. When their Goals are blocked by Activating Events or Adversities (As), such as failure, rejection, and discomfort, they have a choice of making themselves feel and act with healthy Consequences (Cs), such as sorrow, regret, and frustration, that tend to encourage them to change or improve their As. Or they have a choice of making themselves panicking, depressing, raging, and self-hating and thus creating unhealthy Consequences (Cs) that tend to make their As worse and block their achieving their Goals. Some of the main behavioral Cs they choose to construct are withdrawal, procrastination, inertia, compulsions, and addictions (Ellis 1957, 1962, 2000b; Ellis and Dryden 1997; Yankura and Dryden 1990, 1994).

REBT, in other words, hypothesizes that people do not mainly get disturbed by unfortunate Activating Events or Adversities, which *contribute to* but rarely directly cause their self-defeating feelings and actions. Instead, they largely (not completely) *create and constuct* their neuroticizing by their philosophies or *Beliefs* (Bs). When, says REBT, their *Beliefs* consist only of *preferences, wishes,* or *desires,* they make themselves feel healthily frustrated and displeased when their preferences are thwarted. Thus, if they stick to, "I strongly *want* success and approval, *but* I don't absolutely *need* these desirable results," they feel healthily sorry and disappointed but rarely upset themselves about not achieving their goals and values.

Alfred Korzybski (1951, p. 172) seems to have had a picture of human functioning similar to that of the ABC theory of REBT. Thus he said that when we "perceive" a happening or event we "silently" or "nonverbally" react with *evaluations* about it and our "emotions" and "evaluations" are organismically combined together and interact with our verbalizations, which quickly follow our silent thinking-feeling level. He quotes George Santayana as showing that humans are much better at believing than seeing.

I think that Korzybski would have endorsed REBT's crusading against people's absolutistic, dogmatic, overgeneralized *shoulds* and *musts.* Thus, he noted "the fact that we do abstract on higher orders becomes a danger if we are not conscious that we are doing so and retain the primitive confusions or identifications of orders of abstractions" (1951, p. 218). He also advocated our increasingly using the term "etc." because it "facilitates flexibility, and gives a greater degree of conditionability in our semantic reactions ('thinking about thinking,' 'doubt of doubt,' 'fear of fear,' etc.)" (1933/1990, p. 440; 1951, p. 190).

Once again, Korzybski, from 1920 to 1951, presented some unusual ideas that seem to be constant with REBT. Thus, he endorsed physico-mathematical methods of thinking and said that they link science, "and particularly the exact sciences, with problems of sanity in the sense of adjustment to 'facts' and 'reality'" (1951, p. 189). He warned that "elementalistic or metaphysical terms are not to be trusted and that speculations based on them are misleading or dangerous" (1951, p. 192).

SCIENCE AND SANITY

The more I think about Korzybski's masterpiece, *Science and Sanity*, the more I am enthralled by its revolutionary title. For after practicing REBT for several years and trying to assess its effectiveness by using the scientific method to check its results, and after helping hundreds of self-disturbing people by realistically and logically Disputing—at point D in the ABCs of REBT—their neurosis-producing Irrational *Beliefs*, I saw that REBT and the other cognitive-behavior therapies that Dispute people's dysfunctional *Beliefs* tend to show that neurosis and antiscience are similar and that mental health and science distinctly overlap.

Why is this so? Because science includes four main attributes: First, it is realistic and tries to make its theories consistent with the facts of social "reality." It postulates no absolute "reality," because all "things" and "facts" are viewed phenomenologically, through human perceptions and interpretations. But science thinks that there is some kind of "reality" out there, apart from human perception, and it tries to check and falsify or partially verify its theories in relation to external "facts."

Second, science uses logic, both Aristotelian and non-Aristotelian, to check its hypotheses, and usually ends up with theories that are not self-contradictory and are not falsified by other views of people and the world. It rules out magic, cavalierly jumping to conclusions, and many illogical nonsequiturs.

Third, and perhaps most important, science is invariably open-minded and nondogmatic. It holds even its best theories tentatively and sees them as always subject to change, and does not claim that they describe the nature of things for all possible conditions and for all times. It is exceptionally flexible and never devout.

Fourth, science is alternative-seeking and keeps looking for new, better theories and interpretations. It is never absolutist and has no final or invariant technique or answer.

REBT holds that neurosis, unlike science, tends to be replete with the kind of thinking, feeling, and behavior that is unrealistic, illogical, dogmatic, devout, and rigid. In this sense, as I think Korzybski strongly implied, and as REBT agrees, science and unneurotic sanity tend to be similar.

Why is this so? Why do so many people much of the time think crookedly, misperceive reality, reason illogically, become dogmatic and devout, and stick rigidly to misleading percpetions, overgeneralizations, and conclusions? REBT's answer is that they largely are innately predisposed to do this. They are strongly inclined by their biological tendencies, their human experiences, and their social learning to often make themselves self-defeating and socially sabotaging. As Piaget noted, children actively *construct* their view of the world and their adjustments to it; and REBT and other constructivist therapies say that they keep reconstructing their thoughts, feelings, and actions all their lives. That is their "nature" to do so, even though this "nature" is changeable.

Moreover, once people adopt and create unrealistic, rigid, non-alternative-seeking ideas, they have a strong biosocial tendency to carry them into dysfunctional action, to repeat these actions many times, and to habituate themselves to destructive behaviors. They don't *have to* do this, for they always have *some* degree of choice. But they very frequently are innately *propended* to habituate themselves to dysfunctional thoughts, emotions, actions, and find it difficult, though not impossible, to change them.

Fortunately, however, the very nature of human constructivism includes a strong proactive changing and self-actualizing element. People are not merely born and reared to defeat themselves—for if that were so the human race would soon die out. They are also born and raised with a powerful tendency to choose, to remember, to think, to think about their thinking, to change, to grow, and to develop. What is more, if they choose to do so, they can use their abilities to think and to change to largely, though probably not completely, overcome their propensities to perceive, think, and interpret crookedly.

This, of course, is the goal of general semantics—to show people how they can become aware of their misperceptions, overgeneralizing, and poor judgements, and how they can reconsider and reconstitute them so that they help themselves to more accurately perceive, accept, and live more comfortably with "reality."

This goal of general semantics is remarkably similar to that of Rational Emotive Behavior Therapy. REBT has faith in disturbed people's ability to reconstruct their adopted and self-constructed distorted views of themselves, of others, and of the world with which they needlessly disturb themselves. It teaches them how to strongly Dispute their absolutist musts, shoulds, and demands; to reduce their overgeneralizing, awfulizing, and I-can't-stand-it-itis; to evaluate and rate only what they and others think, feel, and do while rigorously refraining from judging others' *self, being, essence,* or *personhood.*

REBT has two main goals: First, to help people see and correct their dogmatic, absolutistic attitudes and dysfunctional feelings and behaviors and to make themselves, as Korzybski called it, subject to greater sanity. Second, as people are making themselves less disturbed and more functional, REBT tries to help them fulfill more of their human potential, to actualize themselves, and to enjoy themselves more fully (as Epicurus more than Epictetus advocated). Korzybski also strongly urged people to try to achieve more of their human potential. Thus, he said, "With a time-binding consciousness, our criteria of values, and so behavior, are based on the study of human potentialities, not on statistical averages on the level of *homo homini lupos* drawn from primitive and/or un-sane evaluational reactions which are on record" (1951, p. 189).

In other words, both general semantics and REBT hold that if people think about their thinking, and minimize their "natural" tendency to over-categorize, they can significantly—though perhaps never completely—free themselves from some of their thought-language limitations and achieve a more self-fulfilling life.

We can speculate that humans in primitive times had to jump to quick conclusions, to make their wishes into musturbatory demands, and to act overemotionally because they were thin-skinned animals living in a very dangerous world. Perhaps their imprecise perception, their seeing part of the picture as a whole, their rigid ways of approaching life, and their other cognitive weaknesses that Korzybski pointed out and that REBT often details, helped them survive in a grim and hostile world. Thus, by insisting that they *must* perform well and that others *had to* do their bidding, they may have made themselves needlessly anxious and angry thousands of years ago but may have survived better than if they were more reasonable. Perhaps. In any event, they did survive with their innate tendencies to reason better than other organisms *and* to often think sloppily. Now, using general semantics and REBT, they can use more reason and less dogma to survive more freely and more happily.

THE IS OF PREDICATION

Let me continue with the agreements between general semantics and REBT. Korzybski showed that using the *is* of predication leads us to think imprecisely. Thus, statements like, "I *am* good" and "I *am* bad" are inaccurate overgeneralizations, because in reality I am a *person who* acts sometimes in a good and sometimes in a bad manner. In REBT, we teach our clients not to rate *themselves* or their *being* but only what they *do*. All *self*-ratings seem to be mistaken, because humans are too complex and many-sided ever to be given a *global* evaluation. Moreover, REBT holds, if you aim to be a *good person* you are too fallible to achieve that all-good status. And if you say, "I *must* be good," you will fail and then see yourself, quite falsely, as being *bad*. When you think in terms of dichotomous, good and bad terms, you will tend to demand that you *always* act well, for otherwise you will "become" bad. So even when you are doing well, you will be at great risk and will anxietize.

Moreover, when you strive to be a *good person* (rather than a person who tries to do *good things*), you make yourself grandiose, try to be better than other *humans*, tend to deify yourself; and then, when you fall back and do stupid things, you see yourself as a *bad person*, and consequently devil-ify yourself. This is the essence of much neurosis! So REBT specifically teaches people, "*You* are not good and *you* are not bad. You are only *you*, a *person who* acts well and badly."

We can avoid the *is* of predication, as Korzybski points out by saying, "I see myself as good" or "I see myself as bad," for then we do not claim that our "goodness" or "badness" really exists in the universe, but only that we *choose* to interpret ourselves in a "good" or "bad" manner. Because we are entitled to our personal definitions, we can *decide* to see ourselves as "good" because that will help us function better, rather than *decide* to see ourselves as "bad," for that will help us bring about worse results.

So REBT teaches people that they can arbitrarily *define* themselves as "good" and that that will work much better than if they define themselves as "bad." They can attach their "goodness," for example, to their existence and tell themselves, "I am *good* because I am human and alive." This is a pretty "safe" definition of themselves because they then will always be "good" as long as they are human and alive—and will only have to worry about being "bad" after they are dead. Quite safe, you can see!

The trouble with this definition of human worth is that it *is* definitional and cannot be validated or falsified. Thus, you could say, "I am good because I am human and alive" and I can object, "But I think you are bad because you are human and alive." Which of us, then, is correct? Neither of us is, because we are both definitional; and definitions are useful but cannot be checked against "facts" or "reality."

Moreover, both statements—"I *am* good" and "I *am* bad"—are over-generalizations because, as noted above, all people do *both* "good" and "bad" deeds, and cannot really be categorized under a single, global heading —as *being* "good" or as *being* "bad." So the pragmatic solution to the problem of human "worth" is not a very good one, and had better be replaced by the REBT *more elegant* solution: "I *am* neither good or bad; I am simply a *person who* sometimes acts 'well' and sometimes acts 'badly.' So I'd better rate or evaluate what I do and not what I *am*." I am pretty sure Korzybski would endorse this *more elegant* REBT solution to the very important problem of *self*-rating.

Korzybski's writings on the *is* of predication encouraged me to help REBT's clients to stop using several kinds of overgeneralizations. For if they say, "I am good," they strongly imply that they have an essence or "soul" of goodness, that they do *only* "good" things, and *therefore* deserve to live and enjoy themselves. This is misleading, because they cannot prove that they have any *essence* (which is a vague word); and if they do have one, they cannot show that it always at all times *is* "good."

To be more precise, REBT helps clients to say, "I am a person who *does* good things (e.g., helps others in *trouble*) but who *also* does many 'neutral' and 'bad' things (e.g., harms others). I am never really *entirely* 'good,' 'bad,' nor 'neutral.' Because I am, as a human, much too complex and many-sided to perform *only* 'good' or 'bad' or 'neutral' behaviors."

Let me repeat this important point: Following Korzybski, REBT is one of the very few psychotherapies that tries to help people only rate, measure, and evaluate what they *do* and *don't do* and not to rate their *self*, *totality*, or *personhood*. Let me say that teaching clients and other people *merely* to rate their acts, feelings, and thoughts and *not* to give themselves a misleading *self*-rating is quite difficult. For, as Korzybski implied, humans *naturally and easily* conclude that "because I act in a 'good' manner, I am a 'good person' and that because I act 'badly' I am a 'bad person.'" Obviously both these views are mistaken and will often produce poor results, because if you view yourself as a "good person" when you behave well, you will almost immediately see yourself as a "rotten person" and thereby produce anxiety, depression, and self-hatred when you fall back, as you invariably will, to behaving "badly" again.

REBT uses another kind of Disputing (D) of people's irrational *Beliefs* (IBs) when they think and say, "Because I do many bad *things*, I am a *bad person*." I tell my clients, "When you say you are a *bad person* for doing bad things, you are engaging in what Bertrand Russell called a category error. You do *all* kinds of things, good, bad, and indifferent. So if you categorize these things as "good" or "bad," you jump to a different category when you call *yourself*, the doer, "good" or "bad." You are *not* what you do. So you'd better rate only the *things* you do and not identify them with your *youness*, which is quite a different category.

I got the idea for this kind of Disputing from Bertrand Russell (1965); and in recently rereading Korzybski (1933/1990) I was pleased to note that he gives Russell due credit for his "epoch-making work in his analysis of subject-predicate relations" (1951, p. 181). Even before I read Korzybski I was significantly influenced by Russell, so I am happy to acknowledge that REBT owes a real debt to both these modern philosophers. Russell, Korzybski, and REBT all join in examining and revealing the limitations of the *is* of predication.

THE IS OF IDENTITY

Korzybski (1951) objected to the *is* of identity, to people saying, "I am a man," "I am a woman," "I am a good (or bad) person." I think he was correct about this, because once again these statements are all incorrect overgeneralizations. Moreover, as REBT points out, to identify with *any* group or concept implies *loss* of oneself and leads to what Helmuth Kaiser called neurotic fusion. Thus, to identify with your peer group gives you a sense of belonging and security. But ironically it also takes away your *own* identity, makes you over-conforming, and therefore less of an individual in your own right. You are really a *person who* chooses to be in the group but had better *not* be a devout follower of the group. When the latter occurs, you are believing something like, "I absolutely *must* be a group adherent, or else I am *nothing*." That is hardly a good state of mental health!

Identity is a poor word because it has conflicting meanings. I am I, myself, and am not really any other person. So that is fairly clear. But I also call myself a New Yorker, an American, or a man; and as I do so I partly lose my identity as myself, a unique human. Of course, as a person I am normally a member of a social group; and, as Sampson (1989) and others have pointed out, I take *some* of the main parts of my personality from the group—such as the way I dress, the kind of foods I eat, and the language I speak. So I am never *only* myself; nor had I better even be *only* a group member. For me to say that I am *only* I or *only* a member of a certain class is wrong on both counts.

Korzybski seems to solve this problem by noting that I am *neither* only myself *nor* only identified with a group. He would presumably say that I am *both/and* rather than *either/or*. That is what REBT says, too. I am partly an individual in my own right but once I choose to be in or to remain in a group that I was put in at birth (e.g., choose to remain an "American"), I no longer am responsible *only* for me and to myself, but *also* to the group of which I choose to remain a member.

REBT, like Korzybski I think, gives me *some* degree of human choice (for I can even choose to be a hermit) but it also says that I have *limited* choice, because my biology and my upbringing help make me a *social* creature; and therefore I am never completely a person in my own right. If I accept this "reality" I shall probably get along fairly well *both* as an individual *and* as a social person. If I reject or deny it, I shall probably get into both personal and social difficulty.

To make things still more confusing, you will practically insure that you will end up by anxietizing if you believe, "I am a good person when I do good things" for you will tend to "logically" conclude, "And I am a bad person when I do bad things"—as, I would say, most people in the world now often conclude. If so, you will make yourself anxietize even when you are acting in a "good" manner, for as a fallible human you will know that you can easily act "badly" tomorrow and your acts will then "make" you a *bad person*. When you do *behave* "badly," you will then tend to view *yourself* as a *rotten individual* and will thereby depress yourself. So unless you are perfect and *always* perform well, defining your *self* or your *personhood* in terms of your "good" and "bad" behaviors is, as Korzybski held, an antifactual overgeneralization. From an REBT standpoint, it just won't work!

As noted above, REBT helps people to refuse to rate their *self*, their *totality*, at all, but merely to evaluate what they do. Then, when they act "badly," they can tell themselves, "*That* was 'bad' or 'foolish' but I am a *person who* acted that way. I am *not* a *bad person* and therefore I am capable of changing my behavior and of probably acting better next time. If *I* am 'bad' I am hopelessly stuck. But if what I *do* is 'bad' I can usually change."

ABSOLUTIST SHOULDS AND MUSTS

Korzybski did not clearly differentiate between people's preferences and their demands, as REBT does, nor did he show how when they take their *preferably shoulds* and change them into *absolute, unconditional shoulds*, they neuroticize themselves. But he implied that virtually all absolutist, unconditional thinking encourages us to make ourselves "unsane."

Thus, when speaking against identity, he said, " 'Identity' as a 'principle' is defined as 'absolute sameness in "all" ("every") respects.' It can never empirically be found in this world of ever-changing processes, nor on silent levels of our nervous systems" (1951, p. 184).

REBT shows that when you believe, "I *preferably should* succeed and win the approval of significant others," you explicitly or tacitly include *buts* and *alternative solutions* to your desires, such as: "*But* if I don't succeed, I can try harder next time." "*But* if I'm not approved, too bad, but it's not the end of the world." When your *preferably shoulds* are not fulfilled, REBT holds, you normally feel *healthily* sorry, disappointed, and frustrated (rather than *un*healthily panicking, depressing, and self-hating).

On the other hand, when you strongly believe, "Because I want to succeed and to be approved by significant others, I *absolutely, under all conditions and at all times must do so*," you anxietize when you *may not* do well and depress when you *do not* act well or win others' approval. For with your *absolute, under all conditions* shoulds and musts you allow yourself no alternative solutions to your desires, box yourself in, and needlessly make yourself miserable.

Korzybski wasn't as clear as REBT is about this, but he fought vigorously against absolutist, dogmatic, allness and neverness thinking. Therefore, general semantics obviously opposes self-statements like, "Because I want to succeed at my profession and want to win the approval of significant others, I *absolutely, under all conditions, at all times must* do so." In REBT, we frequently encourage people to change their inaccurate self-defeating language to more precise languages, and we therefore show our clients how to change this all-or-nothing sentence to something like, "Because I want to succeed at my profession and to win the approval of significant others, I very much *prefer* to do so. But if I don't, I can find other things to succeed at. If I never succeed at any important project, I can enjoy doing what I can do and can still have a reasonably happy life. As for winning the approval of significant others, I *want* very much to do so, but I never *have* to. If I keep trying, I can practically always find *some* people who will like me as I like them. But if I never somehow do, there are many other aspects of life that I can enjoy, so I'll keep looking until I find them."

PRECISE THINKING AND LANGUAGE

Alfred Korzybski was a pioneer in linguistics and pointed out that when we think imprecisely our crooked thinking works its way into our language and then our dysfunctional language leads us into engaging in more imprecise thinking. Ever since I started doing REBT, I found that people habituate themselves to poor language habits that interfere with their functional living, that they largely are responsible for their own dysfunctional language, feelings, and actions, and that therefore they can change them.

Thus, when my clients say, "Joe lied to me and that made me furious," I interrupt, "How could *that*, or *Joe*, get into your gut and *make* you furious?" "Oh, I see," they often reply. "Yes, Joe lied to me, and I chose to infuriate myself *about* his lying." "Yes," I say. "Isn't that a much more accurate description of what happened and how *you* chose to create your fury?"

Again, a client says, "I'm not getting the love I want Martha to give me, and she makes me feel like a worm." I ask, "Do you only *want* Martha's love, or aren't you telling yourself you *need* it?" "Mmm. Yes, I guess I am believing that I absolutely *need* it." "And does Martha's lack of loving you make you feel like a worm?" "Uh, no. I guess I'm putting the two together and *making myself* feel like a worm." "And how could you lose Martha's love and still not label yourself as a worm?" "I guess I could tell myself that because I want Martha's love and don't have it, my relationship with her is somewhat wormy. But that doesn't give me, a total person, the label of a worm." "Right! So hereafter try to watch your language that includes your *demanding* instead of *wanting* and that keeps you making inaccurate labels of you, rather than descriptions of what you and others *do*."

So REBT often shows people how to correct their language and their thinking, and to stop sneaking in overgeneralizing, labeling, demandingness, and other unscientific verbalizations into their thinking and behaving. It thereby employs a scientific technique called *semantic precision* and in this respect is one of the few therapies that puts Korzybski's theory of language and meaning into therapeutic practice.

BIOLOGICAL UNDERPINNINGS OF BEHAVIOR

Although I was mainly an environmentalist as a young psychologist, after I had practiced REBT for a few years, I saw that people are born as well as reared to think irrationally and dysfunctionally and to sink their crooked thinking into unhealthy feelings and self-sabotaging behaviors (Ellis 1962, 1976a). I believe that Korzybski held similar views, because he consistently shows how practically all people at all times in all parts of the world make profound semantic errors and thereby help upset themselves and others. If our parents and our culture mainly taught us to overgeneralize, label, and to commit the cognitive misperceptions and jumping to conclusions that Korzybski talks about, some of us would do so and some of us would not. But all of us, to one degree or another, often seem to be embroiled in these kinds of errors. So although there appears to be some environmentally-inculcated factors in our doing so, we also seem to be innately prone to distorted semantic processes.

Thus, Korzybski notes: "Practically all humans, the most primitive not excluded, have some types of either-or orientation" (1951, p. 186). And: "Our old habits of evaluation, ingrained for centuries if not [millennia], must be reevaluated" (1951, p. 194).

And again: "A 'name' involves for a given individual a whole constellation or configuration of labeling, defining, evaluating, etc., unique for each individual, according to his socio-cultural, linguistic environment and his heredity" (1951, p. 177).

REBT and general semantics, then, seem to fully acknowledge the important biological as well as environmental roles in human dysfunctional thinking.

SELF-CHANGE AND SELF-ACTUALIZATION

While general semantics and REBT seem to agree that people are innately predisposed to create and construct semantic errors, they also agree that people can learn to minimally do so. REBT says that because humans are active constructivists, rather than being passively conditioned to be disturbed by their parents, teachers, and culture, they also have the innate tendency to change themselves and to choose to behave less defeatingly. Thus they are able to think about their thinking, to realistically assess their unrealistic attitudes, to dispute their Irrational *Beliefs*, and to work hard at reconstructing their disordered thoughts, feelings, and behaviors. Moreover, once they keep working at reformulating their disturbing ideas and feelings, they can also creatively work at growing, developing, and bringing about greater degrees of happiness and involvement.

Korzybski and his followers obviously have similar ideas. The International Society for General Semantics and many members of the Society solidly believe that people can be taught the principles of general semantics and can be shown how to think and communicate more clearly with themselves and each other and thereby help themselves to change. REBT and general semantics are both psychoeducational approaches to helping humans improve their intrapersonal and interpersonal relationships (Ellis and Crawford 2000).

THE USE OF E-PRIME

In order to encourage people to give up the is of predication and the *is* of identity, David Bourland (Bourland and Johnston, 1991) advocated and used E-Prime, the English language without any inclusion of various forms of the word *to be* or its various tenses. Although writing in E-Prime is difficult and does not completely make a writer and the reader avoid all linguistic and semantic errors, it does offer some help. REBT, through the advocacy of Dr. Robert Moore of Clearwater, Florida, of Dr. William Knaus of Springfield, Massachusetts, and myself, has favored E-Prime more than has any other form of psychotherapy; and I think that it is still the only form of therapy that has some of its main works written in E-Prime (Ellis 1957/1975, 1977; Ellis and Harper 1975; Ellis and Knaus 1977).

USE OF FORCEFUL PERSUASION

Korzybski noted that we humans need "to change our habitual methods of thinking, and this is not so easy as it seems" (1951, p. 196). He implied that our overgeneralized, misleading thinking gets into our body-mind system and into our action habit patterns. REBT has always said that thinking, feeling, and behaving are not disparate, but importantly and holistically influence and affect each other (Ellis 1958).

Because of its holistic emphasis, REBT has always favored strong and direct cognitive, emotive, and behavioral methods of showing people exactly what they are doing to needlessly disturb themselves and what they can do to active-directively minimize their self-disturbing. In consonance with Korzybski's disavowal of either/or solutions to human problems, REBT does not favor thinking *or* emotive *or* behavioral methods of therapy. It consciously and actively employs all three kinds of therapy; and, following and/also and etcetera formulations, it has no hesitation in combining psychotherapy with pharmacological treatment, with environmental changes, and with any other kinds of psychophysical methods that are likely to help various clients (Ellis 1988, 2000a, 2000b, 2001, 2002; Ellis and Velten 1992, 1998).

REALISM AND PROFOUND PHILOSOPHIC CHANGE

Korzybski was in many ways a profound realist and empiricist, and noted that the revised structure of language that he advocated "necessitates 'thinking' in terms of 'facts,' or visualizing processes, before making generalizations" (1951, p. 193). He also noted that while Aristotelian either-or language fosters our evaluating "by definition" or "intension," his own "non-Aristotelian or physico-mathematical orientation involved evaluating 'by extension,' taking into consideration the actual 'facts' in the particular situation confronting us" (1951, p. 194).

REBT's original method of helping people to Dispute (at point D) their self-defeating ideas, inferences, attributions, and overgeneralizations, showed them how to scientifically challenge these ideas in the light of "reality" or "facts." Thus, if Joan asks Harry to marry her and he refuses to do so, she may foolishly conclude, (1) "I made a mistake in asking him," (2) "He hates me!" and (3) "That proves I'm no good, that I am a bad person!" REBT, and the main other cognitive-behavior therapies often confront Joan with the "facts," which tend to show that her inferences about Harry's refusal are invalid overgeneralizations. Why? Because: (1) Joan was probably right, not wrong, in asking Harry to marry her—for by doing so she has gained some valuable information about his feelings for her. (2) There is no evidence that Harry hates her, but only evidence that he doesn't want to marry and live with her. Actually, he may deeply love her and still, for various reasons, not want to marry her. (3) His refusal to marry her never proves, of course, that she *is* no good or *is* a bad person, though it may possibly show that "factually" (in Harry's eyes), she has some undesirable traits.

REBT and cognitive-behavior therapy (CBT) therefore use "facts" or "reality" to show Joan her dysfunctional Beliefs and they therefore accord with Korzybski's views. But REBT goes further than the other therapies and asks, in Joan's case, "What is the underlying musturbatory overgeneralization that leads an intelligent woman like Joan to make such silly inferences that are obviously unsupported by the 'facts' or 'reality'?"

Seek and ye shall find. Looking for Joan's tacit, implicit, or unconscious *musts* that she probably believes and from which she largely *derives* her antifactual inferences, we find that she very likely *brings to* her proposal to Harry the basic, core philosophy: "Whenever I ask *any* person I really like, such as Harry, to grant me *any* important favor, such as marrying me, he *absolutely must under all conditions* accede to my request—or else (1) I made a mistake in asking, (2) he or she hates me, and (3) that proves I am no good and that I am a bad person."

I am contending, in other words, that if Korzybski were a psychotherapist—which, actually, he partially was—he would surely have Disputed Joan's irrational inferences and refuted them "factually" and "empirically." But he would also, I suggest, look as REBT does (and as some other cognitive-behavior therapies do not) for the higher-order abstractions that seem to lie behind and to help instigate many of Joan's disturbance-creating inferences.

Korzybski noted that "making us *conscious* of our *unconscious assumption* is essential" (1951, p. 195). He also said that "abstracting by necessity involves evaluating, whether conscious or not, and so the process of abstracting may be considered as a *process of evaluating stimuli*" (1951, p. 172). Again: "The fact that we do abstract on higher orders becomes a danger if we are not conscious that we are doing so and retain the primitive confusions or identifications of orders of abstractions" (1951, p. 178).

If I interpret Korzybski correctly, he is saying here that to understand ourselves *in depth* we had better not just look for our conscious inferences about unfortunate events in our lives (such as Joan's conscious inferences about her self when Harry rejects her) but we had better *also* look for our unconscious, tacit assumptions that underlie many of our self-disturbing inferences. This is what REBT does when it looks for core musturbatory philosophies behind Joan's (and other people's) antifactual inferences. In this respect, REBT is not only more depth-centered than most other cognitive-behavior therapies, and is not only one of the many constructivist therapies in today's world, but it also—ironically enough!—seems to be considerably more depth-centered than psychoanalysis. Why? Because psychoanalysis is not particularly philosophic; does not explore and look behind people's disturbing assumptions; creates vague, almost undefinable higher-order abstractions of its own (such as ego, id, and superego); and almost entirely ignores the depth-centered semantic problems that Korzybski raised and went a long way toward solving.

A purely Korzybskian analysis of people's cognitive-emotional-behavioral problems, such as Wendell Johnson (1946) attempted, will, I wager, do people more good and much less harm than will psychoanalysis. When REBT is employed, incorporating as it does much of Korzybski's work with other important elements of cognitive-behavior therapy, even more depth-centered, philosophically profound therapy will, I predict, often occur. Compared to this kind of "deep" analysis, psychoanalysis seems to be quite superficial!

As I think can be seen by many of the parallels between rational emotive behavior therapy and Korzybski's general semantics, the two disciplines overlap in many important respects. This is hardly coincidental, as I was distinctly influenced, when formulating and developing REBT, by several of Korzybski's ideas. This does not mean that were Alfred Korzybski alive today he would enthusiastically endorse REBT and place it above all the other psychotherapies. Perhaps he would—and, quite likely, for one reason or another, he wouldn't. In keeping with his own extensional thinking, I would guess that he would agree with *some* of REBT's theory and practice *some* of the time under *some* conditions. As my own life and my practice of REBT continues, I try and take a similar attitude. REBT works quite well some of the time under some conditions with some people. It is not, and never will be, a panacea for all of all people's cognitive-emotive-behavioral problems. There is no reason for it to take an either-or position, or to claim that all people with all disturbances have to be treated with REBT or else they will not improve. Rubbish! As Korzybski would probably have recommended and as I have previously noted, REBT had better be integrated with the most useful of other therapies so that it becomes and remains effective with many (not all) people much (not all) of the time.

SELF-HELP SUGGESTIONS

- Alfred Korzybski fully recognized the limitations of human thinking because of our strong tendencies to generalize and abstract—which are fine! —and also to overgeneralize—which are not so fine! To help yourself stop overgeneralizing and musturbating, read Korzybski's *Science and Sanity*, or if you find that tough reading, try some of the more readable writers on general semantics, such as S. L. Hayakawa's, *Language in Action*.
- Particularly watch your falling into what Korzybski called the "*is* of identity"—that is, "I am a good person" or "I am a bad person." You *are* a person who *has* good or bad *traits* and who *does* good or bad *acts*. You are not totally good or bad—who *always* does good or bad actions; and even if you were that unique, you would hardly know that you would *always* act in good or bad ways in the future. Therefore, try to evaluate or measure the (individual and social) usefulness of your *behaviors* without falling into the overgeneralization of rating your entire *self*.
- Watch your either-or, black-or-white thinking! Most things have good *and* bad elements, advantages *and* disadvantages. Try not to rigidly label people or events. Instead, be flexible and pluralistic.
- As noted throughout this book, you are a unique individual who has many possible ways of changing yourself—some quite workable and some less workable. Therefore, keep experimenting. But you also are born into and choose to remain in a social setting. Being *totally* for yourself and your own interests or being *totally* for the interests of your social group probably won't work out too well. Consider Korzybski's view of and/also rather than either-or!

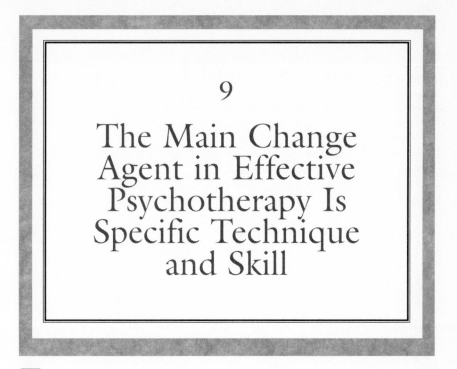

9

The Main Change Agent in Effective Psychotherapy Is Specific Technique and Skill

I shall perhaps be taking a peculiar or "perverse" view in this chapter, namely that the relationship between the therapist and client is often, but definitely not always, a main change agent in effective psychotherapy *if*. If what? *If* the therapist has a specific theory and *if* he or she has workable techniques and skills, including social and persuasive skills, to bring to the therapeutic relationship.

Am I caviling in taking this and/also rather than either/or position? I think not. For I doubt whether any either/or position, especially in a complex field like therapy, is adequate. As I have said for many years, therapy takes many guises (and disguises). It is exceptionally multifaceted and includes procedures overloaded with relationships, such as individual sessions where one client relates to a therapist, and such as group therapy sessions where one therapist intensely relates to eight or ten clients. It also—believe it or not!—includes forms of therapy where clients, and sometimes a large number of clients, have no personal or human relationship with a therapist, but significantly change their thoughts, feelings, and actions when they "relate" to a book, an audiovisual cassette, a computer—or even to a guru who has been dead for five hundred years!

This chapter is partly adapted from "The Main Change Agent in Effective Psychotherapy Is Specific Technique and Skill," in *Controversies in Psychotherapy*, ed. C. Feltman (London: Sage, 1999), pp. 86–94. Used with permission.

Therapy, then, is almost infinitely varied. So are therapists! Thus, one therapist is cool, another cold, another warm, and another very warm. One says practically nothing for many months, another compulsively talks; one dialogues, another incessantly monologues. One therapist rigorously sticks to conversation; another discreetly keeps physically touching clients; still another has passionate sex with his or her clients. One therapist is over-whelmingly cognitive with almost all clients; another is exceptionally emo-tional; still another is mainly behavioral.

What the devil, then, *is* psychotherapy? A good question! It is obviously many things to many different therapists—and to their clients. For what the given therapist does can easily be given widely different interpretations by different clients—or even by the same client on different occasions. Thus, when a male therapist asks a client about her sex life, she may see this as properly teaching her to become more orgasmic, as arousing her more than she wants to be aroused, as showing her that sex is shameful, or as revealing that he's trying to sneakily seduce her.

Relationship itself has many different forms and meanings in therapy. Like Carl Rogers, I have always tried to give my clients unconditional acceptance, or what Rogers termed "unconditional positive regard." I therefore show them that I fully accept them as *persons* even when I deplore many of their behaviors. Some of my clients really see this and appreciate it. But others misinterpret what I am doing and wrongly conclude that I like or love them personally (which I rarely do); or that I hate their behavior and therefore loathe them (which is def-initely not true); or that I accept them because they are bright and competent (which is *conditional* accepting, that I am definitely trying to avoid doing).

So it goes! Therapists use techniques, including relationship with their clients, because *they* think these will work. Clients interpret and for them-selves use the therapist's techniques because of what *they* get—or think they get—out of them, and the twain often meet and produce "effective" results. But even when this happens it is quite unclear why a particular method *some-times* worked for *some* clients *some* of the time.

Just a few of the important variables to consider here are:

1. What the therapist says and how the client takes it.
2. What the therapist doesn't say—and how a client takes this omission.
3. What the client says and how the therapist takes it.
4. What the client doesn't say—and how the therapist takes it.
5. How the client reacts to how the therapist reacts to what the client says.
6. How the therapist reacts to how the client reacts to what the therapist says.

Etcetera!

Let me now address the main theme of this chapter and make a case for my thesis: namely, the main change in effective psychotherapy is a specific therapeutic theory and the therapist's technique and skill to apply this theory.

HISTORY OF THE IMPORTANCE OF THERAPEUTIC THEORY AND TECHNIQUE

Early therapy—such as the philosophic therapies of the ancient Asians (especially Confucius, Gautama Buddha, and Lao-Tzu) and of the ancient Greeks and Romans (especially Epicurus, Epictetus, and Marcus Aurelius)—largely insisted that personality change stems from having a good theory of human disturbance and change and the teaching of effective techniques and skills, so that people can use this theory to minimize their self-disturbing. Modern psychotherapy, beginning with Charcot, Janet, and Freud, and continuing with Adler, Jung, Perls, May, Kelly, Ellis, Beck, and others, largely continued this psychoeducational view of therapy; and it still is very important.

Many of the older therapists—especially Freud, with his emphasis on the transference—included important interpersonal and relationship elements in their theory and practice of therapy; but in the 1940s several therapists—such as Klein, Sullivan, and Rogers—stressed them more than ever. Carl Rogers (1961) went to extremes and insisted that a fairly close relationship between a therapist and her or his client is a "necessary and sufficient" condition for therapeutic personality change.

During the last two decades a good deal of research has largely supported the position that the main change agent—or at least a main change agent—in effective psychotherapy is the relationship between therapist and client. Another body of research has also backed up Jerome Frank's suggestion that nonspecific or common factors, including relationship factors, are significant ingredients in successful therapy.

EVIDENCE AGAINST THE THEORY THAT THE MAIN CHANGE AGENT IN EFFECTIVE THERAPY IS THE CLIENT-THERAPIST RELATIONSHIP

As I shall note later, although a main change agent in effective therapy is the client-therapist relationship, there is considerable evidence that it is often not *the* main agent, and certainly not—as Rogers claimed—a "necessary and sufficient" condition for therapeutic change. Here is some of the evidence:

1. Probably millions of people over the centuries have made a remarkable personality change by listening to a lecture, a sermon, a teacher, a friend, or an acquaintance, and taking to heart the message received—yes, whether it was delivered emotionally or unemotionally.

2. Other millions have changed through reading a papyrus, pamphlet, article, book, computer message, or other written statement.

3. Millions of people today change by attending to audiocassettes, records, CDs, audiovisual cassettes, telephone therapy, and other listening procedures.

4. Millions of people, over the centuries and in recent times, have significantly and sometimes radically changed by having some important, dramatic, or even everyday experience, many of which do not involve other people. Thus, they experience an accident or illness, a near-death occurrence, a success or a failure, a view from a mountaintop, a confinement, a visit to a museum, or any number of events that encourage them to see themselves and the world differently. People can be—and often are—constructive and creative in changing themselves—yes, with or without much help from others.

5. Rogers (1961) gives several specific conditions for clients to experience with therapists if personality therapeutic change is to occur:

> (a) Two persons must be in psychological contact.
> (b) The client must be in a state of incongruence, being vulnerable or anxious.
> (c) The therapist should be, within the confines of this relationship, a congruent, genuine, integrated person.
> (d) The therapist must experience unconditional positive regard for the client.
> (e) The therapist must experience an accurate, empathic understanding of the client's awareness of his own experience.
> (f) The client has perceived the acceptance and empathy which the therapist experiences for him.

Granted that these six therapeutic conditions are usually desirable, obviously thousands of therapists have considerably helped their clients when several of them—or even all of them—did not exist. In fact, points (c) and (d) in the foregoing list frequently are missing, but I have seen many clients who benefited from their therapy sessions in spite of their therapists lacking these traits.

6. Many therapists—not to mention mentors, teachers and religious leaders—consciously and unconsciously ignore Rogerian aspects of therapy and emphasize other aspects—such as dogmatic moral teachings or Zen Buddhist critical and confusing tactics. Nonetheless, some of their clients and students remarkably improve!

7. Many therapists, because of their own personalities or for other rea-

sons, follow conditions and procedures that are almost opposite to what Rogers and other therapists consider "good" attitudes. Thus, they are in poor psychological contact with their clients; are severely disturbed; are incongruent and unintegrated; are often hostile to their clients; and are autistic and unempathic. I agree that such therapists usually do little good and much harm. But not always! I have seen some cases where they considerably helped their clients with these "untherapeutic" ways.

EVIDENCE FOR THE THEORY THAT THE MAIN AGENT IN EFFECTIVE THERAPY IS THE CLIENT-CENTERED RELATIONSHIP

As noted above, a large number of research studies have indicated that the main agent in effective therapy is the client-centered relationship. Among other things, these studies have tended to show the following:

1. The process of therapy is shortened when good client-therapist relationships are achieved and maintained.
2. Various kinds of breaches of the client-therapist relationship block progress or help bring therapy to an end.
3. Therapy progress is deepened and extended when clients feel that they have a good therapeutic relationship.
4. As Jerome Frank has said, it is not so much how the therapist relates to the client but the fact that the therapist believes in a certain method and persuades the client to believe in it too that leads to therapeutic change. Therapeutic *persuasiveness* is what really matters.

WHY I DISAGREE WITH THE FINDINGS THAT A GOOD THERAPEUTIC RELATIONSHIP LEADS TO MORE EFFECTIVE THERAPY

I disagree with the findings about therapeutic relationships for several reasons:

1. Practically all the many studies of therapy that have been done ask clients how they *feel* better after therapy, rather than probing to see if they actually *get* better. When they get better, I hypothesize, they accomplish several things:

   (a) Reduce their main presenting symptom (for example, public speaking anxiety).

    (b) Reduce their related, though perhaps not as presenting, symptoms (for example, social anxiety and test-taking anxiety).

    (c) Maintain their reduced symptoms several years later.

    (d) Rarely experience severe symptoms again even when serious adversities occur in their lives.

2. If I am right about this, people fairly easily feel better when they are carefully heard and fully accepted by a therapist, when this therapist is confident that his or her theory and practice is effective, and when he or she convinces the client that this particular therapy works. So this kind of therapeutic relationship quite often helps people feel better—even when therapists use radically different techniques.

3. In addition, because clients are usually overfocused on failures, rejections, and discomforts, and also frequently are overly concentrated on their disturbed feelings, many kinds of distraction therapies often help them feel better—including meditation, yoga, relaxation methods, biofeedback, sports, recreation, work, and almost anything—including therapy itself—that they find absorbing. Relationships and distraction therapy, however, may mainly cover up and sidetrack people from their basic disturbance-creating philosophies (Ellis 1999, 2000a, 2001).

According to REBT, individuals who disturb themselves have several core absolute musts and demands which largely create their dysfunctioning: notably, "I must do well at important tasks and win the approval of significant others or I am an inadequate person!" "Other people must treat me kindly and fairly or they are rotten humans!" "Conditions must give me what I really want and never seriously deprive me or else the world is *awful*, I *can't stand* it, and it will *always be* that rotten way!" Unless clients—and other people—see these musturbatory philosophies and work hard and persistently—cognitively, emotively, and behaviorally—to replace them with preferences, they rarely will *get* better even though they manage to *feel* better on many occasions.

4. Relationship therapy—especially when it is Rogerian—is designed to help people unconditionally accept themselves *whether or not* they succeed in important areas of their lives and *whether or not* they are approved by significant others. When therapists are unconditionally accepting, as I think Rogers himself almost always was, many of their clients wrongly jump to the conclusion that they are okay as persons *because* their therapist fully accepts them. They base their own acceptance on that of their therapist's respect. They then, of course, only achieve *conditional* self-acceptance!

Can unconditional self-acceptance (USA) be achieved without any form of therapy? Yes, for a few people seem to arrive at it on their own, largely through thinking about their life experiences. Can USA be achieved through a therapist's modeling it and giving clients unconditional acceptance? Yes, because a few clients seem to conclude, "Because my therapist fully accepts and respects me, I can do this for myself. So I will work at thinking through and acting on this unusual philosophy of unconditional self-acceptance."

Can people achieve USA by learning about it, its value, and methods of achieving it, through educational means—books, articles, cassettes, lectures, sermons, and workshops? Yes, and my guess is that this will ultimately prove to be the most efficacious and thoroughgoing way. That is because, again, rating ourselves globally while also rating our "good" and "bad" behaviors seems to be the human condition—both innate and learned. To do differently and to only evaluate what we think, feel and do, and acknowledge but refrain from rating our self, being, essence, or personhood is most difficult and almost alien to human functioning.

Thus, in REBT sessions we therapists do our best to give all our clients unconditional acceptance. We actively teach its value and use many cognitive, emotive, and behavioral methods of explaining and instructing our clients how to achieve it. We encourage them to employ a number of psychoeducational techniques, especially suitable pamphlets, books, and cassettes. We give them in-session and out-of-session homework exercises and assignments to work toward USA. We do quite well with these modeling and active-directive therapy methods much of the time.

But hardly always! We have little trouble teaching the virtues of USA and helping most of our clients to acknowledge them. We actually succeed, I would say, teaching most of them to become considerably more self-accepting than when they first began therapy—and often accomplish this in a few weeks or months. Nonetheless, we still have trouble helping our clients to fully accept themselves, their personhood, *even* when they behave dysfunctionally; and we have more trouble helping them to only rate their specific thoughts, feelings and actions and to refrain from rating their *self* or *being* at all. As noted above, the mere unconditional acceptance by therapists of their clients doesn't quite work, because the clients then almost always accept themselves *conditionally*.

Unconditional self-acceptance is very difficult for most people to learn, truly believe in, and consistently follow. So, according to REBT, are the other two major philosophies and actions that lead to clients' *getting* as well as *feeling* better: Unconditional other acceptance (UOA) and high frustration tolerance (HFT). All of us humans are sometimes treated shabbily and unfairly by other people; and we frequently encounter frustrating conditions. To *get* better, therefore, we preferably should nondamningly accept other *people* even when their *behaviors* are abominable and accept the potential goodness or enjoyment of life even when it is quite troublesome. Yes, *accept* many people and things that we do not *like*.

This is hard to do—by ourselves as well as with the kind and wise help of others. REBT therefore holds that to help people feel *and* get better, therapists preferably should have a good theory of what constitutes disturbance and improvement plus effective techniques for implementing this theory. Both! Teaching clients that they can make themselves less disturbed and less disturbable is important—but so is teaching them how to get there. Yes, *some* clients are bright and creative enough to largely help themselves as they dialogue with a therapist. But to assume that all or most clients are this way is highly unrealistic. Active-directive teaching of therapeutic theory and technique is probably required for most of our clients much of the time.

Active-directive therapy has its distinct limitations and hazards. But so has passive therapy—especially considering that many clients, because of their own deficiencies or those accompanying their disturbances, got themselves into difficulties and, under their own power, are at first unable to resolve them. So we therapists had better be prepared to be persuasive teachers. This very much includes our subscribing to Carl Rogers's important conditions for effective therapy. Thus, we had better be in psychological contact with our clients; be congruent, genuine, integrated persons; experience unconditional positive regard for our clients; and experience an accurate, empathic understanding of clients' awareness of their own therapeutic experience. Fine! None of these traits are absolutely necessary—as I noted above—but all are highly desirable for therapists and, as Rogers himself pointed out, for teachers.

I can think of other important traits for effective therapists to have to aid their effectiveness. For example: have a strong desire to help the client; be open-minded and nondogmatic; be a creative problem-solver; be highly ethical; be clear and understandable; have wide experience and knowledge; have high frustration tolerance; enjoy doing therapy; have a good sense of humor; be experimental; and so on. I doubt whether any of these characteristics or habits are necessary for good therapy. But they can help!

Unless therapists in some ways adequately relate to their clients, the greatest theory and techniques may not help. Clients rarely intimately converse with or actively listen to therapists they dislike. So relating well to clients is an important part of a therapist's method. In regard to clients' *feeling* better, both during and after therapy, it may well be the most important part. In regard to their *getting* better, it is still important, but not crucial or necessary. I still maintain that the therapist's theory and methods are even more important. Now all that I—and other researchers—have to do is to test this hypothesis!

A final word. When we talk about psychotherapy techniques, we usually mean those employed with what I call "nice neurotic" clients and describe a variety of conversational methods that work with these individuals. We often fail to mention clients with severe personality disorders, such as phobic-avoidant personalities and obsessive-compulsive personality disorders. Such individuals, who constitute a fairly large percentage of our clients, often have biological deficits as well as psychological distortions and irrationalities. Many—perhaps most—of them are so fixed in their disordered behavior that no amount of therapeutic conversation alone will help alter it. Consequently, it has been found that behavioral techniques plus suitable medication will help (Cloninger 1999; Ellis 2000b). Unconditional positive regard may well encourage them to make the required behavioral changes and to take their medication, but by itself may not work. As I show in the final chapters of this book, specific cognitive, emotive, and behavioral techniques are also required.

SELF-HELP SUGGESTIONS

- If you are thinking about having therapy, try out several therapists if you can, and pick one who really listens to you and seems to definitely be on your side—that is, a therapist who, in REBT, gives you unconditional acceptance but also points out your weaknesses and tries to help you grow stronger. Among other things, he or she *actively* accepts you *and* pushes you to change some of your self-defeating ways.
- Your goal, if you try therapy, and even if you mainly try to help yourself through books, cassettes, workshops, and other self-help sources, had better be not only to *feel* better and actualize yourself more, but also to *get* better, as defined in this chapter and this book. In REBT terms, this means your making a profound cognitive-emotional-behavioral change, maintaining it over the years, and preferably getting yourself to the point where even some of the most severe Adversities (As) will help make you healthily, strongly sorry, regretful, and frustrated—but not unhealthily panicking, depressing, and raging. At least, not for long!

10

Brief Therapy

THE RATIONAL EMOTIVE BEHAVIOR METHOD

I originated Rational Emotive Behavior Therapy (REBT) because I discovered, from working as a psychoanalyst from 1947 to 1953, that just about all forms of psychoanalysis are long-winded and inefficient. REBT was specifically designed from the start to be brief but effective for many (not *all*) clients. It assumes that some clients are severely disturbed, for biological as well as environmental reasons, and usually require somewhat prolonged therapy, but that a large number of self-neuroticizing individuals can be significantly helped in five to twelve sessions and can appreciably help themselves by continuing to practice the main REBT principles they learned during these sessions.

Although REBT brief therapy uses a number of relationship and experiential methods, it stresses self-help and homework. It actively teaches clients how to understand and help themselves in between sessions and after formal therapy has ended or has been temporarily suspended (Dryden, DiGiuseppe, and Neenan 2001; Ellis 1996; Ellis and Dryden 1997; Ellis and Harper 1961/1997; Walen, DiGiuseppe, and Dryden 1992; Yankura and Dryden 1990).

This chapter is partly adapted from "Brief Therapy: The Rational Emotive Method," in *The First Session in Brief Therapy*, ed. S. H. Budman, M. F. Hoyt, and S. Friedman (New York: Guilford, 1992), pp. 36–58. Used with permission.

REBT assumes that, because the human condition is both self-actualizing and self-disturbing, people had better work *all their lives* to use their self-helping to minimize their self-sabotaging (and social-sabotaging) tendencies. In this sense, good psychotherapy is a lifelong process. However, by far most of this ongoing process can often be taught and activated for hard-working clients in a brief period of time and then steadily reactivated by clients themselves thereafter.

The main therapeutic aspect of REBT is the disputing (D) of Irrational *Beliefs* (IBs). Disputing is first done with a number of cognitive techniques, such as: by discovering clients' dysfunctional attitudes; by logically, empirically, and philosophically discussing and debating them; by using rational coping self-statements; by reframing the As of clients' lives; by using bibliotherapy and audiotherapy; and by reviewing the disadvantages of self-defeating thoughts and behaviors. Emotively, REBT teaches clients a number of forceful affective methods of changing their feelings, including shame-attacking exercises, rational-emotive imagery, role playing, the use of rational humorous songs, and strongly reiterated self-statements. Behaviorally, clients regularly arrange homework assignments with the therapist, do in vivo desensitization, use reinforcements and penalties to help change their thoughts and actions, and often engage in skill-training activities.

CASE ILLUSTRATION

The client was a thirty-eight-year-old African American male, Ted, a high school graduate, manager of a retail store, married ten years, with two young children. He was referred by his physician, an ex-client, because of Ted's pseudo heart attacks, which were really panic attacks, for which he had been given nitroglycerin for reassurance. Two years before coming to therapy, after worrying about the death of a boyhood friend from a heart attack, he was on a PATH train, returning to Manhattan from Jersey City, when he started having chest pains and immediately hospitalized himself for two days, only to find that he was in perfect physical condition with no heart problems. Despite medical reassurance, he then panicked whenever he took the train to work or back to his office, and whenever he even thought about taking a train. In addition, whenever he thought about having intercourse with his wife he panicked and lost his erection. He borrowed some Xanax from his mother, and it calmed him down temporarily, but he hated taking medication and only used it infrequently.

With clients like this, who I quickly diagnose as self-neuroticizing, in the first session I get a brief family and personal history (partly from the four-page questionnaire we have all clients at the Albert Ellis Institute fill out just before the session). I especially want to know when the presenting symptom (panic) started, how intense it is, if other close members of the family have it or other symptoms, how anxious and self-downing the client is about having it, and what he or she is doing to cope with and change it. I usually focus the first session on explaining some of the ABCs of creating disturbance to the client, showing him how he mainly constructs and maintains his symptoms, and what he can quickly start doing to ameliorate them. I assume that most of the treatment can be done in ten or twenty sessions, and that significant improvement may be effected in perhaps a few weeks.

I feel that the most important things to accomplish in the first session include:

1. Finding the core dysfunctional philosophies the client is strongly believing to create and maintain his or her symptoms.
2. Showing the client what these self-defeating Bs are.
3. Showing the client that, in all probability, he or she constructed his or her own irrational shoulds, oughts, and musts and did not merely learn them from his or her parents and culture.
4. Showing the client that he or she can find these core irrationalities and work cognitively, emotively, and behaviorally to change them and ameliorate their influence.
5. Working out some suitable, practical thinking, feeling, and action-oriented homework assignment to perform before the next session.
6. Giving the client some reading material on REBT to start perusing at home.
7. Summarizing the first session by emphasizing that the client is to make a note of any dysfunctional Cs during the week, observe what As preceded these Cs, and look for his or her Rational and Irrational Beliefs with which he or she largely created these disturbed feelings and behaviors.

THE FIRST SESSION

After I spent less than ten minutes determining the client's symptoms, when and how they started and are being perpetuated, and a little background about his family (especially his mother's proneness to anxiety), he says that he borrowed some of his mother's Xanax and took three or four of them.

Therapist: And does it help you when you take it?

Client: Yes. But the one thing I don't like is to take pills. I know that sometimes you need medication, but I hate it.

Therapist: Well, if we can help you to change your ideas and attitudes about taking trains and about having a heart attack, that will really help you and you probably won't need medication. You see, you said you were a perfectionist. So you're first making yourself anxious about doing things perfectly well. "I *must* do well, I *must* do well!" Instead of telling yourself, "I'd *like* to do well, but if I don't, I don't. Fuck it! It's not the end of the world." You see, you're rarely saying that. You're saying, "I've *got* to! I've *got* to!" And that will *make* you anxious—about your work, about sex, about having a heart attack, or about almost anything else. Then, once you make yourself anxious, you often tell yourself, "I *must* not be anxious! I *must* not be anxious!" That will make you *more* anxious—anxious about your anxiety. First, if we can help you stop horrifying yourself about it; if we can help you, second, to give up your perfectionism—your demandingness—then you would not keep making yourself anxious. But you're in the habit of demanding that things *have* to go well and that, when they don't, you *must* not be anxious about them. "I must not be anxious! I must be sensible and sane!" That's exactly how people make themselves anxious—with rigid, forceful shoulds, oughts, and musts.

Client: Like yesterday. Yesterday was my worst day in a long time.

Therapist: Yes, because?

Client: What I did is when I was going to the train, I said: "I need to put something in my mind."

Therapist: To distract yourself from the anxiety that you expected to have when you got on the train?

Client: Yes. I said, "I am going to buy some sports things for the children." So I went to one of the stores and I bought some things, and as soon as I got on the train I started deliberately reading. Ten minutes after I was on the train, I still didn't have any anxiety. I was okay. But then I remembered and I said, "Jesus, I feel okay." At that moment, I started feeling panicked again.

Therapist: That's right. What you probably said to yourself was, "Jesus, I feel okay. But maybe I'll have another attack! Maybe I'll get an attack!" You will if you think that way! For you're really thinking, again, "I *must* not get another attack! What an idiot I am if I get another attack!" Right?

Client: Yes.

(After briefly showing the client that whenever he has a panic attack he really upsets himself and does not merely get upset by the train or anything else, I jump right in and try to teach him that it is not his preferences or wishes for good behavior and good health that upset him but his powerful conscious and unconscious demands, and that if he gives them up, changes them back to preferences, he will surrender his anxietizing about having a heart attack—and also his anxietizing about his anxietizing. In REBT, whenever a client like this one anxietizes, and especially panics, I assume that there is a good chance that he also panics about his panic, and mightily exacerbates his original panic. So

I try to make him aware of this immediately, and I find that very often as soon as he or she sees that this is so, panicking about panicking subsides—and, often, so does the original panicking.)

Therapist: Well, let me explain to you in a little more detail how humans disturb themselves—what they think and do to make themselves anxious and panicked. They don't *get* disturbed because of the happenings in their early childhood. That's largely psychoanalytic hogwash. They almost always needlessly disturb *themselves*—first by listening to their nutty parents and, more importantly, by taking the goals and standards they are taught and insisting that they absolutely have to live up to them, that they completely must do well. They are born with the tendency to "*mus*turbate"; that's their nature. But they can teach themselves not to do so and mainly remain with their preferences. Let me give you a model of most neurotic disturbance, and I know you'll understand it. Suppose you go out of this building at the end of this session into the streets of New York, and you don't know how much money you have in your pocket. It could be a dollar or it could be a thousand. You're ignorant of how much you have. And the one and *only* thing you think to yourself is, "I *wish*, I'd *like*, I'd *prefer* to have in my pocket a minimum of ten dollars. Not one hundred, not two hundred, only ten. I'd like to have ten dollars in my pocket, because I might eat, take a cab, or go to a movie." Then you actually look in your pocket and you find nine dollars, one less than ten. Now, how would you feel if you preferred ten and had nine, one less? What would your feeling be?

Client: That I don't have enough of what I want.

Therapist: Yes, but how would you *feel* about not having enough of what you want? You'd like to have ten dollars, but you have nine, one less than ten.

Client: Slightly disappointed.

Therapist: Fine. That's a very healthy negative feeling, because we wouldn't want you to feel good about not having what you want.

Client: Yeah.

Therapist: Okay. Now the second time you're going out, this time you're saying foolishly to yourself—you know it's foolish but you still say and believe it—"*I must, I must, I must*, at all times, at all times have a minimum guarantee of ten dollars. *I have to! I've got to! I must!*" That's what you believe in your head. Then again, you look in your pocket and find only nine dollars and you can't get the tenth. Now how would you feel?

Client: I would feel very upset.

Therapist: Yes, because of your *must*. It's the same nine dollars, but this time you're insisting that you absolutely *must* have it—and, of course, you don't. You see, we humans don't get upset by a bad condition that occurs in our lives. We largely get upset—or upset ourselves—because of our *musts*. We take our preferences, our wishes, our desires and we often make them into absolute demands, musts, shoulds, oughts. That—your *must*—would be what's upsetting you.

Client: I see. My musts.

Therapist: Now finally, the third time, you go out again and you're still saying to yourself the same thing as the second time: "I *must*, at all times, have a minimum guarantee of ten dollars in my pocket!" And you look in your pocket and this time you find fifteen dollars—more than enough. Now how would you feel?

Client: I'd feel okay.

Therapist: That's right. But a minute later, something would occur to you to make you anxious. Now, why would you be anxious a minute later? First you say to yourself, "Great! I've got fifteen dollars—more than enough!" Then something would occur to make you anxious. Now, why would you become anxious a little later? You've still got the fifteen dollars. You haven't lost it and you haven't said, "I must have twenty or I must have thirty." You're still saying, "I must have a minimum of ten. Great, I've got fifteen!" Now what would make you anxious?

Client: Well, I—. I don't really know.

Therapist: Well, don't forget: You're saying to yourself: "I must have a minimum of ten dollars *at all times*. I *now* have fifteen. But suppose I spend six. Suppose I lose six. Suppose I get robbed!" All of which could happen, you see, because there *are* no guarantees in the real universe! They don't exist, and you're demanding one.

Client: Yes, I see. So I'm still anxious.

Therapist: Right! Now this model shows that anybody in the whole universe—and it doesn't matter what their status is, black or white, young or old, male or female, rich or poor. Anybody who takes any desire, any goal, any preference for anything and makes it into a must, a *got to*, first is miserable when they don't have what they think they must and, second, they're anxious when they do have it—because they could always lose it. Now do you see how that applies to you?

Client: Yes, I do. Any must, any real demands.

Therapist: Yes, and you've got two main musts that make and keep making you anxious: (1) "I *must* do well; I *must* be perfect. I *must* do the right thing and not bring on a heart attack!" And (2) "I *must* not be anxious! I *must* not be panicked! I *must* not be panicked!" With these two musts, you're really going to be off the wall. You see?

Client: I never thought of that before.

Therapist: But can you see it now?

Client: Yes, I think I can.

Therapist: Fine. Now if we can just help you to think, "I don't *like* being anxious, but if I am, too damned bad, it won't kill me," you'll then get rid of your anxiety about your anxiety, your panic about your panic. If you can convince yourself, "Anxiety is uncomfortable but it won't kill me. It won't lead to a heart attack. And it won't make me an idiot for bringing on my anxiety. It's merely uncomfortable. It's not *awful*." Then you'll get rid of most of your problem. Then, as you rid yourself of your anxiety about your anxiety, you can much more easily go back to your original perfectionism—your demand that you always do well and not make serious errors. Then you'll work on being less perfectionistic. You'll still very much want to do well, *prefer* to do well, but you'll give up the idea that you *have* to. There's no necessity, you see, in doing well; no necessity for you to be unanxious.

(During the first session, I often use this model of someone wanting something and not making themselves anxious about its loss and needing the same thing and producing considerable anxiety and often self-hating: first, when they do not have what they think they need and, second, even when they do have it—for then they could always lose it. Most of my clients understand this model of self-disturbing and many of them begin right away to use it in their own lives, and keep mentioning to me how useful it is to them.)

Client: What is the best way to react—when you feel that stress is too strong? How can you overcome it?

Therapist: When you're anxious?

Client: Yes.

Therapist: You say to yourself very strongly, until you really mean it: "Fuck it! So I'm anxious! It'll pass; it'll pass in a few minutes. It won't kill me. It won't turn my hair gray. It won't send me to the loony bin. Nothing will happen if I just go with the anxiety and relax." So you relax. You sit down and relax. And you strongly tell yourself, "Too damned bad—so I'm anxious. But it's not the end of the world." Anxiety won't kill you.

Client: Well, I know that. But—

Therapist: Well, you don't know that *well enough*. You're probably saying to yourself, "Yeah, it won't kill me. But maybe it will! Maybe it will! Maybe it will!" Then you'll be *more* anxious!

Client: Yeah, I think that I need to be anxious to keep living, to stay alive.

Therapist: Well, you don't! You'd better accept the fact that at times we're all anxious, depressed, or upset. Too bad; tough; that's the way it is. That's the human condition—humans often make themselves anxious. But all you have to do is relax—do some deep breathing or other relaxation exercises. Do you know any relaxation exercises?

Client: Yes, I bought a tape the other day. I think I have it here. It shows you how to breathe freely.

Therapist: What's it called? *How to Turn Stress into Energy*. That may be all right. If you really follow this tape, or one of our own relaxation tapes that you can get downstairs, then you'll learn to immediately relax, and your anxiety will temporarily go away. But if you go back to being a perfectionist and insist that you *must* do well, you *must* not be anxious, your anxiety will come back.

Client: Someone told me that when you have great stress, if you do a lot of exercise, you can drain it out.

Therapist: You can distract yourself and feel better. That will temporarily work. But you'd better also change your philosophy—that will work much better. You'd better do two things: (1) distract yourself with some exercise; then your anxiety will go away temporarily. But it will come back because you're still telling yourself, "I *must* do perfectly well. I *must* not be anxious! I *must* not be upset!" (2) You therefore had better change your attitude, as well as relax. Show yourself that you don't have to do that well and that your anxiety won't kill you. Relaxation alone will help, but it will not cure you. Changing your basic musturbatory core philosophy will help you permanently.

Client: So you have to do it physically and mentally?

Therapist: Exactly! You have to do it physically and mentally. And you really have to tell yourself—and *believe*—"Fuck it! I'm anxious, I'm anxious. Too damned bad! This too will pass. And if I work on it and change my philosophy, I can make it rarely come back."

Client: You see, that's what I'm trying to do in regard to the train. I think that my problem is that I think that if I have an attack on the train it will be awful.

Therapist: So suppose you do have an attack on the train? What's going to happen to you then?

Client: Something will happen to me.

Therapist: What?

Client: Most of the time I've said to myself, "Okay, nothing will happen. Because I know that whatever I have is not a heart problem—it's a mental problem, and I create it myself." So I then relax. But what's getting to me is that I have to deal with the same thing every day. Everyday I have to deal with it.

Therapist: I know. Because you're saying, "I *must* not be anxious! I *must* not be anxious!" Instead of, "I don't *like* being anxious, but if I am, I am!" You see, you're terrified of your own anxiety.

Client: That's exactly what it is!

Therapist: Okay. But anxiety is only a pain in the ass. That's all it is. It doesn't kill you. It's only a pain. Everybody gets anxious, including you. And they live with it!

Client: It's a big pain in the ass.

Therapist: I know. But that's all it is. Just like—well, suppose you lost all the money you had with you. That would be a real pain, but you wouldn't worry about it too much, because you know you'd get some more money. But you're making yourself terrified. "Something awful will happen. Suppose people *see* I'm so anxious! How terrible!" Well, suppose they do.

Client: I don't care about that.

Therapist: Well, that's good. Most people are afraid of that and it's good that you're not.

Client: When I walk to the train, I know that I am going to start feeling anxious.

Therapist: You know it because you're afraid of it happening. If you said to yourself strongly and really believed, "Fuck it! If it happens, it happens!" Then it won't even happen. Every time you say, "I must not be anxious! I must not be anxious!"—then you'll be anxious.

Client: I'm getting—not in the train, I mean—yesterday I was like that in the office all day.

Therapist: It doesn't matter where you are. Anytime you say to yourself, "Suppose I'm anxious," you'll be anxious. Sexually, for example, instead of saying to yourself, "What a great piece of ass my wife is! I'm going to enjoy this!" you say, "Suppose I'm anxious and my goddamned cock goes down!" Then you'll be anxious, not be thinking of sexual enjoyment, and it won't work. Anxiety will take over. But if you didn't give that much of a shit about your anxiety, and went back to thinking, "Look: I'd better focus on her body and on sexual enjoyment. That's how I can get and stay erect," then you'll maintain your erection. But, you see, you're not doing that.

Client: A couple of months ago when I was anxious, I did what you're saying. I put a picture in my head, about my wife or about some other sexy woman, and then my anxiety would leave and I'd be all right sexually.

Therapist: Yes, as soon as you focus on anything else, your anxiety will temporarily go. Let me tell you a famous fable. A king didn't want to marry his daughter to a favorite prince, who passed all the tests he was given, so that it looked like he would marry the daughter. But the king was horrified at that, so he said to his wise men, "Look! You find a test this son-of-a-bitch can't pass, or I'll cut your balls off!" The wise men were very panicked about this. So they thought and finally came up with a test that the prince couldn't pass. Do you know what it was?

Client: No, I can't think of one.

Therapist: "Don't think of a pink elephant for twenty minutes!" You see, if you say to yourself, as the prince did, "I must not think of a pink elephant! I must not think of a pink elephant—"

Client: Then you're going to think about that very thing.

Therapist: Right! And that, you see, is exactly what you're doing. You're saying, "I must not be anxious!" Then you'll be anxious. Or, "I must be good sexually." Then you'll make yourself so anxious that you won't be able to concentrate on sexual enjoyment. Because to do well at sex, you have to focus on sexual thoughts—on your wife or on some other desirable woman. You'd better have sexy thoughts. But if you say to yourself, "Oh, my God! Suppose I get anxious! Suppose my cock won't go up and stay up!" Then it won't! So that's what you're doing. You're demanding that you have to do well; and you're also insisting that you must not be anxious. So if we can get you to say to yourself, and really believe, "I'd *like* to do well, but I never *have* to," And, "I'd very much prefer to be unanxious, but fuck it, if I'm anxious, I'm anxious!" then you'll get over this nonsense that you're now telling yourself. Whenever you take a preference, a goal, a desire, and you say, "I have to achieve it! I must perform well!" you're making yourself immediately anxious. That's where your anxiety comes from. And that's what people do: They take their strong desires and say, "I absolutely must achieve them! I have to; I've got to!" Instead of, "I'd like to achieve them, but if I don't, tough! The earth won't stop spinning!"

Client: Okay. So the best way is for me to think, if I am anxious?

Therapist: "Too damned bad! It's only uncomfortable! It won't kill me!" Because nothing terrible does happen if you're anxious. You see? Just like my diabetes. It's a pain in the ass, and I have to take care of it. But it's only uncomfortable, and I don't whine and scream about having it. "I must not have diabetes! I must be perfectly healthy!" If I did that, I'd be in trouble. So I have diabetes! So?

Client: And there's nothing that you can do about it?

Therapist: I take care of it. I stick to my diet and take my insulin regularly. Too fucking bad! I don't like it, but I don't whine and scream and make myself miserable by intoning, "I must not have diabetes! I must not, I must not!"

Client: There's nothing you can do. So you just accept it.

Therapist: Yes, we *invent* the horrors. They really don't exist in the world. Many hassles, many problems do exist. But as a store manager, you know how to take care of problems. That's your business.

Client: Yes, I do that pretty well.

Therapist: So you don't get yourself too excited when there's a problem. You don't say to yourself, "Oh, my God! I absolutely must solve it!" Then you'd make yourself anxious and wouldn't be able to solve it very well.

Client: That's right.

Therapist: So if we could get you to take the same attitude toward your anxiety that you take toward your work, you would do very well and rid yourself of most of your neurotic problems.

Client: See, I never thought of that.

Therapist: Yes, but that's what you'd better think of. That's the thing. Life is a series of hassles, and you've had a number of them in your life. So when your children get sick, you don't like it, but you take care of it. Or if you have problems with your wife, you cope with them. Now, we want you to cope with your anxiety, and also give up some of your perfectionism. For when you say, "I have to do well! I have to do well!" you're going to make yourself upset. There are no absolute necessities in the universe—only things we would like, prefer, desire. There are many of those, but we don't *have* to get them. When people like you change these preferences into musts, they upset themselves needlessly. The three main musts are (1) "I *must* do well and be approved by significant others, or else I'm no good!" (2) "*You* have to treat me well, or you're a shit!" And then people become angry, enraged, homicidal. (3) "Conditions *must* be arranged so that they give me exactly what I want when I want it, and never, no, never give me what I don't want!" Then people have low frustration tolerance and, when conditions are pretty bad, depress themselves. Those three musts really upset people. But, of course, there is no reason why you *have* to do well, or why other people *must* treat you nicely, or that conditions *must* be easy. So whenever you feel upset, or behave foolishly against your interest, about anything, look for your shoulds, look for your musts. You can easily find them, but it takes a good deal of work and effort to give them up. But you can do it!

Client: I see what you're saying. It looks like I can do it.

Therapist: Fine. I am sure you can. Now what I want you to do is take all these forms home with you [the Millon Clinical Multiaxial Inventory], fill them all out and bring them back together and we'll give you some interesting personality scores. Then, for your homework—because we always give homework in REBT—make a note of anything that really bothers you during the week, of any feelings of anxiety, panic, depression, self-hatred, or rage against others. Just a little note to yourself, so that you'll remember these feelings next time you come here. Then note exactly what's happening at point A, your activating event, just before each of these feelings happens. Then look for your B, your rational and irrational beliefs, about A. Rationally, you have preferences and wishes, that unfortunate As (or Adversities) not occur, and these lead to healthy feelings at C, your emotional and behavioral consequences, such as sorrow, regret, frustration, and disappointment. But we are particularly interested in your unhealthy consequences at C—as I said before, your really upset feelings. So bring me some of these ABCs—and you can take one of our REBT Self-help Forms, down at the desk downstairs, to remind you what they are and to help you remember them.

Client: Down at the desk?

Therapist: Yes, we always have free forms for you to take and fill out as homework, during the week, down at the desk. Bring me a few filled out, and especially try to find your Irrational *Beliefs* (IBs) at point B—the shoulds, oughts, and musts by which you disturb yourself. But if you don't find them, just bring me in a few As and a few Cs and I'll show you how to figure out your IBs at point B.

Client: Is that all I have to do during the week?

Therapist: Yes, that's all for this week. Except that we gave you a group of pamphlets, so start reading these REBT pamphlets. And preferably get a copy downstairs of two paperback books: *A Guide to Rational Living* and *How to Stubbornly Refuse to Make Yourself Miserable About Anything—Yes, Anything!* And start reading those books. You don't have to finish all the reading, but let's see if you can at least start it. The more REBT reading you do and the more you listen to some of our tape cassettes, the quicker and better you will see how to help yourself.

Client: Oh, I like reading. I find it helpful.

Therapist: Fine. And, as noted in the instructions for therapy, which we gave you in that envelope, we find it desirable for our clients to record their sessions and then listen to them later. So next time you come, if you want to do so, you can bring a blank cassette, or get one at the desk downstairs, and record your session and listen to it a few times in between sessions. I think you'll find that helpful. Anything else you want to bring up in the last minute or two of this session?

Client: No, I don't think so. I got quite a lot out of this session. I've had some therapy before, but nothing like this! Thank you for helping me. I got a lot.

Therapist: Fine. I am glad you enjoyed this session. Just make another appointment downstairs to see me in a week or so, and I'll look forward to continuing to see you.

Client: Fine. Thank you.

(Notice how I go over some of the essentials of REBT several times, and particularly the point that the client upsets himself with his musts and then makes himself anxietizing about his anxiety with more musts. I directly, forcefully, and briefly keep repeating this message, especially during the first session, to achieve several results: (1) explain some of the basic principles of human disturbing and of REBT to the client; (2) try to get quickly to a central problem, so that he or she can see right away how it is largely created by himself or herself and that he or she can immediately start to do something about it; (3) try to get over the idea that the client can quickly start changing himself or herself but that to do so permanently will require a longer period of time; (4) try to show the client that the REBT sessions themselves can be relatively brief (usually, half-hour sessions) and short-term (from five to thirty sessions for most clients), but only because the client does most of the therapeutic work himself, in between sessions; and (5) give bibliotherapy homework as well as some kind of cognitive, emotive, or behavioral homework.

The REBT Self-Help Form that I instruct this client to get at our reception desk and fill out during the week as one of his homework assignments is used with most clients and especially with those who try for brief therapy results. Our present form was devised by Windy Dryden and Jane Walker in 1992 and revised by me in 1996. It is shown on the following page.

REBT Self-Help Form

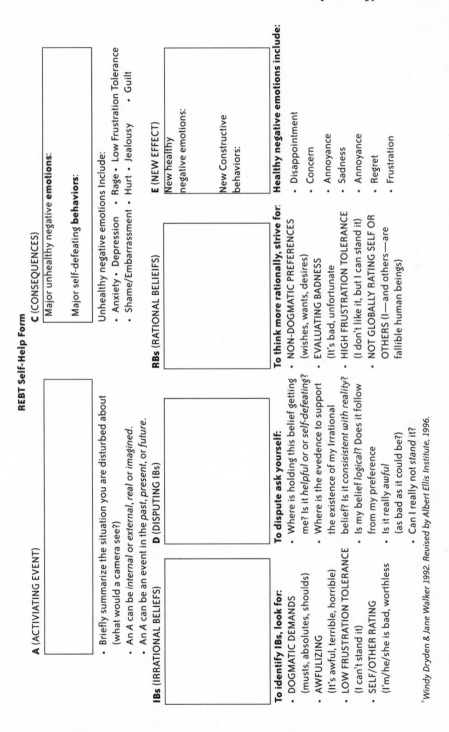

A (ACTIVATING EVENT)

- Briefly summarize the situation you are disturbed about (what would a camera see?)
- An A can be *internal or external, real or imagined.*
- An A can be an event in the *past, present, or future.*

IBs (IRRATIONAL BELIEFS)

To identify IBs, look for:
- DOGMATIC DEMANDS (musts, absolutes, shoulds)
- AWFULIZING (It's awful, terrible, horrible)
- LOW FRUSTRATION TOLERANCE (I can't stand it)
- SELF/OTHER RATING (I'm/he/she is bad, worthless

D (DISPUTING IBs)

To dispute ask yourself:
- Where is holding this belief getting me? Is it *helpful or or self-defeating?*
- Where is the evedence to support the existence of my Irrational belief? Is it *consistent with reality?*
- Is my belief *logical?* Does it follow from my preference
- Is it really *awful* (as bad as it could be?)
- Can I really *not stand it?*

C (CONSEQUENCES)

Major unhealthy negative **emotions:**

Major self-defeating **behaviors:**

Unhealthy negative emotions Include:
- Anxiety • Depression • Rage • Low Frustration Tolerance
- Shame/Embarrassment • Hurt • Jealousy • Guilt

RBs (RATIONAL BELIEFS)

To think more rationally, strive for:
- NON-DOGMATIC PREFERENCES (wishes, wants, desires)
- EVALUATING BADNESS (It's bad, unfortunate
- HIGH FRUSTRATION TOLERANCE (I don't like it, but I can stand it)
- NOT GLOBALLY RATING SELF OR OTHERS (I—and others—are fallible human beings)

E (NEW EFFECT)

New healthy negative emotions:

New Constructive behaviors:

Healthy negative emotions include:
- Disappointment
- Concern
- Annoyance
- Sadness
- Annoyance
- Regret
- Frustration

Windy Dryden & Jane Walker 1992. Revised by Albert Ellis Institute, 1996.

As can be seen by inspecting this form, it includes the main ABCDEs of REBT. Clients first fill in A (Activating Event or Adversity) and C (Consequences of A). Then they fill out their IBs (Irrational Beliefs) and D (their Disputing of these IBs). Then they fill in their RBs (Rational Beliefs) that stem from their Disputing. They finally fill in their E (new Effect) that follow from their Disputing (D) and their Rational Beliefs (RBs). They do this by themselves, as homework assignments, and they then can bring them to their therapy sessions to have their therapist check them for accuracy; or they can check them with a friend, a partner, or another person who knows something about the ABCDEs of REBT.

The second session with this client took place one week after the first session and showed fair progress:

Client: I feel okay, this week only a couple of times have I had some anxiety.

(On a fairly crowded train, he forced himself to read my book How to Stubbornly Refuse to Make Yourself Miserable About Anything—Yes, Anything!, *and distracted himself from his feelings of panic.*

He kept strongly convincing himself that he was creating his panic and that he was not going to have a heart attack and felt uncomfortable rather than anxious.

In his office, he began to tell himself that he did not have to do everything fast or perfectly well. Here are some excerpts from his second session:)

Client: And two minutes later, I feel like I can face myself. My anxiety— it is gone . . . . Last week when I got on the train, I started getting anxiety. This week I got anxious only one time. I got to the train and I said to myself, "There's nothing to worry about. Nothing will happen. So you're creating your anxiety, just like you put wood on a fire. So you can go the other way." So five minutes later I forgot about it and I didn't have that problem. Before last session, I didn't understand what was going on with me. Now I know my anxiety is a problem that I am creating. I can live with that, and one of these days, I won't have that problem. I think I can really convince myself. I don't feel the way that I felt a week ago. Then I was getting crazy. Now I know that anxiety doesn't matter that much. Any time I can take the train and maybe the first couple of minutes I have to deal with myself, and I say, "You don't have to feel panicked. You can feel the other way."

(For the first time, he confessed to some of his friends that he had an anxiety problem and was seeking help.)

Client: I no longer care that much what they think. Because I don't think I'm that crazy. I just have a minor problem. You don't have to be crazy to see a psychologist.

(He kept repeating that he was creating his anxiety and that he didn't have to do so. Two weeks later, during the third session, the client showed that he

had several real breakthroughs as he kept working on his anxiety and kept reading. Here are some excerpts from the session.)

Client: I'm feeling better. Whatever I'm feeling, like anxiety, is not it. I'm creating it. Whatever I'm feeling I can make it go away in a couple of minutes, and if I get upset about my anxiety, I can talk to myself about that. When I get to the train I'm not that anxious. Like this morning, I completely forgot about it until I was on the train. Then I remembered and started saying to myself, "It's nice to be feeling the way I'm feeling now." It doesn't bother me anymore. . . . And last week, a couple of days, I'm going home, I fall asleep on the train, and I wake up at my station and I said to myself, "Whatever happened a couple of months ago is gone."

And even in my work I don't feel anxious. I am working better than before without getting that, uh, anxiety to make everything fast and quick. I can pace myself better than before. . . . Another thing I learned to do: not to upset myself about the others in my office who act badly. If I got upset, they're going to act the same way.

Before, I thought my anxiety meant something was physically wrong. Now I see that I'm creating it. It's not that I am sick. . . . I used to say, while going to the train, "I'm sure I'm gonna get sick." Now I see that I'm creating that sick feeling. Two or three minutes later, I am okay. Two weeks ago it would have taken me fifteen minutes to be less anxious. Now it takes me two or three minutes, and there are days when I don't feel panic at all.

The other day I got to the train when it was almost full, and I couldn't sit down and read and distract myself. But it didn't bother me and I didn't wait for another train as I used to have to do. . . . I can talk to myself and say, "Look, whatever anxiety you feel, you created it. And you can uncreate it." Your book *How to Stubbornly Refuse to Make Yourself Miserable About Anything—Yes, Anything!* is not only helping me with this anxiety problem, but it's also helping me to deal with other people. If they didn't do things the way I wanted it, I would get upset. Now if they don't, it's not like before, I don't upset myself. I can deal with people better and I can deal with myself—not making myself crazy. . . . I used to get angry with them and feel enraged for a long time. But now I tell myself, "If I'm getting angry it's because I'm creating the anger." . . . It doesn't pay for me to do that and feel like that.

I still try to do things better in the office but when I think that I have to do it perfectly, I say to myself, "Please! That is impossible. I will do as best I can—and that's it."

Sexually, I am better now than before. Less anxious. I was having problems with erections because I started thinking, "I won't have it. Suppose I don't have it!" Now, I'm doing what you say in the book: "Maybe I can make it, maybe I cannot. Okay, if I don't, maybe it will be better tomorrow." And things like that. I am enjoying it more. . . . The whole thing is changing because if I start thinking, "I can't," then I won't be able to. But if I don't think like that, then it will be fine. That's what's helping me a great deal.

Since I was feeling better this two weeks, I thought I don't have to be here every week. I would like every two weeks or every three weeks, to see how I can do by myself. I know that I am not 100 percent better, but I feel I am getting there. I think the book helped me a lot. The way you described in it how to overcome your—to deal with just about any problem you have. . . . The chapters that I read, I read them intensely, like trying to absorb a hundred percent of it, you know. It's not that I have the will to practice everything I read over a month. But I was feeling so awful that I said that the only way for me to get better is to really confront my problem and then to follow through on it in whatever way I can.

Therapist: Anything else that's been bothering you at all recently?

Client: Not really. What was bothering me was worrying about when I get to the train. And then I was feeling anxious in the office. But now with that and in the home and in the office, I said I couldn't control my anxiety and that I had to do so. But now I think that it's better to see what the problem is and use my thinking to make the problem go. Work it out, no matter how bad it is.

FOLLOW-UP

I expected to have several more sessions with Ted, because I usually see people like him from five to ten times, but actually this was his last individual therapy session. He and his wife started to attend my regular Friday night workshops at the Albert Ellis Institute in New York, where I interview volunteer clients each week before an audience of one hundred or more people. After working with the clients for about a half hour, I throw the discussion over to the audience and let them question and advise the volunteers under my direction. Ted has participated in these workshops quite actively, as well as in several of our four-hour workshops for the public, such as one on "Overcoming Low Frustration Tolerance." He has continued to read REBT books and to listen to Institute cassettes, especially my tapes *Solving Emotional Problems* and *Unconditionally Accepting Yourself and Others*.

I have spoken with him several times and also with his wife, Myra, who agrees that he is continuing the gains that he indicated during his third session and that he is making still further progress. He has almost completely stopped panicking about trains and has also begun to take plane trips, which he was previously afraid to do but had never spoken about it in his sessions with me. He is rarely anxious or angry at the office, and sex with his wife is "by far the best I have ever had." His wife corroborates his progress, and almost every time I see her she loudly tells me, in the presence of my other workshop participants, what an "absolute miracle on Ted" I performed. Both Ted and Myra keep sending their friends and relatives to me for therapy, and some of these referrals also comment on "what a new man" Ted is.

At the present writing, three months have passed since I saw Ted for therapy, and he continues to hold his ground. I expect that I will see him occasionally again, as new crises may arise in his life, but that he will generally hold the gains he has already made. My guesses about why he was able to make such good gains in the course of three half-hour sessions in one month's time include these: (1) He was a classic neurotic, unlike many clients I often see who have severe personality disordering. On the Millon Clinical Multiaxial Inventory II, his only really high score was on the anxiety scale, with his compulsive and somataform scores somewhat above average. (2) He was highly motivated to reduce his anxietizing and from the first session worked hard to do so. (3) He was competent and hardworking in his business and social life. (4) He took well to my highly active-directive REBT approach and kept echoing my insistence that he was responsible for his own anxietizing and angering and that he had the ability to work at reducing these feelings. (5) He read and listened to our REBT self-help materials most intently and frequently used *How to Stubbornly Refuse to Make Yourself Miserable About Anything—Yes, Anything!* (6) After therapy ended, he continued assiduously to attend REBT workshops and to work with REBT materials.

EDITORS' QUESTIONS

Question: It appears that the client was a man who liked the therapist from the beginning. His personality seems to fit well with the REBT model. He was enthusiastic and willing to comply with your requests. What if the patient had been resistant, difficult, and ornery and had a significant personality disorder? How would your method and technique vary?

Answer: If the client had been resistant, difficult, ornery, and had a significant personality disorder I probably would have tried to show him that he was going to have a difficult time changing and that therefore he had better work harder and longer at doing so. I would often let him know that he very likely had a strong innate tendency to be the way he was, exacerbated by his life experiences and reinforced by his own creating and practicing dysfunctional thoughts, feelings, and behaviors, and that only very hard work and practice—yes, work and practice—to overcome this tendency would probably be effective in his case. I would stress the pain he was in and how disadvantageous it would be for him to prolong it, and I would vigorously show him that, in all probability, he could significantly change if he chose to keep working at doing so. I would try to get him to learn REBT and to keep using it to help others, and would encourage him to spend a good part of the rest of his life helping himself be much less miserable than he presently was.

Question: What do you usually tell a patient about the course and prognosis of treatment? When and how do you determine and discuss length of treatment? How do you motivate the patient?

Answer: I usually tell clients that the treatment will be relatively brief—a matter of months rather than years—if they work very hard in between sessions at using the REBT methods we go over during the sessions. I motivate them in several ways: (1) by emphasizing their present emotional-behavioral misery and showing them that they definitely can reduce or eliminate it; (2) by strongly showing them that they largely create their *own* disturbances and that therefore they can almost invariably alleviate or undo them; and (3) by pointing them toward the greater pleasures they can have if they work at reducing their disturbances *and* at enhancing hedonistic pursuits and at personal self-actualization.

Question: There was a flexible use of time in this case. You advised having the next appointment in a week or so, but later the patient indicated spacing out the sessions. What guides about length of sessions, frequence, and spacing do you use?

Answer: I usually suggest fewer or more-spaced-out sessions after several weeks of therapy, providing that the client is improving. If clients want fewer sessions than I suggest, I say, "Let's try it your way and see how it goes. If you will work hard in between sessions, and keep reading our material and doing your homework, you will probably do a good therapeutic job on yourself and therefore require fewer sessions. If not, we'll soon see a lack of progress and you can arrange for more sessions again."

Question: Did you screen for alcohol abuse? Suppose the patient were alcoholic—would you approach the problem in the same way?

Answer: Yes, I asked the client about alcohol abuse and he indicated that he did only mild social drinking, and I accepted this answer. If there had been alcohol abuse, I would have worked on his problem drinking from the start, ferreted out the dysfunctional beliefs leading to it—including his self-denigrating, his low frustration tolerance, and his squelching of other emotional problems by his drinking—and I would have helped him to stop denigrating himself for his drinking, to work on his low frustration tolerance, and to use a number of cognitive, emotive, and behavioral techniques that are commonly used in REBT with problem drinkers (Ellis and Velten 1992).

Question: If the patient had come to you on medication for panic disorder, how would you proceed?

Answer: I would proceed in much the same way that I did in this case, but I would talk to his psychopharmacologist to see what medication he was taking, what dosage, how long he was expected to take it, what side effects he might have, etc. Depending on the information received from the psychopharmacologist, I might possibly modify some of my treatment methods and the homework assignment worked out with the client.

Question: How would you focus with a client whose problems were more vague or unclear?

Answer: I would get him to clarify his problems by asking him questions about when and where the problems occurred, why they troubled him, what his goal was in regard to them, what he was thinking when the problems occurred, etc. Usually, after a few sessions, I would wind up with a pretty clear idea of his central problems and I would almost always discover at least one specific issue that was clear to both of us and that he or she wanted to work at.

Question: In the case presented, if the patient had not responded well, what are some of the issues you might consider? How might you change your approach?

Answer: I would consider: (1) how well the client understood the ABCs of REBT and knew what he could do about disputing his dysfunctional Bs; (2) how he was actually working to use the ABCs of REBT and how he was doing the homework that we had agreed upon; (3) what he was specifically telling himself when he did not do his cognitive, emotive, and behavioral homework; (4) whether he was really willing to change and to work at changing himself; (5) what, if anything, were his "neurotic" gains from remaining the way he was and from not changing; (6) what unexpected problems he had that may have been blocking him from working on the expressed ones; and (7) how he was reacting to me, and if his positive or negative attitudes toward me were interfering with his working at changing himself.

Question: If the client said that he saw what he was telling himself, was doing his REBT disputing of his irrational and dysfunctional beliefs, and was still not changing, what would you then do?

Answer: I would tell him that he quite probably was seeing his dysfunctional beliefs and disputing them, but mainly doing it lightly, unvigorously, and not often enough. I would show him, if I had not already done so, that practically all self-disturbing people have *two* simultaneous sets of *Beliefs*: one rational and self-helping and the other irrational and self-defeating, and that one is usually held lightly and mildly, while the other is held strongly and powerfully. In his case, the Irrational *Beliefs* were probably *still* being held much more powerfully than the Rational *Beliefs*, and therefore he had better see that this was so and keep vigorously and powerfully disputing the former and replacing them with the latter. At the same time, he had better work very strongly to change his feelings and work powerfully and repetitively to change his behaviors, so that these also interacted with his crooked thinking and significantly helped him change that thinking. I would show him that REBT always has highly emotive and behavioral components, and not merely important cognitive techniques, and that therefore he had better keep working and practicing—yes, keep working and practicing—the REBT methods, and do so very strongly and committedly until he truly believed, felt, and acted on the rational philosophies that he was now (at times) presumably telling himself.

Question: How did you become a brief therapist?

Answer: I became a brief therapist in the early 1940s, when I started to do a great deal of sex and marital therapy and found that most clients only wanted to come for a few sessions and had no intention of making basic personality changes. To help some of them who wanted depth therapy, I was analyzed, trained as an analyst, and practiced psychoanalysis for six years. Doing so, I found that psychoanalysis goes into every irrelevancy under the sun and, alas, misses just about all the philosophic relevancies by which people mainly disturb themselves. Like many therapies that stem from it, psychoanalysis is obsessed with people's past history, which influenced their goals and values but did not really make them disturbed. It largely ignores how they mainly constructed their dysfunctional behavior and what they are now actively doing to keep constructing it. So in 1955 I founded and started using Rational Emotive Behavior Therapy and specifically designed it to be an efficient and brief therapy for most neuroticizing clients, although it is often more prolonged and intensive for seriously disturbed individuals.

SELF-HELP SUGGESTIONS

- Although any process of changing your thinking, feeling, and behaving takes some period of time, and although maintaining your changing also requires time and effort, REBT shows you how you can promptly start changing, with therapy and with self-help materials. It was originally designed to be a relatively brief form of therapy and has proven to be so for almost half a century.
- To get quickly started in using REBT, assume that your emotional dysfunctioning largely (not completely) stems from your thinking, and that the thinking that accompanies your distressing importantly includes your escalating some of your strong *preferences* for success, approval, and comfort into absolutistic *shoulds*, *oughts*, and *musts*.
- Also assume that you can actively and forcefully Dispute your absolutistic demands while still expressing the preferences and desires that go along with them; and that you can do so with a number of counteracting REBT

thinking, feeling, and acting methods. No matter how strongly—that is, emotionally—you hold a dysfunctional must, you can still actively change it back into a preference.

- The human tendency, however, is to restore and reenact to some degree your musturbatory behavings; so you may briefly accomplish this but may have to keep repeating your dysfunctional urges and habits throughout your life. Brief therapy may not mean *final* therapy!

- Like most people, you may greatly desire to minimize any disturbing symptoms you have, such as anxietizing and depressing. But you can easily *Believe*, "I must not anxietize! I must not depress myself!" Then, very often, you will anxietize about your anxiety and depress about your depressing! Your original dysfunctional feelings then worsen! So look for this kind of *double* self-disturbing, Dispute your commands that you *must not* anxietize or depress, and go back to Disputing your original musts and self-distressing.

- No matter how quickly you get going to use REBT methods and how much you reduce your disturbing, as well as your possibly disturbing yourself *about* your anxietizing and depressing, remember the *homework* aspects of therapy. *Keep* looking for your self-upsetting behaviors and *keep* actively and forcefully counteracting them. Ultimately, if you work hard enough, you will probably tend to automatically minimize your self-disturbing without making much conscious effort to do so.

11

Vigorous REBT Disputing and the Technique of Rational Emotive Therapy

VIGOROUS REBT DISPUTING

Disputing (D) your dysfunctional or irrational *Beliefs* (IBs) is one of the most effective REBT techniques. But it is still often ineffective, because you can easily and very strongly hold on to an IB (such as, "I absolutely must be loved by so-and-so, and it's awful and I am an inadequate person when he/she does not love me!"). When you question and challenge this IB you often can come up with an Effective new philosophy (E) that is accurate but weak: "I guess there is no reason why s/he must love me, because there are other people who will do so when s/he does not. I can therefore be reasonably happy without his/her love." If you believe this new philosophy *lightly*, you can easily slip back into believing that "Even though it is not awful and terrible when he or she does not love me, it really is! No matter what, I *still need* his/her affection!"

Lukewarm disputing therefore will often not work very well to help you truly disbelieve some of your powerful and long-held IBs, while vigorous, persistent disputing is more likely to work.

This chapter is partly adapted from "Vigorous REBT Disputing and Rational-Emotive Imagery," in *The REBT Resource Book for Practitioners*, ed. M. E. Bernard and J. L. Wolfe (New York: Albert Ellis Institute, 2000). Used with permission.

147

One way to do highly powerful, vigorous disputing is to use a tape recorder and to record on it one of your strong Irrational *Beliefs*, such as, "If I fail this job interview I am about to have, that will prove that I'll never get a good job and that I might as well apply only for low-level positions!" Figure out several Disputes to this IB and strongly present them on this same tape. For example: "Even if I do poorly in this interview, that will show only that I failed this time; but it doesn't show that I'll *always* fail and can never do well in other interviews. Maybe they'll still hire me for the job. But if they don't, I can learn from my mistakes, can do better in other interviews, and can finally get the kind of job that I want."

Listen to your Disputing. Let other people, including your therapist or members of your therapy group, listen to it. Do it over in an even more forceful and vigorous manner and let them listen to it again, until they agree that you are getting more powerful at doing it. Keep listening to it until you see that you are able to convince yourself and others that you are becoming more powerful and more self-convincing.

RATIONAL-EMOTIVE IMAGERY

Rational-Emotive Imagery was invented in 1971 by Maxie Maultsby, M.D., and used effectively by him in his clinical work and that of his trainees. I found it to be quite useful but also found that it overlapped too much with REBT disputing because Maultsby usually instructed clients, when doing the imagery, to go back to their rational coping statements they had previously figured out with him, and use them to change their unhealthy negative feelings to healthy ones when they thought about an unfortunate Activating Event or Adversity. I therefore began to use Rational-Emotive Imagery in a more emotive-evocative and less disputational way.

In Maultsby's version, you imagine an unfortunate Activating Event (A) happening in your life—and let yourself spontaneously feel very anxious or depressed at point C, a harmful Consequence of A. Then you look at your Rational *Beliefs* (RBs) about A (e.g., "I don't like my failing this task, but I can stand it; it doesn't make me a complete failure") and you strongly say them to yourself, thereby replacing your Irrational *Beliefs* (IBs) that you used to create your anxietizing and depressing (C1). In doing this, you change your unhealthy feelings (C1) to much more appropriate feelings (C2) of disappointment, regret, or frustration.

To use the REBT version of Rational-Emotive Imagery (REI), proceed as follows:

1. Imagine one of the worst things that might happen to you, such as failing at an important project, getting rejected by people you really want to like you, or

being in very poor health. Vividly imagine this unfortunate Activating event or Adversity (A) occurring, and bringing a string of problems into your life.

2. Let yourself deeply feel the kind of unhealthy, self-defeating feeling that you often experience when the unfortunate Activating Event or Adversity you are imagining actually occurs. Thus, let yourself strongly feel—at point C, your emotional Consequence—very anxietizing, depressing, raging, self-hating, or self-pitying. Get in touch with this dysfunctional, happiness-destroying feeling (C1) and really, really *feel* it. Don't prescribe the unhealthy feeling by telling yourself something like, "Now that I am imagining myself being treated badly, I should make myself feel very enraged," because you may actually spontaneously feel panicked or depressed instead of enraged. So, as you imagine this bad Activating Event or Adversity happening, let yourself spontaneously feel whatever you feel and not what you think you are "supposed" to feel at point C1.

3. Once you feel unhealthily upset as you imagine this Adversity, hold this feeling for a minute or two—really, really feel it—then work on your dysfunctional feeling until you truly change it to a healthy or self-helping negative feeling (C2). Which one? Well, you can actually prescribe a healthy negative feeling (C2) that will take the place of your unhealthy one (C1). Thus, if you enrage yourself (C1) at the image or visualization of people treating you unfairly (A1), you can prescribe changing your raging to making yourself feel very displeased with and sorry about their acts, instead of enraging at and damning them for these acts (C2). If you feel panicking (C1) about your imagining you are doing poorly at an important interview (A1) you can change your panic to a feeling of real disappointment at how you are doing instead of horror at yourself for doing so badly (C2). You can also prescribe other healthy self-helping negative feelings when you vividly imagine Adversities—such as sorrowing, regretting, feeling concern, frustration, and sadness (C2)—instead of making yourself dysfunctionally feel depressing, terrorizing, worthless, and raging (C1).

4. When you work at changing your feelings from self-defeating to potentially helpful negative emotions, be sure that you do not do so by changing the unfortunate Activating Event (A) that you are vividly imagining. Thus, when you are visualizing people treating you very unfairly and letting yourself feel raging and murderous (C1) (unhealthy because they will probably obsess you and make you unable to deal adequately with this Adversity) you could instead make yourself feel strongly *displeased* with these people's behavior rather than raging at *them*. You might do this by visualizing that they are not really treating you that unfairly or imagining that they have special "good" reasons for treating you that unfair way. This, however, is an incorrect use of REI. In doing Rational-Emotive Imagery the REBT way, make yourself *keep* the exact adverse image that you made yourself raging about, and then work at changing your *feeling* to a healthy one.

5. Don't merely use distraction techniques, such as relaxation, biofeedback, or meditation methods, to change your dysfunctional feelings to healthy ones. Thus, when you visualize people really treating you unfairly (A) and you make yourself feel raging about this (C1), you could relax or meditate and thereby temporarily rid yourself of your rage. But by doing so you would not be changing your underlying *Beliefs* (Bs) or philosophy about people's unfairness, such as, "They absolutely *must* not treat me in this unfair way! I can't *stand* their acting the way that they must not! They are *horrible* people for acting this way and they deserve to be damned and punished forever!" (IBs).

By using cognitive distraction techniques like relaxation or meditation, you may temporarily put aside your people-hating philosophy (IB), but you will not really get rid of it. Almost inevitably, you will return to it the next time people treat you unfairly and will again enrage yourself at them. So if you want to at first relax and then go back to changing this underlying hatred-creating philosophy, fine. But don't just stop with distraction methods: go on to real Rational-Emotive Imagery.

6. To do this, really work at changing your spontaneous disturbed negative feeling (C1) to a prescribed healthy negative feeling (C2)—such as sorrowing, regretting, frustration, irritation, or displeasure. How? By telling yourself—strongly and repetitively—a sensible Rational *Belief* or coping statement. For example: "Yes, they really did treat me shabbily and unfairly, and I wish they hadn't. But there's no reason why they *must* treat me fairly, however *preferable* that would be. Alas, that's not their way—and may never be! Too bad! Tough! But I can hate their *behavior* without completely damning *them*. And if I refuse to upset myself unduly about that unfairness, I might be able to show them, without raging, why I think they are unfair and perhaps get them to change. But if I can't, I can't! I'll just try to stay away from people like that and give them little chance to keep treating me unfairly."

7. If you do Rational-Emotive Imagery correctly, you'll usually find it takes you only a few minutes to change your unhealthy, self-sabotaging, negative feelings (C1) to healthy, self-helping ones (C2). Don't give up—persist! Remember that you created your own destructive feelings of panicking, depressing, raging, self-hating, and self-pitying. Yes, you—with your Irrational *Beliefs*. Therefore, you can always replace them with healthy negative feelings that will help you deal with unfortunate Activating Events or Adversities, and then either change them or live a reasonably good life in spite of them. So persist until you really feel the healthy negative feelings you are prescribing for yourself as a substitute for your self-damaging feelings.

8. Once you have made yourself feel healthfully sorry about the unfortunate Activating Events that have happened to you—or that you have brought upon yourself—you can use Rational-Emotive Imagery as well to work on your secondary feeling of disturbance. Thus, if you feel guilty and self-downing (C1) about your rage at someone (A), you can first vividly imagine

yourself continuing to create raging at someone and let yourself feel spontaneously self-hating for a short while because of your raging. Then change your self-talk and philosophy (B) so that you feel only the healthy negative feelings (C2) that you prescribe for yourself about your self-defeating raging (A); e.g., make yourself feel only sorry and disappointing (C2) and not self-downing (C1) as you very vividly imagine continuing to feel enraged (A).

9. You can fairly easily, at any given moment, use REI to create healthy instead of unhealthy negative feelings about unfortunate Activating Events that you vividly imagine in your life. But to use it effectively, you usually have to repeat it many times, such as thirty days in a row, for each unhealthy negative feeling you are trying to change. So if you really work for a number of days at strongly imagining people treating you unfairly (point A) and if you forcefully work on changing your destructive raging (C1) to the healthy feeling of disappointment and regretting (C2), you will usually find that when you thereafter imagine A, or when it actually occurs in your life, you will much more easily and automatically begin to feel the new healthy emotion rather than the former, unhealthy one.

10. Rational-Emotive Imagery, if repetitively done, thus becomes a useful REBT tool to train yourself more thoroughly to feel healthy instead of unhealthy negative emotions when unfortunate Activating Events enter your life. By consistently using it, you can change both your thinking and feeling habits and make yourself not only less disturbed, but eventually less disturbable.

11. Give yourself the homework assignment to do REI at least once a day for several weeks to overcome a specific dysfunctional feeling. If you find yourself carrying out this assignment regularly, you can reinforce yourself with some pleasure you really enjoy, such as reading, listening to music, jogging, or eating a special food. If you fail to do regular REI, you can penalize (but never damn!) yourself with something you find unpleasant, such as cleaning, ironing, talking to boring people or making a contribution to a cause you loathe. If you force yourself to do REI regularly, however—even when you find it unpleasant—you will soon find the new emotional Consequences you achieve by its use quite rewarding. Even though it is a negative feeling, it is a healthy one that helps you.

SELF-HELP SUGGESTIONS

The leaflets, "Vigorous REBT Disputing" and "Techniques of Rational-Emotive Imagery" that are adapted in this chapter were both written for REBT and other clients of psychotherapy to be used as self-help materials. Whether or not you are in therapy, you can use them to help yourself strongly Dispute any of your Irrational *Beliefs* (IBs) and to change your unhealthy anxietizing and depressing into healthy negative feelings of sorrow, regret, frustration, and annoyance. The material in this chapter is self-explanatory and you can easily read it and try to follow it.

12

REBT and Marriage and Family Therapy

R ational-emotive-behavior family therapy follows the principles and practice of rational-emotive-behavior therapy (REBT). REBT holds that when family members become emotionally disturbed or upset at point C (emotional and behavioral Consequence) following a significant Activating experience or Adversity (Point A), A may significantly contribute to but does not actually "cause" C. Instead, disturbed Consequences (in individuals and in families) are largely (though not exclusively) created by B— the family members' *Belief* System. When undesirable or disruptive Consequences (C) occur, these largely include people's Irrational *Beliefs* (IBs)— absolutistic, *must*urbatory, unrealistic demands, commands, or expectations on (1) themselves, (2) others, and/or (3) environmental conditions. When these Irrational *Beliefs* (IBs) are effectively disputed (at point D) by challenging them logically, empirically, and pragmatically, the disturbed consequences are minimized and are less likely to recur (Ellis 1957, 1962, 1994, 2000b, 2001, 2002; Ellis and Dryden 1997; Ellis and Harper 1961/1997).

This chapter was partly derived from "Rational Emotive Behavior Marriage and Family Therapy," in *Family Counselling and Therapy*, ed. A. H. Horne (Itasca, Ill.: Peacock, 2000), pp. 489–513. Used with permission.

HISTORICAL DEVELOPMENT

I started to develop marriage and family therapy during the late 1940s and to create REBT in the early 1950s, after I practiced classical psychoanalysis and analytically oriented psychotherapy and found them inefficient. I saw that, no matter how much insight my clients gained, especially about their early childhood, they only partly improved and still retained strong tendencies to create new symptoms. This was because theywere not merely indoctrinated with self-defeating ideas but also actively *invented, accepted,* and *kept reindoctrinating themselves with* these dysfunctional *Beliefs.*

I also discovered that my clients often resisted changing their irrational philosophies, because they *naturally* tended to musturbate: to absolutistically demand (1) that they *must* do well and win others' approval; (2) that people *had to* act considerately and fairly; and (3) that environmental conditions *ought not* be frustrating and ungratifying. I concluded that humans, simply because they are humans, are naturally constructivist and problem-solving. But they also have innate and acquired tendencies to construct strong dysfunctional ideas and often take their healthy preferences—such as desires for love, approval, success, and pleasure—and irrationally define them as "needs" or "necessities." They especially tend to do this when they live intimately, in marital or family groups; and therefore their disturbed interactions are partially intrinsic to family living but are also part and parcel of the easily held premises that they frequently bring to intimate relationships (Ellis 1957/1975, 1994, 2000b, 2001, 2002; Ellis and Dryden 1997; Ellis and Harper 1961, 1961/1997; Ellis, Sichel, Yeager, DiMattia, and DiGiuseppe 1989).

By experimenting with different therapeutic procedures, I also discovered that deep-seated human irrationality is rarely changed by most therapy techniques: because individuals and family members are so strongly habituated to their dysfunctional thinking and dysfunctional behavior that they weakly challenge them—and this is unlikely to work. Passive, nondirective methodologies rarely help them change. Warmth and support often enable clients to live more "happily" with unrealistic notions. Suggestion and "positive thinking" sometimes encourage them to cover up and live with basic self-devaluations but seldom help them remove these notions. Abreaction and catharsis enable them to feel better but often reinforce their unrealistic demands. Behavioral desensitization sometimes relieves clients of anxieties but does not consistently change their anxiety-arousing core philosophies.

What works more effectively, I found in the early days of REBT, is an active-directive, cognitive-emotive-behavioral challenging of clients' self-defeating assumptions. Effective psychotherapy, in group, family, and individual settings, includes full tolerance of people *as individuals* combined with showing them how to campaign against their dysfunctional *ideas, traits,* and *performance.*

When still using psychoanalysis, I began to do conjoint marital counseling and family therapy but found these methods were more efficient and briefer as I replaced analysis with REBT. For REBT marriage and family therapy not only gets to the fundamental premises that underlie people's disillusionment with themselves and their family arrangements, but also uses cognitive, emotive, and behavioral methods of teaching them communication, sexual, relating, and other skills that will help them enhance their relationships.

CURRENT STATUS

REBT and CBT have been investigated and found to be effective in family relationships in a number of research studies which have been summarized by Baucom and Epstein (1990), Beck (1988), Hayes, Jacobson, Faletta, and Dougher (1994), Jacobson (1992).

The first major books applying the principles of REBT to marriage and family problems were *How to Live with a "Neurotic"* (Ellis 1957/1975) and *A Guide to Successful Marriage* (Ellis and Harper 1961). Subsequently, a large number of articles and books have been published that demonstrate how REBT can be efficiently applied to marriage and family therapy and to parenting problems.

In the specialized area of sex therapy, REBT has been one of the prime influences in the treatment of sexual problems. Even before William Masters and Virginia Johnson published their notable work on sex therapy, I pioneered the cognitive-behavioral approach to sex problems in the 1950s and 1960s in such books as *The Art and Science of Love* (1960) and *Sex and the Liberated Man* (1963/1976). The REBT and CBT approach to the treatment of sex problems has led to considerable outstanding work in sex therapy, including that of Arnold Lazarus, Joseph LoPiccolo, Lonnie Barbach, Janet L. Wolfe, and Bernie Zilbergeld.

THE ABCs OF REBT APPLIED TO FAMILY LIFE

REBT hypothesizes that when family members feel upset about anything or behave dysfunctionally at point C (emotional or behavioral Consequence), C is usually preceded by A (an activating Experience or Adversity) such as a family member failing at some important task or being rejected by someone whose love he or she seeks. When A occurs, it does not directly "cause" or create C, although it may indirectly contribute to it. Instead, B (the family member's *Belief* system *about* what is occurring at A), more directly "causes" C.

More specifically, REBT hypothesizes that if, say, a husband feels upset about almost anything at point C (Consequence), he has both Rational *Beliefs* (RBs) and Irrational *Beliefs* (IBs) about what the family members are doing (or supposedly doing) to frustrate or bother him at point A (Activating Experience). His Rational *Beliefs* at B take the form of wishes, wants, and preferences—for example, "I would like to be a good husband and have my wife love me. I don't like failing as a father or mate and having her despise me." These Rational *Beliefs* (RBs) almost invariably lead him to feel healthy negative emotional Consequences, such as sorrow, regret, or annoyance, when he fails and gets rejected at A.

If this husband stayed rigorously with Rational *Beliefs*, REBT contends, he wouldn't feel and act in a disturbed manner when Adversities (As) occurred. He would rationally tell himself, at point B, something like: "Too bad! I have not yet succeeded in being a good husband and having my wife love me. Tough! I'll try harder to succeed and thereby to feel better about my family life. But if I can't, I can't. That's unfortunate, but hardly the end of the world! I can still be a happy, though not quite so happy, person."

Sadly enough, however, this husband often adds to his Rational *Beliefs* (RBs) a set of Irrational *Beliefs* (IBs) along these lines: "I *must* be a good husband and have my wife love me! How *awful* it is I don't succeed in these respects! I *can't stand* failing and being rejected by my family! What a *rotten person* I am for doing so badly!" As a result of these Irrational *Beliefs* (IBs) and not merely as a result of his failing and being rejected at point A, this husband tends to feel the Consequences (C) of horror, low frustration tolerance, and self-downing, and he thereby becomes what we often call "emotionally disturbed." Also, at C, he may resort to dysfunctional behavior, such as abusing his wife and children, alcoholism, staying away from home, or a hasty divorce.

The ABC theory of REBT, then, states that the "cause" of disturbed emotional Consequences (C) in family life is not merely the Activating Experiences that happen in the family at A but also includes the spouses' and children's Irrational *Beliefs* (IBs) about these As. Although people can theoretically have a large number of Irrational *Beliefs*, these are subheadings under three major absolutistic *musts*: (1) "I *must* (or *should* or *ought to*) perform well and/or be approved by significant others. It is *awful* (or *horrible* or *terrible*) if I don't. I *can't stand* it! I am a pretty rotten *person* when I fail as I *must* not!" (2) Other people *must* treat me considerately and fairly. It is *horrible* if they don't! When they fail me, they are *bad individuals* and I *can't bear* them and their crummy behavior!" (3) "Conditions *must* be the way I want them to be, and it is *terrible* when they are not! I *can't stand* living in such an awful world! It is an *utterly abominable place!*"

If family members subscribe to one or more of these three basic *musts* and their various derivatives, they will often create emotional disturbances and dysfunctional behaviors. If they clearly see their absolutistic and unrealistic commands on themselves, on others, and on the universe, and if they work hard at replacing them with strong preferences, they will rarely disturb themselves about life's Adversities, although they will still often have strong healthy negative feelings of displeasure, frustration, disappointment, and sorrow.

Insight and REBT. While REBT emphasizes cognition, it holds that psychodynamic insight seldom leads to profound personality change and instead is usually wasteful and sidetracking. It rarely discovers and disputes people's dysfunctional philosophies. Instead, REBT stresses a number of rational-emotive-behavioral insights.

Thus, REBT shows how family problems often lead to interrelated ABCs. When a husband criticizes his wife at point A, she may *Believe*, at point B, "He *must* not do this to me and is a rotten person if he does what he absolutely *should* not do!" and may thereby create the Consequence (C) of rage. But he then may take her rage (C), make it into his own Activating Event (A), then tell himself at B, "I *must* not make her angry! What a worm I am for doing what I *must* not do!" He may thereby make himself guilty and depressed at C (Consequence).

Then the wife may take her husband's Consequence (C1), make it into her own Activating Event (A2), tell herself, "He *must* not be depressed! I can't stand it!" at point B and thereby bring about her own Consequence (C2) of self-pity and low frustration tolerance. So in all close relationships, one person's Cs may easily be used or interpreted to produce another's As. That is why in REBT family therapy we try to help reduce the emotional and behavioral distress (Cs) of all the interrelated individuals.

Humanistic Outlook. REBT takes the humanistic and existentialist position that family members largely create their own world by the phenomenological *views* they take of what happens to them. It also accepts the philosophy that people had better define their own freedom and cultivate a good measure of individuality but at the same time, especially if they are to live successfully in family ways, adopt an attitude of caring, sharing, and social interest. In accordance with its humanistic outlook, REBT especially emphasizes what Carl Rogers calls unconditional positive regard and what I term unconditional self-acceptance (USA) and unconditional other-acceptance (UOA) (Ellis and Harper 1961/1997; Ellis and Tafrate 1997). As a consequence, REBT takes the unusual stand that we'd better not rate ourselves, our essence, or our being, but only our deeds, acts, and performances. We can choose to do this limited kind of rating not in order to *prove* ourselves—that is, to strengthen our ego and self-esteem—but in order to be ourselves and *enjoy* ourselves.

Behavioral Outlook. REBT holds that family members are easily disturbable and that, even when they have persuaded themselves to give up Irrational *Beliefs*, they easily fall back into self-defeating pathways. It sees people as being biologically and socially prone to dysfunctional behaviors and to resisting giving up these activities. It therefore employs a great deal of behavior modification or retraining experiences. In fact, REBT practitioners often use more operant conditioning and in vivo desensitization procedures than do many classical behavior therapists. Along with the usual behavior therapy methods, however, REBT almost always employs many cognitive and emotive approaches. Therefore, it is intrinsically a form of what Lazarus (1997) calls "multimodal behavior therapy."

Disturbance About Disturbance. REBT has always emphasized the self-talking or self-indoctrinating aspect of human disturbance and family malfunctioning. In addition, it particularly stresses that individuals and family members frequently have secondary as well as primary symptoms of disturbance. Thus, a wife may, at point A, experience criticism from her husband, tell herself, at point B, "I must not be criticized so severely! I am sure that there is something very wrong with what I am doing!" At C (emotional Consequence) she then feels depressing. But, being human and having self-downing tendencies, she then makes C into another A and notes to herself, at her secondary B: "I see that I am depressed. I must not be depressed! It's foolish for me to depress myself! I'm a stupid, worthless individual for being depressed!" She then depresses her self about her depression, and her secondary symptom may be more intense and prolonged than her primary one.

RATIONAL EMOTIVE BEHAVIOR FAMILY THERAPY AND OTHER SYSTEMS OF FAMILY THERAPY

There are many systems of family therapy today, but the main (or at least most popular ones) seem to be the psychoanalytic, systems, and behavioral schools. Here, briefly, is how REBT family therapy overlaps with and differs from these systems.

REBT and Psychoanalytic Family Therapy. REBT differs considerably from classical Freudian analysis and also from object relations theories and practices, because both of these systems overstress deeply hidden and repressed unconscious states; they exaggerate the crucial importance of early childhood experiences in causing adult disturbances; they deify the automatic health-producing qualities of insight into one's past; and they encourage intense transference and countertransference relationships between clients and therapists. REBT is highly skeptical of these theories and practices.

REBT reveals family members' unconscious thinking—especially when they are unaware of their hidden musts and demands—but quickly shows that most of it is barely below the surface of awareness and is only occasionally deeply repressed. It helps clients see that their early experiences were traumatic because they partly told themselves awfulizing philosophies about them. It gives family members insight into their self-damaging *Beliefs* about their histories rather than an obsessive review of its happenings. It provides clients with unconditional acceptance by their therapists, but does not make their relationship with him or her an intensive love-hate part of their lives. In many ways REBT family therapy is much more present-centered, more philosophically-oriented, and more realistic and problem-solving than is psychoanalytic therapy.

REBT AND SYSTEMS FAMILY THERAPY

REBT largely goes along with a great deal of the "systems theory" perspective, including these propositions: (1) In studying families and family therapy, we had better pay attention not only to interpretation of individual thoughts, feelings, and behaviors, but also to wholeness, organization, and relationship among family members. (2) We had better also seriously consider general (as well as reductionist) principles that might be used to explain biological processes that lead to increasing complexity of organization (for the organism). (3) We had better concentrate on patterned rather than merely on linear relationships and to a consideration of events in the context in which they are occurring rather than on isolating of them from their environmental context. (4) The study of communication among family members often shows how they become disturbed and what they can do to ameliorate their disturbances.

   While agreeing with these basic views of systems theory-oriented family therapy, REBT would offer a few caveats as follows: (1) Focusing on wholeness, organization, and relationship among family members is important, but can be overdone. Families become disturbed not merely because of *their* organization and disorganization but because of the serious personal problems of individual family members. Unless, therefore, these are considered and dealt with, too, any changes that are likely to occur through changing the family system are likely to be superficial and unlasting. (2) Family systems therapy tends to require an active-directive therapist who makes clearcut interventions and who engages in a great deal of problem solving. REBT is highly similar in these respects. But family systems therapists often ignore the phenomenological and self-disturbing aspects of family members' problems and mainly deal with the system-creating aspects. In REBT terms, they often focus on solving A-type (Activating Events-type) family problems and *not* on the more important B-type (*Belief* System) problems. REBT *first* tends to show family members how they philosophically disturb themselves *about* what is happening to them at point A and how, at B, *they* basically create their family and personal problems at C. Its approach is double-barreled rather than single-barreled in this respect. (3) Family system therapists often miss the main reasons beyond most people's emotional problems: namely, their absolutistic *musts* and *shoulds* and their own and other family members' behaviors (Huber and Baruth 1989).

Systems therapy covers many widely differing "systems," many of which significantly differ from each other and had better be given specific names. Some of them, like Murray Bowen's and Jay Haley's, are quite cognitive-behavioral and significantly overlap with, and may easily be integrated with REBT.

REBT subscribes to virtually all the main principles of behavioral oriented family therapy, since it is a form of behavior therapy itself and invariably uses (as noted above) many behavioral theories and methods. However, it uses behavioral techniques mainly to help family members change their basic philosophic assumptions and to make an "elegant" change in their thinking, feeling, and acting, rather than the symptomatic change that some of the "pure" behavior therapists, such as Joseph Wolpe, aim for. As Neil Jacobson (1992) finally realized, "pure" behavior therapy may help family members to gain relationship skills but fails to help them unconditionally accept each other with their shortcomings. REBT teaches them better relating skills and unconditional self-acceptance and other-acceptance.

GOALS OF THE THERAPEUTIC PROCESS

The main goals of rational emotive behavior family therapy include: (1) To help all the family members, if feasible, to see that they largely disturb themselves by taking the actions of the other members *too* seriously; and that they have the choice, no matter how these others behave, of *not* seriously upsetting themselves *about* other persons' misbehaving. (2) To help the members continue to keep their desires, wishes, and preferences, but to become keenly aware of and to revise their absolutistic *musts*, demands, and commands that others in the family act the way they would *prefer* them to act. (3) To encourage parents and children to feel strongly sad, regretful, frustrated, annoyed, and determined to change things when they are not getting what they want in and out of the family setting, but to clearly differentiate these healthy negative feelings from their unhealthy feelings of anxietizing, depressing, raging, and low frustration tolerance and to minimize the latter while still feeling the former emotions. (4) To learn a number of cognitive, emotive, and behavioral techniques that will reduce their self- and family-defeating behaviors and encourage them to think, feel, and behave more sensibly and self-enhancingly. (5) As they change their basic disturbance-prone attitudes, to work at solving practical problems that may be preventing them and other family members from being as happy and effective as they would like to be. In REBT terms, as they work at changing Irrational *Beliefs* (IBs), clients also work at changing their As (Adversities) that contribute to these Bs and that also contribute to their Cs (dysfunctional Consequences).

THERAPIST'S ROLE AND FUNCTION

REBT is one of the most active-directive therapies, and this also applies to REBT family therapy. The therapist is a highly trained individual, who understands how people needlessly upset themselves and that they can often refuse to do so. REBT therapists, therefore, are authoritative without being authoritarian; bring up discussions of basic values without foisting their own personal values onto clients; and push, coach, persuade, and encourage—but never command!—clients to think and act against their own self-sabotaging tendencies.

Some of the specific skills that REBT practitioners display in family therapy include: (1) They empathize with clients' thinking and feeling and *also* with their basic disturbance-creating philosophies. (2) They monitor clients' reactions to other family members and to the therapist and show them how to become highly involved but not overinvolved and dependent on others (including the therapist). (3) They show clients how they are relating well and poorly and teach them communication skills. (4) They at times are questioning, forceful, and action-encouraging, just as a successful teacher of children or adults would be. (5) They teach sex, love, relating, and other skills as these seem appropriate for different clients. They actively Dispute clients' Irrational *Beliefs* (IBs) and show them how they can do so on their own (Ellis and Crawford 2000).

PRIMARY TECHNIQUES USED IN **REBT** THERAPY

The main techniques used in REBT family therapy include the following:

Cognitive Techniques. Clients are shown many REBT cognitive techniques such as are described in chapters 1, 2, 5, 8, and other chapters of this book. They are given several different forms of cognitive homework to do, such as to look for their and their family members' absolutistic *shoulds* and *musts*; and to steadily fill out their *REBT Self-Help Report Forms* and to check these with their therapist. They are taught several practical problem methods.

Emotive and Behavioral Techniques. REBT family therapy employs many emotive, evocative, and dramatic techniques and many behavioral techniques that are also designed to show people how they feel and think and to help them to change their unhealthy to healthy feelings. These are described in chapters 1, 5, 6, 7, 11, and other chapters of this book.

CASE EXAMPLE

The following is a typescript of part of the initial family treatment session with a mother, father, and their fifteen-year-old daughter, Debbie. The mother is forty-five years of age, and is a housewife who has done a little professional dancing during the last few years. The father is also forty-five and runs his own business in New York's garment center. They have a twenty-one-year-old and a seventeen-year-old son, both of whom are doing well in school and without serious difficulties, and they are both very upset about their daughter because she has always shown herself to be quite bright—has an IQ of 140 on regular intelligence tests—but she doesn't do her schoolwork, refuses to cooperate with family chores, doesn't look for a job when she promises to do so, fights with her brothers, steals from her family and from the neighbors, and is otherwise disruptive. She acknowledges some of these failings but makes innumerable excuses for them.

At the beginning of the first family therapy session, Debbie admits that she is a "kleptomaniac" and that she uncontrollably steals money. But she denies using it for alcohol and marijuana, which she also denies using regularly. She and her parents agree that she had two good years, in the seventh and eighth grades, when she was in a strict Catholic school. But she has now lost her goal in life—which was to be a lawyer and a politician—and feels purposeless and hopeless and has no incentive to work at school or anything else. Early in the first session, she notes that she had a purpose during the two years she did well: "I knew I wanted to be a lawyer."

Therapist: Yes?

Debbie: And I worked on that.

Therapist: But you've now given it up?

Debbie: Yeah.

Therapist: Why did you give that up?

Debbie: Because I really wanted to become a politician.

Therapist: And you don't want to become a politician anymore?

Debbie: No. They have bad practices and stuff.

Therapist: So that's out of the window?

Debbie: Yes, I have no goal.

Therapist: You're right. If you had a goal in life that would probably help you be happier and avoid the trouble you're getting in. But if you no longer want to be a politician, what stops you from picking some other profession and working toward that?

Debbie: Well, I usually only pick one goal and don't think of other things.

Therapist: Well, you could still choose to be a lawyer, even if not a politician. And there are lots of other things that you could pick that you are capable of doing. Do you think you're capable of doing what you really want to do?

Debbie: For the most part, yes.

Therapist: You had really better give some more thought to that. When bright people like you screw up and give up on goals they frequently feel that they're incapable of succeeding at them. So perhaps you are in that category, too.

Debbie: Maybe.

(The therapist's main hypotheses, which he uses in many cases like Debbie's, are: (1) She has low frustration tolerance and refuses to do things, such as disciplining herself, which are hard and uncomfortable; and (2) she has severe feelings of inadequacy that block her from trying hard to achieve anything and encourage her to cop out at tasks at which she thinks that she might not do well enough. He tries to help her bring out information to back these hypotheses and only partly succeeds in doing so. But the manner in which she replies to him and to her parents, who are present during the entire session, lead him to believe that his hypotheses are plausible.)

Therapist: Do you want to keep getting into the kind of trouble that you're in with your parents, with the school, and with your brothers?

Debbie: No.

Therapist: Why do you think you steal?

Debbie: 'Cause I can't control myself.

Therapist: That's a nutty conclusion! You have *difficulty* controlling yourself. But that doesn't mean that you *can't*. Suppose that every time you stole, the authorities cut off one of your toes. How long do you think you'd continue to steal?

Debbie: (mumbles something like "Many times.")

Therapist: Many times? Well. That's a strong belief you have—but it's not true. You most probably wouldn't. You would then have a powerful *impulse* to steal; but you don't have to give in to your impulses. For two years you weren't doing self-defeating things and did well at school and at home, you didn't steal. Doesn't that show that you're *able* to control your impulses?

Debbie: Yes, to some degree.

Therapist: Yes, for two whole years you were apparently okay. You were obviously able to control yourself.

Debbie: Because I had a purpose. And I was working on that purpose.

Therapist: Yeah. And that was fine. If you have a purpose, you'll use your energies in that direction, and then you will rarely use them in self-defeating ways.

(Although it is quite early in the first session, the therapist tries to show Debbie and her parents that, in REBT terms, Activating Events or Adversities (A) do not directly cause emotional Consequences (C). Instead, they are importantly accompanied by Beliefs (B). So he tries to help Debbie to see that just before she gives in to her urge to steal she is telling herself something; and that this set of Beliefs (B) is a main cause or contributing factor to her dysfunctional Consequences (C).)

Therapist: Why do you think you take money?

Debbie:I want it.

Therapist: You mean, "I want the money I take?"

Mother: I think the main thing she wants is to buy liquor or dope with the money.

Therapist: That may be. But let's go along with Debbie's views. You're saying that you want the money. Right?

Debbie: Yes.

Therapist: But if you only stuck to that belief—"I want the money"—you probably wouldn't steal. Do you know why?

Debbie: Because I'd see that I often get caught and wouldn't want to get caught stealing it.

Therapist: Right! Whenever we have a want or a wish, we tend to see the consequences of having it, and we often reject it. So you're probably saying something much stronger than "I want the money" when you steal. Do you know what that stronger belief probably is?

Debbie: No. Uh, maybe: "I need it."

Therapist: Correct! "I need the money that I want! I MUST have it because I want it!" And that NEED and that MUST will often drive you to steal, even when you know you may get caught and suffer poor consequences. But is your NEED or MUST true? MUST you have the money? Or MUST you have what you get with the money—alcohol, pot, or anything else?

Debbie: No.

Therapist: That's right: No! But if you keep insisting that you MUST have the money (or anything else), you're probably going to feel not only uncomfortable but horrible, off the wall, when you don't have what you think you MUST. Then, when you feel exceptionally uncomfortable, you may well go on to another MUST: "I MUST not feel uncomfortable. I CAN'T STAND this discomfort of not having what I MUST have!" Is that what you're saying, too?

Debbie: Yes. I CAN'T stand it. I CAN'T!

Therapist: Stop a minute, now! CAN'T you really stand it? CAN you actually bear the discomfort of being frustrated and not getting exactly what you want at this very moment that you want it?

Debbie: I don't like it.

Therapist: Right. But you're not merely sticking to, "I don't like it." That would be fine, if you did. I hear you saying, "BECAUSE I don't like it, I CAN'T STAND it! It's AWFUL if I don't have it!"

Debbie: But I really want it!

Therapist: Yes, of course. But your want is not what drives you to stealing. Your basic belief, "I MUST HAVE what I want!" is what does so. And we call that attitude and the feeling that goes with it low frustration tolerance. You're apparently telling yourself, "I WANT, and MUST HAVE, what I want right now! I CAN'T BEAR frustration and deprivation." Isn't that what's really going on in your head?

Debbie: Yes, I CAN'T stand it!

Therapist: Well, as long as you have that basic philosophy—"I absolutely NEED what I want and I CAN'T STAND not having it!" you'll be driven, driven by those beliefs, to steal, fight with your family, break things, goof at school, and do other things that tend to get and keep you in trouble. But you could have, instead, the philosophy: "I want what I want and am determined to try to get it. But if I don't get it right now, tough! So I don't! I do not NEED everything I immediately want!" But you are saying to yourself, as far as I can see, "I DO need it!"

Debbie: Well, perhaps I'm doing it because I'm escaping.

Therapist: Escaping from what? What are you escaping from? Feelings of inadequacy, you mean? The feeling that you haven't the ability to get some of the things that you want and think you need?

Debbie: That could be one.

Therapist: Let's talk about those inadequacy feelings for a moment. What are they? Are you willing to talk about them in front of your parents?

Debbie: It doesn't matter.

Therapist: Well, what do you feel inferior about?

Debbie: I'm confused. I haven't figured out what's the purpose of it all. I don't see how to react to certain problems.

Therapist: Such as?

Debbie: Well, some domestic problems. And I just don't get along with people. I like them but I don't understand them.

Therapist: And you think that you SHOULD, you MUST understand them?

Debbie: Yes. And that's why I often try to get high.

Therapist: And do you blame yourself, for getting high?

Debbie: Yes, sometimes.

Therapist: Well, let's assume that getting high won't solve things and won't make you understand people better, and it's therefore something of a mistake. And let's suppose you're not yet very good at understanding and getting along with people. Why do you put yourself down for these failings?

Debbie: Because I know that it's not right.

Therapist: Yes, well let's assume that. Suppose what you're doing is wrong. How does that make you a worm, that wrong behavior?

Debbie: (silence)

Therapist: Suppose your mother and father do something wrong. Are they worms for doing that wrong thing?

Debbie: No.

Therapist: Then why are you?

Debbie: Because then I'm a wrong person.

Therapist: But you're NOT a wrong person! That's your nutty thinking! That's what we call an overgeneralization. If we can help you to give up that kind of irrational thinking, and get you to completely accept YOURSELF, even when you are doing the wrong THING, then you can usually go back and correct your error. But if you put YOURSELF down and define yourself as a no-goodnik for acting wrongly, there's no good solution to the problem! For how can a worm be dewormified? (Debbie and her parents all laugh fairly heartily at this statement.) Your feelings of inadequacy don't come from doing the wrong thing. They come from CONDEMNING YOURSELF for doing it—putting yourself into hell. That makes things much worse.

Debbie: Yes, it does.

Therapist: But do you really see all of what's going on here? You first do badly—or think that you will do badly at something. Then you put yourself down, MAKE YOURSELF feel inadequate as a person. Then you tend to do something like drink or smoke pot, to make yourself relax temporarily and feel a little better. But then you get into more trouble, because of the alcohol or pot or the stealing that you did to get the money for it, and then you blame yourself more and go around and around in a vicious self-damning circle.

Debbie: I guess I do. I keep thinking that I'm really no good. And then things get worse.

Therapist: Right!

Debbie: But how can I stop that?

Therapist: The best solution is to see very clearly what I said before: that some of your acts are wrong and self-defeating but that YOU are not a worm for doing them. If we could get you to fully accept YOURSELF, your BEING, your TOTALITY, even when you are screwing up and acting stupidly or badly, then we could get you to go back and work on improving your screwups. And you could change most of them, which you are quite capable of doing—if you weren't wasting your time and energy and making things worse by your self-damning. That isn't going to work.

Debbie: It doesn't. I just feel worse. And then I think that I have to keep repeating this, uh, inadequate behavior.

Therapist: Right! The more you condemn YOURSELF for your poor BEHAVIOR the more you lose confidence in your ability to correct that behavior.

Debbie: (smiling) A worm can't be dewormified!

Therapist: Exactly! If you are, to your core, a thorough turd, how can you change your turdiness? No way!

Debbie: But how do I stop blaming myself?

Therapist: By changing your fundamental MUSTS. For, at bottom, you seem to be saying: "I MUST, I HAVE TO do well." Not, "I'd LIKE or PREFER to do well." And you're also saying to yourself, and very strongly, "I MUST NOT suffer inconveniences. It's AWFUL if I do." You could tell yourself, instead, "I'd LIKE to avoid inconveniences. But if I don't, I don't! I can experience them—and still be a happy human!"

Debbie: I see what you mean. But how am I going to *keep* seeing that and believing it?

Therapist: By darned hard work! By continuing *to think about* what you say to yourself and do. And by changing your perfectionistic demands into preferences and desires.

(The therapist, without having the full details of the history of Debbie and her parents, uses some data that he quickly discovers from them and that he hypothesizes from REBT theory that she demands that she perform well and insists that the universe treat her kindly. He tests these hypotheses with Debbie, gets some evidence to support them, and then quickly and forthrightly challenges her unrealistic Irrational Beliefs. He also shows her that she can do this herself, and can change them and create better emotional and behavioral results. As he talks to Debbie, he from time to time shows her parents that they, too, have MUSTS about Debbie, and that they are unrealistically demanding that she act well and are condemning her and upsetting themselves when she doesn't. So he encourages their listening to his disputing of Debbie's Irrational Beliefs (IBs). But he also indicates that they often think the same way as she does, that they also have IBs—and that they do not have to perpetuate them. Toward the end of the session the therapist speaks to Debbie and then to her parents.)

Therapist: If I can help you, Debbie, to keep your desires and give up your MUSTS, you'll begin to feel and act better. By so doing, you'll most probably get more of what you want and less of what you don't want. But you won't get *everything* you want! No one does. (To Debbie's parents): "She has many healthy preferences, but then she tells herself, "I MUST, I MUST fulfill them!" And: "I MUST get what I want IMMEDIATELY!" Now, if I can get all of you, including her, to look for the SHOULD, look for the MUST, as you are all bright enough to do, and if I can persuade you to tackle these *demands* and change them to healthy *wants*, you will all upset yourselves much less and tend to solve your problems of getting along together and living happily in this difficult world. (To Debbie, again): If I can help you do *that*, then you'll get along with your parents and siblings and live more successfully. What you now often do is to overwhelm your desires with impractical MUSTS. "I MUST do this and MUST do that! But maybe I won't. And that would be TERRIBLE!" Then you feel depressed and anxious and start copping out. Then you blame yourself for acting badly and feel more anxious and depressed. A very vicious circle! Have you read any of my writings on this?

The therapist closes the session by assigning all three of them, Debbie and her parents, to read a group of pamphlets on REBT that the Albert Ellis Institute gives to clients at its clinic in New York and also to read A Guide to Rational Living *by Ellis and Harper (1961/1997), which many clients find helpful. Debbie and her parents are to make another appointment, next week; and in between, to make a note of all the times they feel upset during the week, especially about each other, and what is happening in the family. They are to look for the absolutistic SHOULDS and MUSTS that accompany these feelings, to try to Dispute them, and to bring them up during the next session, to see how they are doing at discovering and challenging them.*

Following the first session, Debbie and her parents were seen once a week for a total of sixteen weeks. Debbie was largely seen for individual sessions by herself, but usually one or both parents were also seen with her for a half hour, while she was seen by herself for an additional half hour. On a few occasions her parents were also seen by themselves to deal with their anger and other feelings of upsetness about her "rotten" behavior and about their own problems with each other and with outsiders—especially her father's problems with his business associates and her mother's problems with her women friends. A number of REBT family therapy techniques were used with Debbie and her parents during these sessions.

It would have been preferable as a part of their therapy to see her two brothers, too, for some of the sessions. But the parents insisted that the brothers had no problems and might be harmed by participating in therapy. The brothers themselves also resisted coming, as they thought that Debbie had a serious emotional problem, but that they did not. Under more usual conditions, the brothers would have been seen along with the other members of the family.

Here are some of the REBT methods that I used as the family's therapist:

Cognitive Methods. Whenever Debbie or her parents showed any feelings of anxiety, depression, anger, and self-pity (which they frequently did) or when Debbie continued her antisocial behavior, they were shown the ABCs of REBT: That their Cs (emotional and behavioral Consequences) did not merely stem from their As (Adversities) but also from their own IBs (Irrational *Beliefs*) *about* these As. They were shown their absolutistic *shoulds* and *musts* and how to Dispute them. They were given the cognitive homework of doing the REBT Self-Help Form form published by the Institute (see pages 135–36), and these were gone over with them and discussed with the therapist. They were given bibliotherapeutic materials on REBT to read and discuss, particularly *A Guide to Rational Living, How to Live with a "Neurotic", How to Stubbornly Refuse to Make Yourself Miserable About Anything—Yes, Anything!* and *How To Stop People from Pushing Your Buttons.* They were also encouraged to listen to some of the cassette recordings distributed by the Institute, such as *Conquering Low Frustration Tolerance* and *Unconditionally Accepting Yourself and Others.* They also participated in one of the four-hour workshops on parent-child relationships and on overcoming depression that the Institute regularly holds.

Cognitively, too, the members of this family, especially Debbie, were given practical suggestions on how to solve certain practical problems that arose (such as how Debbie could get and keep a job in spite of her poor reputation in the community). They were shown how to write down and focus on the real disadvantages of their avoidant behaviors. They were taught some of the principles of general semantics dealing with overgeneralization and allness. They were shown how to use cognitive distraction methods, such as Edmund Jacobsen's progressive relaxation methodds, when they wanted to temporarily calm themselves down. I, as their therapist, sometimes used humor and paradoxical intention with them—for example, encouraged Debbie to deliberately fail at certain tasks, to prove to herself that the world did not come to an end when she did, and helped her to see the humorous side of her taking things too seriously and of blaming herself for her poor behavior. They were continually taught how to accept themselves fully, and to stop condemning themselves for anything, even when they made obviously stupid mistakes.

Emotive Methods. Emotively, even though I pulled no punches in showing Debbie how she was being irresponsible to herself and others, she could always see that I fully accepted her as a human in spite of her failings, and that I had confidence that she definitely could—if she would—change. I also helped her, as a homework assignment, to do rational emotive imagery: to imagine that she really did very badly, at work or socially, that others despised her for her poor behavior, to first allow herself to feel very depressed about this image, but then to make herself feel only sorry and disappointed rather than self-downing. I did role-playing with her and her parents, let her confess to them some of the things she hadn't yet told them and then persist at the confessions and work through the shame she felt about their shocked responses. I encouraged her to do out-of-session REBT shame-attacking exercises, such as to wear very "loud" clothing, and to work at not making herself feel embarrassed or humiliated when she did this. I helped her write out some rational self-statements, such as "I do not need immediate gratification, no matter how much I really want it!" and to repeat these to herself very vigorously ten or twenty times a day until she strongly agreed with them. I used George Kelly's fixed role playing method with both Debbie and her parents, and had them write scripts about the kind of people they would like to be and then enact these scripts for a week, until they became used to acting in that unfamiliar way.

Behavioral Methods. With Debbie in particular, I used several behavioral methods and taught her parents how to use them with her. Whenever she spent at least two hours a week looking for a part-time job, she was permitted to socialize with her friends or do other things she enjoyed. And whenever she lied or stole, she was confined to her room for several hours at a time. When her parents criticized her in an angry, damning manner, they were also to refrain from socializing with their friends for that day. These reinforcements and penalties worked fairly well—as long as they were enforced. But her parents had to keep after Debbie and she, to some extent, had to keep after them to actually carry out their reinforcements and penalties.

Debbie was encouraged to take several different kinds of activity homework assignments, including looking for a job, doing various family chores, and behaving in a cooperative instead of disruptive manner with her parents and her siblings. Some of these she quickly carried out, and benefited from seeing that she was able to do them, and was not totally out of control, as she often said she was. Other assignments, such as the chores, she did sporadically but still seemed to derive some benefit from doing them.

At the end of sixteen weeks of rational emotive behavior family therapy, Debbie was doing her school work regularly, had ceased stealing, and was getting along much better with her family members. Even more than this, she was distinctly accepting herself with her imperfect performances. Her mother and father were considerably less angry at her, even when she fell back into her old disruptive behavior; and they used some of the rational ideas and procedures we were discussing and began to feel much less angry at each other and to behave more cooperatively. Their sex life also improved considerably, mainly because of their better relationships with themselves and with Debbie. The father returned for several therapy sessions a year and a half later, because he was avoiding some of his office work and was putting himself down for this; and at that time it was ascertained that Debbie was still acting remarkably better and that much more family harmony existed.

SELF-HELP SUGGESTIONS

- If you have marriage or relationship problems, you probably have dysfunctional thinking, feeling, and behaving that significantly interrelate with your partner's dysfunctionings. So both of you can well go for marriage and family therapy to discuss these interconnections and to try to correct them. You may have to change the family system in order to function better.
- At the same time you, as an individual in a relationship, largely create your own emotional-behavioral problems, according with the ABC theory of REBT that is outlined in this book. You partly *construct* your own *Beliefs about* your partner(s), and only you can change some of them. Effective marriage and family therapy, therefore, had better show you how you *choose* to react to your partner(s) and how you can also change some important aspects of the marital *system*.
- Although the romantic view of relationships indicates that marriage and family involvement adds greatly to your pleasures and joys, it often fails to note that marriage also appreciably adds to your problems and limitations. In viewing it, therefore, you had better realistically see that it often frustrates you in many ways and taxes your frustration tolerance. REBT prepares you for the three main difficulties you are likely to encounter in marriage and—especially!—family relationships: (1) It fosters both your and your partner's acquiring unconditional self-acceptance (USA), even

when you are failing at family responsibilities, and gaining sufficient love from family members. (2) It helps you achieve unconditional other-acceptance (UOA) and thereby fully accept family members even when they are behaving unideally and badly. (3) It fosters your and family members' gaining high frustration tolerance (HFT), so that you and they can bear with and even enjoy some of the hassles of intimate relationships.

- As usual, REBT provides you with many cognitive, emotive, and behavioral methods of therapy that are described in several chapters of this book and that you and your marital and family partners can use when you encounter personal and/or relationship problems. Experiment with several of them.

13

REBT and Its Application to Group Therapy

I began to do group therapy in 1949 with adolescents at the New Jersey State Diagnostic Center when I was still practicing psychoanalysis, and got reasonably good results helping my delinquent clients to open up and reveal themselves. I helped them to accept responsibility for their delinquencies, to work with other group members, to understand themselves, and to make some useful changes. But I soon discovered that psychoanalytic group therapy, like psychoanalytic individual psychotherapy, was woefully inefficient for several reasons:

1. It focused on people's pasts, especially their early life, mistakenly assuming that *that* made them disturbed.
2. It gave them false explanations for their neurosis (and other personality problems), especially the idea that unfortunate or traumatic Activating Events (As) gave them neurotic Consequences (Cs), no matter what they Believed (B) about these As.
3. It obsessively explored their "transference" relationships with their therapists and other group members and assumed that these were caused by prior deep relationships in their childhood.

This chapter is partly adapted from "REBT and Its Application to Group Therapy," in *Special Applications of REBT: A Therapist's Casebook*, ed. J. Yankura and W. Dryden (New York: Springer, 1997), pp. 131–61. Used with permission.

4. It deified the expression of group members' feelings and wrongly held that if they got in full touch with these feelings and honestly expressed them they would win the approval of others and minimize their serious panicking, depressing, and raging (Ellis 1962, 1988; Ellis and Harper 1961, 1997).

For the first several years that I was in full-time practice in New York City, and even when I started doing REBT with my individual clients in 1955, I still avoided doing group therapy because of its usual insufficiencies. But I saw that one analyst had three of my individual clients in his groups, and that almost every time they attended his group sessions they became more disturbed, while after most of their individual sessions with me they became less disturbed. So in 1959 I decided to start my first REBT group. Soon I had four of these groups going—and going strong—every week, and I discovered that for most clients most of the time, my kind of group therapy was more effective, often in a brief period, than was my individual therapy—and much more effective than any form of psychoanalysis. Why? For several reasons:

1. In individual therapy, I mainly Dispute and show my clients how to Dispute their self-defeating Irrational *Beliefs* (IBs). But in group therapy, several other group members do active Disputing and thereby present better and stronger Disputation.
2. In individual therapy, clients rarely get practice in talking me out of my IBs (because we are mainly focusing on them and their IBs). But in group they have many opportunities to discover others' IBs, to actively Dispute them, and thereby receive excellent practice in Disputing their own similar irrationalities.
3. In group therapy, all the group members can, and often do, suggest bigger and better homework assignments for each of the other members.
4. When accepting homework, group members are more likely to carry it out than individual therapy clients, because they have to report back to the whole group as to whether or not they actually did it.
5. When people feel very upset during group sessions, which they often do, we can immediately zero in on what they are telling themselves to help them, right in the here and now, to undo their upsetness and to work to give it up.
6. Homework assignments and other emotive-evocative exercises, which are often used in Rational Emotive Behavior Therapy, can be carried out during group sessions, and not only outside of therapy. Thus my groups are often given—or give themselves—shame-attacking, secret-revealing, hot-seat, risk-taking, and other encounter-type exercises in the course of regular group sessions and are then able to express their

feelings about these exercises and to receive feedback both from the therapist and from other group members.

7. The many cognitive, emotive, and behavioral methods that are commonly used in individual REBT can also be employed in group REBT—and, again, feedback from and interactions with other group members often adds to their effectiveness.

8. Most people come to REBT (and other forms of therapy) with some significant interpersonal and relationship problems. Because the group is a *social* situation, many such problems may be more easily assessed and worked on than they often can be in individual treatment.

KINDS OF REBT GROUPS

Most of my groups are small, weekly meetings, lasting two and a quarter hours. They include a maximum of eight people, because REBT small group sessions are less rambling and more structured than other kinds of groups, and can include more than the six or seven members that other therapies usually set as their top limits. My own groups include males and females, usually ranging from eighteen to seventy years of age, with many different kinds of problems.

However, at the psychological clinic of the Albert Ellis Institute in New York, we also have some same-sex groups, for men and women who prefer to open up only in such a group. We also have time-limited groups—usually for only six or eight sessions—where all the members have a main common problem such as procrastinating, overeating, relationship troubles, and anxietizing. In addition, we regularly arrange one- and two-day rational encounter marathons and nine-hour large group intensives (with fifty or more people at a time).

We also have my famous Friday night workshop, "Problems of Daily Living," with as many as 150 people in the audience watching while I (or, if I am out of town, one of my main associates, such as Dr. Nando Pelusi or Dr. Mitchell Robin) interview individual volunteer clients in public and then throw the discussion of the interview open to all the members of the audience who choose to participate (Ellis et al. 1989).

Again, we have regular 3 1/2-hour workshops, with from ten to ninety participants, in special topics such as managing difficult people, creative personal encounters, panic disorders, post-traumatic stress disorders, and sexual problems.

SELECTING PARTICIPANTS FOR ONGOING GROUPS

No one is usually allowed into any of my ongoing small groups at the Albert Ellis Institute in New York City unless he or she has had at least one individual therapy session. Often, potential members have a number of individual sessions at the Institute before joining group; and only if their individual therapist thinks that they are unsuitable for the group process are they refused entry into a group.

If people desire to become group members without having previous individual sessions, they are required to have at least one individual interview for screening purposes. They are almost always allowed to enter a group, even if they are seriously neurotic, have a personality disorder, or have some psychotic behaviors, as long as they are not considered to be disruptive or too combative. Thus, those who are compulsive talkers, who have frequent angry outbursts at other group members, who are too narcissistic, who come to group under the influence of alcohol or other substances, who cannot follow normal group procedures, or who otherwise would take up too much time in group, or would prove unhelpful to other members are not admitted. If they somehow do get into one of my groups, they are dealt with very firmly and trained to be more "normal" group participants. Or else they are told to enter individual therapy instead and to return to group only when their individual therapist advises that they are ready to do so.

A few members are also dropped from group when they violate its basic rules, such as that they remain confidential outside of group about everything that goes on during the group sessions. In conducting my regular groups steadily since 1959, and having many hundreds of different participants, I (in collaboration with other members of the group) have only insisted that fewer than ten people leave group. However, several dozen more have participated so poorly in group that they have spontaneously seen that they are not suitable members and have quit on their own. Frequently, instead, they have gone into individual therapy with me or other therapists at the Institute.

PROCEDURE OF SMALL GROUP REGULAR SESSIONS

REBT group sessions can be arranged with different procedures and still be effective. I usually start each session by asking each member, one at a time, whether she or he has done the agreed-upon last homework assignment (a list of which I have in front of me). "If not," I ask, "Why not?" I look for the dysfunctional, Irrational *Beliefs* (IBs) that probably stopped her or him from doing the homework, such as: "It's *too* hard to do it. I *should* improve without doing it!" Or: "I *have* to show myself and the group that I'll do it beautifully.

Else, I'm a no-goodnik!" I and other group members Dispute this person's low frustration tolerance (LFT) and perfectionism, and encourage her or him to do the assignment next week or we modify it and add to it.

We then ask the member what problems occurred this week, what Irrational *Beliefs* (IBs) accompanied these problems, what was done to Dispute them, what other REBT techniques were used, what progress or lack of progress was made, what could best be done now, etc. If the group is working well, I alone do not question, challenge, and encourage each member, but several other members also do so, and there is much lively interaction and interchange.

By the time each session ends, all the members present have usually been checked on their homework, led to discuss continuing or new problems, shown how their IBs are often remarkably similar to other members' dysfunctional BELIEFS, led to do some active Disputing, helped to discuss other REBT methods they can use, encouraged to talk to other members and to help them, and asked to accept another homework assignment. If time runs out before important issues can be discussed, they are put on the agenda for priority handling during the following session.

USEFUL REBT GROUP TECHNIQUES

As noted previously, nearly all the regular REBT techniques are used during group therapy sessions, as well as some encounter-type exercises that are specially designed for group processes. Here are some of the techniques that have been found to be most useful.

Cognitive Techniques of REBT

Active disputing. Members are all taught the ABCs of REBT, shown how to find their self-defeating, absolutist shoulds and musts, their awfulizing, their I-can't-stand-it-itis, their damning of self and of other persons, their over-generalizations, and their other dysfunctional inferences and attributions, and are shown how to Dispute these with empirical, logical, and pragmatically useful challenges.

Rational coping self-statements. In group and in their outside life, members are encouraged to prepare Rational *Beliefs* (RBs) and coping statements to substitute for their IBs, and to keep using them steadily until they consistently believe and act on them. Such self-statements can be factual and encouraging (e.g., "I am able to succeed on this job, and I'll work hard to show that I can"). Or, preferably, they can be more philosophical (e.g., "I'd like very much to succeed but I don't *have* to do so; and if I fail I am never a failure or a worthless individual").

Cost-benefit Analysis. Group members can make a list of the real disadvantages of their harmful addictions (e.g., smoking) and a list of the real advantages of changing their dysfunctional behaviors (e.g., procrastination or avoidance of sex-love relationships). They can review and think about this list several times every day (Ellis and Velten 1992).

Modeling. Participants are urged to model themselves after the healthy behavior of the leader, of another member, of friends or relatives, or of other good models they hear of or read about (Bandura 1997; Ellis 2001).

Cognitive homework. Members use the ABCDEs of REBT, observe some of their unfortunate Adversities (As), figure out their IBs, Dispute them (at D) and arrive at Effective New Philosophies (E). They do so either in their head or on one of the REBT Self-Help Forms.

Psychoeducational techniques. Group members use REBT books, workbooks, pamphlets, audio- and videocassettes, and other self-help materials to understand and solidify their working at REBT cognitive, emotive, and behavioral methods.

Proselytizing. Members are encouraged to use REBT to try to help other members, as well as their friends and relatives, to overcome their IBs and thereby help themselves overcome their own disturbances.

Recording therapy sessions. Participants may record the parts of their sessions where the other participants are largely trying to help them with their personal problems, and listen to these recordings in between the sessions.

Reframing. Members are shown how to look for unfortunate As to see that they include good things as well. They learn to accept the challenge, when "bad" As occur, of making themselves healthfully sorry and frustrated, rather than unhealthily panicking and depressing.

Emotive Techniques of REBT

Forceful coping self-statements. REBT hypothesizes that group members (and other people) often hold their IBs quite strongly (with "hot" cognitions) and that, therefore, they had better vigorously and powerfully think, feel, and act against them. Among its emotive-evocative methods is the use of forceful coping self-statements, such as, "I NEVER, NEVER need what I want. I ONLY prefer it!" "I can ALWAYS accept *myself*, my personhood, even when I do stupid and wrong *acts*!"

Rational-Emotive Imagery. Maxie Maultsby Jr., an REBT psychiatrist, created rational emotive imagery (REI) in 1971 and I added more emotive and behavioral elements to it (Ellis 2000c; Maultsby 1971). Group members do REI, both during group sessions and as homework, by imagining one of the worst things that could happen to them (e.g., continuing failure); letting themselves feel very upset about this image (e.g., panicking);

imploding this disturbed feeling; and then working on their feeling, to make themselves have healthy or appropriate negative feelings (such as sorrow, disappointment, or frustration). They can do this every day for thirty days (it usually takes only a minute or two to do) until they automatically experience their healthy negative feelings when they imagine, or actually encounter, similar "horrible" happenings.

Role-playing. Group members often role-play with other group members or with the therapist, as when one plays the interviewee for an important job and the other plays the interviewer. During this form of behavior rehearsal, the rest of the group critiques how well the member is doing in the role-play and suggests how she or he could improve. If either of the role-players shows anxiety, the role-play is temporarily stopped and this person is asked what he or she was thinking to create the anxiety and how he or she could think, instead, to allay it.

Reverse role-play. One group member takes another's irrational Belief (e.g., "So-and-so must always love me completely!") and holds onto it rigidly and forcefully while playing the irrational member's role. The person with the IB then has to talk the other role-player—actually himself or herself—out of this firmly held IB.

Forceful taped disputing. A group member tapes one of his or her main IBs as homework (e.g., "Everybody always has to treat me fairly!") and vigorously Disputes it on the same tape. The other members listen to this Disputing to see if it is really rational and also to see how vigorous and forceful it is (Ellis 1988).

Use of humor. Members are shown how to not take themselves and their mistakes too seriously, and encouraged to humorously assail the IBs of other group members—but only to put down and laugh at the other's ideas and behaviors, and not to denigrate the person himself or herself (Ellis and Harper 1961/1997). REBT group members at the psychological clinic of the Albert Ellis Institute in New York City are given a group of rational humorous songs to sing to themselves when they panic, depress, or enrage themselves. The whole group, as an exercise, may also sing some of these humorous songs or others which they create or contribute to the group themselves. A typical rational humorous song is:

I Wish I Were Not Crazy!*

(Tune: *Dixie*, by Dan Emmett)

Oh, I wish I were really put together—
Smooth and fine as patent leather!
Oh, how great to be rated innately sedate!
But I'm afraid that I was fated

To be rather aberrated—
Oh, how sad to be mad as my Mom and my Dad!
Oh, I wish I were not crazy! Hooray, hooray!
I wish my mind were less inclined
To be the kind that's hazy!
I could agree to really be less crazy,
But I, alas, am just too goddamned lazy!

Relationship methods. Members are given unconditional self-acceptance (USA) by the therapist, no matter how badly or selfishly they behave, and are taught how to give it to other group members and to people outside the group. They are helped to relate better to people in their regular lives and are often taught interpersonal and social skills training in the group.

Encouragement. Members are encouraged to encourage other troubled members to think, feel, and act less disturbedly and more enjoyably; and to do their therapeutic homework, even when it is arduous or difficult to do.

Encounter exercises. Members are given group encounter exercises in their regular group and in special all-day marathons that are arranged for them once or twice a year. Nine-hour intensives are also run by the Albert Ellis Institute in New York for group members (and other people) who want to participate in larger-scale group exercises.

Behavioral Techniques of REBT

In vivo desensitization. Group members are encouraged to do a number of harmless acts, such as making a public speech or talking to strangers, that they are neurotically afraid to do, and also to use several other active-experiential behavioral methods of REBT. They are encouraged to use exposure to past or present traumatic scenes n order to face and work through their horror of imagining or thinking about traumas in their lives, particularly if they have post-traumatic stress disorder (PTSD) or other forms of panicking.

Avoiding running away from obnoxious events. When group members find other members obnoxious or "horrible" and overreact to them, they are encouraged *not* to leave the group until they modify their feelings of rage or horror, and to practice doing so in spite of the "terrible" situation they are in. Once they make themselves considerably less disturbed, they are advised to *then* decide whether it is more advantageous or disadvantageous for them to tolerate being with "obnoxious" group members. Similarly, they are often encouraged not to run away from "bad" people outside the group until they modify their rage or I-can't-stand-it-itis about staying with these people.

---

*Lyrics by Albert Ellis. Copyright 1977 by the Albert Ellis Institute.

Use of reinforcement. Being strongly behavioral, REBT shows group members how to suitably reinforce themselves by doing something enjoyable only after they have done something onerous—such as working on a term paper —that they are avoiding. In group itself they may be allowed to speak up about their own problems only *after* they have tried to help other members with their difficulties.

Use of penalties. Many clients won't stop their addictive or compulsive behavior because it is too immediately pleasurable or reinforcing; and they will not change it for a normal reinforcement. Thus they will not give up smoking or problem drinking for allowing themselves to read or enjoy television. Consequently REBT encourages some group members to penalize themselves after their destructive indulgences—for example, to spend an hour with a boring person every time they gamble, or light every cigarette they smoke with a $50 bill. Clients also encourage other group members to enact suitable penalties and monitor their doing so.

Skill training. Group members often learn and practice particular important interpersonal skills in the group sessions, for example, learning to listen to others, accepting them with their poor behavior, communicating openly with them, and forming relationships with them. They are also urged to acquire suitable personal and interpersonal skills by taking courses and practicing outside of group.

Relapse prevention. Members are shown how to ward off relapses, to accept themselves when they relapse, and to revert to self-helping thoughts, feelings, and behaviors when they fall back to dysfunctional behaving. To do this, they are taught the relapse prevention methods of Marlatt and Gordon (1989) and other cognitive behaviorists and the specific relapse-preventive methods of REBT, particularly monitoring and Disputing their own musturbatory philosophies that lead to relapse.

PROCESSES OF REBT GROUP THERAPY

Various theorists and practitioners have described processes that therapy groups and their leaders go through, or are supposed to go through (Yalom 1955). Some of these processes are emphasized in REBT groups and some are not. Let me discuss them.

Transference. REBT views transference, first, as overgeneralization. Thus, because group members were once treated badly by their fathers and treated well by their mothers, they may tend to put other males in the same category as their father, and may feel hostile or indifferent to men and warm toward women. They may—or may not!—also react to the therapist as a father/mother figure and to other group members as siblings. These are overgeneralizations but, unless they are extreme, may not lead to major emotional and behavioral problems. Because REBT is not preoccupied with this kind of transference (as psychoanalysis is), it does not obsessively look for it and consequently invariably "find" it.

When normal, nondisturbed transference reactions are observed in my groups, I largely ignore them; but when they escalate into disturbed reactions in the group itself or in the members' personal lives, the other group members and I point to these reactions and show members how destructive they are and how to minimize them. Thus, if Miriam avoids sex-love relationships because her father kept rejecting her, we show her that all males are *not* her father, that she can sensibly choose a different type of man, and that if she makes a mistake and picks a partner who is as unloving as her father, that doesn't prove either that she needs his love and she is worthless without it, or that she'll never be able to have a long-term loving relationship. The group and I dispute her disturbed overgeneralizing but not her normal generalizing.

Similarly, if a male member deifies or devil-ifies me, the group leader, and sees me as a loved or hated father figure, we point out his disturbed transference reactions, show him the distorted thinking that lies behind it, and encourage him to adopt less dysfunctional thoughts, feelings, and behaviors. Or if a woman fights with female group members the way she fights with her sisters, we point out her transference and the irrational cognitions behind it and show her how to break her rigid women-are-all-like-my-sisters reaction.

The term *transference* is also used in psychotherapy to denote the close relationship that usually develops between clients and their therapist. I find that such relationship factors do develop in my group, but not nearly as intensely as they do with my individual therapy clients. However, REBT actively espouses the therapist's giving all clients close attention, showing real interest in helping them solve their problems, and especially giving what Rogers (1961) calls unconditional positive regard and what I (Ellis and Harper 1997) call *unconditional other-acceptance*. So, although I am often confrontational with group members, I try to show them that I really care about helping them; that I will work hard to hear, understand, and empathize with them; that I have great faith that they can, despite their handicaps, improve; that I can poke fun *at their irrationalities* without laughing *at them*; and that I totally accept them as fallible humans, no matter how badly they often think and behave. I also use my *person* in my group sessions, and consequently am informal, take risks, reveal some of my own feelings, tell jokes and stories, and generally am myself as well as a group leader. In this way I hope to model flexible, involved, nondisturbed behaviors.

Countertransference. I frankly like and dislike some of my group members more than I do others, and I especially tend to dislike members who often come late, act unhelpfully to others, fail to do their homework, and behave disruptively in group. When I see that I am feeling this way, or possibly telling myself, "They *shouldn't* be the way they are and are rotten people for being that way!" I immediately dispute those damning beliefs and convince myself, "They *should* act the poor way that they do, because it is their nature to act that way right now. I dislike what they do but I can accept *them* with their unfortunate *doings*."

By decreasing my *demands* on my clients, I largely (not completely) overcome my negative countertransference, and I am able to deal with "bad" group members more therapeutically. I sometimes, depending on their vulnerability, confront them and honestly tell them, "I try not to hate *you*, but I really do dislike some of your *behavior*, and I hope for my sake, the group's sake, and especially your own sake, that you change it." When I find myself prejudicedly favoring some members of my groups, I convince myself that they are not gods or goddesses, and I make an effort to keep liking them personally without unduly favoring them in group (Ellis, in press).

Methods of Intervention. Most of my interventions take place with each individual member as he is telling about his homework, talking about his progress and lack or progress, presenting new problems, or returning to old ones. I speak directly to him, ask questions, make suggestions, ferret out and dispute his dysfunctional thoughts, feelings, and behaviors, and suggest homework. My interventions are mainly about his personal problems, especially as they relate to his outside life, but also as they relate to what he says and doesn't say in group.

I often show a member that her actions (and inactions) in group may well replicate her out-of-group behaviors. Thus, I may say, "Johanna, you speak so low here that we can hardly hear what you say. Do you act the same way in social groups? If so, what are you telling yourself to *make* yourself speak so low?"

My interpersonal interventions include commenting on how group members react to one another; noting that they often fail to speak up to or interact with other members; noting their warm or hostile reactions to others, encouraging the former and questioning the latter; giving them relationship exercises to do during group sessions; having a personal interaction with some of the members, pointing out that their group interactions may indicate how they sabotage themselves in their outside relationships and giving them some in-group skill training that may help them relate better outside the group.

My intervention with the group as a whole largely consists of giving all its members cognitive, emotive, and behavioral exercises to be done in the group; giving them all the same homework exercise, such as a shame-attacking exercise to do before the next session; giving them a brief lecture on one of the main theories or practices of REBT; and explaining to them some of the group procedures and discussing with them the advantages and disadvantages of these procedures.

Most of the time, as noted above, I intervene on the individual level, but when interpersonal problems arise, such as two or more members failing to relate to each other, I often intervene with duos or trios. I also plan in advance group-as-a-whole interventions, or else I spontaneously promote them as I deem them advisable (or as the spirit moves me!).

Focusing on Group Processes. Most of the time in my group sessions I use an individualized content focus. I assume that the group members come to therapy to work on their own individual problems and mainly to help themselves in their outside lives. Therefore, I induce them largely to talk about the things that are bothering them in their self-oriented and interpersonal relationships and, with the help of the group, try to show them how they are needlessly upsetting themselves in their daily lives and what they can do to think, feel, and act more healthfully.

The purpose of REBT group (and individual) therapy is to show clients how they are not only assessing and blaming *what they do* but also damning *themselves* for doing it; how they are also evaluating others' behavior *and* damning these others for their "bad" behavior; and how they are noting environmental difficulties and (externally and internally) whining about them, instead of constructively trying to change or avoid them. Therefore, whenever members bring up any undue or exaggerated upsetness, and feel unhealthily panicking, depressing, self-hating, or raging (instead of healthily sad, disappointed, and frustrated) when unfortunate events occur, the other members and I focus on showing them what they are doing to upset themselves needlessly, how to stop doing this, and how to plan and act on achieving a more fulfilling, happier existence. When they are, as it were, "on stage" in the group, almost everyone focuses on them and their difficulties and tries to help them overcome these in the group itself and in the outside world. So a majority of the time in each session is spent on dealing with individual members' problems.

When, however, any of the members displays a problem that particularly relates to the group itself, this is dealt with specifically and groupwise. Thus, if a member keeps coming quite late to group or is absent a good deal of the time, either I or other members raise this as an issue, and we speak to this member about it. We determine, for instance, why he comes late, what core philosophies encourage him to do so, how he defeats himself and the other members by his lateness, how he can change, and what kind of homework assignment in this respect he will agree to carry out. At the same time, the general problem of lateness—as it relates to group and also as it relates to the members' outside lives—is also frequently discussed, and it is brought out how latecoming is disadvantageous to other members and how it interferes with a cohesive and beneficial group process.

Similarly, if a group member only speaks about her own problems and doesn't take the risk of speaking to the others, disputing their self-defeating thoughts and behaviors, and making some suitable suggestions for their change, she is questioned about this and shown how and why she is blocking herself in group, and how and why she probably behaves similarly in her outside life. But the general problem of members being too reserved—or, sometimes, too talkative—in group is also raised, and various members are encouraged to speak up about this problem and to give their ideas about how the group process would be more effective if virtually all the members talked up appropriately, rather than said too much or too little.

Also, if the group as a whole seems to be functioning poorly—for example, being dull, uninterested, apathetic, or overly boisterous—I raise this issue, encourage a general discussion of it, get members to suggest alternative ways for the group to act, and check on these suggestions later to see if they are being implemented. Once in a while I go over some of the general principles of REBT—such as the theory that people largely upset themselves rather than *get* upset—to make sure that the members as a whole understand these principles and are better prepared to use them during the sessions and in their outside affairs.

I keep looking for cues for underlying issues that are not being handled well in group. Some cues are members being interested only in their own problems and not those of other members; not being alert during the group; being too negative to other members who may not be working at helping themselves improve; giving only practical advice to other members, rather than disputing their irrational philosophies; being too sociable, rather than being serious about their own and others' problems; not staying for the after-group session; and "subgrouping" or talking privately to others when the group is going on. I usually intervene soon after these issues arise, and raise the issue either with the individual who is interfering with the group process or with the group as a whole.

My strategy of intervention is usually direct and often confrontational. Thus, I may say, "Jim, you always bring up your own problems in group and seem to have no trouble speaking about them. But I rarely hear you say anything to the other group members about their problems. When you sit there silently while the rest of us are speaking to one of the group members, I suspect that you are saying quite a lot to yourself that you are not saying to the group. Am I right about this? And if I am, what are you telling yourself to *stop* yourself from speaking up to the others?"

A more general intervention will also usually be direct and will go something like this: "Several of you recently are not doing your agreed-upon homework or are doing it very sloppily. Let's discuss this right now and see if I am observing this correctly and, if so, what can we do about it to see that the homework assignments are more useful and to arrange that you tend to follow them more often and more thoroughly."

If the group process is going well and the members are fairly consistently bringing up and working on their problems, both in the group and outside the group, my interventions are relatively few in regard to the group process. But I frequently question, challenge, advise, and confront members about their individual problems. I am an active teacher, confronter, persuader, encourager, and homework suggester, and I usually talk more than any of the other members during a given session. I try to make sure, however, that I do not give long lectures or hold the floor too long. My questions and comments, therefore, are usually frequent but brief.

Although I can easily run one of my groups by myself, without any assistance, I am usually assisted by one of our trainees, a Fellow or Intern of the Institute, because the Albert Ellis Institute in New York is a training institute and because we want all of our trainees to be able to lead a group by themselves. This assistant leader is with me and the group for the first hour and a half of each session and takes over the group by himself or herself for the after-group, which consists of another forty-five minutes. The assistant leader is also trained to make active-directive interventions, but not to hog the floor at any one time, and to encourage the other members to keep making interventions too. A few of the members in each group usually become quite vocal and adept at making interventions, but I tactfully correct them if they seem to go too far off base. The assistant leader and I particularly go after the nonintervening members and keep encouraging them to speak up more and more about other people's problems. If they are recalcitrant or resistant in this respect, we fairly often give them the assignment of speaking up a minimum of three times in each session about *others'* issues.

I keep showing the members how their behavior in group often (but by no means always) mirrors their behaviors and problems outside the group. Thus if one member speaks sharply to another member, I may say, "Mary, you seem to be angry right now at Joan. Are you merely objecting to her behavior, with which you disagree? Or are you, as I seem to hear you doing, damning *her* for exhibiting that *behavior?*" If Mary acknowledges her anger at Joan, I (and the other members) may then ask, "What are you telling yourself right now to make yourself angry? What is your Jehovian *demand* on Joan?" If Mary denies that she is angrily carping at Joan, I may then ask the rest of the group, "What do you think and feel about Mary's reactions to Joan? Am I inventing her anger, or do you sense it too?"

We then get the group reactions to Mary; and if the group agrees that she probably is quite angry at Joan, we go back to the question: "What are you telling yourself right now to *make* yourself angry?" The others and I will also try to get Mary to see that she is making the same kind of demands about those at whom she is angry as she is now making about Joan in the group.

Again, if Ted only offers practical advice to the other members and never helps them to see and to dispute their self-defeating philosophies by which they are upsetting themselves, I, my assistant therapist, or one of the group members may say to him, "Look, Ted, you just ignored Harold's perfectionist demands that are making him refuse to work on the novel he is trying to write, and instead you only offered him some practical advice on how to take a writing course. You often seem to do this same kind of thing in group. Now isn't it likely that in your own life you don't look for and dispute your Irrational *Beliefs* and that you mainly look for practical ways of your acting better with those irrationalities, so that you do not have to tackle them and give them up?"

Working with Difficult Group Members

One kind of difficult group member is the one who interferes with the group process, such as Mel, who interrupted others, indicated that they were pretty worthless for not changing their ways, and often monopolized the group. Other members and I pointed this out to him several times, but he persisted in his disruptive behavior. So we insisted that he stop and consider what he was telling himself when, for example, he interrupted others.

His main musturbatory beliefs appeared to be (1) "I *must* get in what I have to say immediately, or else I might lose it and never get to say it, and that would be *awful!*" and (2) "If I don't make a more brilliant statement to the group than any of the others makes, I am an inadequate person and I might as well shut my mouth and say nothing at all!" We showed Mel how to dispute and change these ideas to *preferences*, but not *necessities*, that he speak and be heard and that he make fine contributions in group. We also gave him the homework assignment of watching his interrupting tendencies and forcing himself for a while to speak up in group only after he had given some other member the choice of speaking up first. After several more sessions, he had distinctly improved his interruptive tendencies, and reported that he was doing the same thing in his group participations and individual conversations outside the group.

Another difficult type of member is the one who rarely completes the homework assignment he has agreed to do, or else completes it occasionally and sloppily. I (and other group members) then ask him to look for the irrational ideas that he is overtly or tacitly holding to block his doing these assignments, such as: "It's hard to do this goddamned assignment; in fact, it's *too* hard and it *shouldn't be* that hard! I can get away with improving myself *without* doing it, even though other people have to do their homework to change. Screw it. I won't do it!" We keep after this member to look at the beliefs he holds which block his doing the homework; to make a list of the disadvantages of not doing it and to go over this list at least five times every day; to dispute his Irrational *Beliefs* strongly and forcefully; to keep telling himself rational coping self-statements in their stead; to use rational emotive imagery to make himself feel sorry and displeased, but not horrified and rebellious, about having to do the homework; to reinforce himself whenever he does it, and perhaps to also penalize himself when he doesn't do it; and to use other suitable methods of REBT to undercut his dysfunctional thinking, feeling, and behaving about doing the homework.

Another type of difficult group member is the one who is overly passive, polite, and nonparticipative. I usually do nothing about such a member until she has been in the group for several weeks and had a chance to acclimate herself to its procedures and to some of the principles of REBT. But then I directly question her about her passivity and lack of participation. If she acknowledges these behaviors, I encourage her to look at her blocking thoughts and actively to dispute them. Thus one member, Josephine, kept telling herself, just before she thought of speaking up in group, "What if I say something stupid! They'll all laugh at me! I'll be an utter fool! They are all brighter than I and know much better how to use REBT. I'll *never* be able to say something intelligent or to be helpful to the other group members. I'd better quit group and only go for individual therapy, where it is much easier for me to speak up, because I only have to talk about myself and don't have to help others with their problems."

In this case, the group and I did what we usually do: we disputed Josephine's unrealistic attributions and inferences and showed her that she wouldn't necessarily say something stupid; that the group might well not laugh at her even if she did; that all the members were not necessarily brighter than she; and that if she kept trying, she most probably would be able to say something intelligent and to be helpful to the other members. As usual, however, we went beyond this—as we almost always do in REBT—by showing Josephine, more elegantly, that even if the worst happened, even if she did say something stupid, even if she was laughed at by the group, even if all the others were brighter than she, and even if she never was able to say something intelligent or to be helpful to the others, she still would never be an inadequate or rotten *person*, but would only be a person who was now behaving poorly and who could always accept and respect herself while remaining unenthusiastic about some of her traits and behaviors.

This is what we usually try to achieve with difficult clients who continually down and damn themselves and who steadily, therefore, feel depressing, panicking, and worthless. The group members and I persist in showing her that we accept her as a fallible human, and that she can learn to consistently do the same for herself. REBT group therapy, like REBT individual therapy, is particularly oriented toward helping all clients give themselves unconditional self-accepting; that is, to reject and to try to change many of their dysfunctional behaviors but always—yes, always!—to accept themselves as humans. Yes, *whether or not* they perform well and *whether or not* they are approved or loved by significant others.

This is one of the cardinal views of REBT; and one that often—though, of course, not always—works well with difficult clients. This aspect of REBT is probably more effective in group than in individual therapy, because all the members of the group are taught to accept both themselves and others unconditionally; so that when an arrant self-denigrator comes to group, she is not only accepted unconditionally by the therapist (who is especially trained to do this kind of accepting) but is almost always also accepted by the other group members, thus encouraging and abetting her to unconditionally accept herself.

Activity of the Therapist and Group Members.

In cognitive-behavioral therapy in general and in REBT group therapy in particular, the activity level of the therapist tends to be high. I am a teacher, who often shows my clients how they upset themselves and what they can do to change, but I also keep encouraging and pushing them to change. The romantic view in therapy is that if clients are provided with a trusting and accepting atmosphere, they have considerable ability to change, and will healthfully use this ability to get themselves to grow and develop. I take the more realistic view that they *can* but that they often *won't* choose to modify their thoughts, feelings, and behaviors unless I actively and directively push them to do so. Consequently, as noted previously in this chapter, I speak more than any other group member during each session; I purposely and purposively lead the group in "healthy" rather than "unhealthy" directions; and I keep each session going in an organized, no-nonsense, presumably efficient way. I try to make sure that no one is neglected during each session; that no one monopolizes the group; and that sidetracking into chit-chat, empty discussion, bombast, endless philosophizing, and other modes of problem avoidance is minimized.

As leader, I try to maximize honest revealings of feelings, cutting through defensiveness, getting to members' dysfunctional core philosophies, Disputing of these philosophies, acceptance of present discomfort, and the carrying out of difficult in-group and out-of-group experiential and behavioral assignments. For example, I (or the other members) may suggest that Sam, an unusually shy person, go around the room and start a conversation with every member who is present. I will then direct Sam to do so, will encourage him to keep going around the room, will ask him about his feelings as he does so, will get him to look at what he is thinking to create these feelings, will ask the other members for the reactions to his overtures, and will lead a general discussion on what has just transpired and how Sam and other members can gain from this exercise. Once, when we did this exercise with an exceptionally shy man, he not only became very much more active in group from that session onward, but also, for the first time in his life, began to approach people in his neighborhood bar, where previously he had always waited for them to approach him. He noted that my actively persuading him and the group to participate in this encouraging exercise was a real turning point in his life.

The activity level of most of the members of my five weekly groups is usually quite high, not only in the expressing of their feelings and ideas, but in their disputing other members' self-defeating beliefs and helping them with their problem solving.

In the section that follows, I provide a case example of how one particular client benefited from her participation in an REBT group.

CASE PRESENTATION OF A GROUP CLIENT

Barbara came to group because of her business and social unassertiveness. A thirty-six-year-old secretary, she had always worked below her potential level because she nicely followed her supervisor's instructions but never took any initiative herself. She therefore failed to become a supervisor or office manager herself, although she definitely seemed to have the ability to do that kind of work. She married at the age of twenty-one and stayed with her alcoholic and irresponsible husband for eight years because of her horror of being alone. Although quite attractive, she practically never went to singles functions, but stayed in her apartment by herself most of the time, because she was afraid to socialize and be rejected by any "good" men she might meet. She felt that she had "nothing really to offer," except to an inferior male. So she only occasionally dated unsuccessful, inadequate men whom she found "safe" but too boring to stay with for any length of time. She had one close woman friend, Selma, who, like herself, was painfully shy and who only socialized with Barbara.

At first Barbara talked freely enough about herself in group, especially about her unassertiveness at work and about her accompanying depression. But she would only give practical advice to other group members and never found or Disputed their Irrational *Beliefs*. When asked about this in group, she said that she did not know how to do REBT well enough to do good Disputation, even though she had read several REBT self-help books and pamphlets.

To show Barbara that she *was* able to do Disputing adequately, she was asked to fill out the REBT Self-Help Form; first about one of her own problems, and then about another group member's unassertiveness with her husband. When Barbara did very well on these homework assignments and admitted that she could do adequate REBT Disputation, she was encouraged to do live Disputing of some other group members' Irrational *Beliefs* during several group sessions, and was again shown that she could do this well. After several weeks she became one of the group's most frequent and persistent Disputers, and began to obviously enjoy the process. She also spontaneously began, outside of therapy, to teach REBT to her shy friend, Selma, and to help Selma considerably with some of her neurotic difficulties.

For several months, Barbara complained and put herself down for her unassertiveness with her supervisor at work. She saw that it stemmed from her dire need for this woman's approval, but did nothing to change her love slobbism or to act more assertively. After doing some assertiveness-training role-playing in group, and after being urged by all the other members to follow it up on the outside, she forced herself to speak up at work. Doing so, she soon arranged to get the promise of a raise in pay, also arranged to come in an hour earlier and to leave work earlier on Tuesdays and Thursdays so that she could take a special word-processing course, and was able to ask for a few other favors at work that she had been terrified to request for more than two years. Both Barbara and the group were delighted with her increased assertiveness, and she was encouraged to look for a better job— which, after four months, she finally attained.

Barbara's social anxiety proved more difficult to tackle than her unassertiveness at work, because she invented innumerable excuses to avoid going to singles affairs and to respond appropriately to males who tried to approach her at church, when she walked her dog, and at the other few "safe" activities in which she allowed herself to participate. She even refused to try a date with an eligible male cousin of Selma, who talked to this cousin and got him interested in seeing Barbara. She was sure that he would lose all interest in her if they actually met, and was terrified that he might have sex with her because he was only interested in her body and would then never want to see her again. She broke two tentative dates with him and per-petuated her perfect record of not having a single date in three years.

The group and I tried several REBT techniques to help Barbara overcome her extreme fears of rejection. We used cost-benefit analysis and had her list of many disadvantages of being socially reclusive and read these over many times to sink them into her consciousness. We tried to help her model herself after other group members who were overcoming their social shyness. We had her say several forceful coping statements to herself a number of times—such as, "I *can* find some males who will like me for more than my body! And if any of them have sex with me and then reject me, that means something about *them* but never, never proves that I am an inadequate person!"

The group showed Barbara how to use rational emotive imagery by imagining that she did get rejected by one of the few men she really liked, letting herself feel very depressed and self-hating about this rejection, and then working on herself until she only felt quite sorry and disappointed but *not* depressed. Most of all, the group and I gave Barbara unconditional acceptance and showed her by our attitudes, tone, and manner that we always accepted *her*, as a person, even when she failed to work on herself, when she sabotaged our suggestions, and when she made up poor excuses for staying in her rut. In addition, of course, we consistently and vigorously taught her unconditional self-acceptance (USA)—that is, fully to accept *herself* no matter how badly, foolishly, and self-defeating she often *acted*. After going over this important point many times, Barbara improved greatly at refusing to blame herself for her mistakes and failures; and she also helped talk several other group members into unconditionally accepting themselves even when they acted quite foolishly.

All this REBT work by Barbara and by her therapy group eventually began to pay off. After attending group regularly for five months, she finally agreed to do the paradoxical homework assignment of going to a dance and making sure that she got at least three rejections by suitable males. She was enormously afraid, at first, to carry out this assignment, and for several weeks copped out on doing it. But she finally painfully forced herself to go to a "safe" church dance and get three men to refuse to dance with her. After the first refusal, she almost ran shamefully back home. But she made herself stay, to her surprise got several acceptances, and just barely, by the end of the evening, got her required three rejections. She was elated with her social assertiveness—and so were the other members of her group.

From then on, Barbara's battle with herself went almost swimmingly smoothly. She dated with increasing frequency, and was disappointed, but not depressed, when the "good" men she occasionally met didn't turn out to be suitable for a long-term relationship. She became active in other ways, such as by participating in a regular discussion group. She became even more active in her therapy group and was voted, in one of the exercises we did, as being the most helpful member. She got a job as an office manager, liked it very much, and did more socializing at the new office in a few weeks than she had previously done in any of the previous jobs that she had kept for years.

After being in group for a little over a year, Barbara decided to leave, partly because she now had so many other things to do in the evening that spending several hours once a week traveling to and from and being in group was getting too exhausting. But she mainly felt that she had achieved her goals of socializing better and becoming more assertive, and that she could continue therapy with intermittent individual sessions. She was still socially anxious at times, but was practically never severely depressing as she had often been previously.

The group members were very sorry to see Barbara leave and hoped she would invite them to her future wedding, which they were sure would not be too far away. Several of them continued to have personal friendships with her for quite a while after she left group. She herself was very happy about her group experience, remarked that she would have never benefited so much with only individual therapy sessions, and kept referring her friends and business associates to the Institute, particularly for group therapy.

Not every member of my groups, of course, makes the dramatic and steady progress that Barbara made, and some take two or three years of participation before they do significantly improve. But if people really work at it, and keep using REBT in group as well as in their outside lives, a large percentage of them make notable gains, minimize their anxiety, depression, and rage, and begin to lead much more self-actualized lives.

Conclusion

Rational emotive behavior and cognitive behavior therapy are partly indigenous to most group therapy, because when several people regularly meet together with a leader in order to work on their psychological problems, they almost always talk about their thoughts, feelings, and behaviors and try to help one another change their cognitions, emotions, and actions. Moreover, they usually give advice to one another, show how others' behavior had better be changed outside the group, and check to see if their homework suggestions are actually being carried out. Again, they normally interact with one another in the group itself, comment on one another's in-group behaviors, and give themselves practice in changing some of their dysfunctional interactions.

Even when a therapy group tries to follow a somewhat narrow theory of psychotherapy, for example, a psychoanalytic or a Jungian orientation, it tends to be much wider-ranging in its actions than in its theory, and often takes on a surprisingly eclectic approach (Yalom 1985). The advantage of REBT group therapy is that it very consciously deals with members as people who think, feel, *and* act; who get disturbed, or *make* themselves disturbed, in all three interacting ways; and who therefore had better consciously see how they largely *construct* their dysfunctioning and how they can reconstruct and improve their patterns of living (Ellis 1994, 1999; Ellis and Dryden 1997).

REBT and CBT group therapy, moreover, in principle accept the fact that humans are social animals and live interpersonally and in groups. It is therefore desirable, though not always necessary, that they work out their cognitive-emotive-behavioral problems together as well as in individual therapy. Group work also covers a wide variety of goals and problems. Thus, therapy groups may be homogeneous—e.g., all the members may be involved in skill training, overcoming alcoholism, or overcoming procrastination—or may be heterogeneous—e.g., the group may include several kinds of disturbed people. While one specific type of treatment is unlikely to be helpful to members of all these different kinds of groups, REBT includes so many different kinds of techniques that it can fairly easily be adapted to almost any kind of group process. With the use of group treatment, more opportunity for learning positive and unlearning self-defeating behavior is provided than one therapist can provide in individual therapy and than one group therapist can provide in a one-sided form of group process.

From a research standpoint, rational emotive behavioral group therapy offers unique possibilities for exploring the effectiveness of group techniques. For it always includes many specific procedures, such as the Disputing of dysfunctional attitudes, the disclosure of "shameful" feelings, and the assigning of homework activities, and each of these methods can be used and not used in controlled experiments, to determine how effective or ineffective each of them is in different kinds of groups and settings. If enough of this kind of experimentation is done, the wide variety of methods now used in REBT (and in CBT) may eventually be pared down to a relatively few effective ones.

For reasons such as these, then, I think that REBT and CBT group therapy will, first, become more popular as the years go by and, second, be increasingly incorporated into or merged with many of the other modes of group treatment. At the same time, cognitive-behavioral group and individual therapy will continue to change as the entire field of psychotherapy grows and develops. Some of its more popular present-day methods will wane and other methods, including some not yet invented, will flourish. Like its sister, behavior therapy, and unlike many of today's other treatment methods, CBT favors scientific experimentation, and already has led to literally hundreds of controlled studies (Hollon and Beck 1994; Lyons and Woods 1991). If this characteristic continues, as I predict it will, REBT and CBT will continue to change and develop.

SELF-HELP SUGGESTIONS

- If you are considering personal REBT or CBT therapy, by all means consider group therapy, for some of the reasons listed on page two of this chapter.
- If you are considering joining an REBT or CBT therapy group, see that the group you select uses some of the techniques listed under "Useful REBT Group Techniques" in this chaper. If not, you can suggest to the group that it starts using some of them.
- Some groups, even when led by a competent thereapist and following regular REBT or CBT procedures, are simply not for you. The members of the group may be too uneducated, too seriously disturbing, or too uncooperative to be very helpful for you. Try being a member of it for a while, but if it doesn't seem to be helpful in spite of your best efforts to use it, try another group or try individual psychotherapy.

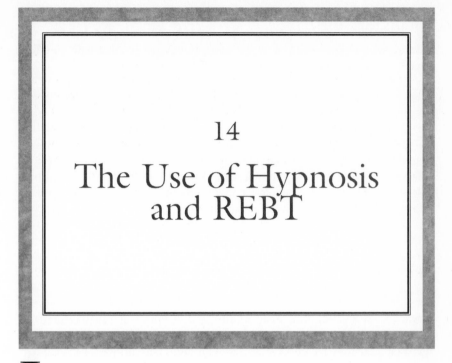

14

The Use of Hypnosis and REBT

I started using hypnosis in 1949 when I was supervised, at the New Jersey State Diagnostic Center in Menlo Park, by a psychiatrist, Dr. Ralph Brancale. I found it useful in some instances, especially to reveal my clients' thoughts and feelings that they didn't easily disclose. I became a Diplomate in Clinical Hypnosis in the 1950s and kept using it from time to time when I originated and started using Rational Emotive Behavior Therapy (REBT) in 1955. At first, I mainly used authoritarian-oriented hypnosis.

Various other therapists have also combined REBT with hypnosis, and have presented studies showing that it can be useful. Donald Tosi and his students have published a number of these studies (Tosi and Murphy 1995). Stanton (1989) has also published two studies showing the successful use of REBT with hypnosis. Several clinical cases back up these studies (Araoz 1983; Ellis 1986; Golden, Dowd, and Friedberg 1987; Hoellen 1988).

In spite of these reported successes of using REBT in conjunction with hypnosis, I at first used this combination only occasionally because it seems to have distinct disadvantages as well as advantages. These are some of its

This chapter is partly adapted from *Changes in the Therapist: A Casebook*, ed. E. Fromm and S. Kahn (Mahwah, N.J.: Erlbaum, 2000), and from *Handbook of Clinical Hypnosis,* ed. J. V. Rhue, S. J. Lynn, and I. Kirsch (Washington, D.C.: American Psychological Association, 1993), pp. 173–86. Used with permission.

advantages: (1) As indicated in the case presented later, I usually conduct REBT hypnotherapy by recording the hypnosis session and having the clients listen to this recording twenty or thirty times. As they do so, they keep hearing the REBT messages on the tape over and over and keep getting urged to do REBT homework. They therefore are likely to respond to the rational self-statements that are on the tape to keep doing their REBT homework. (2) Each hypnotic taped session usually includes working with one or two of the client's main problems and helps the client concentrate on solving this problem before going on to other issues. (3) The general philosophy of REBT—that people largely upset themselves and can therefore choose to unupset themselves—is repetitively shown to clients, so that they can adopt it and keep experimenting with applying it. (4) REBT hypnotherapy is rarely used by itself but is combined with regular REBT non-hypnotic individual or group therapy, so that clients are fully encouraged to think for themselves as well as to follow the suggestion of the hypnotist.

On the other hand. these are some of the disadvantages of using hypnosis along with REBT: (1) REBT holds that people preferably should think for themselves and not unthinkingly adopt the suggestions of a hypnotist (or of anyone else). Suggestion is a low-level form of thinking and not high-level falsification practiced by good scientists. Old-fashioned authoritarian-oriented hypnosis, which I used in the 1950s, includes too much suggestion and therefore conflicts somewhat with the REBT emphasis on self-directed thinking. (2) REBT holds that people had better be fully conscious of their dysfunctional beliefs and not merely cover them up with more productive rational beliefs that they tend to parrot—as in Emile Coué's and Norman Vincent Peale's positive thinking—but not really hold and follow. (3) Clients often want to be hypnotized because, having low-frustration tolerance, they view hypnotism as an easy and magical way of changing themselves. However, REBT emphasizes that people almost always have to work hard and consistently practice new ways of thinking, feeling, and behaving, until—after some time—they automatically begin to become self-conditioned to them. (4) REBT aims to show clients how to be on their own and independently construct self-helping methods for the rest of their lives. When I first used hypnosis I sometimes did it too much in an authoritative manner and I found this to be inconsistent with REBT. Today, hypnosis is used much more permissively and counteracts clients' tendencies to use it by rote and to let the hypnotist do all the work.

For several years I rarely used hypnosis with REBT because some of my clients relied too much on me rather than on their own constructive abilities and because it often took me several sessions to put my clients into a fairly deep trance state. In that period of time I could teach them regular REBT and frequently show them how to use it successfully with themselves. So why bother to add hypnosis to its methods, which include a number of cognitive, emotive, and behavioral techniques?

I got a different slant on using REBT along with hypnosis when, in the late 1970s, I worked with Susan, a forty-year-old teacher who had been severely depressed since childhood, who had obsessive-compulsive attachments to several "wrong" men, and who had made little progress during twelve years of psychoanalytic and interpersonal therapy. When I saw her, she was still obsessed with a twenty-seven-year-old male, Steven, a "loser" and an alcoholic, who had lived with her for two years and then cruelly broke off their relationship ten months before I saw her.

Susan was impressed with REBT because she had read an early edition of my book with Robert A. Harper, *A Guide To Rational Living*, and for the first time in her life started to unconditionally accept herself in spite of her foolish obsessive-compulsive behavior. During our first five sessions, Susan worked hard at finding and disputing her main irrational *Beliefs*, especially: (1) "I *absolutely must* be loved by a bright and attractive man, or else I am worthless!" (2) "If I treat my lover well and he treats me badly, as he *absolutely must* not do, he is a rotten person!" (3) "Conditions in New York are so bad that a really good partner is almost impossible to find. Such atrocious conditions *absolutely must not* exist and I *can't stand it* when they do!"

By actively disputing these irrational, self-defeating *Beliefs*, Susan made some progress and felt less self-damning, less enraged, and less self-pitying. But even by using a number of REBT's cognitive, emotive, and behavioral methods, she only *mildly* accepted herself, her delinquent lovers, and the world. She still *more strongly* felt that all three of these people and things definitely *had to be* better than they were.

Using some of REBT's forceful emotive methods helped Susan most of all. For example, she used Rational Emotive Imagery to vividly imagine being rejected and alone, to let herself get solidly in touch with her unhealthy feelings of severe depression, and to work at changing them to the healthy negative feelings of keen disappointment and sorrow. She very strongly kept repeating rational coping statements to herself, such as, "I can stop thinking about Steven! There is *no reason* why I *must* obsess about him and avoid getting involved with someone else!" She reverse role-played with me, in the course of which I took some of her irrational ideas, deliberately held on to them very strongly and rigidly, and gave her practice in forcefully arguing me out of them.

All this worked—*lightly*. For a week or two, Susan would feel much better: less depressed and less obsessed with thoughts about Steven. Then her obsession would return. She would blame herself both for not being more patient with him and for not leaving him sooner. She would tell herself, "I knew he was an alcoholic and I never should have lived with him." But then again: "I *should have* insisted he go to AA meetings—and even should have gone with him for at least ninety days." Blame, blame, blame—and back to her obsessing. Temporarily, her strong and persistent REBT methods would work. But then she would convince herself that she *absolutely should have* got Steven to change, that she hadn't done that, and that she was therefore a *weak, stupid person*. No go. Her use of REBT then fell off.

During my ninth session with Susan, I suddenly realized that I was not following REBT too closely myself, but was downplaying one of its main aspects. REBT holds that people like Susan keep *insisting*—not merely strongly *wishing*—that they, others, and world conditions must, must, must improve, that it is *awful* when they don't, and that they and their intimates are therefore no damned good. A great many studies have now shown that disturbed people actually do have several irrational, imperative *Beliefs* and that, when they are helped by REBT and by other forms of Cognitive Behavior Therapy (CBT), they often significantly improve (Hollon and Beck 1994, Lyons and Woods 1991).

Fine. But REBT holds that many disturbed people such as Susan also have irrational demands about their upsetness. They insist, "I *must not* be disturbed! It's *awful* to be neurotic! *I'm no good* for upsetting myself!" Then they make themselves depressed about their depression, obsessed about their obsessions. They thus create a secondary disturbance that is even worse than their primary disturbance—and, moreover, one that often pre-occupies them so much that if effectively stops them from dealing with and eliminating their primary symptoms.

In Susan's case, she clearly blamed herself for her primary behavior—her getting attached to wrong men, her being impatient with them, her not insisting that they take care of their serious problems, etc. So I rightly fig-ured out with her that her main symptom was self-denigration and that, pre-sumably, if she stopped seriously putting herself down she would distinctly improve. She agreed with this, and we kept working with REBT to help her overcome her abysmal self-downing.

During her ninth session, Susan indicated that she was most upset because she wasn't using REBT well enough to stave off and continue to overcome her self-flagellation. She still hated herself for her "stupid" behavior with Steven; but she seemed more concerned with her "idiotic" failure to use REBT, "which is such a fine form of therapy," to overcome her original "stupidity."

I then saw that Susan really had two main secondary symptoms: (1) She severely put herself down for being depressed and obsessed about her attachment to Steven—as well as for acting weakly with him. (2) She clearly berated herself for not using REBT effectively.

Led by Susan herself, and by her insistence that she now was more upset about her symptoms and about not overcoming them than she was about her original weaknesses with Steven, I jointly planned with her an attack on her secondary symptoms—and, then, we agreed, we would also get back to her original problems of acting too weakly with Steven.

At this same ninth session, Susan indicated that she had taken a teaching job in Europe and would only be available for a few more sessions in New York. Could we therefore do something to help her work better on her problems before she left? I at first thought of continuing our sessions on the phone—which I do in a number of cases and which I find usually works very well. But the phone rates to Europe, especially in those days, would have been very expensive. So I thought about recording some sessions with Susan—which I also encourage many of my clients to do—and giving her the recordings to take with her when she went abroad.

Susan herself then suggested that perhaps we could speed up things by using hypnosis. So I immediately agreed that, yes, we might try that, and might combine REBT with hypnosis and also with recording.

We quickly arranged to do this. I had Susan bring in a cassette tape, and we recorded three hypnotic sessions. During each of these sessions I put her into a light state of trance, using Edmund Jacobson's progressive relaxation technique for ten minutes. I then told her that posthypnotically she would use REBT in three main ways: First, she would clearly see that she was telling herself, "I *absolutely must* work harder with REBT to overcome my depression and my obsession for Steven! If I don't succeed, as I absolutely *must*, I am an ineffective, *inadequate person*!" Second, Susan was to get in touch with her depression about being depressed and obsessed, and would see that she was telling herself, "I *must not* be obsessed! I *must not* be depressed! It's awful to be afflicted in these ways! I'm a *stupid person* for indulging in my depression and obsession!" Third, she was to get back to her original symptoms, and see that she was strongly convincing herself, "I *must* succeed in getting Steven to really love me! I can't bear losing him! I need him, need him, need him, and must do anything to get him back! I can't be happy *at all* without him!"

As she saw her irrational musts, demands, and insistences about ineffectually using REBT, about making herself depressed and obsessed, and about *needing* Steven and not succeeding in getting him to truly love her, Susan was to do the homework I firmly told her to do during the hypnotic sessions: strongly dispute and challenge her Irrational *Beliefs*; act against them by forcing herself to cut off all contact with Steven; use several other regular REBT cognitive, emotive, and behavioral methods to give up her depression and obsession; and stop deprecating herself for being disturbed and for not using REBT methods effectively enough.

My three hypnotic sessions worked very well with Susan, because she listened to the tape recordings of the sessions at least once a day for the next few weeks that she was in New York. She found that she kept going deeper and deeper into a trance state as she listened to the tapes; and she reported that the posthypnotic instructions to dispute her Irrational *Beliefs* and use other REBT methods became easier and easier to carry out. Some of her original resistance to doing this vanished, and she was able to use disputational methods more forcefully and effectively. She continued to use the three tapes that we made when she was teaching in Europe and wrote me to say that they kept working. At first she used them every day, but after a few months did so only occasionally. She also discovered that the first of the hypnotic recorded sessions was sufficient in itself and that the subsequent ones were repetitious and unnecessary.

During the time I was working with Susan, I also used REBT to thoroughly overcome my own guilt about not seeing more quickly that her main problem was not castigating herself severely when she did not achieve a permanent relationship with Steven. In addition to this, and often more importantly, her secondary symptoms of severely blaming herself for making herself disturbed and for not using REBT effectively to overcome her disturbances created more emotional havoc for her. I honestly admitted to myself—as well as to Susan—that I had not used REBT with her as carefully and thoroughly as I could have used it. But I worked on criticizing only my careless behavior, and not my self or personhood for doing this behavior. So I remained healthily sorry and disappointed with my performance but not damning of my self or being.

As a result of working with Susan, of inventing my new technique of using hypnosis with some of my more difficult clients, and of giving them the tapes of only one or two recorded sessions, I have continued to use this method over the years. I usually first have several sessions of regular REBT with my clients, and work on both their primary and secondary problems during these sessions, to show them how to use several cognitive, emotive, and behavioral REBT methods. Usually this suffices and they get going on their way to significant improvement. When unusual resistance occurs, and especially when they are quite willing to undergo hypnosis, I use the method just described, and often find that it works well to overcome their resistances, to help them use REBT disputing of irrational beliefs and other methods more forcefully, and to persist at therapy largely on their own by listening repetitively to the tape or tapes that I have made for them.

What were my important feelings as this case progressed? They covered quite a range!

First, I liked working with Susan from the beginning, because she favored Rational Emotive Behavior Therapy, knew something about it from reading my book, *A Guide to Rational Living*, and made some real progress during the first few weeks of therapy. I concluded that she was not a difficult customer, and was optimistic about her improving in spite of her long history of depressing herself and her obsessive-compulsive behaving.

Soon, however, I felt somewhat discouraged because she only cavalierly followed the main REBT procedures, only lightly and temporarily gave up her abysmal self-denigration, and sank back to doing little therapeutic homework. I became almost impatient with her insistence that she really *was* doing badly with her obsessiveness and therefore *couldn't* realistically stop blaming herself for this. I forgave her for having some degree of obsessive-compulsive disorder, because even in the 1970s I was beginning to see that it included some biological tendencies. But I insisted that even if she were responsible for some of her stupid behaviors, she never had to damn herself for *any* failings and could still give herself unconditional self-acceptance. I felt irritated when I worked so hard to get this philosophy over to her and when she stubbornly refused to buy it. Her insistence that REBT was not working was "catching" and was almost hypnotically convincing me that it might never work for her.

During our ninth session, when I began to see clearly that Susan was excoriating herself more for her depressing and other symptoms and for not surrendering them than she was for her weak and foolish behavior with Steven and other men, I came close to feeling quite upset. I felt disappointed and guilty about my partial misdiagnosis of Susan's main problems and had to strongly use REBT disputing on myself. As noted above, I finally convinced myself that *I* was okay, though some of my therapy was not. REBT really worked for me!

When Susan and I, spurred by her approaching venture to Europe, decided to try some hypnotic sessions, I was happy that I was sufficiently trained and practiced in hypnotic methods to experiment with them. I also was very curious to see if my unusual use of recording our hypnotic sessions would really work out. So I welcomed this experiment. I also was happy when I learned from Susan that the recorded hypnotic sessions were quite effective, and that using only a few of them seemed to suffice to produce good results.

Over all, I had my own ups and downs in the course of this case, but I was grateful that I learned a lot from it and obtained some evidence that hypnosis can be combined effectively with REBT, especially in some cases where clients at first fail to use regular REBT methods successfully. The additional forceful and highly emotive quality that recorded hypnosis adds to therapy has some real advantages. In Susan's case, her being able to take me with her on tape, and feel that I was still on her side, may possibly have helped her do the work that I was trying to encourage her to do. Hypnosis has a relationship and an emotional quality that can serve as one of the emotive-evocative techniques that are commonly used in REBT, and that makes it a multimodal form of therapy.

SPECIFIC TECHNIQUE OF USING HYPNOSIS WITH REBT WITH A CLIENT WHO PANICKED ABOUT HER PANICKING

I first have a least one session, and frequently several sessions, of regular REBT with my clients and ask them to go over with me one or two major problems that they want to deal with during our hypnotic session. They usually pick a problem such as social anxiety, depression over loss of a loved person, or overeating. I tell each of them to bring a blank cassette for recording our session.

At the beginning of the hypnotic session, I review the main problem we are going to work on. I tell them to lie down comfortably on a sofa in my office, with their shoes off, and with their hands and arms at their sides. They are not to say anything to me during the session, but to listen carefully to everything I say. Then I put their blank cassette into one of my recorders and begin to record the session. For the first eight or ten minutes of the session, I try to put them into a light trance state by using Jacobson's (1938) progressive relaxation technique and getting them to go deeper and deeper into a state of hypnotic relaxation. Almost all of them report that they become exceptionally relaxed, but few of them become deeply hypnotized.

After ten minutes, at most, of deep relaxation, I spend the next ten minutes telling them how to use REBT posthypnotically to work on their problem. Thus, if a man has social anxiety and is afraid to approach women at a dance or party, I will instruct him under hypnosis: (a) "Look for the Irrational *Beliefs* you are holding when you fail to approach a woman and keep looking until you find them." (b) "Particularly discover your dogmatic *shoulds* and *musts*, such as 'I *have* to succeed with her and I'm an *inadequate* person when I don't!" (c) "Vigorously dispute your grandiose demands. Keep challenging them with questions such as 'Why do I *have* to succeed? How do I become a totally *inadequate person* if I don't?'" (d) "Tell yourself, many times, very strong rational coping statements such as, 'It's uncomfortable to get rejected, but it's not *awful*! I don't like it but I definitely *can* stand it!'" (e) "Use Rational Emotive Imagery by imagining the worst thing that can happen to you, such as being rejected several times at a dance or party, let yourself feel very upset about this, such as feeling very anxious or depressed, and then work on your feelings to make yourself feel *only* appropriately sorry and disappointed but *not* anxious or depressed." (f) "Practice this same Rational Emotive Imagery every day for twenty or thirty days in a row, until you automatically begin to feel healthily disappointed instead of unhealthily depressed about rejection." (g) "Make sure that at least a few times every week you do in vivo desensitization by risking getting rejected by suitable women you talk to." (h) "Begin to see that just about all your neurotic problems stem from your rigid *shoulds* and *musts* and that you can always choose to change these to *desires* and *preferences*."

After ten minutes of REBT instructions for posthypnotic use, I end the hypnotic session by telling the clients that they will have had no bad effects after the session and will have a subsequent good, happy day. I then give them the cassette to take home with them, with instructions to listen to it at least once a day for the next thirty to sixty days. I also see them for (usually a few) subsequent sessions to see whether they are listening to the tape, whether they are following its instructions, and what good or bad results they are getting. If they are doing well with the problem addressed on the hypnotic tape, we may have other sessions dealing mainly with their other problems, and especially with their self-denigration, which is usually their greatest neurotic hangup. We may also return to regular REBT, with occasional reliance on special hypnotic sessions.

I have not done any detailed follow-up studies with the clients with whom I use REBT hypnotherapy, but, on the basis of their informal reports I estimate that about 15 percent of them get unusually good results and 50 percent get fairly good results compared with nonhypnotic REBT. About 5 percent get little or poor results, and about 30 percent get the same kind of results they get with regular REBT. All told, the use of this method produces favorable findings, but this may be because I generally use it with clients who ask for it, who are prejudiced in favor of it, and who may therefore do their REBT homework more consistently and forcefully because they favor hypnosis.

Because it would require too much space to include a transcript of a complete session of REBT hypnotherapy in this chapter, I provide excerpts from a case that I have published in full elsewhere (Ellis 1986). The client was a thirty-three-year-old unmarried woman with severe personality disorder, who had been in therapy since the age of thirteen for severe anxiety about her school, work, and love and sex performance: she was especially anxious about her anxiety and was afraid that it would make her go crazy and wind up in a mental hospital. Although she was attractive and did well as a sales manager, she was terrified about becoming homeless without any friends, lovers, or money.

After thirteen sessions of REBT, the client was using REBT to notably decrease her terrors of failing, but she would tend to fall back (as individuals with severe borderline disorder often do) to feeling panicked again, and especially to feeling panicking about her panic. Hearing that one of her friends stopped smoking by using hypnotherapy, she asked me if I would use it with her, and I agreed to do so and had a single hypnotic session with her.

As usual, I spent the first ten minutes of our session putting her into a light hypnotic trance using Jacobson's (1938) progressive relaxation procedure. As the following verbatim transcript shows, I then continued as follows:

You're only focusing on my voice and you're going to listen carefully to what I'm telling you. You're going to remember everything I tell you. And after you wake from this relaxed, hypnotic state, you're going to feel very good. Because you're going to remember everything and use what you hear—use it for you. Use it to put away all your anxiety and all your anxiety *about* your anxiety. You're going to remember what I tell you and use it every day. Whenever you feel anxious about anything, you're going to remember what I'm telling you now, in this relaxed state, and you're going to fully focus on it, concentrate on it very well, and do exactly what we're talking about—relax and get rid of your anxiety, relax and get rid of your anxiety.

Whenever you get anxious about anything, you're going to realize that the reason you're anxious is because you are saying to yourself, telling yourself, "I *must* succeed! I *must* succeed! I *must* do this, or I *must* do that!" You will clearly see and fully accept that your anxiety comes from your self-statements. It doesn't come from without. It doesn't come from other people. *You* make yourself anxious, by demanding that something *must* go well or *must* not exist. It's *your* demand that makes you anxious. It's always you and your self-talk; and therefore *you* control it and *you* can change it.

You're going to realize, "I make myself anxious. I don't *have* to keep making myself anxious. If I give up my demands, my musts, my shoulds, my oughts. If I really accept what is, accept things the way they are, then I won't be anxious. I can always make myself unanxious and less tense by giving up my musts, by relaxing—by wanting and wishing for things, but not *needing*, not *insisting*, not *demanding*, not *must*urbating about them."

You're going to keep telling yourself, "I can *ask* for things, I can *wish*. But I do not *need* what I want. I never *need* what I want! There is nothing I *must* have; and there is nothing I *must* avoid, including my anxiety. I'd *like* to get rid of this anxiety. I *can* get rid of it. I'm *going* to get rid of it. But if I tell myself, 'I *must* not be anxious! I *must* not be anxious,' then I'll be anxious.

Nothing will kill me. Anxiety won't kill me. Lack of sex won't kill me. There are lots of unpleasant things in the world that I don't like, but I can *stand* them. I don't *have* to get rid of them. If I'm anxious, I'm anxious—too damn bad! Because *I* control my emotional destiny—as long as I don't feel that I *have* to do anything, that I *have* to succeed at anything. That's what destroys me—the idea that I *have* to be sexy or I have to succeed at sex. Or that I *have* to get rid of my anxiety."

In your regular life, after listening to this tape regularly, you're gong to think and to keep thinking these things. Whenever you're anxious, you'll look at what you're doing to *make* yourself anxious, and you'll give up your demands and your musts. You'll dispute your ideas that "I *must* do well! I *must* get people to like me! They *must* not criticize me!" You'll keep asking yourself, "Why *must* I do well? Why do I *have* to be a great sex partner? It would be nice if people liked me, but they don't *have* to. I do not *need* their approval. If they criticize me, if they blame me, or they think I'm too sexy or too little sexy, too damn bad! I do not *need* their approval! I'd *like* it, but I don't *need* it. I'd also *like* to be unanxious but there's no reason why

I *must* be. Yes, there's no reason why I *must* be. It's only *preferable*. None of these things I fail at are going to kill me!

"And when I die, as I eventually will, so I die! Death is not horrible. It's a state of *no* feeling. It's exactly the same state as before I was conceived. I won't feel *anything*. So I certainly need not be afraid of that!

"And even if I get very anxious and go crazy, that too isn't terrible. If I tell myself, 'I *must* not go crazy! I *must* not go crazy!' then I'll make myself crazy! But even if I'm crazy, so I'm crazy! I can *live* with it even if I'm in a mental hospital. I can *live* and not depress myself about it. *Nothing* is terrible— even when people don't like me, even when I'm acting stupidly, even when I'm very anxious! *Nothing* is terrible! I *can* stand it! It's only a pain in the ass!"

Now that is what you're going to think about in your everyday life. Whenever you get anxious about anything, you're going to see what you're anxious about, you're going to realize that you are demanding something, saying, "It *must* be so! I *must* get well! I *must* not do the wrong thing: I *must* not be anxious!" And then you're going to stop and say, "You know— I *don't* need that nonsense. If these things happen, they happen. It's not the end of the world! I'd *like* to be unanxious. I'd *like* to get along with people. I'd *like* to have good sex. But if I don't, I don't! Tough! It's not the end of everything. I can always be a happy human *in spite of* failures and hassles. If I don't *demand*, if I don't insist, if I don't say, 'I must, I must! Musts are crazy. My *desires* are all right. But, again, I don't *need* what I *want*!"

Now this is what you're going to keep working at in your everyday life. You're going to keep using your head, your thinking ability, to focus, to concentrate on ridding yourself of your anxiety—just as you're listening and concentrating right now. Your concentration will get better and better. You're going to be more and more in control of your thoughts and your feelings. You will keep realizing that *you* create your anxiety, *you* make yourself upset, and *you* don't have to, you never have to keep doing so. You can always give your anxiety up. You can always change. You can always relax, and relax, and relax, and not take *anyone*, not take *anything* too seriously.

That is what you're going to remember and work at when you get out of this relaxed state. This idea is what you're going to take with you all day, every day: "*I* control me. I don't *have* to upset myself about anything. If I do upset myself, too bad. I may feel upset for a while but it won't ruin my life or kill me. And I can be anxious without putting myself down, without saying, 'I must not be anxious!' At times I will make myself anxious, but I can give up my anxiety if I don't *demand* that I be unanxious."

And you're going to get better and better about thinking this rational way. You'll become more in control of you. Never *totally* in control, because nobody ever is totally unanxious. But you'll make yourself much less anxious and able to live with it when you are anxious. And if you live with it, it will go away. If you live with it, it will go away. Nothing is terrible, not even anxiety. That's what you're going to realize and to keep thinking about until you really, really believe it.

Now you feel nice and free and warm and fully relaxed. In a few minutes I'm going to tell you to come out of this relaxed, hypnotic state. You will then have a good day. You will feel fine when you come out of this state. You will experience no ill effects of hypnosis. You will remember everything I have said to you and will keep working at using it. And you will play this tape every day for the next thirty days. You will listen to it every day until you really believe it and follow it. Eventually you will be able to follow its directions and to think your way out of anxiety and out of anxiety *about* being anxious without the tape.

You will then be able to release yourself from anxiety by yourself. You can always relax and use the antianxiety technique you will learn by listening to the tape. You can always accept yourself with your anxiety and can stop telling yourself, "I must not be anxious! I must not be anxious!" Just tell yourself, "I don't *like* my anxiety. I'll work to give it up. I'll conquer it. I'll control myself, control my own emotional destiny. I can always relax, make myself feel easy and free and nice, just as I feel now, get away from cares for a while and then feel unanxious. But I can more elegantly accept myself first with my anxiety, stop fighting it desperately, and stop telling myself it's awful to be anxious. Then I can go back to the original anxiety and get rid of it by refusing to awfulize about failing and by vigorously disputing my irrational beliefs, 'I must do well! I must not be disapproved.'"

Now you feel good, you feel relaxed, and in a couple of minutes I'm going to count to three, and when I count to three you will awake and feel quite alive, have a good day, and experience no bad effects, no headaches, no physical discomfort! Everything is going to be fine and you'll have a good day. You will remember all this and, as I said, you will listen to this tape whenever you possibly can, at least once a day. And you will think and act more and more on its message. You'll be able to control yourself and reduce your anxiety appreciably. And when you do feel anxious you'll live with the anxiety, accept it, and refuse to panic yourself about it. All right. I'm going to count to three and when I say three you'll wake and be fully alive and alert and feel great for the rest of the day. One, two, three!

This client replayed the recording of her hypnotic REBT session at least once a day for forty-five days and said that her anxiety, and especially her anxiety about her anxiety, had significantly decreased. She was no longer phrenophobic, mainly because she convinced herself that she probably would never go to a mental hospital but that if she did it would be extremely inconvenient but not horrible. She also worked on her fears of sex and other failures, conquered them for a while, and then they partially reappeared and she was able to cope with them.

I saw her for regular, nonhypnotic REBT sessions for fourteen months more but had only eighteen thirty-minute sessions with her during that period. I see her occasionally now, not as a client but as a participant in my regular Friday night workshops at the Albert Ellis Institute in New York, where I do public demonstrations of REBT with volunteer participants. She has largely maintained her nonanxious demeanor, with a few setbacks when a crisis occurs in her life, and is now happily married and highly productive. Once in a while, she still listens to the original hypnotic tape and feels that it is helpful and that it was instrumental in her making greater progress than she had previously made with REBT.

SELF-HELP SUGGESTIONS

- Hypnosis combined with REBT can be effective for many people, but you can also use REBT *without* aid from a hypnotist and realize that it is your own self-suggestion that actually works to help you change emotionally and behaviorally.
- If you really convince yourself, with or without help from hypnosis, and you work hard at changing your thinking, feeling, and behaving, you *can* change—and control the change process *yourself.*
- You can make your own self-hypnosis tapes and on them tell yourself that you *can* change your thinking, feeling, and behaving and that you *can* assign yourself REBT homework designed to effect these changes. Your self-hypnotic tape may be just as effective as a hypnotic therapist making one for you. Listen to your own tape or that of a therapist at least once a day for several weeks to remind you to carry out your REBT homework.
- With the repeated use of your own tape or the hypnotist's tape, you will internalize the general REBT corrective and self-actualizing philosophy into your head and heart and be ready to apply it to your emotional and behavioral problems.
- If you use hypnosis or self-hypnosis to apply REBT, remember that there is no magic in doing so. Your *work and practice* to change yourself and keep changing is what *really* helps you do so.
- Hypnosis or self-hypnosis combined with regular REBT may add a strong emotional quality to helping you to forcefully work on changing your dysfunctional thinking, feeling, and behaving. If it thereby strengthens your use of regular REBT methods, by all means use it!

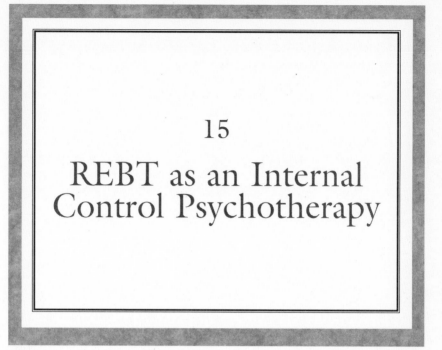

15

REBT as an Internal Control Psychotherapy

Since I am giving this paper at the First National Conference on Internal Control Psychology, I shall mainly discuss the theory and practice of Rational Emotive Behavior Therapy (REBT) and its relationship to internal control. I originated REBT in January 1955, after I had practiced different kinds of external control therapies for several years, particularly psychoanalysis, which largely holds that people who feel and act disturbedly are crucially influenced by the childhood teachings of and experiences in their family. Once they are in the tight control of these powerful conditioners, they have a most difficult time of thinking and choosing their own ways and require several years of intensive analysis to stop entrapping themselves in the past and to give up on external controlling (Freud 1965).

I was also persuaded, in my first decade as a therapist, by the strict behavioral theories of Ivan Pavlov and John B. Watson, which were somewhat similar to the psychoanalysts in that they believed that what we usually call emotional dysfunctioning results from early behavioral conditioning. That is, people's dysfunctional responding gets attached to influential

This chapter is partly adapted from "Rational Emotive Behavior Therapy as an Internal Control Psychology," *International Journal of Reality Therapy* 19 (1999): 4–11, and *Journal of Rational-Emotive and Cognitive-Behavior Therapy* 18 (2000): 19–38. Used with permission.

stimuli; and once their stimulus-responses become persistently conditioned, they control the individual. They supposedly then can extinguish or recondition them, especially with external manipulating by a behavior therapist.

I was never an orthodox psychoanalyst or behaviorist, so my therapy was always heavily eclectic and experimental. When I practiced psychoanalysis, I soon saw the futility of obsessing about the gory details of my clients' past lives. I discovered that, whatever happened to them in their childhood, it was their *present* thoughts, feelings, and actions with which they maintained their self-disturbing. I especially saw this when I became a pioneering marriage and family therapist and well-known sex therapist. I realized that my clients had better clearly understand and change how they *currently* were dysfunctionally thinking and behaving, instead of obsessively ruminating about their past histories.

Internal Control Theory, as used in REBT, does not mean that people only choose to indulge in disturbing themselves by their *Beliefs*. As I noted in my first paper on REBT in 1956 (Ellis 1958), people do not experience thoughts, feelings, and behaviors purely or disparately. Instead, their cognizing importantly influences their feeling and behaving, their feeling influences their thinking and behaving, and their behaving influences their thinking and feeling. Human living processes are enormously interacting and cybernetically oriented. Nonetheless, external control theory says that things and events largely control people's behaving. REBT and internal control theory say instead that their *Beliefs* also are largely influenced by what they feel and do, and often more directly and thoroughly than by outside events. More importantly, people rarely change their emoting and acting without first changing their *Beliefs*, and by changing them they can significantly change how they feel and act. They can usually do so more effectively than if they try to change how they feel and act *without* restructuring their *Beliefs*. Indeed, sometimes major revising of their *Beliefs* is the only way to change their unhealthy emoting and behaving.

This means that cognitive changes are very important in therapy, and therefore are stressed in REBT. Practitioners of REBT emphasize D—Disputing of Irrational *Beliefs* which importantly (though not exclusively) lead to human dysfunctioning. People, REBT holds, importantly create their disturbing emotions and actions by unconsciously and consciously elevating their Rational *Beliefs* (RBs)—which consist of *preferences* for success, approval, and pleasure—into Irrational *Beliefs* (IBs)—which mainly consist of absolutistically demanding and insisting that these preferences must be fulfilled (Ellis 1962, 1994).

In other words, REBT theorizes that when people merely *desire* that their basic goals and values be fulfilled, they healthily strive for this fulfillment and rarely bring on serious trouble for themselves and others. Their *preferences*, however strong, include an explicit or implicit *but*, and this *but* leads them to healthy or useful feelings of sorrowing, regretting, and frustrating when they do not fulfill them. Preferring rarely leads to unhealthy feeling and behaving such as depressing, obsessively worrying, or angering when people's desires are seriously thwarted.

For example: "I greatly *prefer* to win your approval and have your sincere friendship or love. *But* I don't have to fulfill my preferring. Therefore if you ignore or dislike me, I will feel sorrowing and disappointing. I will not destroy or devastate myself, because I may not *now* fulfill my preferring. *But* I will be open to *later* win your approval and/or be approved by significant others and/or to please myself in various other ways even if I am never approved by you and/or others. Because I *prefer* but do not *absolutely need* your approval, I can choose many other ways to fulfill many of my basic desires."

With this kind of *preferential* or *choice* thinking and desiring, people will rarely disturb themselves when their goal-seekings, because of their own shortcomings or because of external Adversities, are thwarted. However, when they raise their preferring to absolutistically demanding and musting—resort, in REBT terms, to musturbating—they almost always create a radically different set of feeling or acting Consequences. For example: "I strongly believe and feel that I *absolutely* must win your approval and/or love and I *have to* fulfill my desiring. Therefore, if you ignore or dislike me, I will panic, depress, or enrage myself. I will conclude that I will *never* gain your approving, will *always* have disapproving by significant others, and will not be able to experience any real enjoying as I go through life. All my days will be *awful* and *terrible*, and I *can't stand* living under those conditions. Because I have failed to win your approving as I *absolutely must*, that proves that I am an *inadequate, worthless person* who is incapable of fulfilling any of my basic desiring."

REBT, again, is a complicated and comprehensive theory and practice of human disturbing and of how people can deal with it therapeutically. As shown in the last two paragraphs, it is clearly an *internal choice* therapy. It says that when thwartings and blockings occur to interfere with people's achieving their desiring, they usually have a clear-cut *choice* of rationally and functionally *preferring* that they not be thwarted and that they achieve some reasonable fulfilling of their desiring. Or they have a choice of irrationally and dysfunctionally demanding and commanding that their *desiring* absolutely must be achieved. If they distinctly select rational *preferring* rather than irrational *demanding*, they will most likely experience healthy negative emoting, such as sorrowing and regretting, instead of unhealthy negative emoting, such as panicking, depressing, and raging. Because people are born and reared with constructive and creative tendencies to think, feel, and act, as well as unconstructive and self-defeating ones, they almost always have a *choice* of using several thinking, feeling, and behaving methods of changing their ineffective feelings and actings to much more effective living.

REBT, as noted, teaches people many thinking, feeling, and acting ways of making themselves less self-disturbing and more enjoying. Among these ways, it especially reveals to people how they both consciously and unconsciously raise their healthy purposing and preferring to unhealthy insisting and demanding, and how they can actively Dispute their self-destructive and relationship-destructive dogmatic insisting and turn it back to effective preferring. REBT particularly educates people to use empirical, logical, and practical forms of Disputing which help them to surrender their arrogant necessitizing.

At the same time, self-disturbing people had better use several of REBT's emotive and activity-oriented methods to arrive at healthy, self-helping and relationship-helping behaving. Their rational thinking is central to their making themselves emotionally and behaviorally healthy. But their feeling and their acting are also integrated with—and are an essential part of—that thinking. So REBT tries to help people think rationally in order to feel and act well; but it also teaches them how to feel and behave efficiently in order to think well. All three pathways are useful and indispensable. All three can be *chosen* by people to promote healthy living.

To show how REBT is a theory of choice and of internal control, let me compare it to the Choice Theory of William Glasser, as he describes it in his book of the same name (Glasser 1998). As noted above, REBT was the first of the major Cognitive Behavior Therapies (CBTs). It preceded the Reality Therapy of Glasser (1965) by ten years, the Cognitive Therapy of Beck (1967) by twelve years, Cognitive Behavior Modification of Meichenbaum (1977) by fourteen years, and the Constructivist Cognitive Behavior therapy of Mahoney (1974) by nineteen years. Actually, George Kelly (1955) had a pioneering constructivist-cognitive theory of therapy, but he used only one behavioral method—fixed role playing—and almost no cognitive methods in his therapy. In fact, he somewhat downplayed the Disputing of Irrational *Beliefs* which is importantly used in REBT and also taken over by most of the other Cognitive Behavior Therapies.

Although Glasser's Choice Theory seems to do much less Disputing of Irrational *Beliefs* than most of the other CBT Systems, I have always felt that it and his Reality Therapy (RT) are somewhat closer to REBT than are most of the other CBTs. This is because Reality Therapy and Choice Theory emphasize teaching and education; they are active-directive; they focus on changing behavior as well as cognitions; they are constructivist; and they particularly, of course, emphasize people's choice of letting external happenings crucially affect them or selecting, instead, to deal with their internal control abilities and thus take more charge of their living.

To see more precisely how REBT is an internal control psychology, it may be instructive to compare some of its main aspects to those of the ten axioms of Choice Theory as described by Glasser (1998).

William Glasser: "The only person whose behavior we can control is our own" (p. 332).

REBT position: Yes, we cannot help *influencing* people, since human nature makes us quite influenceable by things and individuals in our environment (Ellis and Crawford 2000). Sometimes, when we are their parents, intimates, peers, or teachers, people let us profoundly influence them. But in the final analysis they *choose* to take, to reject, to cooperate with, or fight against our influence. Glasser and REBT give several techniques, such as listening closely to people, which may help us influence them more than other techniques, such as ignoring and contradicting them. But even when we go to extremes and coerce and imprison people, they basically react to our coercion in individualistic, personal ways. Moreover, they largely react to what they tell themselves—what they *Believe* (B) about our restricting them (A). They do not *simply* react to what we coercively do to them.

William Glasser: "All we can give or get from other people is information. How we deal with that information is our or their choice" (p. 333).

REBT position: Yes, if under the heading of *information* we include other people's acting. Their acting, like their verbalizing, tells us how they think, feel, and behave toward us. How we react to their thinking, feeling, and behaving is to a large extent our own choice. Even if people tie us up and beat us, our body has limited reactions (e.g., restraint or movement and pain of the beatings). But our thinking and our feeling about their coercion are idiosyncratic to us.

William Glasser: "All long-lasting psychological problems are relationship problems. The cause of [our] misery is always our way of dealing with an important relationship that is not working out the way we want it to" (pp. 333–34).

REBT position: No, not exactly—unless we include under relationship problems our relationships to (1) ourselves, (2) others, and (3) the world. We certainly can depress ourselves when important relationships are not working out well—and most of our depressing is probably over relationship lacks. But we can also depress ourselves when we insist that we *absolutely must* get what we want at work, at sports, and at pleasures. These wants may sometimes involve other people relatively little. Whenever we *insist* that our desiring *must* be fulfilled by ourselves, by others, or by life experiences we will tend to make ourselves miserable when we are deprived. This especially goes for our relationships with others, but it also comes from our *needing*, rather than merely *wanting*, success, power, money, athletic prowess, beauty, and innumerable other goals. Achieving these things we prefer usually involves some degree of relating to others but sometimes not. For example: running five miles a day or dieting successfully may not involve relating to others. However, *most* lasting psychological problems, as Glasser states, involve relationship problems.

William Glasser: "There is no sense wasting time looking for all aspects of our lives for why we are choosing misery. . . . The problem is always part of our present lives" (p. 334).

REBT position: Quite so! We originally chose to upset ourselves for various reasons in the past, such as maltreatment by our parents and our peers. We demanded that these Adversities absolutely must not exist and we awfulized about them. But if we are miserabilizing about these or similar things today, we are still carrying on our demandingness and awfulizing in the present. Thus, we are still *insisting* that our parents, peers, or others *absolutely* must not have unfavorably acted or must now act favorably to us. Our*present* irrational philosophizing therefore upsets us today. We may have *started* to think that way many years ago but we still *continue* to do so currently. So let us deal largely with our present thinking, feeling, and acting, and let us *currently* change them and also modify them *for the future* if we are to stop disturbing ourselves. This rarely involves a detailed consideration of our past, though doing so may sometimes help us to change our present ways. Glasser and REBT mainly agree about the uselessness of historical probing and analyzing—as is obsessively done in psychoanalysis.

William Glasser: "We are driven by five genetic needs: survival, love and belonging . . . power, freedom, and fun" (p. 335).

REBT position: We have strong innate and learned *desires* or *preferences* for survival, love and belonging, power, freedom, and fun. But when we self-defeatingly insist, demand, and command that we *absolutely must* survive, *must* be loved by others, *must* have power over people, *must* be free, and *must* have fun, then we choose to make our *desires* and *preferences* into dire *necessities* and thereby defeat ourselves.

This, alas, seems to be the human condition—for us to take a perfectly natural desire, such as the desire that we live and get along with significant other people, and then we frequently—not, of course, always—turn this into a *dire need* for their approval.

Obviously, our demand for others' approval is not really a necessity, since if we are not approved by someone—say, a parent or mate—whose love we greatly want, and even if we are hated by them, we rarely will die (though we may neurotically kill ourselves). So being loved and approved is hardly a *necessity* for survival. Many people who are little cared for are consequently very sorrowing and wanting, but they still manage to enjoy other things (such as work, art, or science).

When, however, we *think* that love is a necessity and that we *absolutely* need it to be a worthy and happy person, we frequently fail to get it sufficiently (partly because we are too needy to be lovable) and we make ourselves exceptionally panicking and depressing. But it is our *Beliefs* about love that we choose to depress ourselves *about*—not the mere *fact* that we lack it. So, also, *choosing* to raise our strong *desires* for power, freedom, and fun into *dire necessitizing*, instead of greatly *wanting* these goals, often makes us *less* capable of achieving them—and emotionally destroys ourselves when we fail to do so.

This is really, it seems to me, the essence of choice theory. We consciously or unconsciously *decide* to get what we desire, such as love, power, freedom, and fun, which we are born and raised with strong tendencies to want. Then we often *exaggerate* those preferences into musts and demands, convince ourselves that we *absolutely need* approval at practically all times and under all conditions, and thereby depress ourselves when our presumed needs are not fulfilled. We take our *healthy* goals and aspirations and make them into unhealthy insistences. We thereby *create* emotional trouble for ourselves, with and for other people, and with realistic world conditions which, of course, never provide us with everything we foolishly think we *need*.

REBT agrees with Glasser and his Choice Theory that we naturally want survival, love, power, freedom, and fun—for they often add to our enjoying life and help us survive, if we get them. But Glasser often implies that we need—that is, *absolutely must have*—these goals fulfilled. He especially, from his first book, *Reality Therapy* (Glasser 1965), posits love and approval as a need rather than as a very powerful human desire. Perhaps this is mainly a semantic problem.

Perhaps Glasser uses the term *need for love* to mean the REBT term *strong desire for love*. If so, he and REBT are on a similar track. But if, by using *need for love*, he means that in order to survive and be *at all* happy, we must love others and be loved by them, then I think he exaggerates and somewhat distorts our healthy *preference* for love, cooperation, socializing, and getting along with others and makes our healthily preferring them into unhealthy necessitizing. If so, I think that he gets into serious contradiction and conflict with his own Choice Theory. He is first saying we *choose* to love and be loved, but also saying that it is a *necessary* choice for survival and personal worth. Isn't this contradictory?

William Glasser: "We can satisfy these needs [for survival, love, power, freedom, and fun] only by satisfying a picture or pictures in our quality worlds. Of all we know, what we choose to put into our quality worlds is the most important" (p. 335).

REBT position: Here again I disagree with Glasser's calling our strong *preferences* for survival, love, power, freedom, and fun *needs*. If we substitute powerful desires for his use of the word needs, however, his position seems to be close to the REBT position. I agree with him that we have weak and moderate desires—e.g., our desires to win a ping pong game—and also have strong and *powerful desires*—e.g., our urge to win the ping pong championship. Glasser seems to be saying that when we satisfy a weak set of desires we are reasonably happy; but only when we satisfy our quality desires—the goals and ideas that we hold quite strongly and consistently—are we truly happy. If we win a game, or a bet, or someone's temporary favor, we are pleased. But if we consistently win a game we enjoy or win the intense and steady approval of those we favor, then we profoundly affect our lives and can easily weather other difficulties and hassles. Our quality worlds are our main or core desires and, as Glasser says, they are most important. But, REBT holds, it is not necessary that we fulfill them. If we do *not* foolishly *define* them as imperatives, we can still be happy, though obviously not as happy, when we don't achieve them.

William Glasser: "The most freedom we ever experience is when we are able to satisfy a picture or pictures in our quality worlds. If we put pictures into our quality worlds that we cannot satisfy, we are giving up freedom" (p. 335).

REBT position: Not quite! Glasser makes an important point, but also misses some of the point. When we satisfy the goals and aspirations in our quality worlds, we are naturally happier than if we satisfy our weaker goals. But are we freer? Not necessarily. Freedom is the ability to minimally restrict ourselves and to avoid interfering with our main wishes. We feel temporarily free to go after and to try to get things we really want. But if we *need* what we want, we easily worry about not getting it, about not *completely* gaining it, and not always getting it in the future.

Satisfying our quality worlds when we think we absolutely must satisfy them is a pyrrhic victory. Much greater—and lasting—freedom comes from having pictures in our quality worlds and strongly *preferring* but not *demanding* that we fulfill them. Then we are free to desire love, power, freedom from restriction, and fun, and we are free to make ourselves only feel frustrated and disappointed when we don't fulfill our desires, but also free to *not* feel panicking, depressing, and raging. Our main freeing is to keep ourselves free from emotionally paining ourselves, instead of frequently choosing to bring pain on ourselves. We largely bring on this needless self-paining by *choosing* our quality worlds and actively working to achieve them—but at the same time not imperiously demanding that *we must* have good quality and *must not have* bad quality experiencing.

William Glasser: "All behavior is designated by verbs, usually infinitives and gerunds, and named by the component that is most recognizable. For example, I am choosing to depress or I am depressing instead of I am suffering from depression or I am depressed" (p. 335).

REBT position: Glasser is definitely on a better verbal track here—as was, before him, Alfred Korzybski. Korzybski pointed out in *Science and Sanity*, "I am depressed" is an overgeneralization, since it implies, "I am *totally* depressed" or "I am *only* depressed and have no other feelings or behaviors." But this is very rarely accurate! My whole *being*, my *totality*, and my *future* may include many feelings besides my depressing myself.

Moreover, "I *am* depressed" implies that since depressing is my *essence*, my *core*, I will *always* depress myself, now and in the future. "I *am* what I *do*," Korzybski noted, constitutes the "is of identity," which supposedly makes me *totally* and *always* what I do. Obviously this is vast overgeneralizing and constitutes unverifiable and unfalsifiable hypothesizing.

Again, if you do badly—say, depressing yourself—and you say that therefore "I am bad" or "My depressing myself makes me a *bad person*," you think and behave most negatively and pessimistically. Now, how will that pessimizing help you overcome your depressing? It won't. So REBT teaches you that you act unhealthily when you keep using the *is* of identity or otherwise overgeneralize. It helps you to think and verbalize more precisely and factually, and thereby optimistically tackles your self-disturbing. It endorses Glasser's use of language and opposes self-disturbing grammar as much as he does.

William Glasser: "People think the miserable feeling [such as depressing] is happening *to* them or is caused by what someone else does. As soon as we say, *I'm choosing to depress* or *I am depressing*, we are immediately aware it is a choice, and we have gained personal freedom. This is why designating these choices by verbs is important" (p. 336).

REBT position: A good point! Glasser is very helpful here. But he seems to miss something. Suppose you say, "I am *choosing* to anger myself at you by seeing that you keep lying to me and harming me. Therefore you absolutely *must not* lie the way you are doing and you are a louse if you do keep lying."

If you note this, you can recognize that your anger stems from your damning me as a person and not merely from my lying, my *actions*. Therefore you can choose to stop angering yourself by changing the demands you are making on me, even though I still continue to lie. You give up my external control over your anger, take internal control over it, and can reduce or eliminate it by giving up your grandiose demands that because you see my lying as wrong and harmful, I absolutely *must not* resort to it. Obviously, you cannot *make me* stop lying. But you can change your ideas and feelings about my doing so. Good!

Suppose, however, you not only believe that my lying is wrong and harmful, but you can also get most people to agree with you about this. But you also believe that lying is so harmful that there is absolutely *no excusing* it, that it absolutely *must not* exist, and that a liar like me is a *thoroughly rotten person*.

If you strongly hold these absolutistic musts and you thoroughly damn people like me who do not tell the truth as you say they *must*, you may want to get rid of your anger—because it rips up your guts and it may be against your religious or other principles—but you probably won't be able to do so. You may even *know* that you produced your own anger, may be very guilty about doing so, but still you will keep angering yourself.

Why? Because you intensely and devoutly *Believe* not only that my lying is wrong, but that I *absolutely should not and must not* behave wrongly. This damning judgement of me will almost inevitably enrage you against me. Practically any demand that I refuse to obey will incense you and obsess you —or lead to your panicking, depressing, or angering yourself.

Let me say again that if you only *wish* that I (and other people) stop lying (or doing anything else that you displease yourself about), you implicitly tell yourself, "I *wish* this happens *but* it doesn't *have to*. Too bad if it doesn't." Result: You have healthy feelings of sorrow, regret, and frustration. But if you also *demand* and *insist* that I stop lying (or doing anything else), you consciously or unconsciously give up your *but* and tell yourself, "His lying *absolutely must* stop; and if he doesn't do as he *must*, it's *awful*, I *can't stand* it, and he is a*rotten person*. No buts about it!" Result: You have self-defeating, other-defeating, and world-defeating feelings of horrorizing, depressing, and raging. Try turning any of your preferring to absolute necessitizing and see for yourself.

So Glasser sees one way—a very important way—to stop your self-upsetting. Take internal responsibility for it. Don't blame it on external people and events. Then you will most likely see that because you largely create it, you can also uncreate it. Yes, you can replace your dysfunctional feeling and behaving with much more healthy functioning. Fine!

REBT says yes, fine, but not quite good enough. First, it says, by all means accept what Glasser and REBT both emphasize: that you control your feelings and behaving. No, not completely, for you have biological and environmental limitations. But you are mainly, if you choose to be, in your own emotional saddle. As I have often said to my clients and readers, you largely control your emotional destiny.

Second, REBT says—and Glasser doesn't deny but also doesn't emphasize—the way you use your internal control is by all means sticking with your quality world—your basic and strong *desires* and *preferences*. But—here's the catch!—you had better stubbornly resist your natural, innate and learned, tendencies to make these preferences into godlike musts, demands, and commands. By all means want, powerfully want, what you want. But don't convince yourself that you utterly need what you want, whether it be love, power, freedom, or fun. These are fine, beautiful strivings. But if and when you don't achieve them—which frequently happens to all of us—you won't die, you don't have to make yourself utterly miserable and devastated, and you can still have many pleasurings and enjoyings. Providing that you *decide* that you can—yes, *choose* to be reasonably happy even when you are experiencing frustrations and restrictions.

Third, REBT says—and Glasser would appear to agree—once you (unupsettedly) select goals, interests, and desires to follow, you can actively work at pursuing them. You educate yourself about the best ways to get what you want, such as success and love, and you work at following these ways. As we say in REBT, you PYA—push your ass—to try to fulfill your desiring. You do what you'd better do to achieve practically anything—*work and practice* to get it and *work and practice* to remove obstacles to getting it. When you fail to get what you want, you then return to the three main philosophizings of REBT that lead to your strongly *preferring* instead of absolutely *needing*:

One: You acquire USA, unconditional self-accepting, and never castigate yourself when your own efforts fail to achieve your desires. You accept *yourself* while disliking your *failures*. You see yourself as a *person who failed*, never as a *Failure* with a capital F.

Two: You acquire UOA, unconditional other-accepting, and you thereby never damn others who, even unfairly and cruelly, keep you from achieving your desires. You accept *them*, as persons, while deploring their interfering, and perhaps unjust, *behaving*.

Three: You acquire high frustration tolerance, and stop whining about conditions and events when they block you from achieving your desires. When you try hard but can't change and improve thwarting circumstances, you accept the *world* while disliking its frustrating *conditions* and *events*.

To summarize: Along with Glasser, REBT *first* advises you to accept internal control and to consciously *choose* many of your emotional and behavioral reactings instead of letting other people and events control you. Once you get yourself off to that excellent start, REBT more specifically helps you to strongly *prefer* rather than decide to *absolutely need* what you want. It helps you to make yourself see that you don't have to win success and approval, don't need others to follow your rules, and do not *have* to get your desires fulfilled. Once you do this self-helping and misery-destroying philosophizing, you work like hell to get what you want and avoid what you don't want. Undisturbedly! Determinedly but unfrantically!

You then use a number of hardheaded, realistic cognizing, emoting, and behaving methods of REBT to keep working—yes, working for the rest of your life—to think, feel, and act in a more efficient and pleasure-producing manner than you innately do and have learned to often do. You keep fighting against your self-destructing and fighting for your creative and self-helping tendencies. It's quite a fight—well worth it!

William Glasser: "All total behavior is chosen, but we have direct control over only the acting and thinking components. We can, however, control our feelings and physiology indirectly through how we choose to act and think" (p. 336).

REBT position: *Usually*, but probably not *always*. Thinking, feeling, and acting are integrally and interactionally united, not disparate. By using our internal control, we usually control our feelings by willfully forcing—yes, forcing—ourselves to look at our thoughts and actions when we feel upset, and to change them. This is *easier* and *more thoroughgoing* than if we directly work on our feelings to change our self-disturbing thinking and acting. Because that's the way the human mechanism usually is designed to work: when we feel bad (say, panicking or depressing) we can *reflect* on our awfulizing thinking that accompanies our feelings (e.g., "Something *terrible* may happen and I can't handle it!") and change it to nonawfulizing thinking (e.g., "Something unfortunate may happen, but if it does I can cope with it and still live and experience happiness. Too bad!").

Or we can change our panicking and depressing activities. For example, change our running away from possible failure at a job interview to deliberately facing and risking several interviews until we see that even when we fail at them nothing "terrible" happens.

So thinking and acting *directly* can change our feelings, and probably do so more quickly, effectively, and thoroughly than working on these feelings themselves. But not necessarily, REBT says. Thus, if you panic about a job interview, you may be able to deliberately get in touch with your panicking, instead of denying or avoiding it. By working to face and escalate the feeling of panic itself (e.g., feeling it as long and as intensely as you can) you may see (that is, think) that it is not terrible and won't kill you and you can act against it (e.g., by going more easily for "dangerous" job interviews). If you do this kind of confronting, experiencing, and imploding your panicking feelings, you may somewhat *directly* change them and the thoughts and actions that go with (and are an intrinsic part of) them; therefore REBT includes some emotive or feeling techniques which to some extent directly help you change your disturbing feelings themselves.

Nevertheless, REBT largely agrees with Glasser that the *main* direct way to change your unhealthy negative feelings is to force yourself—yes, actively and directively force yourself—to change your Irrational *Beliefs* (IBs) and your dysfunctional acting that almost always accompany them. Push yourself to *think* and to *act* less disturbedly and you will thereby best achieve internal control over your panicking and depressing.

From this review of the main points of William Glasser's Choice Theory and the corresponding theories of REBT you can see that the two systems of therapizing overlap in many respects. Glasser's treatment of psychological disturbing is an internal rather than an external control approach. So is REBT's. Definitely.

However, Glasser and I had both better watch our human tendencies to illogically jump from generalizing to overgeneralizing. If we say that people disturb themselves only or always by their internal choices to external Adversities, that is misleading. How they make themselves happy about events they favor and make themselves miserable about those they disfavor is, modern psychology shows, a very complicated mode of interacting. No man or woman, as John Donne said, is an island. People exist, react to, and interact with an environment. They think, feel, and act in context, as recent psychological observing and experimenting has particularly shown (Hayes, Strosahl, and Wilson 1999).

People disturb themselves, as REBT has always indicated, by encountering Adversities (A) and reacting to them with their Belief-Behaviors (B). So they produce their disturbing Consequences (C) by the formula $A \times B = C$.

If, therefore, people thoroughly wish to change C, their miserabilizing, they'd better ideally change A and B, and not merely, as internal control sometimes implies, change B. Thus, when someone treats them "unfairly" (A) and they make themselves angry at him or her (C), they'd better change their Beliefs (B) that create their anger—e.g., "People *absolutely must not* treat me unfairly and they are *thoroughly rotten* when they do!"

Fine. But instead of *angrily* trying to get others to treat them fairly, they preferably should *un*angrily assess the "unfairness" of others and try to induce them to be "fair." In Alfred Korzybski's terms, they can best change their external-internal, either/or philosophizing to both/and viewing. That is, change *both* their internal controlling (self-control) *and* their dealing with external "controlling" situations (Adversities that happen in their lives).

Ivey and Goncalves (1988) and Rigazio-DiGilio, Ivey, and Locke (1997) have given this matter of internal and external control some serious thought and have come up with counseling theories and practices called development counseling therapy (DCT) and its extension, systematic cognitive-developmental theory (SCDT). Their theories hold that because the Adversities people experience are frequently antisocial and humanity-destroying—e.g., rape, child abuse, and war—counselors have a moral responsibility to help their clients not only to internally make themselves less panicking and depressive about these Adversities (A) but also to help their clients, as individuals and as members of their social groups, to change and ameliorate A *and* B (their internal *Beliefs* about these As). Thus, the clients would be helped to change themselves (internal control) and *also* change the inhumane environment (external control) in which they and other members of their social group reside.

Urging counselors to try to help clients use this kind of dual internal/external control is perhaps controversial, as I note in chapter 3. But actually this is what Glasser's Choice Theory and REBT both try to do. They first emphasize internal control and encourage people to choose to change their own reacting to others who act badly, so that they do not needlessly upset themselves about these unfortunate happenings. But at the same time they show people how to deal with and cope with others calmly, so as to help these others to some degree act more cooperatively and less adversarily.

In the final analysis, then, Choice Theory and REBT both encourage people to change themselves *and* thereby be able to arrange better their relationships and situations with others. They therefore effectively promote internal control but at the same time help people to exert better external influence on other people and events. In these ways they strive for the best of both possible worlds—but had better not insist that they have the right answers for all the people and all the conditions these people encounter all of the time. Our understanding of the causes of human disturbing and how to treat it in different people still has a long way to go.

SELF-HELP SUGGESTIONS

- Although you may have partly been trained or conditioned by your childhood relationships to act disturbedly today, you do not have to *carry on* these early trainings by engaging in your acquired thinking, feeling, and behaving *today*.
- You therefore have the *choice* of distressing yourself today, as you may have previously done—or the *choice* of thinking and acting more functionally. REBT, since its inception in 1955, is one of the leading choice therapies—as also is William Glasser's Reality Therapy, which started a decade later and has recently been renamed Choice Theory.
- Both REBT and Choice Theory accept the fact that external events—such as the Adversities you may easily encounter—as well as your biological makeup, influence and control you, and may significantly contribute to your dysfunctioning. But both these forms of therapy say that you, as a unique human, have a good measure of internal control over your emotional destiny—if you *choose* or *prefer* to use it.
- In particular, REBT provides you with many thinking-feeling-behaving *options* for correcting your dysfunctioning and making yourself more functional. It particularly shows you how to Dispute your Irrational *Beliefs* (IBs) that are often basic to your disturbing, and how to replace them with preferable, Rational *Beliefs* (RBs). It stresses your acquiring the crucial *philosophies* of unconditional self-acceptance (USA), unconditional other acceptance (UOA), antiawfulizing, and high frustration tolerance (HFT).
- REBT, along with Glasser, emphasizes the importance of your learning to deal well with your human relationships, but it also emphasizes your merely *wanting*, and not absolutely *needing*, performance, business, athletic, and other kinds of success. It shows you how to unupsettedly deal with both things and relationships.
- You have *strong* preferences and *quality* desires, and you will be *very* frustrated when you do not fulfill them. But it would be wise if you restrict your natural tendency to escalate even your quality desires into dire *necessities*. If you think that you *absolutely must* fulfill *any* of your preferences, you greatly risk making yourself anxietizing and depressing.

16

The Importance of Cognitive Processing in Facilitating Accepting in Psychotherapy

The term *acceptance*, which I am mainly referring to as *accepting* in this chapter, is an elusive term, as Haas (1994) pointed out in his comments on Hayes's (1994) and others' use of it in the book, *Acceptance and Change: Content and Context in Psychotherapy* (Hayes, Jacobson, Follette, and Dougher 1994). Hayes himself (1994, p. 11) says that "acceptance is of different types, and not all of them are psychologically healthy." *Webster's New World Dictionary*, if anything, adds to this confusion by defining *acceptance* as "1. An accepting or being accepted. 2. Approving reception; approval. 3. Belief in; assent." And it defines *accept* as "to receive favorably; approve."

This dictionary definition is particularly unhelpful in psychotherapy because we often try to help clients accept behaviors that they disapprove of but can't change, and to accept their feelings simply because they exist, without necessarily approving or disapproving of them.

How, then, can we accurately define *accepting* when it has several different, and sometimes contradictory, meanings? Not very precisely! However, let me try to mention several forms of accepting or nonjudging that

This chapter is partly adapted from "The Importance of Cognitive Processes in Facilitating Accepting in Psychotherapy," which I gave as an invited address to the 25th Anniversary Annual Convention of the Association of Behavior Analysis on May 29, 1999, and which was published in the *Journal of Cognitive Behavioral Practice* 7 (2000): 288–99. Used with permission.

have been commonly advocated by several philosophers—such as Gautama Buddha, Lao-Tsu, Jesus, and Martin Buber—as well as by a number of therapists—such as Carl Rogers, Fritz Perls, and myself. According to these writers, it is important for people to have several kinds of accepting:

- To accept yourself unconditionally, even though you have many failings.
- To unconditionally accept other people with their shortcomings. To accept the sinner but not the sin.
- To accept the grim conditions of life when they cannot be changed.
- To accept your dysfunctional feelings when you cannot change them.
- To accept present restrictions and pains when they will produce future gains.
- To accept the fact that your past history cannot be changed but your present reactions to it can be.
- To accept your biological and socially learned limitations and not demand that they do not exist.
- To accept your ultimate death, even if you would like to live forever.
- To accept your and other people's fallibility and imperfection, to give them and you the right to be wrong.
- To accept that you can change your thoughts, feelings, and behaviors—but usually only with much work and practice.
- To accept that few things are wholly good or wholly bad. They are good and bad for a given purpose at a given time under certain conditions.
- To accept that you and other people are often easily disturbable, and without trouble can act quite unreasonably and upsetting. Consider the source! Accept others with their self-upsetting.

My list grows apace—and I could probably add to it considerably. To be both physically and mentally healthy you may well try for these and various other kinds of accepting. But how? Ah, that's the problem!

ACCEPTING VERSUS MUSTURBATING

Unfortunately, accepting yourself and others unconditionally is somewhat antibiological or superhuman. As Alfred Korzybski showed in *Science and Sanity*, just about all of us humans are unsane—no, not insane—because we create, especially with the use of language, the is of identity, or "I *am* what I *do*." Thus, we say, "I treated someone badly, and therefore I *am* a bad person." Or: "I created a great work of art, therefore I *am* a great artist." Or, worse yet, "Therefore I *am* a great person." This is arrant overgeneralizing—which, Korzybski pointed out, is the human condition, since we are both born and reared to think in that inaccurate manner.

Moreover, as I noted some forty years ago (Ellis 1962) and as Karen Horney (1950) pointed out earlier, we find it almost impossible to accept ourselves unconditionally, because we have innate and learned tendencies to take our strong preferences and easily turn them into musts and demands. Thus we frequently tell ourselves, "I hate my weaknesses and would greatly prefer to change them. So if I keep them, as I *must* not, I am a *weak person* and a *no-goodnik!*" Or we think, "I want very much to be loved by Joan (or John), so I absolutely must win her (or his) love. Otherwise, I am an unlovable, worthless individual!"

Whenever we turn a desire into a necessity, we tend to illogically conclude that when we do not achieve what we absolutely must, we are worthless for not achieving it, or other people are rotten for blocking us from getting it, or the world is a horrible place for not providing it for us. The frustration of our *wants* leads to our healthy feelings of sorrow and regret—and to further efforts to get them fulfilled. But the blocking of our escalated (and quite fictional) "needs" leads us to panic and depress ourselves—and to dysfunctional efforts to attain these "needs." We are able to accept the blocking of our desires and motivate ourselves to ultimately achieve them. But we damn ourselves and others—which is the very opposite of accepting—when we fail to fulfill our so-called needs.

Worse yet, when we fail to achieve success, power, love, or pleasure that we think we absolutely must have, we frequently create primary negative feelings, such as raging at ourselves, because we tell ourselves, "I must succeed, and I stupidly failed; therefore I'm a Failure!" Result: self-downing and depressing. But then we observe our severe depressing feelings, and frequently tell ourselves, "I must not have these depressing feelings! It's terrible to feel depressed." We consequently depress ourselves about our depressing. This secondary disturbing ourselves comes from our refusal to merely observe and sorrowfully accept instead of depressingly damn, our primary symptom.

In other words, our refusal to accept the unpleasantness of our disturbing frequently leads to our doubly disturbing ourselves. This is especially true when we make ourselves feel dramatically disturbing, such as panicking. We define panicking as so undesirable that we tell ourselves, "I absolutely must not panic! I must not even think about panicking!" Then we not only make it impossible to stop our panicking, for how can we not think about something when we are commanding ourselves not to think about it? If we told ourselves, "I want to stop thinking about panicking," we might be able to think of something else, such as a movie or a sporting event. But if we say, "I must not think about panicking," our command to not think about it will almost inevitably make us think about it.

Hayes (1994, p. 17), a prominent radical behaviorist, specifically acknowledges how our absolutistic musts get us into strongly nonaccepting behaviors, by noting that, "For someone who must not think a negative thought, they must contact a verbal rule that is normally designed to help a person contact a thought, but in fact produces it. It's not possible to follow a rule, 'do not think of X,' without also thinking of X." This is exactly the REBT position on musts, which I stated in 1962.

Along with the human tendency to overgeneralize and to musturbate are the somewhat related traits of exaggerating, catastrophizing, and awfulizing. People are not only natural storytellers but tend to be dramatic, theatrical storytellers. Thus, they create heroes and heroines who always win out against the greatest odds—and who, of course, live in perfect bliss for-ever after. That, naturally, is unrealistic—because of human fallibility and life's uncertainties—and leads to frequent disillusionment by overoptimistic and pollyannaish people. But optimism, and even pollyannaism, have some motivational advantages and may encourage self-efficacy, as Martin Seligman and Albert Bandura have shown.

Exaggerated pessimism is much worse than overoptimism and is fre-quently involved in emotional and behavioral disturbing. A good deal of it may have possibly been biologically built into the human race, in order to make us able to deal with primitive dangers, such as floods, forest fires, rape, and murder. If people awfulize about such adversities, they may be moti-vated to prepare for and deal with them. Perhaps!

In any event, even in the relative safety of modern civilization, we con-siderably awfulize. We take a minor setback in the stock market and predict disaster. We fail at two job interviews and say, "I'll never get a job." We have a bad year in business and see ourselves well on the way to bankruptcy, to living on welfare, and to being ostracized by all our friends.

Awfulizing and exaggerated pessimism are, once again, almost the opposite of accepting. When we accept some of our failings we don't awfulize about them and tell ourselves, "I'll always fail! I'm a hopeless failure!" When we accept pain and illness, we rarely conclude, "It's bound to get worse! I can't bear it! I'll soon die of it!" When we accept the death of a loved one, we don't conclude, "My whole life is devastated! I can't enjoy anything! I think I'll kill myself !"

So far I have shown that overgeneralizing, musturbating, and awfulizing are three major forms of cognizing—or making cognitive errors—that lead to nonacceptance of ourselves, of other people, and of unfortunate world conditions that can't at the moment be changed. Are there other important cognizings that block therapeutic acceptance? Yes, there probably are, but for brevity's sake I shall name only one more—absolutizing. When bad things happen to good people, the way to solve them or accept them without quite solving them is, first, to consider several possible *alternative ways* of improving them; also to consider several possible *alternative ways* of reacting to them—since we humans often have a good degree of *choice* or *freedom* in both of these matters. Thus we have several ways of preventing weak bridges from falling, dealing with a failing business, getting a more than satisfactory job, and winning the approval of significant others. But if we rigidly consider and inflexibly stick with only one possible solution to a problem event, we will have less chance of remedying it.

Similarly, if an Adversity occurs and cannot for the moment be improved, we have several things we can do to feel and behave about it. Thus, emotionally, we can cry, whine, and scream; or feel sorry and regretful; or agonize, panic, depress, rage, or feel hopeless about the Adversity. Or we can joke about it, take it lightly, reflect on it, or even try to enjoy some aspects of it.

Behaviorally, when an Adversity happens, we can work to change it, flee from it, distract ourselves, engage in other activity, ineffectively and compulsively keep trying to fix it even when it is unfixable, and take other forms of action or inaction.

Many people faced with Adversity, however, stick themselves inflexibly on a single form of dealing with it. Thus they beat a dead horse, stay in a highly unsatisfactory job, leave a series of mates very quickly, or declare bankruptcy when they could work at keeping a failing business alive and make it go.

Similarly many people, when Adversity hits, mire themselves emotionally in the one feeling that comes easily to them, even though it only creates misery. Thus they cry for years over a lost loved one, or continue to panic about the falling stock market, or continuously enrage themselves over someone who treated them unfairly during their childhood.

People, then, have choices of how to act and feel about Adversities. If one action—or inaction—doesn't work to improve problem situations, they can experiment with an alternative plan. If they bring on themselves a single miserable feeling about or reaction to a life difficulty, they can experiment with and select an alternative reaction. But to do so they had better:

- Look for alternative feelings and behaviors,
- Accept that some probably exist,
- Consider the results of trying them,
- Actually try them out,
- Check the results,
- Revise their approaches, and
- Keep revising them on the basis of new results and experiences they perceive.

Accepting, then, seems to go hand in hand with trying, experimenting, and open-mindedly continuing to try to experiment. It is fairly equivalent to the scientific method: Scientists are open-minded and flexible; set up only tentative hypotheses; keep planning experiments to test their hypotheses; keep revising their experiments on the basis of the obtained results; and keep revising their theories to fit the discovered empirical data. No rest for the weary! Constant trial-and-error seeking. Constant flexibility.

We can do the same with accepting. We constantly look for possible solutions to adversities and to our emotional and behavioral reacting to these adversities by seeking and choosing among several likely alternatives. We flexibly assume that none of the answers we arrive at are absolute, are fixed, are perfect, or are certain. Accepting is open-minded and flexible, nonaccepting is dogmatic and one-sided.

VERBAL BLOCKS TO ACCEPTING

This is a relatively short chapter and summarizes some of the main characteristics of therapeutic accepting I have culled from being a therapist for fifty-eight years; doing rational emotive behavior therapy for forty-six years; attending many lectures and workshops; and reading many theoretical and research writings. It is based only lightly on specific empirical studies, but it would probably be endorsed by many practitioners of humanistic-experiential therapy such as Carl Rogers and Fritz Perls, who would agree with much of its philosophic assumptions but would insist that they can be achieved only when clients are in an intimate, fully accepting relationship and/or they experience dramatic-evocative exercises that somehow show clients, through actual emotional experiences, how to follow an accepting rather than a nonaccepting life.

To some extent, the radical behavioralist position of Hayes (1994) and his associates (Hayes, Strosahl, and Wilson 1999) agrees with the humanists that accepting had better be shown rather than didactically taught to clients by a combination of arranging a close relationship with the therapist and arranging a series of behavioral exercises that include paradoxical thinking processes. Hayes demonstrates to clients that their usual nonaccepting methods have not worked and will not work, and thereby teach them how to have unusual, almost nonhuman, accepting attitudes and actions.

Hayes takes a somewhat equivocal stand regarding the use and disuse of cognition, or what he calls verbal processes, in accepting and nonaccepting. On the one hand, he points out that "barriers to acceptance are verbal" (1994, p. 22) and on the other hand he states, "radical forms of acceptance require a manipulation of verbal processes" (1994, p. 31).

Actually, however, Hayes's theory of nonacceptance appears to my prejudiced ears to be quite cognitive and to overlap with much of the theory that REBT has proposed since 1962 and that has been largely adopted by most of the other cognitive behavioral therapies.

Thus Hayes states: "If I must not be anxious, and yet I am anxious, then something dangerous or even invalid has occurred. The trauma this causes goes far beyond the direct experience of the anxiety itself. This 'should not be happening'" (1994, p. 161). Also, Hayes (1994, p. 17) notes: "The real damage comes from people trying not to feel, think or remember what they already think, feel, and remember anyway. That puts them in the untenable position of experiencing something, while at the same time holding the experience to be in some way inherently threatening to them and their survival as a psychological being. That is the essence of psychological trauma." Here again Hayes, a radical behavior therapist, is mainly restating the exceptionally cognitive behavioral position that REBT has held for forty years. Hayes continues:

> There is little in the private psychological reactions of anxious, depressed, angry, or confused persons that needs to be changed. A posture of psychological acceptance, in which the goal of the individual is to get more fully present with what they feel and think and remember, and to bring all of that with them into a successful pattern of adjustment in an overt behavioral sense, changes the negative content functionally, without having to change it topographically or situationally. It is not necessary for a person who is having a panic attack to have fewer panic attacks, or to have less intense panic attacks. What is most important is that the person drain the trauma out of these so-called panic attacks and begin living a valued life. If the person had a different purpose, namely that of psychological openness and healthy living, "panic" need not be viewed as one's own enemy, or as an indication of the failure of one's life.
>
> The paradox is this. In the context of deliberate change, fearsome content is inherently fearsome . . . . In the concept of psychological acceptance, fearsome content is changed functionally even if no change occurs in its frequency. (1994, pp. 18–19)

Hayes points out here that you can have private psychological reactions of panicking and feeling depressed in a healthy manner provided that "you bring all of that with them in a successful pattern of adjustment in an overt behavioral manner [which] changes the negative content functionally, without having to change it topographically or situationally." He gives the relevant example of people who deliberately pay significant amounts of money for roller coaster rides so that they can enjoy experiencing intense periods of fear, strong bodily sensations, and thoughts such as "I'm going to die," some of the behavioral precursors of escape or defense. Why so? Because they accept their panicky feelings, instead of making themselves terrified by these feelings.

This is a good example that restates the REBT theory of panicking I presented in *Reason and Emotion in Psychotherapy* in 1962. I said that panicking consists of (1) fear of failure or danger and (2) fear of panicking itself. What Hayes seems to be saying is that the nonpanicky feelings you have on a roller coaster ride are deliberately chosen when, first, you do not view the ride as really dangerous, but merely dramatic and thrilling, and second, you view your dramatic gut feelings, again, as acceptable and enjoyable and therefore are not horrified about them.

What Hayes calls the "context-oriented approach" consists of (1) a problematic event, such as a "dangerous" situation and (2) your *view* of that problematic event—e.g., a roller-coaster ride—as essentially nondangerous, plus your own view of your panicky feelings as nondisturbed and, in fact, even pleasurable.

Hayes rightly concludes, therefore, that your voluntarily taken "dangerous" roller-coaster ride is seen in a different context than if you were involuntarily forced to ride on a roller coaster that you viewed as rickety and thought was in danger of collapsing. What he calls the content of both situations is similar—the dizzying ride and your psychological and physiological reactions to it; but what he calls the *context* of the ride includes (1) a similar content, the ride; (2) a different *view* of the "danger" of the ride; and (3) a different view of your experience of the panic resulting from (1) and (2). Your purpose is to enjoy the ride and your panicky feelings, so therefore you accept them in this light, because of your *view* of them.

In other words, whenever a problematic situation occurs in your life, which could possibly be dangerous or even life-threatening, you encounter it in the context—that is, your view of (1) how dangerous it "really" is and (2) your view of how "horrible" your private reactions are to it. Not only, Hayes is apparently saying, do you provide a context for every problematic situation you see, but that context consists of two important cognitions: one, your view of how problematic the situation "really" is and, two, your view of how "bad" or "dangerous" is your psychological reacting—your emotional experiencing—to the situation. This seems to mean that because you are a human reactor and have a *choice* of how to react, you bring to most problematic situations at least two important cognitions: First, your view of the situation itself, and second, your reactions to the situation. Your responding to the situation, consequently, consists of its content (the situation itself) plus your multiple cognitions about this content, which Hayes calls the context in which you view it.

THE RATIONAL EMOTIVE BEHAVIOR THERAPY THEORY OF ACCEPTING

If I am correct about this, Hayes seems to be restating the REBT theory of emotional-behavioral disturbance. This theory holds that people often choose to disturb themselves when some Adversity (A) occurs in their lives, not simply because A simply occurs and makes them upset. Instead, they bring to this Adversity (A) a cognitive-emotive-behavioral *Belief* System (B), which has both innate and learned elements. Their *Belief* System is quite complicated, and also has historical elements. But very importantly, and often crucially, it includes two contradictory beliefs: (1) The Adversity that is encountered definitely does exist, but because it is against people's basic goals (G) it must not, absolutely should not *be* as adverse as it is. (2) When people produce disturbing feelings and behaviors (Consequences) by their contradictory *Beliefs* (B), they frequently react to these subsequent Adversities (A_2) by constructing a secondary *Belief* System (B_2) which holds that C_1 (feeling panicky about A_1) once again definitely exists, and is bad. But it, too, absolutely should not, must not be as bad as it is. So they end up making themselves panicking about their panic (C_2) and now have two disturbances for the price of one!

Like Hayes, REBT, since its inception in 1955, says that A (Adversity) does not directly lead to or cause C (disturbing Consequences). Instead, C = A x B (Adversity times your Belief System about Adversity). Also, when A1 x B1 produces C_1 (your first disturbance), you frequently make C_1 into A_2 and construct B_2 (dysfunctional *Beliefs* about A_2) and wind up with C_2 (disturbing yourself about your initial disturbing). So your *Belief* System (B) often includes primary *Beliefs*—cognitions about Adversity (A)—as well as cognitions about your unpleasant Consequences (C_1) or your dysfunctioning.

These sets of *Beliefs* $(B_1$ and $B_2)$ Hayes seems to call the context in which you *view* A_1 and A_2. A_1 is the content of your Adversity and A_2 is the disturbing feelings you produce about A_1. But B_1 and B_2 are the contexts or *Beliefs* about A_1 and A_2 that lead to your dysfunctional feelings and behaviors, C_1 and C_2. In REBT, we say that B_1 and B_2 are largely *Beliefs* (cognitions) about A_1 and A_2.

More specifically, REBT hypothesizes that when you insist (B_1) that Adversities (A_1) that occur must not be as bad as they are, you make yourself panicky and depressing at C_1 (your emotional-behavioral Consequence); and when you insist that the disruptive feelings you produce at C must not be bad when they actually are that bad, you disturb yourself about disturbing yourself.

So REBT, again, agrees with Hayes that you "paradoxically" insist that Adversities that are occurring must not occur, and you thereby make yourself disturbed about them. Then, secondarily, you "paradoxically" insist that your disturbing feelings (especially, panicking) do exist and at the same time must not be as bad as they are—so you make yourself panicky about your panicking because you refuse to accept your feelings, even when you clearly see that they unfortunately do exist. Double nonsense!

Hayes goes on to say that because humans have important language and verbal processes, and they make these dominant in their lives, they close off both the events they experience and also make themselves nonaccepting of their own experience. So their verbal processes bring about great gains (such as science and mathematics) but make them *see* their experiences distortedly and believe much of what is factually incorrect. Hayes's definition of accepting, as Haas (1994, p. 33) paraphrases it, "involves experiencing events fully and without defense, as they are not as you say they are." But verbal processes—such as reasoning—seriously interfere with this kind of accepting.

Let us assume that Hayes is correct and that verbal processes and human thinking often create several types of nonaccepting, as I hypothesized in the first part of this chapter. People overgeneralize and see themselves as bad people when they have merely performed undesirable acts, so they deny or rationalize about verbal processes—for which they have a natural and learned talent—and pretend that they have not performed badly. Or they acknowledge their undesirable behavior and make themselves guilty— meaning *self*-deprecating—about it, then feel depressed, and then think that depressing is awful and that they can't stand it. So they refuse to face their genuine feelings and don't accept them when they actually *experience* them.

If this vicious cycle of nonaccepting occurs—as clinical cases seem to show it often does—how can we, as therapists, interrupt it and help our clients to accept themselves and others unconditionally; to accept adversities that they try to change but can't; to accept that their emotional and behavioral disturbances are partly self-created and not merely brought on by external conditions; to accept their feelings of panicking and depressing as unfortunate and undesirable but as genuine feelings; and to *accept* many other thoughts, feelings, and behaviors that they prefer to but do not need to reduce or remove?

My answer—and the answer of REBT—is that nonaccepting people, including those who are making their problems worse by their nonaccepting, can use a large variety of experiential-emotive techniques which the humanistic therapists tend to employ and can also use the activity homework assignments that cognitive behavior and radical behavior therapists employ.

Thus, Hayes uses a visualization-experiential technique to help a client who damns herself for some performance, thus creating panicking, and who then damns herself for making herself panicking. Hayes gets this client to imagine a child sitting in front of her who is making himself terribly panicky. He asks the client, "Can you love this child even though the child is afraid?" When she replies, "Yes," he shows her how she is prepared to accept the child with his panicking and self-doubting but refuses to accept herself with similar panicky feelings.

In REBT, I often use a similar exercise to show clients how self-discriminatory it is to damn themselves but not others for panicky behavior. But I would also explain to this client that she is first making herself panicking by insisting that she absolutely must *not* feel panicky when she is feeling that way. Then, as Hayes perhaps would do, too, I would help this client to (paradoxically) expose herself to situations in which she might well fail, to thereby *see* that she survives and may even benefit from these situations. But I would primarily help her to see that her *Beliefs* (B_1) about failing performances (A_1), not the failures themselves, largely create her panicking feelings (C_1). Also that her Beliefs (B_2) about feeling panicky (A_2), and not her panicking itself (C_1) lead her to feeling panicky about panicking.

Hayes, as a radical behaviorist, would do something similar to what I as an REBT therapist would do. What then is the difference? If I, using REBT, include in my therapy, as I often do, emotive-experiential methods that humanistic therapists employ, and also include it in activity homework methods that radical behaviorists use, where do I differ?

THE PLACE OF COGNIZING IN TREATING NONACCEPTING

I would say that REBT differs from Hayes's Acceptance and Commitment Therapy (ACT) in the heavy cognitive emphasis that it uses together with its usual emotive and behavioral methods. REBT fully acknowledges the place of language and cognition in creating human disturbing, the frequent nonaccepting of Adversities that lead to such disturbing, and the nonacceptance of feelings of upsetting about upsetting. Yes, verbal processes are often the villains here. But REBT hypothesizes that the best—though not the only—way to change harmful verbal processes is, paradoxically enough, to use higher order cognitive processes, or metacognition, to thoroughly and elegantly solve this problem.

In other words, people think, think about their thinking, and think about thinking about their thinking. Their use of a complex language enables them to do this kind of metathinking—and sometimes causes trouble. Thus some of their thinking, such as when it is obsessive and intrusive, consists of dysfunctional cognizing. People view their thinking, tell themselves, "It is wrong to think that way," and make efforts to stop it. But they also tell themselves, "I *must not* think that stupid way! I *must* immediately stop it!" Then they create panicking about obsessing—and thereby cannot stop their obsessing. Their nonaccepting of their "bad" thinking makes them, as I have been showing in this chapter, and as Hayes also emphasizes, obsess even more.

If thinking about thinking often leads to human problems, it can also be used to uncreate many of those same problems. In fact, REBT hypothesizes that it is the most thoroughgoing and elegant way of dealing with the problem of antitherapeutic nonaccepting, as well as with most other emotional and behavioral difficulties. Thus, simple behavior therapy can be done with pure nonverbal or noncognitive techniques, as when Joseph Wolpe used behavioral methods to make laboratory animals phobic and then used other behavioral techniques to make them unphobicking.

As I discussed with Wolpe at the Evolution of Psychotherapy Conference in 1995, his use of behavioral methods of reciprocal inhibition was much different when he later used it with human clients. I again noted, in commenting on G. T. Wilson's implication that Wolpe's methods were more scientific and more purely behavioral than cognitive methods of treating phobias, that both Wolpe and Wilson were ignoring the important cognitive elements in Wolpe's "pure" behavior therapy. I said:

> Because the people that Wolpe "deconditions" are much more cognitive than the animals with which he first experimented, we might expect that the "deconditioning" of people will involve many more cognitive processes than acknowledged by Wolpe.
>
> Thus, persons with snake phobias first have to *focus* on Wolpe's instructions; then have to *imagine* a snake a mile away; then have to *imagine* getting closer and closer to it; then have to *tell themselves* to use Edmund Jacobson's progressive relaxation technique; then have to *keep reminding themselves* to continue to follow Wolpe's teachings; then have to *observe* if their phobia is lessening; then have to *note* and *report* whether their fear stays in abeyance, and so on. The words emphasized in the example above are all cognitions and tend to show that Wolpe's systematic desensitization method is behavioral *and* cognitive, and not purely behavioral as Wilson implies.
>
> Moreover, assuming that Wolpe successfully desensitizes a client's phobic fear of snakes, does it follow that this client *really* changed their aversive reaction because of counterconditioning by "physical" relaxation methods? Perhaps so. But we could also hypothesize that the more often the client faces snakes imaginally—instead of avoiding thinking about them as was the case previously—he or she will (a) *perceive* them as less dangerous than he or she previously *saw* them; (b) *realize* that even if snakes are dangerous, they are usually locked up safely in zoos, and therefore will do no harm; (c) *conclude* that imagining snakes or even being in the same room with snakes is "exciting" and "challenging" rather than "devastating"; (d) *tell himself* that the great majority of snakes are not poisonous and therefore harmless; (e) *see* that some snakes are actually somewhat attractive; (f) *remember* that in their vicinity—especially if the client lives in a city apartment—few snakes exist and practically never attack people; (g) *decide* to go to a nearby zoo and keep looking snakes in the eye until this form of exposure reduces his or her phobia.
>
> The foregoing are some cognitions that clients with a phobia may resort to as they go through Wolpe's "deconditioning" process. Indeed, because clients are human and because, unlike rats and guinea pigs, they can talk to themselves about practically everything they do, and especially about dysfunctional behaviors like phobias, we can guess with a high degree of probability that their phobic fear *includes* some cognitions—such as

"snakes are very dangerous and I must at all costs avoid them!" "My phobia about snakes is ridiculous and I am an idiot for not overcoming it!" "If people discover how phobic I am about snakes that would be shameful! So I must not let them know how phobic I am!"

In overcoming fears of snakes by Wolpe's systematic desensitization method, persons with such phobias also inevitably have some important cognitions about using this method, such as "Dr. Wolpe is a great innovator and a fine therapist, so I think he really can help me"; "Maybe systematic desensitization won't work, but I'll give it a chance and see"; "It's hard following Dr. Wolpe's instructions, but it will be harder for me if I don't follow them and if I keep indulging in my phobia."

If I am correct about what I have been saying, then there is no such thing as a pure behavioral method of therapy. All behavioral methods of therapy seem to have important cognitive elements and are, therefore, really cognitive-behavioral. Similarly, all cognitive therapies, particularly when they are effective, seem to have important behavioral elements. Thus a person with a snake phobia can use REBT and think, "I don't *have to* run away from snakes, but *can* keep confronting them. They are *not that* dangerous; and, although I find snakes unattractive, I don't have to view them as *awful* and *horrible*. To hell with it—I think I'll get one as a pet!" But this cognitivist client, to actually get over his or her snake phobia, will still have to actively force himself to keep thinking about snakes, keep imagining himself confronting them, and then repetitively *act* on those cognitions. (Ellis 1997, pp. 560–61)

When I made essentially the same comment at Wolpe's paper at the Evolution of Psychotherapy Conference in 1995, he remarked, somewhat to my surprise, "There is an important point that Al Ellis made about cognitive events in therapy. Yes, cognition enters into everything that we do. When we have a conversation, there is cognition on both sides. When Al Ellis and I are talking to you now, we are thinking that you are thinking, and all this is cognition. When I am telling a person to assert himself in certain situations, I am using his intellect, he is taking on what I say cognitively, and will later be using his judgment in carrying out assertive action" (Wolpe 1997, p. 119).

The point I am making is that just about all therapy with humans, including pure behavioral analysis, inevitably has important cognitive elements and would hardly exist without these elements. But I want to particularly emphasize that when clients easily and naturally use their language systems to make self-defeating conclusions about themselves, about others, and especially about the "horror" of their panicking and depressing, probably the best and most thoroughgoing way to help them is to teach them philosophic methods of change, especially how to think better about their thinking.

CASE PRESENTATION

Let me be more specific. Consider one of my clients, Claire, who became panicking at the age of sixteen, when a subway train in which she was riding got stuck in a tunnel for ten minutes. She thereafter, for the next ten years, had many panic attacks when in the subway or thinking about riding underground. I immediately explained to her, in the first few sessions, that people rarely upset themselves without strongly believing in musts and demands; and we figured out together that she was taking her sensible preferences, "I hate getting stuck in the subway, but it won't kill me," and raising them to imperatives: "I *must* not get stuck in the subway! I *can't stand* this inconvenience! Maybe there's a fire in the tunnel—and that would be *awful*! I must get out of here!—and I can't. I'm hopelessly trapped!" With these demands, she brought on her panicking.

Moreover, I quickly questioned Claire—since I knew that most panicking people develop symptoms *about* their feelings of panic—as to whether this was true in her case, and she replied, "Definitely! If I even think of becoming panicky, I panic about that." So we determined her secondary musts about her panicking:

"I *must* not panic! It's *awful* to panic! Not everyone panics like I do, so I'm *a weakling* for indulging in this panic!"

I explained to Claire, with a little lecture on the human condition, that people frequently take their preferences for safety and competency and raise them into musts and demands—and then they create their panicking feelings. Her insistence that she not be uncomfortably stuck in the subway, when, in fact, she was stuck and could not quickly be unstuck, was creating her panicking. No, the stuck subway was not making her upset—though, of course, it *contributed* to her panicking. The stuck subway multiplied by her *demand* that it should not be stuck equaled her panicking.

Moreover, when we determined that Claire was panicking about her panicking, we figured out that, once again, she was healthily desiring that she not feel that way and *also* unhealthily insisting that she fulfill her desire—and do so immediately. So she was stuck not merely in the subway, but in her own stuckness. We figured out that her primary symptom stemmed from her needing to have the subway start up when it was actually halted, and her secondary symptom from her needing to feel unpanicky when she actually felt panicky. She was not only stuck in the subway—which was unpleasant—but was stuck in her own contradictory thinking—"I must not be stuck when I am stuck!" She was also stuck in her own contradictory thinking about her thinking—"I must not feel panicky or even think about feeling panicky, because then I am acting incompetently and that makes me an incompetent person!"

Claire saw that it was largely her thinking about being trapped in the subway, as well as her thinking that she must not panic, that led to her originally making herself anxietizing and then to her making herself panicked about her panicking. She then began using REBT to keep preferring comfort and competency but to give up her imperative demand that she achieve her preferences. She quickly felt less primary and secondary panicking.

At the same time, I showed Claire how her thinking of herself as an incompetent person for panicking and for panicking about her panicking was overgeneralizing. I gave her a little lecture on Korzybski's (1933/1990) theory of the *is* of identity, and showed her that *she* was not her poor *performance*. She was a person who under certain conditions performed badly—panicking herself. But she also performed many things well and was capable, in the future, of correcting her poor performances. So she had better observe her overgeneralizing and change it back to probability statements—and thus think more correctfully and usefully about her thinking. I asked her to come up with a probability rather than an overgeneralizing statement about her panicking and she came up with: "I sometimes panic myself by demanding that I not be stuck in the subway, and that is undesirable behavior, as demanding often is. But that foolish thinking doesn't make me a fool—just a person who stupidly, at times, overgeneralizes, and can see what I'm foolishly thinking and stop it." When she realized that she—and other people—often create emotional problems by overgeneralizing, Claire began to do so much less often. When she reverted to doing so, she stopped her overgeneralizing by thinking about her thinking and the poor results it created.

I also showed Claire how she frequently exaggerated her problems and awfulized about them. Thus, when trapped in the subway, she told herself that restriction was uncomfortable—because her goal was to get to her destination quickly and she didn't want to be hindered. But she also told herself, "Being trapped like this is *awful. I can't stand* it!" And also, secondarily, "Feeling panic like I do is *awful* and I *can't stand* this feeling!" Her disliking being trapped led to uncomfortable feelings which by themselves would lead her to feeling sorry and disappointing. These were healthy and useful since she wasn't getting what she wanted and they would motivate her to try to escape from the trapped train or live with being trapped without horrifying herself about it. But labeling her being trapped as *awful* and *unbearable* was exaggerated thinking that said or implied (1) that being trapped was totally bad, (2) that it was as bad as it could possibly be, (3) that she couldn't stand it and still survive, (4) that she couldn't be happy *at all* if bad events like this existed, (5) that being stuck was *so* bad that the degree of badness *absolutely should not* exist, and (6) that the train being stuck was *so* bad—or perhaps even *more than bad*—that therefore it *absolutely should not* be stuck. Claire's *awfulizing* consisted, first, of her perceiving the stuck subway train and thinking of its stopping as undesirable—that is, against her interests and goals. This was factual and realistic, since her performance was being blocked, and she'd better feel disappointing about that restriction. But her awfulizing consisted, second, of her exaggeratedly *labeling* an uncomfortable situation as *worse* than it was—as life-threatening and as destructive of all possible happiness. Her awfulizing, therefore, turned her feelings of displeasure and frustration into those of horror and panic.

This, I showed Claire, is what usually happens when people awfulize about undesirable life events—and when they also awfulize about their own thoughts and feelings. They thereby *make* them as bad as they could possibly be instead of merely unfortunate. Then they usually create ego-downing ("I am no good for allowing this awful situation to exist and/or not coping well with it!"); and they create low frustration tolerance ("This situation is so awful that I can't be happy at all while it lasts!").

Awfulizing thus takes a realistic thought—"This is bad because it is against my goals"—and *defines it* as *too bad* or *so bad that it must not exist, or even badder than bad*. It takes a fact, undesirability, and makes it into something of a fiction; undesirable things, thoughts, and feelings are *so* bad that they *must not* be that bad or *must not* exist at all. But since undesirable events, like a stuck subway when one is in a hurry, *do* exist, and *should be* just as undesirable as they actually are—should make one late to an appointment if they do make one late—to label them as *awful* is to insist that they shouldn't be as bad as they actually are. Hence awfulizing like Claire's often makes one panicking, depressing, or raging. In a sense, it takes the thought, "I really dislike this!" and adds to it, "Therefore it must not be allowed to be as bad as it is!" So it is a form of thinking about thinking.

Claire had trouble at first stopping her awfulizing, especially about her panicking, because, as she said, "It feels so awful when it's there. I'm almost completely unable to do anything *except* feel awful. I get quite disorganized!"

"Yes," I said, "it does feel awful. And you will never like it. But I still hear you telling yourself that it's as bad as it possibly can be, that it will never go away, and that it will ruin your whole life. Not to mention that you are a stupid and rotten person for reacting so badly to simply being stuck for a while in the subway!"

"Exactly! It's really stupid. And I shouldn't be such a ninny and act so stupidly!"

"Wrong!" I said. "You should act so stupidly when you do act that way. You can't, at the moment, act otherwise. But does that make you a stupid, hopeless *person* who *always* acts that way? Does that make you incapable of any enjoyment?"

Claire held her ground—her neurotic ground—at first and berated herself for being *so* weak and panicking. I helped her see, again, that panicking might well be weak but that she, the panicker, wasn't an *awful* person. Also, that if she kept panicking for the rest of her life, it would be highly inconvenient but not *totally* inconvenient and therefore *awful*. She had been modeling after her parents' awfulizing about things for many years—and I showed her what poor results she and they got from doing so. What would her own present and future life be like if she continued to define stalled subway trains, feelings of panicking, or anything else as awful? She smiled at that question and answered, "My life will be *awful*!" "If you don't want it to be," I said, "then you'd better stop calling inconvenient experiences *awful*!" Claire was struck by my statement and went over it many times until she saw that she had a *choice* about defining unfortunate things as *awful* and that she also could merely *choose* to define them as "very inconvenient." That, she said, made quite a difference.

I consistently showed Claire that she always had a choice, not about what happened to her but how she *thought and felt* about undesirable happenings. I convinced her that if she chose one kind of thinking—defining Adversities as *unpreferable*—she was able to cope much better with them than if she picked the other choice of defining them as *catastrophic* or *awful*. Even calling frustrating events, such as stalled subway trains, "bad" or "pretty bad" was somewhat arbitrary and definitional, because some other riders, who preferred to be late to an undesired appointment, might call the same situation "good." So evaluating things as "good" or "bad" depended upon her goals, which were *chosen*. But calling stalled subways "bad" or "inconvenient" would make her feel less upsetting about them than calling them "terrible" or "awful." Her language, and the thinking processes behind this language, could make quite a difference!

When I helped Claire to see the meaning—the thought process—behind using "inconvenient" and "awful" to describe the same event, sitting for a while in a stalled subway train, she realized that her own selection of languaging and thinking was crucial to her feelings and actions about certain events that interfere with her wishes. So, again, by encouraging her to work against her awfulizing, instead of carelessly indulging in it, I showed her how to think about and change her thinking and thereby achieve much less agonizing results.

Let me give one more example of the thinking about thinking techniques that I commonly use with my nonaccepting clients and that I used with Claire. At first, when she was panicking about stalled subway trains and panicking about her panicking, she engaged in a good deal of rigid, one-sided, absolutistic thinking. Thus, she thought that the subway conductor was completely wrong about not letting riders know what was going on when the train had stalled and that he absolutely should have announced what was happening over the speaker system. Or, if that was not possible, he should go through the train himself and reassure the passengers. When he did nothing of the sort, she damned him thoroughly and thought he was "a complete idiot and a cruel bastard."

Claire also rigidly believed that the transit authority and the city officials who allowed subway breakdowns to occur were thoroughly wrong and criminally lax, and therefore should be dismissed and severely punished. She demanded that stalled trains, which presumably could be avoided if everyone involved did the *right* things, shouldn't happen *at all*. The fact that they did *wrongly* stall, when again they absolutely *shouldn't*, proved of course that she was *right* and that the culprits involved in letting it happen *should* be damned and punished.

Claire, then, thought in rigid, absolutist terms, about what was *right* and what was *wrong*—and, we might say, logically stemming from her one-sided thinking, she believed in and emotionally espoused, total damnation for wrongdoers like the officials of the transit authority. At first, I had trouble challenging her rigid theories of *rightness* and *damnation*. But as we kept collaborating on disputing her musturbating, her overgeneralizing, and her awfulizing, she began to see that her absolutist views of rightness and wrongness went along with her other careless thinking, and she started revising them. She still thought that several city officials wrongly and badly maintained the subway system. But she began to doubt whether they were *totally* wrong and thoroughly damnable for being wrong.

Claire's openmindedness increased appreciably in this respect when I showed her—as REBT therapists commonly do—that her close-minded thinking would lead to poor results. First, it would make her quite incensed at city officials who were fallible individuals but hardly 100 percent wrong. Second, it would make her remain thoroughly obsessing with them instead of contemplating how she could possibly help them be less wrong. Third, it would give her intense feelings of raging, in addition to feelings of panicking, which would rip up her own gut and body. Fourth, her close-mindedness would distract her from looking at the kind of thinking—and the kind of thinking about thinking—that was significantly contributing to her panicking. Fifth, it would reinforce and add to her natural and acquired tendencies to think crookedly and upset herself by her dysfunctioning thinking.

By my showing Claire how to monitor and question the results of her rigid thinking, I encouraged her to *think seriously* about this thinking, and thereby make efforts to minimize it.

My persistently and forcefully driving several of the above cognitive techniques home helped Claire make some profound philosophic changes. After eight sessions of REBT—which included, as it normally does, several emotive-experiential exercises and behavioral homework assignments such as deliberately exposing herself to subway rides instead of giving into her panicking by avoiding them—she began to rarely panic and make herself panicking about her panicking. She was enthusiastic about these results, and urged several of her friends to come for REBT sessions. But I encouraged her to stay for five months of therapy to work on some of her other emotional problems. She often berated herself and felt depressing whenever she compared herself to other teachers, who seemed to keep their students in better order than she did; and she fought bitterly with her righteous older sister who was constantly criticizing her for her "stupid" mistakes.

I helped Claire to see that her depressive self-berating stemmed largely from the same kind of overgeneralizing, musturbating, awfulizing, and rigidly damning thinking that led to her panicking and to her panicking about her panicking. I also helped her realize that her sister's righteousness and overly critical attitude probably stemmed from similar dysfunctional thinking and from thinking about thinking; and that her own upsetting herself about her sister's behavior also included similar ineffective thinking.

After five months Claire achieved what I call the "elegant" benefit from therapy. She was not only much less disturbing, but made herself considerably less disturb*able* (Ellis 1999). When confronted by new adversities in her life, such as a new school principal who acted dictatorially and unfairly with Claire and several other teachers, Claire felt very sorry and regretting, but reacted with much less raging and panicking than she would have reacted before using REBT to change her thinking, emoting, and behaving. Her being able to think about her dysfunctional thinking, and to correct it before it led to her seriously upsetting herself about adversities, convinced her that she was going to safely deal with other adversities that may arise in her life.

THE PLACE OF COGNIZING IN AIDING ACCEPTING

As noted in this chapter, I used several experiential-emotive and behavioral techniques with Claire, some of which would be used by other cognitive-behavior therapists and by those of other persuasions. Especially with clients who are panicking and panicking about their panicking, some of these methods work very well—and sometimes in a few sessions. These include some of the techniques that Steven Hayes uses in his form of radical behavior therapy, ACT.

Let me present several major hypotheses as well. First, nearly all forms of "pure" behavior therapy actually include many cognitive methods that are not really expressed in the published descriptions of what the therapist is doing, but they are still solidly there. Second, as Hayes states, verbal processes and language significantly help people to make themselves disturbed and especially to create secondary symptoms, such as panicking about panicking, that make them doubly disturbing. Third, as Hayes again correctly points out, many therapies inefficiently focus on helping clients to change the Adversities they encounter (e.g., by skill training or by avoiding failure) instead of more effectively tackling the interaction between the adverse environment and how they constructively (or destructively) react to this Adversity.

Fourth, many therapies, as Hayes again notes, inefficiently get people to ignore their disturbing feelings, to distract themselves from them, or to quickly minimize them, instead of fully acknowledging them, possibly enjoying them, and more thoroughly dealing with them when they want to change them.

Fifth, of the many methods of therapy that give people a *choice* of accepting their feelings and a *choice* of dealing with dysfunctional ones more thoroughly in the present and making themselves less disturb*able* in the future, several cognitive methods are probably the most effective. These methods include thinking about and disputing one's dysfunctional thinking. If clients are shown by therapists how their overgeneralizing, musturbating, awfulizing, and rigid absolutizing and damning are prime causes of their needlessly and unhealthily disturbing themselves, and if they will think about this kind of dysfunctional thinking and think about ways of contradicting it and minimizing it, they will be able to minimize it now as well as train themselves to habitually resort to it less in the future. This will especially enable them to unconditionally accept themselves, accept other people, accept world conditions, and accept their own thinking, feeling, and behaving when, for the moment, they can't change them.

I have used rational emotive behavior therapy (REBT) for many years with clients like Claire, who have made themselves panicking about dangerous and nondangerous events and who have then felt panicking about their panicking. I have also supervised many cases of therapists who have had clients with feelings of panicking and depressing and who created disturbed feelings and behaviors *about* their original primary neuroticizing of themselves. My clinical work as well as the perusal of many studies of self-defeating thinking and of therapy methods designed to deal with it have convinced me of the element of truth in Shakespeare's maxim in *Hamlet*: "There's nothing either good or bad but thinking makes it so." In large part—though not completely—people's *Belief System*, with its inevitable emotional and behavioral components, creates their neuroticizing reactions, and can therefore be therapeutically employed to uncreate them.

Moreover, the human ability to think about thinking about one's thinking encourages people to develop primary and secondary symptoms of disturbing themselves that often seem paradoxical but perhaps follow logically from their use of language and their verbal processes. Verbal behavior, as Steven Hayes notes, has many advantages but also has its inevitable pitfalls—especially in regard to the disturbing aspects of nonaccepting and the therapeutic aspects of accepting in psychotherapy.

I try to show in this chapter how thinking about thinking can be used in treating neurotic panicking and panicking about panicking. I also hypothesize that cognizing is consciously and/or implicitly used in nearly all kinds of therapy, including "pure" behavior therapy; and that it is particularly useful in teaching clients how to employ it in accepting therapy.

REBT includes many cognitive, emotive, and behavioral methods—because it holds that thinking, feeling, and acting are processes that all include and interact with each other (Bernard and Ellis 1998; Ellis 2001; Ellis and MacLaren 1998). But it especially stresses teaching clients how to therapeutically think about and restructure their untherapeutic thinking and thinking about their thinking. By so doing, it is proposed, therapists can elegantly zero in on showing clients how to unconditionally accept themselves, accept other people, and accept the undesirable realities of world events that they cannot presently change.

SELF-HELP SUGGESTIONS

- Acceptance is one of the most important and potentially effective aspects of psychotherapy and self-help. It has many useful forms, some of which are listed in the third paragraph of this chapter. Consider these possibilities!
- When you choose to absolutistically demand and musturbate, you nicely sabotage much of your accepting. What a choice!
- Misery loves the company of rigidity. Freedom-oriented alternative-seeking offers you many other choices. Look for them: loosen up your self-inflicted thongs! Flexibility is mind-opening.
- Although your use of language often leads to your overgeneralizing and nonaccepting, REBT recommends that you use many experiential and behavioral methods to stop the language tricks you often play on yourself. But it also recommends that you use your ability to think about your thinking and to think about thinking about your thinking to verbally undo the nonaccepting and musturbating that you have verbally done. Yes, thinking about your thinking can unbind you!
- Probably the best way for you to achieve unconditional self-accepting (USA), unconditional other-accepting (UOA), and unconditional accepting of frustration or high frustration tolerance (HFT) is to *decide* to do so. Your decision or choice had better include determining and acting on accepting. But deciding is also *thinking*. And thinking *about* whether your decision is a good one is thinking about thinking. Try it!

17

The Rise of Cognitive Behavior Therapy

I can't say that I originated cognitive behavior therapy because you can always find some ancient sage who practiced a form of it many hundreds of years ago. Thus, Gautama Buddha became enlightened and founded Buddhism more than 2,500 years ago; and to his cognitive teachings were soon added the behavioral exercises of the Zen Buddhists and other groups. Hindu yoga practices are also definitely cognitive-behavioral, as are the combinings of religious philosophies with various behavioral rituals of the ancient Hebrews and the early Christians.

Indeed, many religious groups intent on creating what might be called therapeutic change in their members seem to use a combination of philosophic education, emotional exercises, and behavioral practices to encourage their adherents to devoutly follow their precepts. We might speculate that their combination of cognitive, emotive, and behavioral methods tends to show that in order to make and maintain profound personality changes, humans often have to strongly and persistently follow these combined methods. Combined cognitive, emotional, and activity procedures are almost essential to basic personality change.

This chapter is partly adapted from *The History of Behavior Therapy*, ed. S. C. Hayes and M. Clayton (Reno, Nev.: Context Press, 2001). Used with permission.

245

When I started to regularly practice psychotherapy in 1943, I was already prejudiced in favor of cognitive behavior therapy. Unlike the vast majority of psychologists, I was well on my way to being a sexologist; and in addition, not only was I very interested in marriage and family relationships, but I had made a special study of love relationships. Since 1939 I had trained myself in these areas by reading thousands of books and articles on sex, love, and marriage, and by voluntarily counseling my friends and relatives on their problems in these areas.

As a clinical sexologist, I followed the procedures of the early twentieth-century practitioners, especially Iwan Bloch, August Forel, Havelock Ellis, and W. F. Robie, who were physicians and who practiced what could be called cognitive-behavior sex therapy. They educated their patients sexually, helped minimize their shame and guilt, and gave them practical in vivo homework assignments. Following their procedures, I found that I could help my early clients to overcome their sex problems, as well as many of their love and marital difficulties, often in just a few active-directive sessions.

I practiced this kind of cognitive behavior therapy from 1943 to 1947 and then mistakenly thought that I could do a deeper and more intensive kind of treatment by getting trained in liberal psychoanalysis, and practiced it for six years. I was really an existentialist analyst, since my supervisor and trainer, Richard Hulbeck, was a training analyst of the Karen Horney Institute and was also a leading existentialist. Moreover, on my own I was opposed to Freudian analysis, since I thought that Freud was exceptionally unscientific, knew very little about the origin of people's sex and love problems, and wrote brilliant fiction which he presented as scientific nonfiction. So I mostly followed the neo-Freudian views of Alfred Adler, Franz Alexander and Thomas French, Erich Fromm, Karen Horney, and Harry Stack Sullivan.

I found that even this kind of liberal psychoanalysis was exceptionally inefficient and superficial, because it was passive, little educational, and lacking behavioral elements which I had effectively used as a sex therapist and love and marriage therapist. So I abandoned it in 1953, did an intensive study of many techniques of therapy in the next two years (Ellis 1955a, 1955b) and started formulating a more efficient form of psychotherapy.

In January 1955 I started to do what I called rational psychotherapy (Ellis 1958), later called rational-emotive therapy (Ellis 1962; Ellis and Harper 1961), and finally retitled rational emotive behavior therapy (REBT) (Ellis 1993, 1999). Although there were a few cognitive behavior therapies before REBT, such as those of Alexander Herzberg and Andrew Salter, they were highly unpopular in 1955. Freudian therapy ruled the roost, especially in the United States, and Rogerian therapy, which I had been trained in while in graduate school, was immensely popular.

Why was REBT, right from its start, heavily behavioral? Mainly because I had used behavior therapy on myself before I even thought of becoming a therapist, and because I had used it successfully for a dozen years in my specialty of sex, love, and marriage therapy. I first used it when I was nineteen years of age and had a severe phobia of public speaking. I was the youth leader of a radical political group, but never dared give a public speech. But by reading the early experiments of John B. Watson (1919) and his associates, I learned that they deconditioned young children in a few sessions to overcome their fears of animals by in vivo desensitization. So I forced myself, very uncomfortably, to speak and speak in public and within seven weeks got completely over my phobia—and since that time, as I frequently tell my workshop audiences, you can't keep me away from the public speaking platform!

Thrilled by my success in getting almost a hundred percent over my panic about public speaking, I soon tackled my second paralyzing phobia—social anxiety. I could talk to young women comfortably after being introduced to them by a friend, but panicked at the thought of approaching them by myself and starting up a conversation. I never did so, just as I had avoided all public speeches up to the time I used exposure to rid myself of this fear. So I gave myself the homework assignment, in the month of August when I was on vacation from college, of sitting next to every young woman I saw sitting alone on a bench in Bronx Botanical Gardens and giving myself no more than one minute—yes, one lousy minute—to start a conversation with her. No nonsense, Albert—*one minute*!

I actually, in one month, sat next to 130 young women—which I had never tried to do before, so afraid was I of being rejected. Whereupon thirty out of the 130 immediately got up and walked away. But that left me with an even sample of one hundred—good for research purposes! Nothing daunted, I opened a conversation with the remaining one hundred women—for the first time, again, in my entire young life. I spoke about the weather, the birds and the bees, the flowers and the trees, the book they were reading—truly, about everything and anything.

As I have often related, I got absolutely nowhere with my efforts to befriend, to date, and perhaps even to marry a few of these women with whom I conversed. If Fred Skinner, who was then teaching at Indiana University, had known of my futile efforts, he would have predicted that I would have been extinguished. Of the hundred women I talked to, I only made one date—and she didn't show up for it! She kissed me in the park, promised to meet me again later in the evening, and didn't appear. Being a novice at this kind of dating, I forgot to take her telephone number, so I never did discover what happened to her. Thereafter, I always took the phone number of the women I arranged to date!

Anyway, I found out that nothing terrible happened when I got rejected by one hundred women in one month. No one took out a stiletto and cut my balls off. Women only do that these days! No one vomited and ran away. No one called a cop. I had many interesting and pleasant conversations. I found out a great deal about women. And I got so relaxed about talking to strange women in strange places that I got good at conversing, and with my next hundred tries, I actually made three dates. Better yet, I got completely over my fear of approaching women for the rest of my life, and have espoused the pickup technique of meeting new partners to hundreds of my clients over the years.

Well, *in vivo* desensitization really worked for me at the age of nineteen. So when I started to practice psychotherapy in 1943, when I was thirty years old, I used it, with much success, with many anxious and phobic clients. Some of them achieved remarkable cures of their long-standing panicking in just a few sessions. So my attempts to use this behavioral technique were nicely reinforced, and REBT has used it more than the other cognitive behavioral therapies, which followed it about a decade after I started to use REBT in 1955.

IMPORTANT DEVELOPMENTS IN THE RISE OF COGNITIVE BEHAVIORAL THERAPIES

As I have noted, the use of cognitive behavioral methods in personality change is centuries old. Modern therapy, which started to become popular in the late eighteenth century with the experiments of Franz Anton Mesmer, was almost always cognitive-behavioral. Hypnotists like James Braid, Jean Martin Charcot, and Hippolyte Bernheim used educational-persuasive and emotive methods to put their clients into trances and then often gave them activity homework assignments to help them work against their disturbed symptoms. Bernheim was quite cognitive, in that he realized that hypnotism worked mainly because clients took the suggestions of the hypnotist and decided to follow them. Emile Coué developed the cognitive aspects of hypnotism in the early years of the twentieth century by realizing that suggestion was not only at the heart of hypnotic therapy, but also that people's negative self-suggestion—or what he called autosuggestion—was a prime element in creating neurotic disturbance and that they could consciously choose to replace it with positive autosuggestion to solve many of their emotive and behavioral problems. Coué also invented positive visualization to help disturbed people improve their psychophysical functioning. So he was definitely a cognitive behavior therapist.

When did modern cognitive behavior therapy (CBT) start? Probably in 1953, when I abandoned psychoanalysis and started to develop REBT. After several futile attempts to reform psychoanalytic thinking and to make it more scientific—in a series of articles I wrote from 1947 to 1953 (Ellis 1950, 1956)—I abandoned it and looked for an alternative system of psychotherapy. I went back to philosophy, especially the philosophy of human happiness, which had been one of my main hobbies since the age of sixteen, and rediscovered the ancient Asian, Greek, and Roman philosophers. I was particularly taken with Epicurus, who preached the philosophy of disciplined hedonism, and with Epictetus, who brought the stoic philosophy from Greece to Rome during the first century C.E. Most of these ancient writers were constructivists who differed from the later Freudian idea that childhood traumas caused early and later emotional disturbance. They also differed from the somewhat similar idea of John B. Watson, who stated that if he trained or conditioned a child during its first five years to behave in a certain way it would take on that personality pattern for the rest of its life.

On the contrary, the ancient philosophers were constructivists. They largely maintained, along with Epictetus, who wrote in *The Enchiridion* or *Manual* in the first century, "People are disturbed not by things, but by the *views* they take of them." This philosophy gives humans some *choice* in making themselves disturbed and undisturbed; and it was solidly reiterated by the existentialist philosophers, such as Soren Kierkegaard, Martin Heidigger, Jean-Paul Sartre, and Paul Tillich, in modern times.

Taking this constructivist or choice theory to heart, I created and started practicing REBT in January 1955. I was not influenced by George Kelly (1955), whose brilliant *Psychology of Personal Constructs* appeared later in 1955 and which I didn't read until 1957. But I was thrilled to see, when I read it, how much his theory of personal choice overlapped with that which I had already incorporated in rational emotive behavior therapy.

As I noted in my first paper on it at the American Psychological Association Convention in Chicago in August 1956 (Ellis 1958), REBT went beyond the previous cognitive therapies of Pierre Janet, Paul Dubois, and Alfred Adler, all of whom worked to change what Janet called the *ideés fixe*—the fixed ideas—of disturbed people. REBT specifically described twelve common irrational or dysfunctional beliefs, which I derived from my clients' formulations of their problems during the first year and a half that I used it. It hypothesized that these and related Irrational *Beliefs* (IBs) almost invariably accompanied and helped to instigate people's neurotic feelings and behavior. As its main cognitive method, it actively-directively showed clients how to empirically, logically, and pragmatically dispute these IBs (Ellis 1957/1975, 1958, 1962). This was much more specific than the previous cognitive therapies, and was largely adopted by most of the other cognitive behavioral systems that originated about a decade later, such as those of Beck (1967), Meichenbaum (1977), and Mahoney (1974).

Moreover, my hypothesized irrational or dysfunctional *Beliefs*—which I soon raised to about 50 common IBs—were put into paper and pencil questionnaires. More than 2,000 research studies using these questionnaires have now been published that tend to confirm my hypothesis that when people hold more irrational or dysfunctional beliefs, and hold them strongly, they are more seriously disturbed than those who hold fewer of them and hold them weakly (Clark 1997; Glass and Arnkoff 1997; Hollon and Beck 1994).

Moreover, more than 2000 empirical studies have also been published by REBT and CBT researchers that tend to show that when clients are shown their irrational and dysfunctional beliefs, and are taught how to use cognitive behavioral methods of changing them, they tend to become less neurotic and less afflicted with severe personality disorders (Engels, Garnefski, and Diekstra 1993; Hollon and Beck 1994; Lyons and Woods 1991; McGovern and Silverman 1984; Meichenbaum 1977; Silverman, McCarthy, and McGovern 1992). So the REBT theories of emotional-behavioral disturbance and their cognitive-behavioral treatment have been backed by many empirical studies.

What about REBT and its place in behavior therapy? I also clearly stated in my first presentations on REBT that it is both highly emotive-evocative and behavioral; and I changed its name in 1961 from rational therapy (RT) to rational emotive therapy (RET). In the 1960s, following the work of Fritz Perls and William Schutz, I also added many experiential exercises to REBT, including my famous shame-attacking exercises. So from the start REBT differed from most other therapies in its regular use of many cognitive, many emotive, and many behavioral methods; and in this respect it has always been, to use Arnold Lazarus's (1997) term, multimodal (Kwee and Ellis 1997).

This is an important aspect of cognitive behavioral therapy: In theory as well as practice, it is eclectic and integrationist. I clearly said in my first paper on REBT (Ellis 1958) that thinking, feeling, and behaving overlap and are holistically interrelated.

I think that all behavior therapy is really cognitive behavioral, since even in its purest form it consists of teaching, educating, and persuading clients to experiment with new behaviors. In pointing this out in a discussion I had with Joe Wolpe in 1955, I got him to admit this, as I stated in the previous chapter.

Behavior Therapy, then, is nearly always cognitive behavioral; and cognitive behavior therapy practically always tends to be integrational, because its theory and practice hold that there are many roads to treating disturbed individuals, and these include various psychodynamic, interpersonal, person-centered, and other therapeutic methods (Ellis 1958, 1962, 1999, 2000b; Goldfried 1995). Even the radical behaviorists, such as Steven Hayes (Hayes, Strosdahl, and Wilson 1999) have fairly recently included distinctly cognitive and emotive methods in their form of behavior therapy and seem to be increasingly headed in that direction. So today, more than ever before, behavior and cognitive behavior therapy are following REBT and Lazarus's multimodal therapy in becoming wide-ranging in their therapeutic procedures.

CASE STUDY OF REACTIONS TO RATIONAL EMOTIVE BEHAVIOR THERAPY

My most cited publication on REBT was my book *Reason and Emotion in Psychotherapy* (Ellis 1962). The reactions to it by leading therapists all over the world were at first almost uniformly negative. Fritz Perls carried on a feud with me for many years, contending that the book was boringly intellectual and completely omitted any emotional element. Carl Rogers never mentioned it publicly but, according to his intimates, was solidly against it. Several leading psychoanalysts called it superficial and made snippy remarks about it.

Psychologists were much kinder. Francis Ilg and Louse B. Ames, prominent child psychologists, called it "a most important, unusually interesting, and at times terribly amusing book." The unorthodox psychoanalyst, Harry Bone a leading Sullivanian, was quite enthusiastic about it, and wrote:

> Aside from his contributions to therapy, Ellis has made many important thoroughly scholarly researches which do not have as many readers as they deserve. I unhesitatingly recommend his unique contribution to psychotherapy and his excellent exposition of his highly original system. It seems to me that Ellis's basic principle of *complete absence of blame* of not "blaming *anyone* for *anything* at *any time*," is essentially identical with Carl Rogers's principle of *unconditional positive regard*. The *thoroughness* with which they espouse this principle and its *implications* together with their respective ways of effectively *implementing* it, distinguishes their systems from other systems. This is the source of their potency and economy. I consider Ellis's *Reason and Emotion in Psychotherapy* the most important contribution to the field since Rogers' contribution. (Bone 1968, p. 174)

Reviews of *Reason and Emotion in Psychotherapy* were almost nonexistent; and *Contemporary Psychology* reviewed it only when John Gullo, already a practicing psychologist who used REBT, convinced the editors to review it and gave it a very favorable review. Otherwise the book would have been ignored by this journal—as it was by all the other professional journals. Despite this fact, *Reason and Emotion* sold more copies over the years than almost any other professional book of its day and a number of therapists learned how to do REBT mainly by reading it. To my surprise, although clearly written for the psychological profession, it became popular in the self-help field and I have many endorsements of it by readers who found it more helpful than some of my other books, which were written for the public.

Speaking of my popular books, they have been much more widely reviewed than my professional ones. *A Guide to Rational Living,* first published in 1961, has sold almost two million copies, has been largely praised highly, and has been one of the books that therapists have recommended most to their clients. It has received very favorable reviews by many mental health professionals, including Cyril Franks, Daniel Wiener, Thomas W. Allen, Harold Greenwald, and Rowena and Heinz Ansbacher. Frank Richardson said that "It is still perhaps the single best 'self-help' book available to lay persons and psychotherapy clients." Sol Gordon noted, "Still, in my judgment, the most sensible and usable of the self-help books" (1980, p. 203).

My popular books which applied REBT methods to sex, love, and marriage problems have sold very well, but been heavily criticized for their liberal views. Conservative professionals and critics have often objected to them strongly and have sometimes objected to the cognitive behavioral techniques they presented, often for the first time, to the public. They have been influential in the field of sex therapy, and have encouraged William Masters and Virginia Johnson, Helen Kaplan, Joseph LoPicolo, Lonnie Barbach, Bernie Zilbergeld, and other authorities to adopt cognitive behavioral methods. But they also have prejudiced some professionals against REBT theory and practices in nonsexual areas, because of their objections to my sexual liberalism. On the other hand, my forthright sex writings have influenced many members of the public and mental health professionals to favor general CBT theory and practice. Prejudice, apparently, goes both ways!

POSSIBLE OBJECT LESSONS FOR THE FUTURE OF COGNITIVE BEHAVIOR THERAPY

Cognitive behavior therapy has come a long way since I first started to do REBT in 1955. It is perhaps the most common form of psychological treatment that therapists actually do today, no matter what system of therapy they say they follow. Many of its common procedures, such as cognitive restructuring and in vivo shame-attacking exercises, are widely used by many different kinds of therapists.

Moreover, in subtle or conscious ways, the use of various kinds of cognitive restructuring is commonly employed in various forms of CBT (such as the constructivist therapy of Michael Mahoney [1991]), and in fairly pure behavior therapy (such as that of Wolpe [1990]), and in radical behavior therapy (such as that of Hayes [Hayes, Stroshahl and Wilson 1999]). So, again, important elements of CBT are almost universally used today in most psychotherapies.

This is exactly, I think, what preferably should happen in the future. Cognitive behavior therapies had better be tested for their effectiveness in their own right—though, actually, this is difficult to do, since they include a number of different cognitive, emotive, and behavioral techniques. But they also can be at least partially integrated with methods derived from psychodynamic, interpersonal, person-centered, and other schools of therapy.

This kind of integration has always been experimentally tried by many therapists. Even Freud gave occasional activity homework assignments; and REBT practitioners have at times used pollyannaish, unrealistic, and irrational methods, to which normally they are allergic. Whatever works works! Though as Steven Hayes (1994) and I (Ellis 1999, 2000b, 2001) have pointed out, some workable methods can also interfere with clients' use of deeper and more elegant methods of treatment.

Cognitive behavioral therapy is probably here to stay—and to be constantly revised and improved. That is the way of scientific endeavor, and therefore the way to continue to go!

SELF-HELP SUGGESTIONS

- Rational Emotive Behavior Therapy (REBT) and Cognitive Behavior Therapy (CBT) have really been practiced for thousands of years—often by religious groups, like the Jews, Hindus, Buddhists, and early Christians. Although they are not foolproof, literally millions of people have derived distinct improvement in practicing them, and in that sense they have been often tested and found effective. So if you experiment with some of their methods, you are in good company!

- Sex therapy since the beginning of the twentieth century has most often been cognitive-behavioral and effective. Again, CBT methods have proven to be reliable—and remarkably brief! Better, frequently cheaper, and more permanent than Viagra!

- When I pioneeringly started using and teaching REBT in 1955, cognitive behavior therapy (CBT) soon followed its main practices, became quite popular, and now is included, in one form or another, in many other kinds of psychological treatment, largely because hundreds of research studies have shown that it is effective. You can therefore have considerable confidence that you can use aspects of REBT and CBT to help yourself. Again, many studies show that they work for self-help purposes.

- Practically all kinds of therapy, including "pure" behavior therapy, include important cognitive and emotional elements and therefore unconsciously, if not consciously, overlap with REBT. Make yourself quite conscious of the fact that the therapy or self-help therapy that you are using has distinct thinking, feeling, and action aspects and try to use all three of these important aspects.

- Most self-help books, once again, are largely filled with cognitive-behavioral techniques and that, I naturally think, is why many of them can help you.

18

The Future of Cognitive Behavior Therapy and Rational Emotive Behavior Therapy

I n writing about the future of counseling and psychotherapy, I shall naturally take a biased view and hold that its future will largely be eclectic and integrative, as that is the way therapy is developing. At the core of this eclecticism and integrationism, however, will be cognitive-behavior therapy (CBT) in general and my own form of CBT, rational emotive behavior therapy (REBT).

Cognitive Behavior Therapy (CBT) is one of the youngest of today's popular psychotherapies, and I think I can immodestly say that I seem to have originated it in January 1955, under the names of Rational Therapy (RT) and Rational Emotive Therapy (RET). Psychoanalysis had previously existed for over a half century, and client-centered, existential-humanistic, and behavior therapy were about a decade old at that time. Cognitive therapy, without the emotive and behavioral aspects included in REBT, originally became popular in the latter part of the twentieth century, and was particularly developed by Alfred Adler. Eclectic and integrative therapy also was becoming fairly well known in the 1950s (Thorne 1950), but grew enormously in the 1980s (Beutler 1991; Goldfried 1995).

Cognitive Behavior Therapy in general, and Rational Emotive Behavior

This chapter is partly adapted from "The Future of Cognitive-Behavior and Rational Emotive Behavior Therapy," in *The Future of Counseling and Psychotherapy*, ed. S. Palmer and V. Varna (London: Sage, 1997), pp. 1–14. Used with permission.

Therapy in particular, significantly overlap with early cognitive therapy as well as with existential-humanistic and behavior therapy, and REBT is exceptionally eclectic and integrative, as is Arnold Lazarus's multimodal therapy. Together CBT and REBT have been tested in over two thousand outcome studies, the great majority of which have shown them to be more effective than other forms of therapy or of waiting list groups (Hollon and Beck 1994; Lyons and Woods 1991; McGovern and Silverman 1984; Meichenbaum 1977; Silverman, McCarthy, and McGovern 1992).

Because of their clinical effectiveness, CBT and REBT have recently become very popular forms of therapy, and even therapists who ostensibly practice other forms of psychological treatment, such as psychoanalysis, transactional analysis, and existential-humanistic therapy include, and one might say, sneak in CBT methods. Therapy that is called eclectic or integrative also often mainly consists of cognitive-behavioral practice.

I predict that the future of Cognitive Behavior Therapy will be exceptionally promising and that it will consciously or unconsciously, overtly or covertly, continue to influence and be used by most therapists in individual psychotherapy. In group therapy it is still not the main modality employed by most therapists but, once again, many of its best procedures, such as cognitive homework assignments, are creeping into experiential and psychoanalytic groups. In marital and family therapy it is also becoming much more popular and will, I prognosticate, continue to grow.

In the field of sex therapy, CBT has practically taken over and is easily the most popular form of treatment (Leiblum and Rosen 1998). It certainly looks as though its preeminence in this important area of psychological treatment will continue and will expand.

So the future of CBT in regular fields of therapy seems quite bright. But in several related fields it appears to be even brighter. For unlike several other forms of therapy that insist on an intimate, intense relationship between the clients and their therapists—especially psychoanalysis and humanistic-existentialist psychotherapy—CBT can be effectively taught in a number of psychoeducational and mass media ways. Let me mention a few important areas in which it is already quite popular and seems well on its way to becoming even more influential.

SELF-HELP MATERIALS

Both REBT and CBT include many psychoeducational approaches that can easily be explained in written and audiovisual materials and thereby set up to teach literally millions of readers, listeners, and viewers. The last two decades have spawned a myriad of best-selling self-help books, such as *Your Erro-*

neous Zones, A Guide to Rational Living, and *The Road Less Traveled*, that are heavily cognitive-behavioral. Millions of CBT-oriented audio and video tapes have also been sold and used. An increasing number of self-help materials by reputable CBT therapists have also been widely employed.

The future of CBT oriented self-help materials looks bright; it is probable that they will be increasingly used by themselves and as adjuncts to individual, family, and group therapy in the next decade and beyond. At our psychological clinic at the Albert Ellis Institute in New York, we have found that clients who use the self-help materials that we recommend often improve more quickly and more intensively than those who make little use of these materials, and several studies have shown that cognitive-behavioral writings and cassettes are effective when used by themselves (Barlow and Craske 1994; Foa and Wilson 1991; Scoggin et al. 1990). Other studies have shown that nearly 90 percent of psychologists use bibliotherapy in their practice and that only 4 percent found this unhelpful. Considerable evidence for the widespread use of self-help materials by different kinds of therapists has also been found. It would be most surprising if the present-day effective use of cognitive-behavioral materials by therapists and by users who are not undergoing therapy does not continue and expand.

SELF-HELP GROUPS

Ever since Alcoholics Anonymous and Recovery Inc. groups started in the 1930s, self-help groups have become very popular and have literally millions of active members today. Most of the groups, like AA, Recovery Inc., Overeaters Anonymous, and Gamblers Anonymous, have a clearcut cognitive-behavioral orientation; and one of the newer groups, Self-Management and Recovery Training (SMART), specifically follows and teaches REBT and CBT in its regular weekly meetings (Knaus 2000; Tate 1997). Virtually all the other self-help groups also use rational coping statements, behavioral procedures, CBT-oriented self-help literature, and other cognitive-behavioral materials. The antiaddiction pamphlets, books, and audiovisual cassettes now used in this large-scale movement sell millions of copies every year and seem to be growing in popularity. The future of cognitive-behavioral self-help groups and paraphernalia appears to be quite assured.

STRESS MANAGEMENT TRAINING

Stress management training today is actually a very popular form of psychotherapy that is mostly done by trainers, educators, employment assistance personnel, and other nontherapists. It reaches great numbers of people, many of whom reduce their stress and anxiety with no other forms of treatment, and it mainly consists of cognitive-behavioral techniques and includes the kind of self-help materials mentioned above. More and more organizations, such as business, educational, nonprofit, political, professional, athletic, and religious organizations, are teaching their employees and members stress management procedures and are using REBT and CBT materials and methods. At the Albert Ellis Institute in New York, for example, we have an active corporate services division that works with business and other organizations to teach their members rational effectiveness training, which is done through workshops, courses, written and audiovisual materials, and other cognitive-behavioral methods (Ellis, Gordon, Neenan, and Palmer 1999; Palmer 1996). Applications of REBT and CBT in the workplace or in other organizations are very likely to have an increasingly active and popular future.

School Programs

Both REBT and CBT are ideally, and perhaps most importantly, suited for school programs from nursery school through graduate school. They are, of course, one of the most didactic forms of therapy, and many studies and reports have shown that their main methods can be taught in large and small groups in the form of classes, lectures, workshops, and audiovisual presentations (Bernard and Joyce 1984; Ellis and Bernard 1983; Knaus 1974; Seligman 1995; Vernon 1989, 1999).

Considering that the vast majority of children, adolescents, and adults all over the world receive schooling of some sort, and that relatively few of them receive any amount of emotional education, and considering that cognitive-behavioral methods of enhancing emotional health are unusually didactic and homework-assigning, the potential use of REBT and CBT in the school system is enormous. Significant beginnings in this direction have already been made and numerous regular education and continuing education programs on personal growth and development are now being offered, almost all of which are heavily cognitive-behavioral. My conviction is that these programs will continue to expand greatly, so that within the next decade or two few high school and college graduates will fail to acquire considerable emotional education along with their academic and vocational learning.

BRIEF THERAPY

Brief therapy has been pushed into unusual prominence in the 1990s, largely because of the insistence of health maintenance organizations (HMOs) and other insurance agencies. However, REBT and CBT have always been intrinsically brief procedures and most of the studies showing their effectiveness have been with subjects who have had from ten to twenty sessions.

This is hardly surprising; I originated REBT in 1955, after I had previously practiced psychoanalysis, because I found psychoanalytic, person-centered, and most other therapies to be too long-winded and inefficient. One of the main theories of REBT is that disturbing people usually have an underlying and core belief system that includes powerful absolutistic musts and demands. They not only get influenced and affected by negative life events, but also create and maintain dysfunctional philosophies that are integrated with their self-defeating feelings and behaviors; and they also have innate and acquired constructivist thoughts, feelings, and behaviors that help them change themselves and become more functional.

In particular, REBT is a highly active-directive, philosophical form of therapy that shows clients how they specifically upset themselves and how to use a number of cognitive, emotive, and behavioral methods to reduce their disturbances and help themselves be happier, more self-actualized individuals. It assumes that effective REBT can often be done in relatively few sessions—though hardly with all clients all of the time (Broder 1995a, 1995b; Dryden 1999b; Ellis 1996). Cognitive-behavior therapy also specializes in relatively brief therapy and has shown some remarkable success in this regard (Beck, Rush, Shaw, and Emery 1979; McMullin 2000).

Because REBT and CBT are experiential procedures that stress efficiency as well as philosophical depth, they are likely to remain in the vanguard of brief therapies well into the twenty-first century.

ELEGANT THERAPY TO HELP CLIENTS FEEL BETTER AND GET BETTER

Since the early 1970s I have stressed the fact that while most therapies try to help people *feel* better, REBT emphasizes helping them *get* better as well (Ellis 1999, 2000b, 2001). I have become even more convinced about this in recent years and have contended that even brief therapy, when it is philosophically done, can be better, deeper, and more enduring than some of the longer therapies, such as classical psychoanalysis.

Although several methods of therapy vaguely try to achieve this elegant goal, REBT is especially oriented in this direction. It hypothesizes that a prime factor in disturbance is cognitive-emotional musturbation—the dogmatic, rigid, and forceful holding of absolutistic shoulds, oughts, and demands on oneself, on others, and on external conditions; and it focuses on showing people how to become aware of and change their core dysfunctional philosophies, including their innate tendencies to overgeneralize, reify, and absolutize, which Korzybski (1933/1990) and others have pointed out (Piatelli-Palmarini 1994; Ellis 1994, 1996, 2000b, 2001).

Some other cognitive-behavior therapists have followed REBT in this respect (Alford and Beck 1997; J. Beck 1995; Mahoney 1991; Meichenbaum 1992). My prediction is that the future of effective psychotherapy lies in this direction and will be much more concerned than it now is with helping clients feel better *and* get better, and thereby make themselves significantly less disturb*able*.

THE FUTURE OF OTHER FORMS OF COUNSELING AND PSYCHOTHERAPY

Assuming that general cognitive-behavior therapy (CBT) and specific rational emotive behavior therapy (REBT) will flourish in the twenty-first century, what will be the future of the other therapies that are popular today? I predict that certain aspects of them will flourish and be integrated with CBT and REBT.

To be more specific, person-centered therapy (Rogers 1961) will continue in the form of unconditional positive regard. But this will be taught to clients more actively-directively and, as is presently the case in REBT, few counselors and therapists will be as nondirective and passive as many person-centered practitioners now are.

Classical psychoanalysis, as practiced by Freud (1965) and his orthodox followers, will rarely be used. But some of the psychodynamic explorations, such as using the relationship between the therapist/counselor and the client and investigating the connection between early experiences and present disturbances, will be employed.

Jungian therapy with its emphasis on exploring archetypes and the collective unconscious will rarely be practiced. But Jung's emphasis on individuation, self-actualization, and creativity will often be incorporated into general counseling and psychotherapy.

Adler's individual psychology will be more popular than ever but its highly cognitive practice will have many of the effective emotive and behavioral methods of CBT and REBT added and routinely incorporated into it. Its pioneering advocacy of social interest will be increasingly incorporated into other therapies (Adler 1964).

Existential therapy will have some of its main values incorporated into general counseling and psychotherapy, as they have already been incorporated into REBT. These values include helping clients to choose their own pathways, live in dialogue with other humans, be more present in the immediacy of the moment, and learn to accept certain limits in life.

Eclectic, multimodal, and integrative counseling and therapy, as I noted above, will become more acknowledged and more popular than it is now. I still think that it will usually be heavily cognitive-behavioral but will include important aspects of other therapies (Ellis 1994; Lazarus 1997; Norcross, Santrock, Campbell, Smith, Sommer, and Zuckerman 2000; Palmer and Laungani 1999).

INDIVIDUALITY AND SOCIALITY

Although the enhancement of human individuality, self-direction, and self-actualization has been a prime goal of most counselors and therapists in western countries up to now, individuals practically always live in social groups; their "personality" is enormously influenced by their social upbringing; and their survival may well depend on a higher degree of social interest than counseling and psychotherapy often promote (Adler 1964; Ellis 1994; Sampson 1989). Twenty-first-century psychological practice had better, and probably will, effectively abet human individuality and sociality. Not either/or but both/and!

The future of counseling and psychotherapy looks good to me for several reasons:

1. Therapy is being experimentally studied and will continue to be investigated, much more than before. This will tend to make it briefer and more effective for more people more of the time.

2. It is becoming more open-minded and integrative—which again will probably increase its efficiency.

3. It is dealing more fully with people's core disturbances and with the thoughts, feelings, and behaviors that go with them. It is on the way to helping them become less disturbed and less disturbable.

4. It is increasingly helping people to achieve unconditional self-acceptance (USA), unconditional other-acceptance (UOA), and higher frustration tolerance (HFT).

5. It is increasingly emphasizing the dual goals of helping people enhance their human individuality and their sociality.

All this looks optimistic. But what we don't know about effective counseling and psychotherapy far outweighs what we do know. If we have high frustration tolerance and scientific flexibility, our future as counselors and therapists looks bright!

SELF-HELP SUGGESTIONS

- If you choose to help yourself by psychotherapy and/or self-help procedures, Cognitive Behavior Therapy (CBT) and Rational Emotive Behavior Therapy (REBT) are now among the most popular and the most scientifically tested procedures. Almost all effective therapies overtly or covertly use their methods. Eclectic and integrated psychotherapies, which are becoming more and more popular, are largely cognitive-behavioral.
- Self-help materials also have been shown to be effective and are usually highly cognitive-behavioral. Today you have a wide choice in using them.
- If you want to join a self-help group, such as Alcoholics Anonymous or different kinds of Recovery groups, you again have a wide choice of groups that largely use cognitive-behavioral educational methods.
- Stress management training is also available in many business and non-profit organizations and almost always uses regular REBT and CBT methods of stress reduction.
- Strive, of course, to help your individual growth and development and that of the people you care for most; but try to put your striving within a broader, socially oriented framework that will help your present and your future community. You are inevitably a social creature who has a great potential capacity for helping yourself and others. Use it

PART II

Treating Specific Emotional and Behavioral Problems and Severe Personality Disorders with Rational Emotive Behavioral Therapy

19

Some Main Treatment Practices of Rational Emotive Behavior Therapy (REBT)

I n the first part of this book, I presented up-to-date revisions of the theory and practice of REBT. This second part will emphasize the use of REBT in treating specific thinking, feeling, and behavior malfunctioning. For readers who want to review some of the material in the first part, I now present an interview I had with Michael E. Bernard, who has practiced REBT for over twenty years, has written several important books on it, and is now a professor at the College of Education, State University, Long Beach, California. I think that the interview I had with Michael amply serves as an introduction to the more detailed treatment methods of REBT that are about to be described in this part of the book.

MICHEL BERNARD: In a recent article I was reviewing that compared multimodal therapy with REBT, I was reminded of the distinctive feature of REBT as being philosophic and that this feature probably separates it from other forms of CBT and multimodal therapy. I'm wondering whether you consider REBT's defining characteristic to be its philosophic basis, both in terms of theory and practice.

This chapter is partly adapted from M. E. Bernard and A. Ellis, "Albert Ellis at 85: Professional Reflections," *Journal of Rational-Emotive and Cognitive-Behavior Therapy* 16 (1998): 151–81. Used with permission.

ALBERT ELLIS: Well, that's a hard question to answer, because there are really several defining aspects of it, and that is one of them. Multimodal therapy includes cognition and my guess is that Arnie Lazarus himself and some of the multimodal people do a lot of it—have philosophical discussions—but they act as if it's only one aspect equal to other aspects of therapy. And I don't think it is. I think humans uniquely talk to themselves—cognize, conceptualize—and that maybe cognition more strongly affects their feeling and their behavior than vice versa, and, maybe, more permanently. Aaron Beck, of course, does cognitive therapy, and in his own way so does Donald Meichenbaum. But I once talked, years ago, to Ray Novaco, who was Meichenbaum's trainee, and he hadn't the slightest notion of what philosophizing was. He was just giving his clients rational coping statements and not helping them to think for themselves. So in REBT we question clients, challenge them, give them coping statements, but largely help them to review their own basic outlook—their own philosophy—and then to see that that's very important in their feelings and behaviors—and then to change their thoughts, emotions, and actions. So we would add that to the usual kind of cognitive behavior therapy.

On the other hand, ironically, we are really the first multimodal therapy. Well, maybe not the first, because maybe somebody like Alexander Herzberg did it before. But of the modern cognitive behavior therapies, we are really the first, because in 1962—and I guess even in 1956, in my first paper on REBT— I said very clearly that thinking strongly influences behaviors and feelings. But feeling and thinking and behaving all are integrated. They go together. They're not separate. Therefore, implicitly and explicitly, REBT has right from the start used a number of cognitive and emotive and behavioral techniques. Now Arnie Lazarus puts them under seven different headings, but really all of his seven could be put under the three main headings that REBT often uses.

BERNARD: Can I ask you, then, even in those early days, when you used all types of techniques, in your own mind were you targeting patient-outlook, philosophy, or were you targeting the ways they were thinking in particular situations, but without an appreciation of the broader outlook?

ELLIS: I was doing both, because—with an individual client we were talking about their problems—so I was specifically showing them that their anxietizing and depressing, let us say, went along with, accompanied, and to some degree was caused by (because they're still interactional with) their thinking. But then I would even give them an educational lecture and show them that humans generally have an overt or implied philosophy. Thus, whenever they make themselves disturbing, the chances are very high that they have some basic irrational philosophies, including one, two, or three core musts.

BERNARD: But the reason that people think in particular ways in particular situations derives from their basic philosophic outlook.

ELLIS: The basic philosophy that is involved in what we call emotional disturbance—as I've said many times—I learned from philosophers, the Asians, who were really among the first. They were about a century before the Greeks and the Romans. The Greeks and the Romans saw it about 400 B.C.E., and I think the Asians figured it out about 500 B.C.E. So the general outlook I got from them, especially that constructivist statement of Epictetus: "People are disturbed, not by things that happen to them, but by their *view* of them."

So, right from the start, I tried to teach my clients, (1) "You specifically are disturbing yourself. Your anxiety largely comes from saying, 'It would be *awful* if I fail. I *absolutely must* not fail!'" And (2) "You and other people generally do this. This is the nature of humans, to often take their desires for success and make them absolute necessities."

Now, at the same time, don't forget what I often show at my workshops on REBT. I would have never created cognitive *behavior* therapy if I had not, at the age of nineteen, overcome my fear of public speaking by forcing myself to behave differently, and then also rid myself of my fear of approaching females by forcing myself to behave risk-takingly.

BERNARD: So did your behavioral change lead to philosophic change in you?

ELLIS: Well, it's interactional. There is no such thing as one or the other. I'm making a point in an article I'm now writing that really there is no such thing as pure behavior therapy. It is *also* cognitive and emotive. So I said right at the start, in my first paper on REBT at the American Psychological Association Convention in Chicago in 1956, thoughts, behaviors, and feelings interact. I first called REBT Rational Therapy—to emphasize the cognitive element in it. But really the client also has to change his or her feelings and behaviors. So I'm the grandfather of cognitive behavior therapy. But REBT also includes a strong emotional component. So in that sense we are the pioneers of multimodal therapy.

BERNARD: Let me just clarify this a minute. People bring with them their outlook about a situation.

ELLIS: Right.

BERNARD: This outlook, presumably, is philosophic.

ELLIS: Yes, you can call an outlook, an attitude, or a philosophy.

BERNARD: Right. They're not emotions. They're not behaviors as much as they are attitudes and beliefs that people have.

ELLIS: Well, but see, there again, that's how clients and therapists mislead themselves. An attitude *includes*, to a large degree, a feeling and a behavior. There probably is no such thing as a *pure* attitude.

BERNARD: But if I enter a social situation with an approval-seeking attitude, what will it mean?

ELLIS: Yes, what does that mean? Let's define it more concretely, which we usually don't do enough. It means that I believe (an attitude) that I must not get rejected. And therefore I feel anxious and maybe stay away from social situations. I have both a feeling and a behavior included in my attitude. Again, an attitude is never pure. Because humans aren't that way. And that's what I specifically point out in my first paper on REBT and in *Reason and Emotion in Psychotherapy*. There isn't any such thing as a pure thought or a pure behavior or a pure feeling, except maybe for a split second. Maybe, but even then you could say that implicitly the three go together. And rather than cause each other, they accompany each other. You see, thoughts accompany feelings and behaviors. They all accompany each other. "Cause" is a bad word.

BERNARD: So you are saying that if you look at your general main irrational beliefs, "I must be successful and approved of," and "Others should treat me considerately and fairly and in the way I want," and "The world should be organized so I get what I want comfortably and quickly . . . ."

ELLIS: Right. If you look at those, they include feeling tendencies, if you want to call them that, or feelings, and also include behavioral tendencies.

BERNARD: Hmm. Does this position represent somewhat of a shift in your thinking from, perhaps, an earlier time when you were focused more on their philosophic . . . ?

ELLIS: No, it doesn't. Yes and no, because I said again, I said in that very first paper in 1956, that there is no such thing as a pure thought or feeling or behavior. Then I expanded that somewhat and gave more detail in *Reason and Emotion in Psychotherapy* in 1962. But I'm saying that if you want to make what we call a profound change, then you had better use all three processes. But you had better focus on your disturbed philosophy, your attitude, more than most of the other therapies do. This is a thing that maybe I see more clearly now than I saw before. I suggested to Windy Dryden, and I may do it myself, a study of how every one of the other therapies, Rogerian, Gestalt, psychoanalysis, all use cognitive methods. If we got the details, complete protocols of what they actually did, we would find that they all are really trying to change basic attitudes in different ways. Second, we would find that if the client's behavior basically changed, in all probability his or her basic attitude—or philosophy—changed.

So I have emphasized cognition partly because other therapies neglect it. But I never said to use it alone. I said the contrary: especially, give behavioral homework assignments. Other therapies usually emphasize something else, such as emotional methods. But implicitly or explicitly they're also throwing in the changing of attitudes. That's why if we really were open-minded, we'd realize that most therapies really overlap to some degree. But I think we would still find that by helping clients emphasize their philosophy and attitude, you can enable them to achieve better, more profound, and quicker change than by putting their philosophies second or third. Most therapies, again, really include clients' basic attitudes but put them in second or third place.

BERNARD: Okay, that's interesting, because I think now when I write about REBT, in terms of what it is, I might emphasize a little bit more that people bring with them to their environment characteristic ways of thinking—their outlook—but also bring feeling and behaving.

ELLIS: That's right. You see, people are prone to do this—and as a matter of fact a lot of research has recently shown this. It didn't show it that much in 1955—that what we call temperament is fairly consistent from early childhood onward and is partly innate.

BERNARD: Right.

ELLIS: But temperament is a bad word, because it includes thinking and feeling and behaving, doesn't it?

BERNARD: Yes, I've always thought that. And I've always thought that innate temperament gives rise to characteristic styles of thinking that reflect an individual's personality.

ELLIS: But also styles of feeling and behaving.

MICHEL BERNARD: I want to come back to the possibility of considering cognition as distinct from emotion and behavior. And the role of philosophy as the core feature of Rational Emotive Behavior Therapy. If you take expectations as a type of rational belief or cognition, people have expectations; they expect people to act fairly and considerately. One, presumably, has rational expectations that are reality based, and demands that are not reality based. Not only would I expect people to act considerately, I think they *must* or they *should*. I could also, I would presume, hold the belief that when people don't act considerately or when they do the wrong thing, they're bad. Now the proposition that I'd like you to consider is if one holds these beliefs, whether they necessarily involve emotion and behavior when the person is not upset and is not engaging in any self-defeating, self-destructive behavior. Can these expectations or beliefs be viewed as basic, fundamental traits distinct from affective experience or action patterns?

ELLIS: I think that people's demands, their unrealistic demands, include feelings and behaviors. They're not just demands. When you have demands that people be some way, you have feelings about your demands and behaviors along with them.

BERNARD: Let's suppose I'm just sitting across from you and I'm not angry with anyone. I'm at peace, happy. Within me resides a belief that people who do the wrong thing are bad.

ELLIS: But that's also a feeling and a behavior, not *just* a belief.

BERNARD: Let's stay with this for a minute longer. Because I don't feel angry at the moment, no one is obstructing my expectation or doing the wrong thing by me, there is no Activating event or Adversity. I'm going to say that Activating events are required to, if you like, occasion or activate the Irrational *Belief* that gives rise to the thoughts and feelings and actions. But in the absence of Activating events that might block my goals or might not fulfill my expectations or beliefs is the basic outlook of the person. My outlook on people, the way I conceive of people, is in this kind of black and white state, potentially in a condemning fashion. But I don't immediately have any affective experience—

ELLIS: Yes, but a demand *is* an affect.

BERNARD: Well, that's why I said let's not take a demand. Let's take the other rating component. Let's say you have the idea that people who do the wrong thing are totally bad.

ELLIS: But that is an affective demand. "They're totally bad people, as I demand that they not be."

BERNARD: But could one define that without having an affective component to it?

ELLIS: I doubt it. Because you're saying, really, that they're totally bad people if they don't go along with your demand and you have both a belief *and* a feeling that they're totally bad people. You're demanding that they behave well, and your feeling and behavior goes along with your demand. Therefore, when they don't fulfill your demand, they are no-good people. So I doubt whether you can have any demands like that without some real feeling and some real action tendencies.

BERNARD: But couldn't the demands only give rise to the affects in the presence of an Activating event? Without an Activating event—

ALBERT ELLIS: But that's the point—that your demand *will* give rise to an affect. So it has an affective dimension or component—whatever you want to call it. You have demands in regard to the people, and you're saying they must not be the way they are. So I don't see how you can have a demand without an affect and a behavioral tendency.

BERNARD: Yes, when you say affect, what do you mean by affect?

ELLIS: Well, you have a feeling that they must not be the way they are. That feeling is an affect. I say that along with your thought is a feeling that they must not be the way they are.

BERNARD: So you're defining the feeling by the cognition. But I must—

ELLIS: Along with your cognition you have a feeling, an affect.

BERNARD: Even in the absence of disturbing events, or potentially disturbing events in the environment?

ELLIS: Well, no. I think you're really saying that when people do not act the way they *should*, they are no good. But they always act in some kind of environment.

BERNARD: I have no problem with the interrelatedness of cognition, emotions and behavior. I'm just wondering and, I guess, feel more comfortable with the idea that it might be possible to have assumptions about other people and expectations about the other people that are driven primarily by a sort of outlook, a view of people.

ELLIS: But your outlook includes a demand, again, and along with that demand you're going to have a feeling that they should not be the way they are.

BERNARD: When they're not being the way you demand that they be?

ELLIS: Yes, when they're not going along with your outlook.

BERNARD: And what about when I am alone? What about if I'm on a desert island and there are no people around. I still have that outlook.

ELLIS: You'd still be thinking that if there *were* people around, they *should* go along with your demands.

BERNARD: Right.

ELLIS: So it still includes the belief and the feeling that if people were around they must not be the way you demand that they not be. And if they are the way they must not be, then they are no damn good.

BERNARD: Right.

ELLIS: So I still say you have an unrealistic *demand* on them and a strong *feeling* that they must be the way you want them to be. You don't only have a preference, but a need—demand—for them to be the way you think is the right way for them to be.

BERNARD: What about if I've just got a preference?

ELLIS: Well, if you have a preference and you say, "I *wish* to hell they were that way. But they don't *have* to be," then you have little or no demand that they be a certain way.

MICHEL BERNARD: And how much affect would there be?

ALBERT ELLIS: Well, you could have a *strong* desire, but not a *demand* that they must fulfill that desire.

BERNARD: So the demand itself carries with it the affect; the absolutizing virtually by definition is what brings with it emotion?

ELLIS: Yes. Your preference itself is a desire or affect, and it brings a feeling that they had better not be the way you don't want them to be. You would strongly*prefer* it or evaluate it as good if they were not. But when you say, "They *must* not be that way," that has, it seems to me, a different kind of feeling than your preference.

BERNARD: Yes. I guess I'm having a hard time distinguishing the demand from the affect when one isn't confronted with an Activating event. Let's take, "Life must be easy, and I must always get what I want easily."

ELLIS: When you have a demand that life *must* be easy, then it seems to me that you have a different feeling—usually a disturbed feeling—than when you merely have a preference.

BERNARD: When do I have that feeling?

ELLIS: When you have a demand and people are not fulfilling your demand.

BERNARD: And what happens when . . . . Well, let's take instances when either life is going easily for me, or in fact it's not an issue that is currently arising. I'm on holidays. Do I still have the demand that life be easy?

ELLIS: You have the *implicit* demand that life should, must be easy, and the implicit demand that it's *awful* when it's not.

BERNARD: Right. But is it the Activating event that gives rise to the emotion? Surely, when life is difficult, that's when I start to whine about it. And then I get upset.

ELLIS: Yes, you get upset because along with the thwarting Activating event, you again have the demand that people must fulfill your desires.

BERNARD: Okay. Al, my model is that attitudes or habits of mind exist as a part of the outlook of the individual, and that when they're confronted with Activating events, the Activating itself gives rise to the thinking and the feeling and the behavior. My conceptualization is that these good or bad habits of the mind exist subconsciously, independent from it, at a deeper level. Thinking in specific situations is stimulated by, generated from a deeper structure of thinking, which I call habit of mind or mind-set, that is stimulated by the situation that the individual is confronted with. I feel very comfortable defining these habits of mind fairly cognitively, because when they're at a very basic level, I see them as an outlook as opposed to an affective trait. They're affective when they actually give rise to patterns of negative thinking in certain situations. That's why I'm pushing you a little bit, to get you basically to reject this model and say, "That isn't really the way I see it."

ELLIS: The situation or Activating event is negative, against your outlook. But when you have that negative situation, then you feel that it shouldn't be that way.

BERNARD: Feel and think? Think and feel?

ELLIS: Yes. Think-Feel. Think-Feel. Think hyphen feel.

BERNARD: Right. But does it make any sense to say that the thinking and then the feeling is generated from a deeper cognitive structure or outlook embedded within the personality of the individual that has a very strong cognitive feature, an expectation, or . . . ?

ELLIS: Well, I think that your cognition *goes with* a feeling. It's both a cognition and a feeling.

BERNARD: So you still would prefer not to define that as a cognitive philosophical component of the psychological makeup of the individual? You'd want to include within that, at a more basic deep structure level, also affective qualities?

ELLIS: Yes, because you very much want to have things your way. You have a wish, which is both cognitive and affective. Then you add to that a *need* for your want to be fulfilled—a *demand*. Your need is an additional cognition that includes a new, and usually strong affect.

BERNARD: Do you accept, though, there are any subconscious outlooks that give rise to the cognitions about particular situations and emotions: that there is a more fundamental, deeper structure of musts that give rise to the disturbed thinking and feeling in particular situations? Is it not useful to conceptualize a generative program that underlies the surface thinking and feeling and behaving in specific situations? Is it a valid distinction for you?

ELLIS: Yes, people are born and reared with desires *and* musts. When they have strong desires, they often *tend* to raise them to musts. So I'm not sure you really ever have the deep *belief* that people must do your bidding without a concomitant feeling that they *must* do so and are no damned good or it is awful if they don't.

BERNARD: Yeah. Okay, that's been helpful. Moving on, I've wanted to ask you for some time now about distinguishing between needs that people have and the demands they make of others. Because in some of your writing you subsume both of these categories within musts: "I must be loved and approved of." And "People must treat me in certain ways." And I've always felt that people who have demanding philosophies are somewhat different from those that have high needs for love and approval.

ELLIS: You mean people who feel entitled, for example—who particularly demand that others do good by them? Sometimes called entitlement.

BERNARD: Yeah, people who tend to get regularly upset about others—angry about others' behavior and inconsiderateness—seem to me to be cut from a slightly different psychological cloth than people who have high needs for affiliation. I've always wondered whether we ought to separate those a little bit more, or whether you're still comfortable about subsuming them underneath the same category of musts.

ELLIS: Yes. We could well separate them more and indicate that some people have, almost equally, both beliefs. Some people equally say, "I must win your love, or else I'm no good" and "You must give your love to me, or you're no good." So they're both self-downing and angry. But some people are mainly in one camp—I won't say exclusively, because nobody's exclusively anything—but mainly in one camp or the other. They mainly say, "I absolutely *need* your love, and I'll kiss your ass and do everything for your approval rather than be myself." But then others say, "You should recognize that I'm an entitled person and you should kiss my ass and do my bidding." So people can believe and feel both ways or either way.

BERNARD: Right. Okay. I'd like to ask you about when you do consulting with people concerning REBT and you have a limited amount of time—let's say four or eight hours—as opposed to therapy, but when you're doing an intensive workshop or an in-service series with a group of people who have come together to learn how to, let's say, manage their own stress. A typical type of group might be working with a group of teachers or a group of parents teaching them basic REBT so that they can teach it to their children.

ELLIS: Right.

BERNARD: How much do you think can be accomplished in a short period of time? And from your own experience, what are some things that are useful items for them to take away that they can understand and implement? What are some areas that you think we'd better not introduce because those are harder for them to internalize and apply? Does this question make sense?

ELLIS: Well, let me rephrase it. When I'm working as a consultant with a group of teachers or managers, and trying to get them to use REBT in their work to help themselves and to help whomever they're working with, then what are some of the things I would emphasize and maybe some of the things I would not emphasize?

BERNARD: And what would we expect them to be able to absorb?

ELLIS: Well, I'll answer the second one first. That depends partly and largely on them. Because if I'm working with two managers at different times, showing them how to manage their school or business, one may learn REBT right away and say, "You know I never realized that before, that I upset myself about my coworkers and that they upset themselves about me. I see now that we don't have to react that way." And another vaguely gets the REBT outlook or doesn't get it at all.

BERNARD: So there is a continuum of insight in most groups of people, from those who get it immediately to those that are vaguely aware of the psychology of it and how it works.

ELLIS: Right. And even with those who get it, there's another continuum of those who start *using* it and those who don't.

BERNARD: Right.

ELLIS: At my demonstrations with live volunteer clients—and I was giving one at an out of town workshop just yesterday—most of the volunteer clients, because they had heard my lecture on REBT first, understood what I was talking about. But some people either get it or don't get it, and use it or don't use it. So I assume that the particular person I am talking with can get it and use it, which may be an optimistic assumption. So I make REBT very simple and uncomplicated and get feedback from him or her as to how well they understand it. The basic thing, since I have limited time to work with them, is that they'd better understand the ABC's of REBT and realize that people largely, mainly upset themselves. They don't just *get* upset from Adversities in their lives. Adversities (A) contribute to their disturbed Consequences (C) but A alone does not disturb them. B, their *Belief* System, is also very important. Moreover, they have a great deal of potential control over B, but often don't have too much control over A. So that is the thing I quickly try to get across to them. And that not only goes for a manager, let us say, but for the people they are managing. They, too, don't just *get* upset but also *make* themselves disturbed.

BERNARD: Yeah, that's where I start when I present. What do we do after that?

ELLIS: All right. Then you ask them for specific examples. You ask them, "When were you recently upset about your assistant manager, or your supervisees?" I look for examples of their feeling anger at someone, having low frustration tolerance about poor work situations, and feeling inadequate and depressed because they are not doing as well as they think they should do. In virtually all cases I show them that B, their *Belief* System, and not A, their Adversity alone, leads to C, their upset feelings. A x B = C. At the same time, if they are dealing with a difficult customer—say, a person who is very angry at them—I show them what ABCs this person is probably using to create his anger. So they understand that the ABCs I indicate apply to themselves and to others.

BERNARD: Okay. Then we move on to the next step, which is we've now demonstrated the ABC model and they understand that it's the B that largely causes the C. Now I'm wondering, what are some ideas that we can then introduce that they can start to teach other people. What can parents and teachers start to teach children now that they realize they've got the ability to educate the minds of their children. So I'm wondering, for example, would you introduce self-acceptance, which I typically teach?

ELLIS: Yes. There are a few main things which I would help them to teach children. Let's use an example of teaching a junior high school class REBT. One idea is to teach them that they never have to put themselves down, make themselves depressed, horrified, guilty, ashamed of anything. What they do is bad or unfortunate, but they are never bad people. One, they can always define themselves as good people or as people whose essence is not bad. They can choose to have USA—Unconditional Self-Acceptance—even when they behave badly. Again, when they get angry and hostile, they condemn others—not only their behavior—so I teach them how to do the latter, and not the former. They learn to have UOA—Unconditional Other-Acceptance. Three, when the conditions of their life are rotten—such as rotten parents, rotten teaching conditions, poverty—I show them that they still have the ability to stop their whining and screaming about these conditions—which will probably make them worse—and to try to rectify them. But first, accept them without horror and then try to change those conditions.

BERNARD: So we first teach the ABCs.

ELLIS: Right.

BERNARD: We can teach them self-acceptance, which contradicts the devastating *Belief* that *they* are worthless when their behavior is poor.

ELLIS: Yes, USA—Unconditional Self-Acceptance.

BERNARD: Yes. Then we have tolerance and acceptance of others for their fallibility.

ELLIS: Right. UOA—Unconditional Other-Acceptance.

BERNARD: Right. And then we have the antiawfulizing "I *can* stand rotten conditions, though I greatly dislike them."

ELLIS: High Frustration Tolerance.

BERNARD: Right.

ELLIS: Those are the three main things.

BERNARD: USA.

ELLIS: UOA.

BERNARD: UOA.

ELLIS: And HFT.

BERNARD: And then we say, "Thank you for coming." Do we draw the line there? Is there anything else?

ELLIS: Well, we say, "You seem to agree with REBT theory. But now you'd better use it on your own disturbed feelings and in your working with other people. Then, you can teach them and show them by unconditionally accepting them that they can fully accept themselves. You'd better unconditionally accept the students in your class who act stupidly and who rebel against what you are trying to do. Nonetheless, keep teaching them and demonstrating to them USA, UOA, and HFT. Also show them the value of achieving these traits. That's another thing. Several people at our training practice, when they're dealing with an angry person, say right away, "Well, do you want to change that feeling of anger?" I rarely ask that. I simply assume that their anger is self-defeating and I start showing them that. I don't say, "Do you want to change it?" They'd damn well better change it! So you educate them and show them why conditional self-acceptance often leads to self-denigration and hence to trouble. But intolerance also does. Anger stirs one's own gut and leads to psychosomatic reactions and, of course, gets you in difficulty with other people. And whining about the world doesn't help! Especially when they're angry, people think, "I'm strong. I really told that person off." Or, "I'm in touch with my feelings." They don't see that changing your anger at others to displeasure at their acts is the better way to go.

BERNARD: Well, we have to ask them, "Do you want to change your anger?" because they frequently don't look at the consequences of their anger. They just—

ELLIS: Oh, well that would be okay if that's a prelude to showing them how disadvantageous anger is.

BERNARD: I think it often is.

ELLIS: Yes. But really we want to teach them, if they don't already know it, that anger usually brings bad results, because some people say, "I'm angry and I don't want to get rid of it. I want to express it better." But we want to show people that anger at oneself, at others, and at the world, are somewhat the same—are really forms of whining.

BERNARD: Okay. What would you say about teaching consultees such as parents or teachers about disputing and challenging the thinking of someone else, as well as themselves, especially if you have a relatively short period of time to do that?

ELLIS: Well, I help them see that they'd definitely better first see, in their own heads, they'd better figure out what the other people are telling themselves and see that they're usually not recognizing the ABCs of human disturbance. Then they can show these others how the Bs significantly contribute to their disturbed Cs, and how to Dispute them.

BERNARD: But how long do you think it would take for people to actually understand what disputing is, be able to apply it to themselves, and then be able to dispute someone else's thinking?

ELLIS: Again, it varies widely. Some talk to me and immediately say,

"You're quite right." A person comes in and is angry at his mother for twenty years and guilty as hell. So first I may show him not to damn himself for his anger. But then I show him that she's probably a screwed-up human and she *should* be that way, because she *is*. Now, some of these angry clients come in for their second session and report that they have spoken to their mother for the first time in twenty years. Without any anger! But some clients take thirty sessions to give up their anger.

BERNARD: Right. But if you take a group that varies on the continuum, with both insight and ability to apply it, in terms of efficiency of your teaching during a one-day practicum or consultancy, how much time would you spend on teaching them the process of challenging and disputing?

ELLIS: Oh, I would show them, just as I did those therapists I presented to yesterday, that D, disputing, is very important, and that it first consists usually of realistic disputes—"Where is the evidence that you *must* do well?" Of course there is none. Then I show them how to do logical Disputing. "When you say, 'Because I did poorly, I am a stupid person,' how does that follow?" And I use heuristic or pragmatic Disputes—"Where will it get you if you think that you *absolutely must* do well and that you are a stupid person if you don't?" Then I go on to antiawfulizing and other kinds of overgeneralizing that they and their clients use to disturb themselves. But I assume that most clients will agree *lightly* with their Disputing, but that it will take them a while to solidly believe in the healthy answers to doing it. They'd also better do some reading and cassette listening and go over their Disputing of Irrational Beliefs many times.

BERNARD: So if you want a group to get more immediate benefit from teaching the ABCs, would Unconditional Self-Accepting (USA), Unconditional Other-Accepting (UOA), and High Frustration Tolerance (HFT) be the things that will have the most immediate impact in terms of applying REBT to themselves and to others?

ELLIS: Yes. Don't forget, that's one of the reasons why I think my workshops are very well received—because I give live demonstrations. I show the participants right there, by using it with demonstratees who bring up real emotional problems, that people can quickly zero in on their shoulds, oughts, and musts, and start feeling differently. And I almost always give them Rational Emotive Imagery in my live demonstrations. I induce people to imagine a very bad Adversity happening to them, to feel quite upset, and then to change their feelings to healthy negative emotions. And I give them homework, including activity homework. So I think that helps members of my audience to understand REBT more clearly than they would understand from a merely didactic presentation.

BERNARD: Let me shift over to the treatment of particular problems that you've seen over the years. And what I'd like to do is to ask you about some key interventions or some key things that would help people who present with particular problems. If possible, could you confine yourself to forty- or fifty-word replies summarizing what you've learned? A client comes to you and says, "Dr. Ellis, I am feeling very stressed." What's the thing that would help the most?

ELLIS: I would first try to help her to see that she probably means she feels anxious—*dis*tress. Stress as a symptom is usually anxiety. But it could also be depression. So it's probably either or both. Anxiety and/or depression. Let us say it's anxiety. I would then ask, "What are you most anxious about?"

BERNARD: So you identify the A.

ELLIS: Yes. Work, school, love, sex, etc. And then I would show the anxious person that almost always he is asking for some guarantee. That's what anxiety normally is. "I would like very much to do well and win approval. Therefore, I've *got to*. I *need* a guarantee. I only have a certain degree of probability—because I may have a good history of doing well and getting approval. But I've got to have a *guarantee*." And I show him that's his must. "I must have a guarantee." Then I demonstrate that there is, of course, *no* reason why he or she *must* succeed. Most of the time stress is a form of anxiety.

BERNARD: Okay. A client comes to you and says, "Dr. Ellis, I'm angry." Angry. "I'm angry with my husband." Or, "I'm angry with my boss."

ELLIS: All right. So I say, "Let's take your husband. Give me a typical thing he does right before you get angry." The client might say, "He screams and yells at me," or "He beats the children." Or "He spends too much money."

BERNARD: I recall a great example from one of your clients years ago. There was a husband who was bugging the hell out of his wife because he used to feed the dog at the dinner table. And he'd take his fork and he'd spear food on it and he'd hold it up, and the dog would eat it.

ELLIS: Off the fork?

BERNARD: Was it off the fork? I can't remember if it was off the fork or if it was off his plate. And the wife would get so angry, because he'd continue to do that just to get her.

ELLIS: Just to get her angry?

BERNARD: Just to do what he wanted to do.

ELLIS: Well, if she told me that, I would almost immediately say, as we usually do in REBT, "Well, let's suppose you're right. One, he does this; and two, he does it to get you angry." So we've got A, fairly clear. Let's suppose she's describing it accurately. Actually, I may say to myself, "Maybe she's paranoid." But to her, "Let's suppose you're right. What are you saying to yourself about his rotten behavior or behavior that most people would agree is rotten?" Because she's describing something that most people, not only she, would greatly dislike. And I would help her see that her anger stems from her command, "He *must not* do that rotten thing, and especially *must not* do it to make me angry!" So I'd say, "Well, why *must he not*? And how does he become a *rotten person* by doing it? And if you keep being angry at him, will that help him change?" She gives me A and C, and I help her see B, her Irrational *Belief*, and Dispute it.

BERNARD: Right. What about depression?

ELLIS: In a case of depressing, I'd begin by saying, "Well, what are you mostly depressed about?" And the client would say, "Everything." Or, "I've been depressed since early childhood." I'd say, "When certain things happen today—let's take a recent thing that you felt depressed about, such as rejection or failure—what do you most feel depressed about?" So I get A. And I'd say, again, "Well, when you are depressing, what are you telling yourself?" A client replies, "This rejection *must not* occur. I'm no damn good when I get rejected!" Then I show him why his *Beliefs* are irrational or self-defeating and how to Dispute them.

BERNARD: Self-downing?

ELLIS: Yes, self-downing. I ask, "What do you mostly down yourself for? What are your main failings that you down yourself for? Work, school, love?"

BERNARD: And what has been the most effective way of challenging self-downing?

ELLIS: Well, with fairly well-educated clients, I almost immediately, during the first session, go on to USA, Unconditional Self-Acceptance. I sometimes ask them my famous question, "Why was Hitler not a shit?" I answer, "Because he *acted* shittily *much* of the time, not *all* of the time; but he also was kind to his mother, his dog, and his mistress." "And why was Mother Theresa not a good person?" I answer, "Because she went to Congress and testified against birth control. That's fascistic—trying to force the rest of us not to use it."

So I show my clients that no human is subhuman, that all people are fallible. You see, I'm educational in the first session. I show them that virtually all the six billion people in this world fairly often put *themselves* down as well as put their *behavior* down. I show them that self-downing is an innate, as well as an early learned, human tendency. I've seen hundreds of people who were thoroughly accepted by their parents and family. They're often the worst self-downers. "Because my parents didn't blame me and I still behave badly, I'm really no good for behaving that way."

So I tell them, "That's often the human condition, self-denigration. And you're going to have a hard time giving it up. But you have," and I sometimes say in the first session, "you have two choices: One, to think 'I'm okay because I'm alive and human.' Or two, to think 'I'm not okay and I'm not *not* okay; I'm only alive and human. I'm going to rate *only* what I do, my feelings, my thoughts, and my actions—not me, my me-ness.'" But I tell them that's going to be difficult. I warn them, "You see, it's not easy to acquire Unconditional Self-Acceptance. We're teaching you something that's partly against the human condition."

BERNARD: Right. When you say, "I'm educational, even in my first session," I understand what you mean.

ELLIS: Yes. We really don't follow the medical model. We follow the educational model. Because we are teachers who know in advance, pretty much, what people do to upset themselves. And we're going to teach them what they can do to refuse to make themselves disturbed. And also teach them how to not do self-destructive acts. Now that's partly the medical model too, because a doctor teaches you to eat the right foods, to exercise, and so forth. But we don't have to follow a clear-cut DSM-IV diagnosis to teach emotional health. Because we can teach it to almost anybody. But with people with a specific DSM-IV diagnosis, we usually teach more intensively and for a longer period of time.

BERNARD: But when you say educational, you also mean teaching the concept or idea of human fallibility, don't you?

ELLIS: Yes, that's right. Let's face it. We point out that all humans are fallible, including you, the client. "Now, isn't it silly, therefore, to say, 'I *must* do well! I *must* be perfect!' That's stupid. Why? Because it's against your social and biological reality." Incidentally, I may say parenthetically that I stopped using the term "against reality" because, according to postmodernism, there is no such thing as pure reality. There is no absolute truth about anything. So I say *social* reality. "And it's against social reality that you can always succeed or that you're infallible. Who is? We have considerable evidence for human fallibility."

BERNARD: When you think about educational, just to sidestep for a minute, I think that's one of the powerful characteristics of REBT. Do you ever feel that the educational element of REBT gets lost in the shuffle a bit?

ELLIS: Sometimes. Because you help people to do active Disputing. It isn't as obvious as it could be that you're really teaching them that, as far as we know, the universe doesn't have absolute musts in it. In REBT, you're also teaching people how to Dispute *their* Irrational *Beliefs* by themselves, when their therapist is not present.

BERNARD: Okay, a client comes to you and is guilty.

ELLIS: I say, almost immediately: "When you feel guilty, you're normally telling yourself two things, one possibly correct and one incorrect. The correct one may be, 'I probably did the wrong, stupid, or immoral thing.' You're assessing your behavior. And let's assume it is bad or immoral. But then, two, you say, 'I *must* not do that immoral thing, and since I did what I *must* not do, I am a no-good person.' That is incorrect, since it is self-defeating. When anyone feels ashamed or guilty, almost always he includes that second part of his thinking. You think you're only condemning your act, and I'm not going to deny that may be correct. Whatever your morals are, they're yours. But you are also condemning *you* for the *act*, and that's what we want to change and to help you to say, 'Yes, I did those rotten *things*. That I did, and I'm the person who did them. But I'm not a damnable, *rotten person*.' Your evaluating your behavior may help you change what you did badly. But if you evaluate *you* and conclude that you are a *no-goodnik*, how can a rotter like you change a bad act? Not very easily!"

BERNARD: And over the years, have you seen that this logical argument helps to liberate people from their guilt about their acts?

ELLIS: Sometimes immediately. Some do it between the first and second sessions. They think about it and go over it in their heads and at least partly give up their self-damning. Others do it lightly and then they have to keep doing it, because their guilt comes back. "Yes, but I'm really responsible," said a woman I talked to yesterday in a live demonstration. "I'm truly responsible for my procrastination; doesn't that prove that I am no good?" "No," I said, "It proves that you're *acting* irresponsibly. But how does that make you a no-goodnik?" So clients frequently have to go over it many times. Because I again point out to them that guilt, too, is probably an innate human tendency. You put *it*, your behavior, down and *you*, the doer, down. *Both*. But you can train yourself to accept *you*—and *not* your poor *behavior*.

BERNARD: Right. Are people more self-accepting today or less self-accepting than they were thirty years ago?

ELLIS: Well some of them—a minority—are more self-accepting, because a number of books have copied REBT in teaching unconditional self-accepting to their readers. Other book authors use Asian philosophies, like Taoism, where you try to minimize your ego and accept yourself. So I think even New Age writing has much self-accepting in it. It includes considerable pollyannaism, but it uses some self-acceptance, as encouraged by REBT and other philosophies.

BERNARD: But in society more generally, wouldn't it be the case that we're less moralizing toward people—liberation, sexual liberation, religious liberation, lifestyle liberation?

ELLIS: Yes and no. We were becoming less self-damning until the Moral Majority and the fundamentalists came along. So some absolutist groups are bigger and wider than ever.

BERNARD: But if you look at the recent coming out of the closet of lesbians in Hollywood.

ELLIS: That has improved immensely.

BERNARD: So homophobia . . . ?

ELLIS: But even then, did I tell you what one of our therapists uses with his gay clients? Well, according to the Mormon Bible, he reminded me that it says clearly that if you're gay you roast in hell for eternity. This therapist, who is a psychologist and a Mormon priest, teaches at a leading Mormon university. He does REBT, is in the counseling department, and has clients at the university's clinic. He teaches his students that if you're gay and a Mormon you roast in hell for eternity. But, he shows them, it's not *awful* to roast—it's highly *inconvenient*! You see? So again, there are many more liberal Christians these days. But nondamnation is spotty. In regard to being gay, people have pushed and pushed for the acceptance of gayness, just like the women's libbers have for women's equality. But then a couple of our states passed a law against it. So in general that kind of damnation may have lessened. But damning people, for example, for crime and for addiction, may be as bad or worse than ever.

BERNARD: If you look at self-downing, what proportion of it do you think is biological and what proportion of it do you think is social, cultural?

ELLIS: Well, I think much of it is biological. Do you know my analogy about being raised by wolves on a desert island? Let us suppose you were raised by wolves on a desert island. They took you in at the age of two months and they raised you. You now, therefore, think you are a wolf. But you're handicapped. Because when the other wolves kill an animal to eat, you get to it last. You can't run as fast as the other wolves. And there is another wolf, like you, who is also handicapped. He's lame. So you both get to the carcass last. You both conclude, in wolf language, "I'm handicapped. I'm inadequate at running, in getting to the carcass fast. Isn't that bad!" But only you, the human, say to yourself, "Therefore, I'm a shit." Does the wolf ever really put himself down? I say, No. He doesn't generalize and make *himself* into a *rotten wolf*, as the human often makes himself into a *rotten person*. He feels very sad, upset about his handicap. But I don't think he'd say, "I'm a rotten wolf." But you, a human, would. So I say that humans, for evolutionary reasons, learn (a) to put others down—"We'll kill the bastards before they kill us"—and (b) to put themselves down. Maybe that's helped them to correct their behavior, because to some degree if you beat yourself you may change your behavior. I think humans naturally down themselves as well as some of their 'bad' acts. Then it gets exacerbated by their parents and others saying, "You're a *bad boy*" or "You're a *bad girl*," when you *act* badly.

BERNARD: And the individual difference is in the biological part of it? The innate part is . . . ?

ELLIS: Oh, my guess is—and I have a lot of clinical evidence to support my view—that individuals with borderline personality disorder, and some of the other people with the severe personality disorders, not only put themselves down, but do it with a vengeance, and therapists have one hell of a time helping them to change their self-damning. They are self-downing for both biological and social reasons. While the "nice neurotics" denigrate themselves too—but they much more easily can give it up and criticize only some of their *behaviors*. They are less likely to be innately-inclined self-downers.

BERNARD: Okay. What about the procrastinating client who says, "I'm just not able to get to many things."

ELLIS: Well, I usually tell chronic procrastinators, right at the start, "There is a high degree of probability that first you have low frustration tolerance—that you're saying, 'It's too damned hard to do it right now. It's easier to look at television, talk to my friends, or do something else that's pleasant. I'll do it tomorrow!' Meaning, you hope you'll *never* have to do it. So you have low frustration tolerance. But often it's your perfectionism: 'If I did it right now, it wouldn't be good *enough*, so again I'll put it off, put it off, and perhaps never have to do it, and thus never fail at it and put myself down for failing.'"

BERNARD: Yes.

ELLIS: I also ask procrastinators, "When you procrastinate, how do you feel about you?" And they almost all say, "Well, I'm *no good* for procrastinating." And I say, "That's a secondary symptom, you see. A, 'I have this onerous task.' B, 'It's too hard.' C, you procrastinate. Then you make C into A2. 'I stupidly procrastinate.' At B2, you think, 'I'm a procrastinator, as I *shouldn't* be. Therefore, I'm no good!' And you then feel worthless at C2." So I show them that most procrastinators have both the secondary symptom, self-downing about their procrastination, as well as their primary symptom, procrastination.

BERNARD: Okay. So we identify and challenge those Irrational *Beliefs*.

ELLIS: Yes.

BERNARD: And is there anything else to help a procrastinator that you've, over the years, noticed? Or will that be your main therapy?

ELLIS: Well, they may have various other Irrational *Beliefs* that lead to their procrastinating. But usually they have some degree of both low frustration tolerance (LFT) and perfectionism. They almost all have LFT, but some of them have self-downing: "I *have to do this task well* and be approved by the people I present it to. It *would be awful* if I didn't and they despised me. Therefore I'll do it tomorrow or I won't do it at all."

BERNARD: And what about the . . . ?

ELLIS: And incidentally, some of them have obsessive-compulsive disorders. Like the rat-packers. They can't throw things out. They have a whole house full of junk. But they're not just procrastinators. They probably also have basic disorganization. Some of the serious procrastinators or rat-packers have obsessive-compulsive disorder (OCD).

BERNARD: What about disorganization and poor priority setting?

ELLIS: Well, there again a lot of people with these problems have ADD—Attention Deficit Disorder—not to mention learning disabilities. But especially Attention Deficit Disorder. Therefore, they are confused and disorganized. Others are perfectionistic, in addition to having ADD: "I must do this task well—and I must do it *perfectly* well." Then, they get so anxious about being imperfect that they bollix things up. So it's often a combination of both Irrational *Beliefs* and perhaps having a severe personality disorder.

BERNARD: We covered some of your typical methods of approach to dealing with different emotional problems like anxiety, guilt, depression, and procrastination. We talked about the Irrational *Beliefs* that you tend to go after and change and challenge. I'm wondering if you have favorite behavioral methods or practical advice that you typically give clients in addition to the cognitive restructuring approaches that you suggest. Are there practical things that you routinely suggest to clients to get them moving and going?

I'm wondering, for example, in treating anxiety, are there typical behavioral methods or homework or advice that you give your clients in addition to the disputing of their need to have guarantees for approval or perfection?

ELLIS: I show my clients that when they tell themselves, "I must have a guarantee that this goal or desire of mine will be fulfilled," in order to eliminate or to minimize that demand, they'd better take risks that it won't work out the way they demand that it *must*. So they'd better force themselves to take risks and through this risk-taking see that there is no horror when their desires don't work out.

BERNARD: So you would routinely prescribe risk-taking activities as a part of combating anxiety?

ELLIS: That's right. To act against your horror about things not working out, you take risks to see that there is no horror if they don't. You thereby prove to yourself that it is *uncomfortable* but not *horrible* when your desires are not fulfilled.

BERNARD: And in a similar way, would you prescribe shame-attacking exercises for people who are awfulizing about rejection?

ELLIS: Yes. By doing shame-attacking exercises, people let themselves risk rejection. They do something that they consider "shameful," risk rejection by others for doing it, and show themselves that even when they do get rejected they can have a non-upsetting philosophy and attitude. "Too bad. It's not *awful* that I was disapproved for doing this 'shameful' act, and I can still live and be happy!"

BERNARD: Okay. What about your depressed clients?

ELLIS: Well, with depressed people, when they feel depressed about rejection, is that what we're talking about?

BERNARD: Or failing or losing love.

ELLIS: We would still encourage them to take the risk of being rejected and losing love. While risking failure, they would show themselves, again in *action, behaviorally*, that failing is not *awful*. They would take risks along with convincing themselves cognitively that it's unfortunate to get rejected, but that doesn't lower their worth as a person.

BERNARD: So would a typical behavior method for depressed clients be risk-taking?

ELLIS: Yes, and when people are depressed we want them to keep in motion, to act, to act, to act. And therefore feel less depressed. Physical activity will often help them.

BERNARD: And when you recommend action as homework, are there particular types of action that you suggest to people depending on their type of depression? Or do you have some basic things you get your depressed clients to do?

ELLIS: An important way to get over depression is to act in spite of the feeling of depression. And again, through the action, show themselves that they're okay and that nothing terrible or horrible happens.

BERNARD: Would the actions be in any area of their lives where they might be successful? Or are there particular social interactions or work interactions or hobby activities that you prescribe?

ELLIS: Well, they would, even when depressed, risk social rejection and show themselves that that's not terrible. And also risk business rejection, or school rejection, and show themselves that that's not horrible. And do pleasurable activities, to show themselves that life can still be enjoyable.

BERNARD: So you're saying they're depressed because they're saying, "It was terrible that I was rejected."

ELLIS: "That it was terrible that I didn't get the love I think I need, and it was terrible that I didn't get the pleasure I think I need."

BERNARD: Right. Okay. What about angry clients, behaviorally, are there things that you typically suggest for them to do?

ELLIS: Yes. The angry person—and let's suppose somebody is angry at her mother or her boss—then I would try to get her to stay with the rotten situation where this mother or the boss is still acting badly and not giving her what she thinks she needs. And so I'd say, "Stay in that bad situation. Or actually phone your mother, if you're avoiding contact with her. And show yourself that even when you get rejected or fail with your mother or boss, that it's not okay. It's bad. But you can accept the badness and not damn the rejecting person."

BERNARD: I thought you were going to say also to provide them with evidence that they can stand the miserable behavior for which they're condemning the rejecting person.

ELLIS: Yes, to prove to themselves that they can stand the unfair, miserable behavior of the mother or boss and still get themselves to feel okay—not about it, the situation, but to feel that it's not horrible and it's not so unfair that they can't stand it and can't have any pleasure at all.

BERNARD: So both concentrating on the pleasure that they can have and staying in the situation as well as increasing their frustration tolerance for being in the situation?

ELLIS: Yes, help them see, first, that the pain of rejection is not awful; and, second, that they can still have pleasure in spite of its pain.

BERNARD: Okay. Guilt. Are there any corrective actions that you would prescribe? For example, if someone was feeling guilty about having an affair with someone, one would advise them to . . . .

ELLIS: First, acknowledge that the affair is wrong, if it is against their moral code and their agreement with their mate. Then, perhaps, feel healthy remorse for having it, and preferably stop it. Second, to not feel self-downing for doing this wrong thing. Only feel remorse. Third, discuss the affair, if possible, with their mate and decide about what they are going to do. Their activity homework would be to discuss the affair with their mate or perhaps to stop it.

BERNARD: Okay. And the final one is LFT procrastination. Someone is putting off doing things. You Dispute with them their LFT philosophy that life shouldn't be so hard. What would be the typical activities that you would prescribe to them?

ELLIS: When indulging in procrastination, they would force themselves to do what they're afraid of doing, because they would be afraid of failing at it or because it is "too hard" to do. So they would still force themselves to do that unpleasant or "dangerous" task, in spite of their discomfort.

BERNARD: What's common in all those behavioral methods, it seems to me, is to get the clients to face, to stay with the situation, and to expose themselves to the discomfort of the situation, as opposed to avoiding it?

ELLIS: Yes. To not run away from the situation, to do the unpleasant thing, which they view as "too risky" or "too hard." They would act to show themselves that it's not *that* uncomfortable or dangerous to do. So their actions would help them, along with their cognitions, to do what they needlessly fear, to give up their damning other people for their obnoxious behaviors, and not to be horrified about difficult life situations.

BERNARD: So whether the situation is rejection, or failure, or being treated badly by someone else, or work that is onerous, behavioral methods all involve getting the person to confront the situation and develop high frustration tolerance, self-acceptance, and other-acceptance at the same time as they're confronting the situations?

ELLIS: Right. To confront the unpleasantness of the tasks they are procrastinating on, for example, and not put themselves down when they fail at these tasks. To give themselves USA—Unconditional Self-Acceptance— even though they failed and/or got rejected.

BERNARD: Well, that makes good sense. Okay. Have there been people writing in the field of psychology and psychotherapy who have impressed you, in the last decade, who you think complement what you do and extend your thinking?

ELLIS: Well, the main people are the constructivists who emphasize to self-disturbing people that they have the ability to cope with the situation because they are innate problem-solvers and naturally construct solutions to life's dilemmas. Therefore, they are able to do well despite the fact that they are failing and they don't have to put themselves down. Then the therapists who for the last decade do solution focused therapy, which has its virtues. They show clients that they can discover what they did previously to overcome their emotional problems, and can use those solutions again. However, using REBT, we would also point out to clients that even if they did poorly that they could still give themselves USA—Unconditional Self-Acceptance—*while* they are doing poorly, not berate themselves for doing so, and therefore have a better chance of succeeding in the future.

BERNARD: So in terms of the constructivist approach, you believe that it helps enhance people's efficacy to overcome problems by appealing to their capacity to solve problems and to stress that aspect of human functioning?

ELLIS: Yes—to see that they can achieve self-efficacy and that they can do well partly because they *believe* they have the ability to do so. They can enhance their self-efficacy by *seeing* themselves as efficacious. But on the other hand, they had better not confuse self-efficacy with self-acceptance. Self-efficacy means, again, that "I'm *able* to do well, so let me strive to succeed. But I'm not, *therefore*, a good or great person." So we would show them that even if they were *not* efficacious, they could still have USA—Unconditional Self-Acceptance.

BERNARD: Problem-solving, though, has always been a part of REBT.

ELLIS: That's right. We always have said, first, don't beat yourself for doing poorly. And change your *Belief* system, B, about how you're no good or unable to do well. But then go back to A and figure out more effective ways of solving your practical problems. You're failing with your husband or wife. You're failing at work. You're failing at school. So we show you how to succeed better. Usually, as we deal with your emotional problems and help you feel less disturbed.

BERNARD: I've always felt that you've had a rare talent in that area. Part of your success as a therapist has been in your ability to help people solve problems.

ELLIS: Oh, yes. And don't forget that for a good many years REBT has taught people how to function better sexually, to improve their relationships, to be more effective at business and at school. So we help people to do better; but not to tell themselves, "I'm okay *because* I'm doing better. I'm okay even if I *don't* do better." But, along with accepting themselvees, we help people solve practical issues in many important areas of their lives.

BERNARD: Could you review with me what part of your therapy brings that out the strongest. Or how about your writing on problem-solving? Because I think that is a very strong feature that has always characterized REBT, and I'm just wondering where we bring that out in terms of the way we describe REBT.

ELLIS: Well, certainly, even in the 1940s I was showing people how to function better sexually and not to put themselves down when they failed. I also wrote several books and articles in the 1950s showing my readers how to satisfy their sex and love partners, such as *The Art and Science of Love*, which for many years was a paperback best-seller. Masters and Johnson cited some of my sex therapy papers in their famous manual, *Human Sexual Inadequacy*. I also in many of my books showed people, early in REBT, how to function in industry, in school, in sports, in the arts, and in other areas. How, again, to achieve self-efficacy. But never to put themselves down when they were inefficient or ineffective.

BERNARD: And in teaching people how to improve situations and be more successful, have you tended to focus on teaching them skills or have you tended to get them simply to think about alternative ways of approaching the situation using skills that they already have?

ELLIS: Well, first, I help them think about alternative ways of using the skills they already have; and, second, to gain better skills—sex skills, work skills, educational skills—while not putting themselves down for their poor functioning. So it becomes a matter of not only fully accepting themselves, but also doing better.

BERNARD: Because I'm thinking of the different areas you've written on in terms of marriage and relationships as well as sex, and I'm wondering if you're providing suggestions for different ways of either working or relating, and emphasizing to people the importance of engaging in those behaviors to be more successful, pointing out to people that the successful behaviors that they need to engage in to be more successful in marriage.

ELLIS: Yes. My very first book on REBT was *How to Live With a "Neurotic" at Work and at Home*. Both. So I showed my readers how not to damn themselves and also how to understand their partners and accept them with their poor functioning and then how to get along much better with them.

BERNARD: Did that go beyond accepting them the way they are to more specific forms of advice?

ELLIS: Oh, yes. Especially in the areas of marital functioning, to show them how to be more adequate. In 1971, *Your Perfect Right* by Alberti and Emmons showed people how to be more assertive. But it used some of the REBT methods of functioning better that I had previously published. In 1963, I included a pioneering chapter, "How to Be Assertive Without Being Aggressive" in the first edition of my book, *The Intelligent Woman's Guide to Dating and Mating*. So REBT, from its beginnings, included instructing people in their love life, their sex life, their marital life, their business life, and so on.

BERNARD: I suppose that was one of the motivations for the name change, too. Not only using behavioral methods to get people to change their emotions and cognitions, but also behavioral methods to get people to improve the quality of their life and to solve the problems that they have.

ELLIS: And we were probably among the first therapists to show that individuals could self-actualize and lead a more joyous kind of existence in life. So we were pioneering in that respect, too.

BERNARD: It's useful to cover this ground, because I think sometimes we overlook that aspect of REBT.

ELLIS: Right.

BERNARD: Solving problems and living happier lives at the same time we're overcoming the emotional disturbance that block self-actualization.

ELLIS: Right. Again, REBTers were doing that in the 1950s and 1960s: helping people feel better about themselves, and also enjoy themselves more.

BERNARD: What are your thoughts on the self-actualizing instinct today as a generative force for getting people to experience joy in their lives? Do you see it as a strong force, that if you help people overcome their self-downing and other-rating and develop High Frustration Tolerance that self-actualizing is a dynamic quality that will lead people to experience the things that lead to an enjoyable life? Is it quiet, is it strong? Does it need to be cultivated, encouraged? What are your thoughts on self-actualizing? The "self-actualizing" person?

ELLIS: Well, I've always promoted self-actualizing. I don't like the idea of a *fully* functioning individual, but I have written several papers on a *better* functioning person—because fully functioning implies utopianism. So I think that humans can be shown how to enjoy themselves more, but not *absolutely* or *fully* or anything unrealistically idealistic.

BERNARD: So you'd like to take the absolutism out of self-actualizing?

ELLIS: Right. And I agree with Christopher Lasch that we can try to show humans how to enjoy themselves better but *not only* in their own interest. REBT encourages them to include social interest in their enjoyments: to personally take pleasure in helping other people and their community.

BERNARD: Right. When you think of the self-actualizing tendency, do you see it as a motivational life force that propels people into new areas, or how does self-actualizing operate psychologically?

ELLIS: Well, again, our goal is to help people accept themselves whether or not they do better, but to try to do better and live happier lives.

BERNARD: And you think people's tendency to try to do better is a clear indication of the self-actualizing instinct?

ELLIS: Yes, I think it's a good example of their innate constructivism. I think that humans can creatively try to enjoy themselves more without being utopian and saying, "I *have to be*," or "I've *got to be* perfectly self-actualizing." Their self-actualizing had better be *preferential* rather than *necessitizing*. Otherwise it can paradoxically lead to stuckness!

BERNARD: And that's a distinctly human quality, isn't it? We presume animals don't have the self-actualizing instinct.

ELLIS: I doubt it.

BERNARD: They want to survive, and that's what propels them presumably.

ELLIS: Well, I think we can help humans survive better, be happier, and not to be *desperate* about their goals of functioning better. Desperation, again, leads to stuckness.

BERNARD: Do you have any things that you'd like to say to the practitioners of REBT concerning their continued use of it? Anything that you'd like to address directly to them?

ELLIS: REBT practitioners obviously don't have to be better therapists or better people. But they can definitely strive for greater efficiency, for more acceptance of themselves, and for more fully enjoying as they try to help others.

BERNARD: Would it be your hope that REBT can be of significant benefit to the practitioner—that not only would it help the client, but it would help the practitioner lead a more fulfilled, less disturbed life? Would that be something that you would hope would be a benefit of REBT?

ELLIS: Yes. REBT is designed to help clients and its practitioners to be healthier and happier. That would be nice! REBT has pushed these goals from the start. I have for many years said that therapists who best practice it with their clients quite often use it almost automatically to increase their own mental health.

BERNARD: Do you have any concerns that REBT maybe has become an ideology, an -ism, that you so strongly advocated against in your professional life? Do you see any signs that REBT practitioners are becoming overly dogmatic in their allegiance to the principles and practice of REBT? Do you fear that they are becoming overly dogmatic, the REBT practitioners, in their adherence to REBT?

ELLIS: I hope they aren't.

BERNARD: You hope they're not?

ELLIS: I strongly hope they aren't becoming arrogant or dogmatic. Let them, by all means, keep brainwashing their clients' dogmatism—and their own!

BERNARD: As one of numerous REBT practitioners, I think I am not alone in saying that REBT continues to help each of us not only be successful in our professional lives, but to cope with our own individual personal, bumpy roads. For this, we are indebted to you.

ELLIS: Fine!

SELF-HELP SUGGESTIONS

- Like other cognitive-behavior therapies (CBTs), REBT shows you how to change your dysfunctional thinking, feeling, and behaving; but it particularly shows you how to make a profound philosophical change that will help you get better and stay better for the rest of your life—yes, even if some of the most difficult Adversities occur in your life.
- REBT, however, shows you how your Belief System—your philosophizing—*includes* your emotions and your action tendencies and therefore encourages you, while working to modify your dysfunctional or Irrational *Beliefs*, to *forcefully*, *vigorously*, and *persistently* do so and, at the very same time, to determinedly act against them. Thus it is very cognitive *and* highly emotional.
- When you are upset about something in your life, such as some failure or rejection, you can quickly zero in on *how* you most probably upset yourself by using the ABCs of REBT. Your goal or desire is to get what you wanted or to not get what you don't want. At point A you suffer from Adversity—from being deprived or rejected. You then have a choice, at point C, your Consequence, of making yourself healthily feel sorry and regretful about your Adversity (A) or making yourself unhealthily feel anxietizing and depressing. You execute this choice mainly by thinking *preferential* Rational *Beliefs* (RBs), such as, "I don't like A. I wish it didn't exist"; or by thinking *musturbatory* Irrational *Beliefs* (IBs) such as "A *must not* exist, and because it actually does, it's *awful, I can't stand it*, I am an *inadequate person* for not preventing it!" By your IBs, you created dysfunctional feelings (such as anxietizing and depressing) and dysfunctional acts (such as compulsively avoiding dealing with Adversity).

- If you fully (strongly) acknowledge your partial creation of your destructive feelings and actions, and if you change your (strong) *demands* at point B back to *preferences*, you can usually appreciably improve your dysfunctional Consequences (C) or self-disturbing.
- If you work steadily and powerfully (emotionally) at acquiring three healthy profound philosophies, you can significantly reduce your distressing and your human tendencies to make yourself disturb*able*. These profound philosophies are: (1) unconditional self-accepting (USA); (2) unconditional other-accepting (UOA); and (3) high frustration tolerance (HFT) or antiawfulizing.
- REBT gives you a number of cognitive, emotive, and behavioral methods to work at achieving and consolidating USA, UOA, and HFT. It also shows you how your absolutist musts and demands make you angry ("People must act the way I want them to act!"); make you anxetizing and stressful ("I *must* have a guarantee that I'll always perform well and that others will approve of me!"); make you depressing ("I *must* have all the important things that I want!"); make you procrastinate ("It *must* not be as hard to write a report as it actually is!"); and make you have other emotional-behavioral problems. When you feel disturbing, persist at looking for and finding these *musts* and turn them back into healthy preferences.
- Once you keep using a number of REBT methods to minimize your self-disturbing, you can then creatively find long-range goals, projects, values, causes, and interests to help actualize yourself and use your human constructivist talents to enjoy yourself and to help others to enjoy themselves.

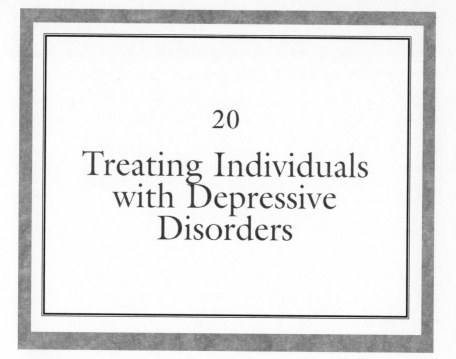

20

Treating Individuals with Depressive Disorders

As noted in the previous chapters, I treat people with depressive disorders actively-directively with the usual theory and practice of REBT. Even though they are severely depressed and perhaps suicidal? Yes, usually. As I noted several years ago, I have had considerable success seeing suicidal clients for only a few sessions, in getting quickly to their intense feelings of hopelessness, and in warding off their suicidal tendencies. Their deeply depressed states, especially when they have endogenous depression, usually takes much longer to change.

As I show in the following case of Flora, who seriously depressed herself after eighteen years of marriage, anxietizing and depressing usually stem from some absolutistic musts—especially self-denigrating musts. So I explore and tackle these dysfunctional self-commands as soon as feasible—normally from the first session onward—to help the client alleviate them. Let me be specific about Flora's case.

This chapter is partly adapted from "Flora: A Case of Depression and Treatment with Rational Emotive Behavior Therapy," in *A Casebook in Abnormal Psychology*, ed. R. P. Halgin and J. K. Whitbourne (New York: Oxford, 1998), pp. 160–80. Used with permission.

THE CASE OF FLORA: CONFRONTING PHILOSOPHIC ABSOLUTISM

Flora came to see me after she had attended two of my Friday Night Workshops at the Albert Ellis Institute in New York City and had been struck with the fact that I was extremely active and directive in the course of interviewing volunteers with live problems and quickly ferreted out the main philosophic sources of their disturbances. She had been in psychoanalytic treatment with three different analysts for the past ten years and was amazed at my ability to zero in on people's neurotic difficulties in a half-hour public session. I showed them that what they seemed to be telling themselves created most of their problems, then demonstrated how they could change their absolutistic musts and demands by making them only into strong preferences, and thereby demonstrated how they could stop depressing themselves. Flora's analysts had mainly listened to her complaints during the ten years, had formed an intense relationship with her, and had endlessly explored her early childhood and her other family relationships. But they had done damned little to reveal her self-defeating core philosophy and to help her dispute and act against them.

Initial Session

"I was particularly impressed," Flora said in the first few minutes of her first session with me, "that you always seemed to know exactly what the volunteers at your workshops were thinking to upset themselves, and that you quickly helped them to see these thoughts for themselves. What was also startling in the case of each of the four people I saw you work with, was that you always suspected that they were not only disturbed, but also disturbed about their disturbances. In all my years of psychoanalytic therapy, this was never quite pointed out to me; and now that I've seen you demonstrate it to several others, all of whom agreed that you were right, I'm beginning to see that this is also one of my main problems. I have not only been anxious for practically my whole life, but I have also been seriously depressed. After watching you in action, I'm beginning to suspect that my depression and my feelings of great inadequacy that go with it mainly stem from my horror of being anxious—from continually putting myself down for my anxiety. I may be wrong, but this is the way it now seems to me, and I want to check this out with you and use your system of Rational Emotive Behavior Therapy—which I see is in many ways the opposite of psychoanalysis—to finally overcome my depression. Also, of course, to alleviate my lifelong feelings of anxiety."

I was very happy that Flora had been benefiting from merely observing my public therapy sessions with several of my Friday Night Workshop volunteers. I thought from the start that she was probably getting on the right track, after years of being sidetracked from it by her classical psychoanalysis, and that with her cooperation we might quickly get to the root of her depressing and anxietizing herself and discover what she could do to work at overcoming deadly feelings.

Like most of my regular clients, as well as the many people I see for public therapy sessions each year, Flora had two major forms of disturbances: First, her original disturbance, which led to severe and almost steady anxiety; and second, her disturbing herself about her disturbance, which led to serious depressing, including frequent suicidal ideation, about her original problem.

According to the theory of Rational Emotive Behavior Therapy (REBT), most people are like Flora in this important respect. They consciously and unconsciously choose to upset themselves by taking some of their important desires and goals—such as to perform well and to be loved and accepted by others—and they irrationally (that is, *self-defeatingly*) make them into grandiose demands: "Because it is good for me to succeed and to win others' approval, I *absolutely must* do so, and it is *horrible* when I don't." Then, when their unrealistic necessitizing—or what I call musturbation—makes them feel quite disturbed and often to act destructively, they note their self-sabotaging, take their *preference* for behaving better and make it into another dogmatic *demand*: "I *absolutely must not* feel disturbed and I *ought not* behave foolishly!" They then make themselves upset about their upsetness, and create an emotional problem that is much worse than their original one.

Not all people and all clients, of course, do this. But probably the majority of them do—as I often quickly show them. I found it refreshing, therefore, that Flora, in her first interview with me, was beginning to see this important facet of human disturbance for herself, and that her attendance at my Friday Night Workshop was already beginning to pay off.

Case History

Flora was a forty-eight-year-old manager of a dress shop who had anxietized since about day one of her life. Her father, an accountant, and her mother, a school teacher, had been very happy to have her as their only child, had given her emotional support all her life, and were still happily married themselves. But they both highly anxietized. The mother was quite hypochondriacal and the father worried incessantly about having enough money for his approaching retirement, even though the family's financial condition was unusually secure. On both sides of her family, her aunts and uncles and grandparents tended to be well-functioning people, but often anxietized. Several of them were also depressed.

Flora, like her parents, married in her early twenties, constantly worried about her husband being unfaithful, and felt devastated when, after eighteen years of marriage, he actually ran off with his secretary, saying that he no longer could stand Flora's pandemic anxiety and her constant checking on his activities. Her twenty-two-year-old son also tended to keep a distance from her, though he said he loved her, because she kept nagging him to lead a highly respectable life and to avoid getting into any trouble.

After her husband divorced her, Flora was so hurt and depressed that she stayed out of the dating scene for a few years, although several men were attracted to her and wanted to form a close relationship. She finally started dating Joe, a fifty-year-old widower who also was wary of deep involvements. He saw her every Saturday night, enjoyed being with her sexually and companionably, but refused to get any closer. She convinced herself that this was all right, but she really yearned for a closer relationship and was afraid to talk to Joe about this, fearing that he would stop seeing her completely.

Recently another suitor, Ed, showed great interest in Flora, and even talked about living with her and marrying her when his divorce became final. But Flora was very anxious about seeing Ed, because she would ultimately have to tell Joe about it and might end up losing both of them. Ed, though a better candidate for a close relationship than Joe, had monetary difficulties, and Flora was afraid that if she decided to live with him, she might not be able to continue enjoying her middle-class lifestyle, and that she would have great anxiety about their monetary difficulties. So she saw Ed, who lived fifty miles away, occasionally, but still saw Joe every Saturday, and felt guilty about having sex with both of them.

Diagnosis

Flora was a college graduate, had done well in school, and I judged her to have high average intelligence. On the Milton Multiaxial Inventory II, her main high scores were for Anxiety, Depression, and Avoidant Personality. Her DSM-IV diagnosis was as follows:

Axis I: Generalized anxiety disorder

            Recurrent depressive disorder

Axis II: Avoidant personality disorder

Axis III: Irritable bowel syndrome

Axis IV: Relationship difficulties

Axis V: GAF (Global Assessment Functioning) 55

Case Formulation

Flora's case was pretty much as she herself presented it during our first session and was similar to hundreds of cases of anxietizing, depressing, and avoidance that I have seen over the years. For both biological and environmental reasons, she first felt severe performance anxietizing. Like most other people in the white middle-class culture in which she was raised, she wanted to do well in school, in her social relations, in her marriage, and in her subsequent life. But she almost always raised her strong preference for doing so into an absolutistic demand: "I *absolutely must* succeed at the important things that I do, I *have to* be seen as competent and as being a nice person by significant others, and I *must* have a guarantee that people will continue to like and love me and never reject me. If I don't succeed in these respects, I am really an incompetent and unlovable person. So I must always make sure that I am doing well and am respected and loved." Flora's demands for guarantees in these respects made her continually anxious and produced constant feelings that, even when she was doing well, she was not doing well enough, and therefore she was never really an adequate and acceptable individual.

In addition to her steady performance and relationship anxietizing, Flora also had some degree of low frustration tolerance. She irrationally believed that she had to be comfortable and must not be frustrated or deprived of life comforts. Thus she strongly believed, "It's *awful* when I am balked or thwarted, and I *can't stand it*!" She consequently angered and upset herself when the conditions of her life were not going well and when people (such as her ex-husband) deprived her of what she wanted—and presumably *should* have!

Flora clearly was damning herself on two levels: First, for not doing well enough in her own life and not having guaranteed approval from others; and second, for making herself so anxious about these "horrible inadequacies." She also damned her life, and especially her love life, for often being "too difficult." We explored her rage against others, including her ex-husband, which depressed people often create. But although she seemed to be at times angry at them, she was much more angry at herself for *her* "awful failings."

Course of Treatment

I used several cognitive methods of therapy with Flora and taught her how to use them between sessions and after therapy ended. I especially showed her how to Dispute (at point D) her Irrational *Beliefs* (IBs) and how to change them. For example, "Why *must* I not foolishly make myself anxious about not succeeding and not being approved?" Answer: "There's no reason why I must not be anxious, though I would highly *prefer* to stop creating such feelings." "Why is it *terrible* for me to fail at important things and get rejected?" Answer: "It isn't. It's distinctly *unfortunate* and *inconvenient*, but I can still accept myself and lead an enjoyable life."

When Flora kept Disputing her Irrational *Beliefs*, she began to feel sorry and disappointed about her feelings of anxiety—but not depressed and self-deprecating about having them. Once she accepted herself *with* her anxiety, she found it relatively easy to also accept herself when she failed or got rejected, and to reduce most of her original anxiety and feelings of inadequacy.

Flora was also taught to use several other cognitive methods of REBT:

Rational Coping Statements. She worked out, wrote down, and steadily told herself several coping statements, such as: "I *want* other people to like me, but I do not *need* their approval." "I'm a fallible human who often does foolish *things*, but I'm never, never a *rotten fool* for doing them!"

Recordings. Flora recorded our sessions together and listened to each of them several times to get their full impact.

Psychoeducational Study. She read a number of REBT books and pamphlets and listened to cassettes of lectures and workshops. She kept attending my Friday Night Workshops and other public workshops at the Albert Ellis Institute.

Modeling. She modeled herself after friends and relatives who were more rational than she was, after effective people she read about, and to some extent after my own refusal to upset myself when she resisted my disputing her Irrational *Beliefs*.

Philosophy. Flora worked on acquiring the philosophy of tolerance, of accepting human fallibility, and of long-range instead of short-range hedonism.

While using these cognitive methods of REBT, Flora kept vigorously using several emotive-experiential methods, including the following:

Rational Emotive Imagery. She imagined some of the worst things that might happen to her—such as failing at an important project—let herself feel very anxious or depressed about this, and then worked at changing her disturbed feelings to healthy negative ones, such as keen sorrow and disappointment.

Shame-attacking Exercises. She deliberately did some foolish and "shameful" things in public, such as singing in the street, and made herself feel unashamed and only sorry and regretful about doing them and being criticized by others for doing so.

Forceful Coping Statements. She said to herself, very forcefully, many rational statements like: "I really *want* to have things go my way, but they never, never *have to*! I can *still* definitely lead a fine life when I am frustrated!"

Forceful Disputing of Irrational Beliefs. She stated, on a tape recorder, self-defeating beliefs, such as "I *must* be liked by all significant people at all times!" and she then very strongly disputed them until she truly disbelieved them.

Reverse Role-Playing. I took the role of Flora, held on vigorously to some of her dysfunctional beliefs, and gave her practice in vigorously talking *me* out of them.

Unconditional Self-Acceptance. I unconditionally accepted Flora, even when she did badly and didn't do the REBT homework that she had agreed to do. But I also showed her how to unconditionally accept herself *whether or not* she performed well and *whether or not* other people (including myself) respected and approved of her.

Interpersonal Relating. Because Flora had an avoidant personality disorder, and was particularly distrustful of men, I at first refrained from attempting to get her attached to me and perhaps rebellious against such an attachment. I showed her that I liked her for her intelligence and honest efforts to change herself, but was neither going to be fatherly (I was about thirty years older than she was) nor husbandly. I was very honest with her about how disturbed I thought she was, but showed confidence that she could overcome her disturbance. I indicated that seeing her was a good learning experience for me, because her depression about her anxiety tested my theory of the importance of secondary disturbances and gave me a chance to partially validate this theory. So I made her into a collaborator, a kind of cotherapist who would look into herself for the data that might confirm or deny my theory, report these data back to me, and help me check on and expand my theory. She seemed to appreciate this collaborator role and became much more trustful of me than she had been of any of her previous therapists. Her trusting me seemed to help her be more trustful of the two main men in her life. In turn, I liked and trusted her for helping me to check on one of my favorite theories.

Flora and I also used a number of REBT behavioral homework assignments which she agreed to do in between sessions, including these:

In vivo Desensitization. She tried "risky" situations, like telling both Joe and Ed that she was dating the other man and would continue to do so until she made up her mind which one of them, if either one, she chose to be monogamous with.

Staying in Difficult Situations While Working on Her Upsetness. She deliberately kept having sex with both partners until she stopped putting herself down for doing so, and then decided that one of them (Joe) was better for her.

Reinforcement. She reinforced herself when she did her cognitive and emotional homework by allowing herself to spend money on herself only *after* she did it. When she ate too many sweets and gained more weight than she wanted to, she penalized herself by restricting her social life until she cut down on her food indulgences.

Skill Training. I talked with Flora about her methods of relating to and managing her relationships with men and showed her how she could be more assertive without being aggressive.

Outcome of the Case

Flora had twelve sessions of REBT over a period of four and a half months. We first worked on her self-deprecating for her anxietizing and helped her unconditionally accept herself with it. Once she was able to do this, she was also able to stop making herself anxious and self-deprecating when she didn't perform "well enough" and when other people didn't accept her as well as she presumably *should* have induced them to do.

Flora actually took only a couple of months to start accepting herself unconditionally, in spite of her long-standing anxiety and not doing well enough and her experiencing rejections by significant others. So she did remarkably well in achieving unconditional self-acceptance (USA), which is almost always a prime goal of REBT.

Paradoxically, she had more difficulty in achieving the second important goal that is usually worked for in effective therapy: achieving higher frustration tolerance or long-range hedonism. When she reduced her ego-demandingness, she kept insisting that life—and sometimes other people—absolutely must give her what she wanted when she wanted it. But by continuing to dispute these Irrational *Beliefs* on her own and by continuing to use REBT materials and workshops, she ultimately decreased her whining about life's "horrors" and made herself less self-indulgent and more disciplined. Three years after ending therapy, she still comes regularly to my Friday Night Workshops. In the discussion period, after I conduct a public session with a volunteer from the audience, Flora often helpfully presents some of her own experiences and makes sensible suggestions to the person with whom I am counseling.

REBT Treatment of Depression

Let me summarize how I usually treat individuals with severe symptoms of depressing. I first try to determine, from their initial presentation and from their (and their family's) history, whether they are mainly reacting to serious losses, disabilities, or traumas, and therefore have reactive depressing. Or, I ask myself, do they suddenly feel depressed, lethargic, and lose interest in many activities out of the blue—for no special reason? If so, they may have endogenous—or biochemically related—depressing. I also ask them about present and past medication for emotional or other problems.

If I suspect that they have endogenous depressing, I elicit more details about their personal and family history, and discuss with them the advisability of getting a psychopharmacological evaluation by a psychiatrist and of considering antidepressant (and other) medication. If they resist medication—as many of them do—I tell them that we will try REBT by itself, which may work quite well *if* they strongly and persistently use it. But I also say to myself, "We'll both try to do our best with REBT. If this client seems to be too disturbing, however, I'll see if I can later make it clear that it is also probably advisable to try medication." Occasionally, when my client is nonfunctional or suicidal, I refuse to continue appointments without psychiatric consultation, and sometimes insist on hospitalization.

By far most of the time, whether or not the client is on medication, I actively reveal the chosen and self-created Irrational *Beliefs* that probably instigate the reactive depression—absolutistic shoulds, musts, and other grandiose demands on herself, on others, and on external conditions. I briefly explain the ABCs of emotional disturbing. I show how the client can independently discover Irrational *Beliefs*, actively dispute self-depressing insistences, and considerably reduce them and change them to healthy preferences.

I particularly show my depressing clients that they frequently have two very debilitating musts: One, "I must perform important tasks well and be approved by people I find important, or else I am an *inadequate, worthless* person!" This kind of self-downing is most common in depressed people. Two, "People and conditions I live with *absolutely must* treat me considerately and fairly, give me what I *really* want, and rarely seriously frustrate me! Or else, I *can't* stand it, my life is *awful*, and I can't enjoy it at all!"

I check my depressing clients to see whether they have either of these two main dysfunctional beliefs—or any of their innumerable variations—and rarely find that they don't have them. Even if they are endogenously depressing, their biochemistry encourages them to think crookedly, so that their thoughts, feelings, and behaviors are *all* involved in their moodiness. So I usually find some of their Irrational *Beliefs* in the first session or two, show them how these contribute to their depression, and also start teaching them how to discover and dispute their particular self-sabotaging beliefs.

So I explore the important possibility of my clients depressing themselves about their depression. If they have this secondary symptom, I show them first how to reduce their upsetness about their depression, and then to reduce or eliminate their original depressing. Quite a trick! But I find that, interestingly enough, many of my clients are at first more likely to conquer their secondary symptom without too much trouble. However, they often benefit about this and yet find it difficult to convince themselves that their original failures or losses are not awful, but only highly inconvenient. So it may take them a much longer time to overcome their primary depression.

As I note in Flora's case, I almost always employ a number of cognitive, emotive, and behavioral methods to help my depressed clients minimize their disturbing and their disturbances about this disturbing. This is because people think, feel, and act dysfunctionally; and their thoughts, feelings, and actions importantly interact with and exacerbate each other. Moreover, although practically all depressing people have significant similarities, they also are unique individuals in their own right. What works easily with one may not work with another. But REBT methods are so many and so varied that they provide much leeway to use different strokes for different folks. And I usually vary REBT techniques with each client.

"How long will it take," many of my clients ask me, "to overcome my depression?" I reply, "It depends on several important factors: first, on how depressed you make yourself and for how long you have been disturbed; second, on whether your biochemistry is seriously out of whack; and third, on the kind, degree, and persistence of the Adversities in your life. Over these kind of factors, you have relatively little control. But you do have a great deal of choice concerning how you think, feel, and behave about the Adversities that afflict you. Like practically all humans, you are born and reared with opposing tendencies. On the one hand, you are easily disturbable, and can upset yourself over both little and big things. On the other hand, you are born and raised with real tendencies to change and to correct your self-defeating behaviors. You are potentially proactive and self-actualizing, if you *use* your healthy potentialities."

"How do I do that?" many of my clients ask.

My response is, "By seeing and using three of REBT's main insights. Number 1: See what we have been talking about in these sessions. You largely, though never completely, help create your own depressing and other disturbing. Especially when you depress yourself after suffering losses and failures. Number 2: No matter how and why you originally depressed yourself, you still, *today*, are thinking crookedly, feeling inappropriately, and acting dysfunctionally. So you are *continuing* to make yourself depressed and, often, depressed about your depression."

"I see. And the third insight for me to achieve?"

"Oh, yes, the important third insight. There is usually no way but work and practice—yes, much work and practice—for you to change your depressed thoughts, feelings, and actions. No magic. No miracles. Only much work and practice."

"So I have to push myself to change myself?"

"Yes, almost always. If you do, within a few weeks or months you will probably make yourself feel much better—much less depressed. No guarantees—but a high degree of probability. However, if you want to achieve what I call the *elegant solution* to your emotional problems and make yourself both less disturbing and less disturb*able*, that usually takes longer."

"And that is?"

"That is, use REBT so strongly and persistently that you first significantly reduce your depressing. Then go on to make a profound philosophical-emotional change where you endorse your healthy goals, desires, and preferences and minimize your absolutistic musts, insistences, and demands."

"Can I really do this?"

"Not easily! But with continued work and practice, you can. If you do, you then will rarely depress yourself in the future—no, not never, but rarely. If and when you do, you will give yourself unconditional self-accepting, refrain from putting yourself down, and return to using the kinds of REBT methods that you used to undepress yourself before."

"Sounds good."

"And fascinating. You control most of your emotional destiny. If you *think* you do and if you *work* at doing so."

Naturally, I don't convince all of my depressing clients to make themselves significantly less depressed. Even when I do, I hardly help all of them to make themselves elegantly less disturb*able*. But I always try, and I often succeed. So do they—sometimes!

SELF-HELP SUGGESTIONS

- If you depress yourself about your lack of achievement, your mistakes, your misfortunes, or about almost anything else, talking to a therapist about your Adversities may make you feel better but rarely get better. This kind of long-term "help" will not get at the self-chosen sources of your depressing, and may easily enhance your awfulizing about the misfortunes and hassles of your life.
- You often can depress yourself by self-downing—the demand that you *absolutely must* do better and/or win more approval from significant others than you actually are doing. Suspect that some significant degree of denigrating yourself as a person, and not merely acknowledging your poor performances, is a key depressing issue. If so, work steadily to

achieve USA—unconditional self-accepting *whether or not* you perform well or achieve greatly. Your deeds do not down you. You do! Work at stubbornly refusing to do so.

- Self-depressing—which we might well call autodepressing—also frequently follows from your awfulizing and terribilizing about undesirable conditions—lack of money, love, companionship, good health, and so forth. All these things may well be bad—because you don't want them. But *defining* them as *awful* usually makes them worse and less correctable. If you can't correct them you *can* find happiness in spite of them. Try!

- Self-depressing is often—very often—exacerbated by your putting yourself down and having low frustration about your original depressing. "I'm no good for being depressed!" and "I *can't stand* my depressing!" will depress you more! See that you're never a worm if you wormily depress yourself; and you *can* stand, though you'll hardly like, depressing.

- Use several REBT cognitive, emotive, and behavioral techniques, as described in this chapter, to interrupt your depressing yourself and to feel healthily sorry and disappointing but not unhealthily self-hating and whining when things go wrong or you make them wrong.

- If you really try to use some of the main cognitive, emotive, and behavioral methods of REBT and CBT to ameliorate your depressing and your self-therapy or psychotherapy still doesn't seem to be working, suspect that you may have an endogenous, innate tendency to depress yourself. Consult a psychiatrist, try to get a specific diagnosis (e.g., severe depression or manic depression), and experiment, if advisable, with antidepressive or other psychotropic medication. Your possible biological tendency to seriously depress may well be alleviated by psychotherapy *and* medication. Experiment and see!

21

Treating Individuals with Anxiety Disorders

I t is difficult to say which is the main cognitive-emotive-behavioral disorder of most people much of the time, but my guess would be that it is fairly severe anxietizing—with self-depressing coming a close second. This is probably because healthy anxietizing—e.g., feeling concern, caution, and vigilance—preserves the human race and has been built into us over the centuries. Frequently, we escalate it to unhealthy anxietizing—feeling overconcerned, panicking, perfectionistic, and phobic. These feelings, too, have distinct drawbacks but are also often life-preserving. To be without any anxiety, therefore, is dangerous; but to be overwhelmed by it may indeed at times preserve your life—and your misery!

I probably formulated REBT because as a practicing young psychologist, from 1943 to 1953 I was inundated with anxietizing clients. Sex, at least in our culture, is seen as a performance, and people with sex problems are usually afraid that they will not perform well, adequately—and, yes, perfectly. At the same time, they may not perform competently at love, marriage, parenthood, school, work, and you name it. What a devastating idea!

This chapter was partly adapted from "Transcript of a Verbatim Session with a Therapist Who Is Anxious About Taking an REBT Training Practicum," in W. Dryden, *Practical Skills in Rational Emotive Behavior Therapy* (London: Whurr, 1996), pp. 91–101. Used with permission.

305

I could easily see, when I rid myself of psychoanalytic prejudices and went back to figuring out my clients' philosophizing, that their performance anxiety almost always stemmed from their *must*urbating about their doing well and being approved by significant others for doing so. They had a strong *preference* for success and approval and that was fine. But, when anxietizing, they also had a *dire need* to do well and win the approval of others. Without the latter, they would make themselves healthily *sorry and disappointed* when they failed to achieve success or love, but rarely *anxious and depressed*. They made important winning *necessary*, not merely *desirable*.

My getting at the main source of anxietizing soon helped me, often in a few sessions, to show my clients how they were creating their anxietizing with *demands* and how to uncreate it by solidly changing these to *preferences*. Great! But I also saw that performance or ego anxietizing was often accompanied by awfulizing or what I called discomfort disturbance (Ellis 1979, 1980). My clients—and people all over the world—demanded comfort, ease, and immediate gratification. When they instead got discomfort, hassles, and deprivation—as, of course, they absolutely *must* not get—they often made themselves anxietizing and/or depressing. Almost inevitably.

The therapeutic answer to much of people's anxietizing? Fairly obviously, helping them keep their desires for success, approval, and comfort and refuse to escalate them into grandiose demands (Ellis 1962, 1994, 1999, 2000b, 2001).

As I briefly noted in the first chapter of this book, people have remarkable ease and talent in raising their wants and wishes into musts and shoulds, but they also can be shown many cognitive, emotive, and behavioral ways of not doing so. REBT, since 1955, has shown them how to do this; and many effective practitioners of Cognitive Behavior Therapy (CBT) have followed its lead since the 1960s.

Partly to show that anxietizing—both healthy and unhealthy—is the human condition, I shall present in this chapter a verbatim transcript of a session with a practicing therapist, Susan (not, of course, her real name), who was a participant in a three-day training practicum in REBT. Also Susan has practiced psychotherapy for several years, and favors using REBT and CBT with her clients, she—like most of the other therapists at this practicum—still anxietized about how well she performed in front of the other trainees.

Every year the Albert Ellis Institute in New York gives several training practica for psychotherapists and counselors and awards a Primary Certificate or Associate Certificate for those candidates who pass it. I give several demonstration therapy sessions with candidates who volunteer to present their own personal problems, to show all the other candidates some of the important aspects of REBT practice. Susan, one of the Primary Certificate candidates, volunteered to be interviewed for a demonstration session and gave the Institute permission to record and publish this transcript of a session with me. The session took place after she had been in the practicum for three days.

After my session with Susan, it was transcribed exactly as it occurred. Windy Dryden, one of the leading REBT theorists and practitioners, and one of the few full professors of psychological counseling in England, made some critical remarks on the transcribed session; and I also made some comments on it.

INTERVIEW AND COMMENTARIES

Albert: Okay, what problem would you like to raise?

[Windy: Note the problem-oriented way that Albert begins this demonstration session.]

Susan: I'd like to raise something that was raised yesterday, that I thought I had, er, completely overcome.

Albert: Yeah, what was that?

Susan: Well, it was pointed out to me that I said, er, "Well I don't torture myself anymore." I mean, that was twenty years ago I tortured myself, no more, and two of the young men in the room said: "Is that so? Because twenty minutes ago [laughing], you know, I heard you torturing yourself."

Albert: Yes.

Susan: And I thought, wow, you know. Right! I just do it in smaller bits now. I used to do it globally, and er. . . .

Albert: And they picked that up that you were still torturing yourself.

Susan: Right. And that . . . er . . . I was very disappointed.

Albert: Because you thought that you had ended that sort of thing?

Susan: I thought I had conquered that.

Albert: And they sort of brought to your attention again that you're still torturing yourself. And in what way would you say you're mainly torturing yourself now that you're looking at it?

[Windy: Albert intervenes to bring specificity to Susan's rather vague description of her problem.]

Susan: Well, what brought it up, er . . . yesterday, was this . . . this whole practicum. Er . . . that I'm very . . . [sighing]. I'm very disturbed by the fact that I don't think I do it well, that when I do the sessions with one partner that, you know, I just seem to be either floating around in the air or . . . or blocking, and everybody else seems to be doing so well. And that was the basis of the torture.

Albert: So, first you see that they're doing better than you, you're not doing that well, and then you torture yourself, if I understand you correctly, about seeing that. Is that right?

[Windy: Here Albert is ensuring that he understands Susan's problems from her perspective.]

Susan: Yes, er . . . but as you say, first you see I . . . I realize . . . something clicks in, and I'm evaluating it that way. I'm perceiving it that way, it doesn't necessarily have to be that way.

Albert: Right. But you could perceive it and evaluate it differently. But first let's assume, because you may be exaggerating, you may not be doing that poorly, but let's just assume for the sake of discussion that what you're seeing, your perception, is accurate. You are doing poorly. Then, how do you torture yourself about that? What is your evaluation, as you just sort of indicated?

[Albert: I know I am only going to have this one session with this client, so I want to quickly, with her assent, determine the ABCs of her disturbance. I tentatively surmise, at this point, that A is her perception of her doing poorly as a therapist in the practicum; B is her underlying demand, "I must do better than this—and at least as well as the other therapists at the practicum. If I don't, I'm an incompetent therapist and something of an incompetent person (IP)." C is her feelings of anxiety and depression. I directively explore to see if my surmises about her ABCs are probably accurate.]

[Windy: Albert has done three things in this intervention. First, he distinguishes between perceptions (at A) and evaluations (at B). Second, he identifies Susan's A—that she is doing poorly and third, he adopts the typical REBT tack at this stage—assumes temporarily that her A is true. You will note that Albert identifies Susan's A a little before her C, but this is okay as there are no hard and fast rules concerning whether to assess C before A or vice versa.]

Susan: I don't know if I would say that I torture myself. I think I, er . . . more or less begin to say, "Well this isn't so important anyhow and I guess I really don't wanna do this really, it's just taking up a week of time and that's great. It's interesting but, er . . . you know, it's not that important."

Albert: So, we would call that withdrawal? You sort of withdraw from the situation, and view it as not very important, is that right?

Susan: Yes.

[Albert: I now have found a behavioral C—withdrawal, and perhaps a defensive philosophy: "This situation is not very important—because if I viewed it as important, I would really have to put myself down for failing at it."]

[Windy: As Albert has just noted, he has identified her C, which in this instance is behavioral, not emotional.]

Albert: But do you think that *underneath* that view, "I'm finding this not important," you're first sort of torturing yourself and there-fore withdrawing? Is that your view of the torture?

Susan: I don't know. I'm not really, er . . . yeah . . . yeah.

Albert: Do you think that may be going on?

Susan: I'm having a little trouble with defining torture.

Albert: All right. But we can even skip torture, because we can just look at what we call C, the Consequence, which would be withdrawal. So, at A, the Activating Event in our system of Rational Emotive Behavior Therapy, you're perceiving that you're not doing well and we're assuming, you and I, that that's true—that may be false, but let's assume that's true—and then at C, you withdraw, maybe defensively. Is that right?

Susan: Yes.

[Albert: Although she agrees to the C of defensive withdrawal, I still hypothesize to myself that she is withdrawing from "torture"—meaning anxiety, depression, self-damnation, and feelings of severe inadequacy.]

[Windy: As Albert notes, by putting "torture" in quotes, this term is very vague and probably encompasses B and C elements. As he notes above, "torture" can be "skipped" and her A and C elements can be formulated using more specific referents. Note also that in his above response Albert is specific in mentioning A and C. Because Susan is a participant on a primary REBT practicum, she will know what these letters refer to. Hence, he offers her no explanation.]

Albert: That maybe you're withdrawing defensively, but at least you withdraw. Now, what do you think you're telling yourself at B, to cause that withdrawal?

[Windy: Again, as Susan is a primary practicum participant she knows the B-C connection. Thus, Albert goes straight to assessing her Irra-tional Beliefs. Note that he does so using open-ended rather than theory-driven questions.]

Susan: Okay, ummm, "I'm not as bright as I think I am." Er . . . "These guys are really far more well-trained than . . . I am." Umm, "They're more perceptive than I am," "I really have no perception . . . I don't know what the hell I'm doing," er " . . . I can't even drag out of a session the kernel of the problem, and if I'm lucky enough to happen on the kernel of the problem, *what do I do?*" You know, er, I'm er . . . I don't know what to do. I don't feel schooled, or trained, or . . . or able, um, to be a therapist.

[Windy: Note that Susan does not offer Irrational *Beliefs* in response to Albert's open-ended enquiry. Rather, she comes up with further inferences at A (or what in his next response Albert refers to as observations).]

Albert: Right. Those are all observations that you're making about your performance compared with their performance. "I'm not bright enough," "I'm not well-schooled enough," "I seem to be confused about what to do"; is that right?

Susan: Yes.

Albert: You're observing those things about *your* performance compared with their performance.

Susan: Well, I thought I was feeling those things.

Albert: Well, but at first; isn't there an observation that that's what you see? We'll get to the feeling in a minute, and we know the behavior to a certain degree already: you're withdrawing. But once you perceive those things, and let's just assume the worst—we like to assume the worst in REBT to show people that they can go with even the worst—so, let's assume you're accurate, that compared with the other practicum trainees, you are below par and that as a therapist compared with them you're not so hot. That's what you're perceiving and evaluating, you're right, you are evaluating that. But that kind of observation and evaluation of performance wouldn't make you withdraw. Do you know why it wouldn't make you withdraw if you only stuck with that kind of observation and evaluation: why wouldn't you with- draw?

[Windy: Here Albert does a number of things. First, he helps Susan to distinguish between her perceptions (or what I call inferences) and her feelings. Second, he reminds Susan that they are still assuming that her A is true. Finally, he distinguishes between perceptions and evaluations of performance (which properly belong at A) and a more central type of evaluation that explains her withdrawal and which constitutes Irrational *Beliefs* at B (as we shall soon see).]

Susan: Possibly because I see others who are equally inept.

Albert: That would be one thing. That's right. You see others who are inept. But also you could conclude, "Even though this is so, I'm glad I now see that. Maybe I'd better throw myself into it more and get more training and overcome these deficiencies." Couldn't that be a legitimate conclusion?

Susan: Yes . . . yes.

Albert: And then you wouldn't withdraw.

Susan: Right.

Albert: But we know that you *did* feel like withdrawing. Right?

Susan: Yes.

Albert: That's your thought and feeling: "I don't wanna be here. I'd better withdraw." Now, therefore, we believe in REBT that there's an additional evaluation. In addition to the evaluation of your performance, you're saying something *stronger* about *it* and about *you*. Now, if I'm right about that, and I could be wrong but I'm just hypothesizing now, what would you be saying that's *stronger* that would make you withdraw?

[Windy: Again, Albert is adopting an open-ended rather than a theory-driven enquiry to help Susan discover her irrational beliefs at B.]

Susan: "If I continue I'm gonna make a real ass of myself."

Albert: And if I make an ass of myself?

Susan: "If I make a real ass of myself (laughing), it's another notch in my belt of asshood."

Albert: Right. And that proves *what* about you?

Susan: That I will die an ass.

Albert: I will *always* be an ass. I'm a *hopeless* ass do you mean, or something like that?

Susan: I am never going to er . . . I am never going to get it all straightened out.

Albert: Right. Now, do you see then, that you have two sets of observations and evaluations? The first one, merely "Compared with them I'm not doing well and maybe I never will." And that *might* be true, you see. It could be that you're evaluating correctly, that your performance is never going to be up to theirs. But *then* you say: "My performance makes me an ass and a hopeless ass and I'll *die* an ass as I *live* an ass," is that right?

[Windy: Here Albert helps Susan to discriminate keenly between her self-downing Irrational *Belief* and her evaluation of performance at A.]

Susan: Yes.

[Albert: More and more she is confirming my inner assumptions about her ABCs. Of course, she is a therapist and knows some REBT, so she may be giving me the "right" ABCs to please me. But I am convinced by her tone of voice and her descriptions that she has a real emotional problem and that the ABCs that I am assuming she has are probably accurate.]

Albert: Now *that's* an evaluation.

Susan: [Laughing] My God, that sounds terrible!

[Albert: I immediately assume from her last statement that she probably has a secondary symptom—that she feels "terrible" about her negative evaluation of herself. So I make a note to myself to get back after to exploring her symptom stress—her symptom about her symptom. But I first return to her primary symptom—self-downing about her perceived inefficiency as a therapist.]

[Windy: Albert notes here that Susan probably has a meta-emotional problem. However, he probably does not want to lose the momentum that he has achieved at this point of the interview and thus he keeps his focus

on Susan's primary problem. You will note that Albert does not
return to her meta-emotional problem in this interview.]

Albert: That's right, you see. And that's what we want to question, and
that's why we go to D, Disputing. Let's suppose the worst again,
that your observation is true and let's even suppose you go on
acting this way, you're not very good at therapy as the other
trainees are. How does that make you, a human, an ass?

[Albert: I could, of course, question her perception of her being inefficacious as a therapist, but instead I go forward to the more elegant
solution of REBT—even if she can provide evidence for this inefficiency, how does that prove that *she*, an entire *person*, is an *ass*?]

[Windy: Note that Albert does not formally help Susan to connect her
Irrational *Belief* with her withdrawal at C. He probably infers
that she understands this. Consequently, he proceeds to the Disputing stage.]

Susan: I guess somewhere I feel that I *have* to excel at *something*.

[Windy: It is interesting to note that as soon as Albert Disputes Susan's self-
downing belief that she comes up with her musturbatory belief.]

Albert: Right. You see the "*have to*"?

Susan: I *have* to excel at something.

Albert: And if you change that "*have to*" to I'd *like* to excel at something, but if I don't, I don't" would you then feel like an ass?

Susan: No, I wouldn't. But I really have to change the whole statement
anyway. I *have* to excel at *everything*. I want to excel at *everything*
I touch.

Albert: Well, but notice you just said two things. "I *want* to excel at
everything," which I think almost every human says. "I'd *like* to.
I *want* to excel at important things." Not tiddlywinks, you don't
care if you don't excel at tiddlywinks, do you?

[Windy: Here Albert helps Susan to distinguish carefully between her
Rational *Belief* and her Irrational *Belief*.]

Susan: No, that would be all right. *That* would show that I was only human.

Albert: Yes, right. But you want to excel at every important thing and
then you say "and therefore I *have* to," is that right?

Susan: Yes.

Albert: Now, in REBT we never question desires, preferences, wishes,
wants, because you could *want* anything. You could want, right
now, ten million dollars, or to be the greatest genius at therapy
in the world, and as long as you were saying, "I *want* it, but I
don't *have* to have it," you wouldn't be in trouble. But we question the "*have to*." Why *must* you excel at an important thing like
therapy? Why must you?

Susan: I don't know.

Albert: Well, think about that.

[Albert: I could easily tell her the "right" answer here. But I prefer that she figure it out herself.]

Susan: Well, I dunno. I suppose . . . er . . . I think it may be that I'm a product of growing up where I've been told, or it's been implied that if you do something, do it well.

[Windy: Note that Susan doesn't directly respond to Albert's disputing question: "Why must you excel at an important thing like therapy?" Note how Albert responds in the next intervention.]

Albert: Right. Let's suppose that's true. And, incidentally, that has sense to it, because if you do something well it would be *preferable* to doing it poorly. We all learn that because that's not false. Our parents and our schools and our books teach us to try to do well. "If at once you don't succeed, try, try again to succeed." Isn't that what it means? And so that's okay. But you're still asking another question, not why it's *preferable* to do well, but why *must* you do what's preferable. Why do you *have* to?

[Windy: Albert shows Susan that her answer to his previous question provides evidence why it is preferable to do well. Then he asks her why she must do what is preferable. That is a typical Ellis inter-vention.]

Susan: I feel better when I . . . when I do accomplish. I feel better about myself.

Albert: Ah, about *yourself*. But you see you've just again said two things, (1) "I feel better about *it*," which we hope is true—that you would feel better about accomplishment rather than sitting on your rump and doing nothing and doing badly. So you'd better feel better about it. But you're saying, "I feel better about *me*, I accept *me* only when I do *it* well." Now, is *that* a legitimate con-clusion? "I can accept *me*, *myself*, my *being*, my totality, only-when I do *it*, therapy, well." Now is that a good conclusion?

[Windy: Albert tracks Susan quite carefully here. You will note that he orig-inally disputed her self-downing *Beliefs*, moved to disputing her demanding *Belief* when she moved to this type of IB, and has now gone back to disputing her self-downing *Belief*. My own prefer-ence is to help the client to dispute fully one type of IB before moving on to a related IB. Thus, I may have helped Susan to dis-pute her self-downing *Belief* fully before disputing her must.]

Susan: You mean, is it accurate?

Albert: Well, will it give you good results?

[Albert: Actually, her conclusion is poor, meaning unrealistic and illog-ical. But I want her to see that in REBT we show clients not *only* that their thoughts are unrealistic and illogical, but also that they won't work—will give them poor results.]

[Windy: You will note that Susan and Albert refer to the three criteria for irrationality—empirical, logical, and pragmatic—in very quick succession. My preference here would have been to slow the pace down so that Susan could have considered more fully each criterion in turn.]

Susan: No, it won't give me good results.

Albert: It'll give you what you have . . . withdrawal and anxiety. Maybe what you said at the beginning of this session, some kind of anguish, terror almost, which may be the thing that is making you withdraw—which we could just guess about. But it certainly *won't give you pleasure* and it won't help you to stay with this training practicum or any other thing that you enter. You'll tend to run away. And by running away will you do as well as you'd like to do?

Susan: No.

Albert: You'll normally do worse, isn't that so?

Susan: Well, I will not have accomplished anything at all.

Albert: That's right.

Susan: Except to have reinforced again, once again, "Susan strikes out!"

Albert: That's the irony, you see. That's really an irony. By demanding that "I must do X well," such as therapy in a practicum, "I *have to*! I *have to*! I've *got to*! I've *got to do it well*!" you will *withdraw* and not even do it *at all*. You see the *need*, the *necessity* of, performing well leads to withdrawal or anxiety, which interferes with your performance. You see that's catch-22. Now, how do you think you can get out of that bind?

[Windy: You will note that Albert focuses on pragmatic disputing of Susan's irrational beliefs in this sequence.]

Susan: By not withdrawing and not being anxious.

Albert: That's right. First, not withdrawing. Then you still would be anxious if you didn't withdraw. Now, how could you get rid of your anxiety? Let's assume you stayed with it, and it was *uncomfortable* to stay. And that's what we recommend in REBT, to stay with your discomfort until you make yourself comfortable. *How* could you get rid of the anxiety by staying with your discomfort?

Susan: By applying myself more, and er . . . learning the techniques.

Albert: Right. That's one way, but that's a little inelegant. That would work, because let's suppose that you stayed with it no matter how uncomfortable you felt and you learned the techniques of doing REBT. You got better at it and you felt *unanxious*. Do you realize why that would be an inelegant kind of solution? It would work, temporarily, but why would it only work temporarily? Why would it be inelegant?

[Windy: By using Socratic questioning, Albert is attempting to get Susan to see that the only elegant way of overcoming her withdrawal

and the anxiety that underpins her defensive behavior is to challenge and change her Irrational *Beliefs*. He makes this point more
explicitly in his next response but one.]

Susan: Because I think it attacks just a very small piece of it.

Albert: That's right. And even in that small piece, suppose you first did
well, and then later did badly. Suppose you finished the
practicum, learned REBT quite well, as well as anybody does,
and then compared yourself with other therapists and *still* did
poorly. Then what would you go back to telling yourself?

Susan: That I really don't belong here. I'll go back to the same thing.

Albert: And "I'm a no-good person for being a no-good therapist." You
see, you haven't got rid of that. So the technique of REBT is,
first, *stay* with the uncomfortable situation and then *work* on the
anxiety by giving up your *must*. Now, how could you give up, "I
must do well," "I *have* to," "I've *got* to?"

[Albert: I don't merely allow Susan to *act* well by staying in the uncomfortable therapy situation. I want her to do that *and* to tackle her
must—to *think* differently and act differently.]

Susan: By telling myself, "Okay, I will continue, and I will try, and I will do
my best, and if it works out, that will be very nice. And if it doesn't
work out, well maybe I'll try another kind of er . . . training."

Albert: Or . . . "Maybe I'll . . . ."

Susan: "I'll go into another field."

Albert: No, no . . . that's okay. Those are okay *practical* solutions. But
better yet, "Maybe I'll stay in this field and not *have* to be so
great. It doesn't *have* to work out well—I don't *have* to do as
well as the others." Isn't that better?

[Windy: Susan doesn't fully see that the real psychological solution to her
emotional problem is to challenge and change her must. So
Albert emphasizes this solution without denigrating her more
practically oriented solutions.]

Susan: Yes, I can be a student, a C student, and survive.

Albert: I often talk about the Sunday painters. They're out in the park
with their easels and their paints every Sunday, painting some of
the most *god-awful* things, and some of them know it and they
still enjoy painting. Now how do they *continue* to paint those *god-
awful* things and still enjoy it? What are they telling themselves?

[Windy: Here Ellis is using a metaphor to reinforce his point.]

Susan: One . . . they *like* those god-awful things.

Albert: Right.

Susan: And two, there's nothing wrong with those god-awful things.

Albert: Or better—there's nothing wrong with *them* for painting god-
awfully. You see. And they even might say, "I don't like my paint-

ings, but I like *painting*." They're doing poorly at the activity but allowing themselves to *enjoy* it. I always quote the statement of Oscar Wilde, "Anything that's worth doing is worth doing *badly*." You see? Because the *activity itself* is worth it. The *results* may *not* be worth it. You may never like the *results*. Now, as a therapist, we wouldn't want you to go on being a really bad therapist. And, as you said before, "Maybe I'd better get into another field or something like that." But that would be later—when you've really determined that you're bad at therapy. First, you stay with your discomfort, as I said. Then you recognize that you are *creating* much of it. You *make* yourself anxious. Third, you see that you mainly do it by your "*have to*," your "*got to*," your "*must*." And by "I am a rotten person if I do badly, rottenly." Then you *dispute*: "Where is the evidence that I'm a rotten person or that I *have* to do well?" And what conclusion do you end up with then?

[Albert: I persist at trying to help Susan get to her *core* dysfunctional belief—that she *must* be good at therapy and is a *rotten person* if she does not do as well as she *must*.]

Susan: I'm beginning to wonder, am I really saying that I am a rotten person or am I really and truly saying, I am a rotten therapist?

Albert: Well, let's suppose you were. Let's suppose that for the moment. That would be . . . that might be sane. If you had enough evidence, if you did poorly time and again, and if you're not that good at therapy and you're concluding, "I am *rotten* at *therapy* and probably I'll never be more than average or mediocre at therapy," then that would be okay. But I doubt whether you'd withdraw from doing therapy so *quickly* if that were so.

Susan: Aaaah.

Albert: You see?

Susan: Aaaah.

Albert: Do you really have evidence?

Susan: I was going to say, I really needed evidence. I see. That I can understand.

Albert: You see, just like those Sunday painters. They might go week after week, fifty-two weeks of the year, to the park and paint, and then finally say, "You know, I like painting, but I don't like the result. Maybe I'd better do sculpture. I would get better results." That would be okay. But if they quit after the first week then we get suspicious of their self-downing. How do they even know they're right about their *painting*, but not about *themselves*, being no good. You see?

[Windy: By continuing to use the Sunday painter metaphor, Albert helps

Susan to see that her defensive withdrawal prevents her from identifying, challenging, and changing her irrational beliefs.]

Susan: I know you might find it very difficult to believe, but at home I have now sitting umm . . . some paint and some canvases [laughing]. Because my daughter is getting me ready for retirement. She said, "Gee, you've always said you'd like to paint." I have not touched the paints for two months because . . . why? Because I know when I get to it the painting's gonna be lousy.

Albert: And it *should* right from the start be great?

Susan: Be terrific! Right.

Albert: Now isn't *that* something you're imposing on yourself? And you see it was interesting that I used painting as an example, and it now turns out that you're really in a position of copping out. But that's a good thing, because in therapy you'd at least have the excuse, "Well if I'm rotten at therapy, I'd better not be a therapist because I might harm others." Or something like that. But in painting, *who would you harm?* If you really work for weeks and months at it and it turned out that you were no good at it, who would be harmed? Would anybody be harmed?

[Windy: Albert now helps Susan to begin to generalize her learning about the role of her Irrational *Beliefs* from the therapy situation to painting.]

Susan: No.

Albert: And you would have *learned* at least the valuable information that, "You know, painting may not *be* my cup of tea." You would have *gathered* some evidence. Now in cases like yours, you're withdrawing too *quickly* and therefore we probably could call it defensive. But don't accept that you are defensive because I think you are or some other therapists think you are. We could be *wrong*. You might be very perceptive and sense quickly that you're not that good at therapy and decide to do something else. That would be legitimate. But *get the evidence*. You see? And the more quickly you withdraw from doing therapy, the less evidence you'll have, you see?

[Albert: I am using evidence and logic here to try to show Susan that she is not necessarily wrong to withdraw from therapy but that her withdrawing *so quickly* tends to show that she *may* be avoiding self-downing about her being poor at painting. I am not trying to prove that she *is* defensively withdrawing but only that she *may* be. My interpretation could be *wrong*. So I do not want to foist it on her.]

[Windy: An important part of REBT is encouraging clients to think for themselves and not to accept what their therapists say because they are therapists.]

Susan: Yeah, that's er . . . .

Albert: Anything else you wanted to raise about this?

Susan: No . . . I think that . . . er, this is something I really have to, er . . . give a lot of thought to. Because it's, er . . . I . . . [sighing]. I think this is the first time I feel that I'm down to the kernel. "Okay, terrific, that was a great session!" and go out and have lunch and forget about it. But I'm gonna make myself sit on that kernel and chew on that kernel.

Albert: That's right . . . .

Susan: . . . And unfold. Try to unfold.

Albert: And that's a very good point you're making. *Don't* assume that what I said was correct because I said it or because I have some status. See whether it applies to you and test it out, keep testing, you see.

Susan: Yeah. Uh-hum [Bell rings.] Was that the end?

Albert: No. That just happened to be the bell to open the door downstairs.

Susan: Because I feel very well satisfied that I have gotten quite a . . . quite a jolt here.

Albert: Now, how can you *use* that jolt to your benefit? That's the main thing.

[Albert: No matter how much insight she seems to be getting, I want to try to see that Susan *uses* it to work against her self-downing, her defensiveness, and her withdrawal, and her basic musts that lie behind these feelings and actions, and to *change* them.]

Susan: [Sighing]. Well, I think what I'm gonna do is sit down at home and go over the past year or so of events where I have tried to do something and er . . . they have not worked out . . . none of them has worked out, and see whether indeed they have not worked out because I realistically evaluated it or er . . . I didn't give it enough time.

[Windy: Susan is suggesting to herself a homework assignment to test for herself the validity of Albert's hypothesis. Albert thus does not need to make the point that one way in which she can deepen her learning is by the use of homework assignments.]

Albert: Withdrew too quickly. Right.

Susan: Which was something that was brought up yesterday too er . . . or, if . . . Have I given the things I have turned my hand to enough time and effort?

Albert: Right. That's a good point.

Susan: Because in my case there was plenty of time, but I don't know how much effort went into these activities.

Albert: Yeah. Because if you're telling yourself what we said before, let's just assume we're right. "I *must* do well and isn't it awful if I don't." And, "If not, I might be a rotten therapist or even a rotten person." If so, you may force yourself to continue at therapy and not really give it your *all*. So, the test of whether you're good at *anything* is: (1) take enough time, don't withdraw, and then (2) really throw yourself in and take it as a *challenge* to learn. You see? If you really are bad at something you still have the challenge of doing better. It's an interesting puzzle to solve if you take that attitude. Like, people don't play tic-tac-toe because it's too easy. Some of them don't even play chequers because it is too easy, so they play chess, or Go, or some complicated game, *knowing* they're going to lose but it's a greater challenge. Now you . . . this is your life, let's see if you can take the *challenge* of finding out whether quitting therapy is a cop-out on your part, which we're not sure about yet, because it could be. Or whether you are quickly ascertaining whether therapy is not for you. But give it more time, give it more effort, stop *must*ur-bating about it and then we'll see.

[Albert: I do not want her to immediately stop doing therapy—or to decide to continue doing it. I would like her to *consider* the hypotheses we have raised about her history of failing and about her consequently defensively withdrawing. I hope that she *experiments* more, without musturbating, to see what her final conclusion about being a therapist might be.]

Susan: Yeah. Fine.

Albert: You see what you can do?

Susan: Yeah. That will be my homework.

Albert: Yes. That will be your homework. To *consider* what we've said and test it as a hypothesis. It's *only* a hypothesis, and see whether you can find evidence for either your appropriately getting out of a situation, or running out pell-mell *de-fen-sive-ly*.

Susan: Yeah. And even as I now think, as you're talking, of the events of the past year or two, it's amazing to me that my conclusions always were, "Well, I am not, I am *not*, I am *not*," and so I dropped all of those efforts. Because I thought, "I am *not*."

Albert: But you could have said, "*Maybe* I am not. Let's see."

Susan: Yeah.

Albert: Right?

Susan: Right.

Albert: Okay. You work on that.

Susan: Fine. Very good.

Albert: All right?

Susan: Well, I appreciate that.

[Albert: I thought that this was a good initial session—which gave Susan some important things to *consider* and *think* about. Her being a therapist probably helped her get some of my points quickly—and perhaps be able to act on them. But, even if she were an accountant, an attorney, or something else, I would have proceeded as I did, but with much more detail, explanations, and examples. I still, however, would have tried to make the main point about her musts and self-downing leading to her possible defensiveness and too-ready withdrawal.]

SELF-HELP SUGGESTIONS

- Realize that psychotherapists, like just about all other people, are prone to make themselves anxietizing, panicking, and even torturing, as the case of the therapist in this chapter shows. So even if you know a good deal of REBT and often use it, on yourself and with others, you may easily fall back to severe anxietizing.
- Even if you do some performances well, you may think that you do not do them well *enough*—and you then may anxietize about them and anxietize about your anxiety.
- If you are in doubt about how good your performance is, you may well benefit by assuming that it *is* quite bad—and then use REBT to make yourself unanxietizing about this *worst* possibility. Then you've really got it made!
- Anxietizing itself is emotionally debilitating, but it may be temporarily avoided by withdrawing and avoiding participating in "dangerous" pursuits. However, your withdrawing into this kind of inactivity significantly limits your life and happiness. It also stops you from actively exposing yourself to "dangerous" pursuits and thereby helping yourself to reduce your panicking.
- If you severely anxietize or panic, you may easily put yourself, and not merely your behavior, down. Your anxietizing about your anxiety may especially lead you to panic yourself more, to withdraw from all "dangerous" performances, and to block your overcoming your panicking.
- Comparing your performances with those of other people does not in itself make you anxietize. Telling yourself that you *absolutely must* do as well as or better than others is the culprit. It would be nice!—but why *must* you?
- In addition to insisting that you invariably *have to* perform well, and what a loser you would be if you did not, you may easily horrify yourself about the frustration, hassles, and possible dangers that you encounter. To *want* to remove or diminish them is healthy; but to *need* to reduce then, when

you often can't, leads you to feel discomfort anxietizing or low frustration tolerance. You thereby *increase* your frustrating feelings.

- When you create performance or ego anxietizing you often correctly rate your feelings and behaviors, but you overgeneralize and rate your *self*, your *being*. You then make yourself into a *loser* or a *rotten person*, see yourself as practically *always* doing poorly—and acquire a self-fulfilling prophecy of general ineptness. The answer, as pointed out in this book, is unconditional self-accepting (USA), no matter what are your failings. You may fail often but you are never, except by your own irrational *definition*, a *failure*.

- Consistent *preferring*, not *needing*, to perform well, and strongly *desiring*, not *insisting upon*, comfort and pleasure, minimizes your ego and discomfort anxietizing. Not completely, but largely!

- Don't withdraw and put off till "tomorrow" what you can harmlessly fail at today. Risk, risk, risk—while making your risks into a learning project. 'Tis better to have tried and lost than to terrifyingly define yourself as a loser!

22

Treating Individuals with Low Frustration Tolerance

I was always heavily into choice psychology and psychotherapy, especially when I created Rational Emotive Behavior Therapy (REBT) in 1955. For I then saw more clearly than ever that nearly all clients anxietize, depress, and hate themselves, mainly by neurotically *demanding* that they *absolutely must* perform well and *have to* be approved by significant others. If they only, instead, strongly *preferred* but didn't grandiosely *insist upon* success and approval, they would be fine and they would rarely put down their entire *self* or their *ego* when they failed and got rejected.

My teaching my clients unconditional self-acceptance (USA) *whether or not* they importantly succeed or are greatly approved by others has, I am convinced, helped literally thousands of them, as well as perhaps millions of readers of my articles and books, over the last five decades. Fine! But not all my clients are serious self-downers—as I importantly learned from one of them a number of years ago. She, Bernice, a thirty-four-year-old teacher, was extremely bright and attractive, but was unusually fearful of dating suitable men. She consequently did a great deal of social dancing—at which she was

---

This chapter is partly adapted from a paper I gave at a symposium, "Lessons I Learned from My Clients," which was presented at the American Psychological Association Annual Convention in San Francisco in 1998.

unusually adept—but practically never dated any of the men who she found attractive whom she met while dancing. I was at first sure that she was a self-downer, and that she did not date because she was afraid that the men who at first found her attractive and a fine dancer would, if she went with them a few times, find her poor at relating, would therefore reject her, and that would lead to her viewing herself as an *inadequate person*. So, knowing that she would then put *herself* down, I hypothesized, she found dating too risky, so she avoided it.

To my surprise, Bernice resisted my interpretation, saying that she *once* felt like an *inadequate person* when men—or anyone else—rejected her but that she now hardly ever deprecated herself for anything—for any kind of failure or rejection. How come? Well, she said, she had mainly given up that kind of self-downing by reading my books—particularly by reading, and several times rereading, my book, *A Guide to Rational Living*. That had helped her so much, in fact, that she had therefore come to see me for therapy so that she could work on her dating phobia.

Was I pleasantly surprised! Most of my clients, especially those who are afraid of rejection, abysmally put themselves down, know that they will do so if they are rejected—and therefore fear, really, their *own* put-downs rather than their rejection by others. It was good to know that Bernice, mainly by reading my books, had minimized this common kind of disturbance. But what *were* her self-sabotagings that created her social anxiety? I was curious to find them out.

Well I soon did. Bernice put her finger on it right away. "I've thought about this a lot—particularly after reading several of your books. I'm really afraid of *discomfort*—of feeling *awkward*. I have what you call low frustration tolerance—LFT."

"How so?" I asked.

"Well, I originally, before I even heard of you, was a self-downer, and also downed myself for downing myself. But by the time I gave up that double-headed kind of self-denigration I already was well practiced in avoiding dates with attractive men. I *easily* and talentedly ran away from going out with them. So when, a couple of years ago, I overcame my self-blaming and forced myself to accept dates with some of my dance partners, I found that I was very uncomfortable on these dates. Having little experience in this arena, I didn't exactly know what to do—what to think about, how to pet with them without winding up with my clothes off, how to tactfully refuse subsequent dates with men who bored me, how to get them to talk about things I was really interested in, and a host of other things that women who date regularly seem to have no trouble doing."

"And did you put yourself down for your ignorance and your awkwardness?"

"A little. But I again used REBT on myself and stopped doing that. But I magnified my discomfort and awkwardness—"

"—like people with LFT often do?"

"Exactly! I told myself—as I see that other clients that you describe in your books do—'It's *hard* to go through this damned hassle of dating! It's *too* hard. It *shouldn't be* that hard! I'll be damned if I keep putting myself through all of this crap!' "

"You're right," I said. "That *is* LFT as I have described it in my books. But usually about procrastinators or other kinds of shirkers, not about people with social anxiety."

"Yes, but I see that it applies to me too. Normally, I don't avoid work and responsibility. But in this dating area I obviously do."

"You mean that even though you see the gains of dating and eventually enjoying it and getting the kind of man you want, you refuse to follow Benjamin Franklin's motto, 'There are no gains without pains.'"

"Precisely. I am in this respect what you call a short-range hedonist. I refuse to go through present pains—the awkwardness and boredom of dating—to get future gains—the long-term enjoyment of an ongoing relationship."

I quickly saw that Bernice was right and had nicely zeroed in on her own major irrationality—defining the *hassle* of dating as an *unmitigated horror.* With this self-defeating philosophy she made herself shy away from practically all dating and therefore remained unhappily alone. Because she wanted to work at overcoming her hangup, we collaborated on actively and vigorously attacking her low frustration tolerance and replacing it with rational self-helping ideas. She was then able to tell herself, "Yes, it's hard to keep dating, and often to go through awkward and boring situations in the course of my dates. But it's harder if I don't go through these kinds of hassles to finally get what I really want. Ben Franklin was right: No gain without pain! I'd better accept that unfortunate reality and work at eventually finding and building a solid relationship!"

I was happy to help Bernice reduce her low frustration and to work at dating and relating. But I was especially happy about her helping me to clearly see that, yes, self-downing is the essence of *much*, but hardly of *all*, social difficulties. People not only terrify themselves about rejection by irrationally viewing themselves as *inadequate, worthless persons* when they are rejected by others. They frequently also horrify themselves about the hassles, inconveniences, and efforts they have to undertake in the process of dating and mating and thereby bring on low frustration tolerance and self-defeating avoidance. Whenever I now encounter clients—not to mention friends and relatives—who have relationship problems, I still suspect, look for, and try to help them ameliorate their self-downing, which almost always is importantly involved in their social phobia. But I also look for—and often find—their self-sabotaging LFT as well.

In my own case, too, I have not put myself down for any of my foolish and mistaken acts for a good many decades. Instead, I acknowledge them and denigrate my behavior but not *myself,* the behaver. Great. But when I act badly and needlessly defeat my own ends and/or treat others unfairly, I suspect my own LFT, often find it, and work to reduce it.

Even with Bernice, I realized as I was seeing her, my mistake in first attributing her social anxiety to self-deprecation mainly resulted from my own low frustration tolerance. For I found it *quick* and *easy* to interpret her disturbance in this way. That is because most of the social avoiders I see do largely damn themselves for being rejected and therefore make themselves phobic. Why not, then, assume that Bernice was in that common class? So I did assume this—wrongly! Now I still *tentatively* assume that avoiders *may* have this self-downing attitude. But I also assume—thanks to Bernice!—that they may have other irrationalities—especially low frustration tolerance or short-range hedonism. That additional hypothesis helps me to help both myself and my clients and to become a more effective therapist. Again, thanks to Bernice!

As I note in the previous chapter, low frustration tolerance is a form of discomfort anxietizing or discomfort depressing. Almost everyone—including therapists—at times suffers from it. As with other forms of self-disturbing, it probably has evolutionary origins and perhaps counters and corrects the human tendency to promptly musturbate and take care of Adversities too quickly—and too sloppily.

Thus, when confronted with a fierce animal or furious human, ancient people often had to act fast. "I must kill this animal (or person) *immediately* or else I am a goner!" "I must run like hell or else I'm dead as a duck!" Quick reaction followed by fast action. Life- and limb-preserving!

But often slow and steady wins the race. If, when confronted with a dangerous animal, I stop and think, climb a tree instead of run, hide in the bush and build a trap for the fierce animal, take time to fashion a weapon before I go out to face danger, my "procrastination" may more effectively save me from harm.

At any rate, doing things—especially onerous or dangerous things—*after* I have thought about them, prepared for them, arranged safeguards for them, rested to gain more energy and face them—all these "delays" may help me. So putting off till tomorrow what I can more riskily and exhaustedly do today may well be to my advantage.

However, I—as a member of the human race—must *decide* what to do and when to do it to save or more fully enjoy myself. The deciding process *itself* often includes delay or my first doing easy tasks instead of more difficult ones. And because delay often takes less energy than prompt task-doing, I frequently *wrongly* choose it while convincing myself it is *best* to do so. So, despite fairly obvious penalties, I put off paying my taxes, writing the great American Novel, going for a job interview, and so on. Tomorrow! *Mañana!*

Of course, I frequently am motivated to do things the easy way because of my ego-anxietizing. I may do a *poor* tax return, write a *lousy* novel, or *abysmally fail* at the job interview. That, in my nutty head, would make me a *failure.* Too risky! Nonetheless, my foolish procrastinating may *also* involve the dire need for comfort, ease, and energy-conserving. Indeed it may!

In doing REBT, therefore, you never neglect the possible ego- or performance-anxietizing of your clients, but you also assume that they may have discomfort-anxietizing or LFT. Their typical Irrational *Beliefs* that help create their LFT are:

- "It's quite hard to quickly do this project I've accepted. It *should be* easier!"

- "It's not only hard to do this thing that I'd better do. It's *too* hard. I can't do it now!"

- "People absolutely must not act as frustratingly and badly as they do to me!"

- "I *can't stand* great or prolonged frustration!"

- "What is happening to me is *totally* bad—therefore it's *awful!*"

- "I can't do anything to cope with this horror, so I can't face it and deal with it!"

- "I *absolutely must* find something enjoyable to distract me from this terrible frustration!"

- "Even thinking about this horrible situation will completely upset me, so I won't think about it!"

- "This frustration is *so* bad that I can't be happy at all if I attend to it!"

In doing REBT with clients who have serious discomfort-anxietizing or discomfort-depressing, you can use many cognitive, emotive, and behavioral techniques, including some of which you use with ego-anxietizing. Particularly, you often show clients the cost-benefit ratio of their pleasurably indulging today—and their paying the grim price tomorrow. You help them make a long list of the *pains* of procrastinating. You show them that, yes, it is quite hard to do onerous things today—but much hard*er* to do them later. You show them how to model themselves after people with great handicaps who nonetheless pushed themselves to be quite productive.

Emotively, you use several REBT techniques that are described in this book and in my other writings (Ellis 1999, 2000b, 2001), such as Rational Emotive Imagery, shame-attacking exercises, forceful coping statements, vigorous disputing, and role-playing.

Behaviorally, you help clients with discomfort-anxietizing (and with ego-anxietizing) to stay in difficult situations and work on their LFT until they improve it; to reinforce themselves when they promptly do difficult tasks they are avoiding; to sometimes penalize themselves when they cop out of doing them; and to use other REBT behavioral methods that are described in this book and my other recent writings.

Of course, if discomfort-anxietizing is one of your own problems, you use the above methods for self-help purposes—and, if required, see an REBT or CBT practitioner to monitor and help you use them.

The ultimate goal with you and your clients? Preferably achieve "elegant" REBT solutions to LFT: (1) Minimize the clients' most destructive aspects of their discomfort-anxietizing. (2) Look for and reduce its other aspects, that they may not at first talk about. (3) Try to help them rarely resort to serious LFT. (4) Encourage them to constructively use REBT methods again when they do afflict themselves with LFT once more. (5) Push them to commit themselves to working against their potential LFT for the rest of their lives. (6) Automatically and unconditionally keep only mildly disturbing themselves even when faced with unusual frustrations and restrictions that may occur.

Quite a curative and prophylactic program! But still, with persistent cognitive, emotive, and behavioral work, achievable!

SELF-HELP SUGGESTIONS

- If you have discomfort-anxietizing or low frustration tolerance (LFT) and you often avoid onerous tasks that you promise yourself to do, look for your self-sabotaging musts—e.g., "These tasks are *too* hard." "They *must* not be that hard." "It is *awful* that they are so hard." "It is impossible for me to promptly do them!" Find your Irrational *Beliefs* and persistently and forcefully show yourself that they are incorrect and debilitating.
- Use a number of other cognitive, emotive, and behavioral techniques that are described in this book to Dispute your discomfort-anxietizing.
- Suspect that you also have some degree of perfectionism or ego-anxietizing that encourages you to delay or avoid important tasks such as, "If I do this project right away and fail at it, I'm no damned good!" If so, use REBT methods to surrender it and to achieve unconditional self-accepting (USA).
- As usual, if you are still afflicted with LFT, fully acknowledge the disadvantages and shortcomings that you create with it, but only criticize your mistaken *behavior* and not *yourself* for misbehaving. Also, see if you have LFT about surrendering your LFT: "It's *too hard* and *too* painful to minimize it. I *shouldn't* have to put so much effort into tackling it! How awful!" Find and Dispute your symptom about your symptom.
- Keep working at reducing your discomfort-anxietizing or LFT until you find it relatively automatic and easy to considerably reduce it. That day may come—or, rather, you may arrange to make it arrive!

23

Treating Elderly People with Emotional and Behavioral Disturbances

As Emmett Velten and I have noted in our book, *Optimal Aging,* there are several different, and yet in some ways overlapping reasons why older people frequently disturb themselves emotionally and are potentially good subjects for psychotherapy. These include: (1) They have poor physical health which, by itself or in reaction to which, they may become emotionally vulnerable. (2) They may be subject to more stresses and life changes—such as financial, retirement, and moving problems—than are younger people. (3) They frequently lack social support from family, friends, coworkers, and neighbors that they may have had in their earlier days. (4) They often are less efficacious than they were in their youth and middle age and lack the feelings of mastery and self-efficacy that they once had. (5) For all of the above, plus other reasons, their mobility and freedom to change may be distinctly limited. (6) They may have had a history of previous personality, relationship, and coping difficulties which ill-prepared them for older age and they may be anxious or depressed about their recurring.

This chapter is partly adapted from an invited address to the 31st Annual Convention of the Association for the Advancement of Behavior Therapy in Miami Beach, Florida, November 15, 1997, and from "Rational Emotive Behavior Therapy and Cognitive Behavior Therapy for Elderly People," *Journal of Rational-Emotive and Cognitive Behavior Therapy* 17 (1999): 5–18. Used with permission.

Older individuals, at the same time, are exactly that—individuals. Some of them use their experiences, including their traumatic and frustrating experiences, to grow and develop by—and thereby fulfill the old saw about becoming older and wiser. They have somehow, for perhaps biological and experiential reasons, used the aging process constructively, and developed a philosophic outlook that has helped them to survive and to adjust to what often would be called grim circumstances. They have been conditioned and/or self-conditioned to roll with the tides, and to be optimistic, tough-minded, and one could say in many ways rational, in spite of—and sometimes because of—the Adversities they have experienced, and in spite of the limitations and restrictions of older age.

It has also been noted by some investigators that older age has its blessings. For in addition to the hazards I indicate at the beginning of this chapter, it has its advantages. Thus, many older people have a steady relationship—or else are not interested in having one. They are retired from their career and are not frantically trying to achieve outstandingly. They may be comfortable financially, although not as wealthy as they would like to be. And they may even be socially secure, especially if they live in a senior citizen community or retirement home.

Nonetheless, the disadvantages, especially the physical ones, of older age usually outweigh the advantages. It is difficult to gauge how many people over sixty-five suffer from significant emotional problems because few older people come to community health centers, and it has been estimated that only 2 percent are served by private therapists. Estimates of people over sixty-five, especially women, who have depressive symptoms, are about 15 percent, and it is estimated that as many as 10 percent more have severe states of anxiety, depression, addiction, and personality disorders.

Not only is there reluctance on the part of older people to go for psychotherapy, but studies of psychotherapists' preference ratings indicate that they prefer to treat middle-aged over older clients and that few of them have seen any number of clients over sixty-five years of age. The prejudice against the psychological treatment of older clients seems to go both ways!

Nonetheless, a number of therapeutic approaches to dealing with the emotional problems of older people have been tried for many years, in spite of Freud's pessimism in this respect. Thus, treatment methods have been devised by psychoanalysts, by existential therapists, by interpersonal therapists, by Gestalt therapists, and by Adlerian therapists.

Very few actual outcome studies have been done by the proponents of these psychotherapeutic methods of treating older people, but encouraging case material has often been presented.

From its beginnings, REBT emphasized that both older and younger people can use its cognitive-behavioral methods to reduce their emotional and behavioral dysfunctions. Other therapists began using REBT in the late

1950s and early 1960s and some of them, such as Maxim Young, emphasized its value in treating older and seriously dysfunctional older clients.

Rose Oliver got her Ph.D. in psychology and received special training in REBT when she was in her sixties and began specializing in the treatment of older and disabled clients thereafter. J. Keller and J. Croake did an early study, the effects of a program in rational thinking on anxiety in older persons, in 1975.

Following the applications of Ellis, Young, and Oliver of REBT to older clients, a number of other articles and books on using REBT with these clients as well as with those who have disabilities, fear of dying and actual fatal illness. These include writings by Manny Alvarez, Rochelle Balter and P. Unger, Louis Calabro, Gerald Gandy, and Larry Hill. Proponents of REBT have been quite busy in this important area of therapy.

A good many outcome studies have been done using cognitive behavior therapy with older clients, and most of these studies have shown moderately effective results. These include a well-known study by Beck, Rush, Shaw, and Emery (1979).

According to the theory of REBT, effective therapy consists not only of changing people's Irrational *Beliefs* (IBs) for more Rational *Beliefs* (RBs), but also of working persistently and forcefully on their emotions and their behaviors. REBT is highly multimodal, to use Arnold Lazarus's term, and has a great many cognitive, emotive, and behavioral techniques. It uses these multimodal methods with elderly, as well as with younger clients.

Most of the other cognitive behavior therapies (CBTs) also use several cognitive, emotive, and behavioral methods, but they tend to be less philosophic, less experiential, and to use less exposure or *in vivo* desensitization. REBT, more so than CBT, is highly active-directive, and it especially stresses clients acquiring unconditional self-acceptance.

The rest of this chapter will consider the main Irrational *Beliefs* (IBs) that seem to be most common in older people and how they may be disputed cognitively, emotively, and behaviorally to help those who hold them. It will largely be concerned with REBT theory and practice, because I have much firsthand experience with this form of CBT. For many years, it has emphasized revealing and Disputing clients' core beliefs and attitudes and not merely their more superficial automatic negative thoughts.

It is easy to find irrational or dysfunctional *Beliefs* in the elderly, but it is not so easy to differentiate them from self-defeating philosophies in the young and middle-aged. This is because irrationality leading to what we call human disturbance is so prevalent at all ages! Humans on the whole, as I have noted for many years, are often "unsane"—and who is to say that the elderly are more or less so? Certainly, being close to ninety myself, I'd better go a little kindly on us elders!

What we had better look for, then, is the *special* Irrational *Beliefs* (IBs) connected with aging that older people have. We can then still deal with their regular IBs and help them minimize them, but we can do them a real service by also assessing their unique irrationalities that seem to go with, or are at least exacerbated by, the aging process. Doing so, moreover, we can probably get a closer therapeutic alliance with them by honoring the fact that they have some general *and* special problems, and that instead of discriminating against them, as people in our culture often do, we are definitely on their side and are determinedly *with* them.

In Rational Emotive Behavior Therapy (REBT), we distinguish between people's basic self-defeating philosophies—their core demands and musts—and the automatic thoughts and inferences that often stem from this absolutistic demandingness. Let me first describe some of the common musturbatory ideas that are often held by most of my clients. These fall under REBT's three major musts: (1) I absolutely must perform well, else I am an inadequate person. (2) You absolutely must treat me kindly and fairly, else you are damnable. (3) Conditions under which I live absolutely must be comfortable, else life is awful and I can't stand it. The whole human race frequently seems to be plagued by these three major IBs and their innumerable subheadings. Older clients, from seventy to ninety, frequently hold them too; but they especially create the following variations on them:

SELF-DOWNING IRRATIONAL BELIEFS

1. I must do as well as I previously did when I was younger and more able, else I am an inadequate person.

2. I must be younger and more attractive than I am.

3. I must not be physically weak and deficient.

4. I should have accomplished more than I did during my life.

5. I must not look as anxious and weak as I now do.

6. I must not die and be forgotten.

ANGER-CREATING IRRATIONAL BELIEFS

1. Other people must treat me kindly and fairly, especially because of my age and the limitations and disabilities that go with it. When they treat me shabbily they are rotten people.

2. My relatives and friends must not neglect me and must treat me as well as they did when I was younger.

3. Other people should treat me as well as they did when I was younger and more able.

4. People should not discriminate against me or look down upon me because of my age and my weaknesses.

LOW FRUSTRATION TOLERANCE IRRATIONAL BELIEFS

1. The conditions of my life must be as good as they previously were, and it's *awful* and I *can't stand it* when they aren't.

2. The special problems and difficulties of old age should not exist and it's *too hard* to live with them.

3. I *need* more pleasure and excitement and life is too boring without it.

4. I *need* more companionship and love, especially from those I care for.

5. I should have the work I used to have to fill my life and make it more interesting.

6. I should have the health I used to have and not be ill or disabled.

7. I should not have to be as dependent on others as I now am.

8. I should not have to die and be deprived of life.

These are some of the main Irrational *Beliefs* that I find are often a function of aging—or at least are much more prevalent in old age. Like the *Beliefs* of younger people, they frequently include two opposing musts. Thus, both young and older individuals may strongly believe, "I must be superior to other people" and "I must be universally loved by others." Fat chance that they can achieve both demands!

Similarly, older people may strongly believe, "I must not be weak and deficient," and "Because I am weak and deficient other people should especially treat me with unusual kindness and consideration." Either one of these demands is unrealistic and self-defeating. Taken together, they may easily lead to self-denigration, anger at others, and low frustration tolerance about unchangeable conditions.

These are only a sample of special Irrational *Beliefs* of older clients. Much research has yet to be done to determine which are the most common, which are more strongly held, and which lead to unhealthy results. Similarly to its application to younger disturbed people, REBT uses many cognitive, emotive, and behavioral techniques to minimize and uproot the IBs of elderly clients, as the next few paragraphs show.

Cognitively, for example, it actively disputes dysfunctional *Beliefs*.

Empirically, it asks where is the evidence that older people must do as well as they did when they were younger and more able. Logically, it questions whether they will *always* perform poorly and will be an *inadequate person* if they sometimes or often do. Pragmatically, it encourages them to ask themselves what results will they achieve if they command that they absolutely must do as well as they did when younger and are worthless individuals if they don't function as well as they did in their youth.

REBT uses many other cognitive techniques of disputing Irrational *Beliefs* of the elderly. Thus, it encourages them to devise and to use rational coping statements, such as "I can still greatly enjoy my life in spite of my restrictions and handicaps!" It helps them model themselves after older people they personally know and hear about who overcome their limitations. It shows them how to reframe some of the hassles of old age and even find enjoyment in them. It gives them psychoeducational reading materials and audiovisual cassettes to teach them more constructive attitudes and coping skills. It uses cognitive distraction, relaxation techniques, and the acquiring of vital absorbing interests to interrupt their negative focusing and enhance their lives. It emphasizes problem-solving methods as they deal with their emotional difficulties and helps them become more able and skillful to face practical issues.

Emotively and behaviorally, REBT uses a number of active techniques in regular sessions and as homework assignments for older individuals. Therapists not only form an active therapeutic alliance with them that compensates somewhat for their losses of familial and social support; they also give unconditional acceptance even when older clients have real limitations and deficiencies. More importantly, they teach clients to have unconditional self-acceptance (USA) whether or not they function well and whether or not they are liked by others.

REBT also uses my famous shame-attacking exercises with older people, and encourages them to do foolish things in public and not to put themselves down when others criticize them. It employs Rational Emotive Imagery, where clients imagine one of the worst things that could happen to them actually happening, let themselves feel very upset, then work on their feelings to make themselves experience healthy negative emotions like regret and disappointment instead of unhealthy ones like panic and depression. It also shows elderly clients how to vigorously and powerfully change their self-defeating thoughts and feelings to firmly held self-helping cognitions and emotions, and thereby acquire emotional as well as intellectual insight. It is important that they really believe and feel that they can cope with life difficulties instead of lightly parroting to themselves that they can.

REBT also uses a wide variety of behavioral methods with older clients, in keeping with its multimodal approach to therapy and with its theory that rigidly held Irrational *Beliefs* can often be modified by encouraging clients to act against them. Thus when people in their seventies and eighties resist giving up ideas that make them enormously anxious about minor inconveniences, they are given imaginary or in vivo desensitization assignments. They are encouraged to stay in uncomfortable situations until they get over their low frustration tolerance, and then perhaps to change the situations. They agree to take reinforcements for taking social risks and sometimes penalties for not taking them. And they are given skill training involving tasks and recreations that will keep them so occupied that they will forget about some of their obsessive fears.

As noted, many REBT methods are at the disposal of the REBT therapist who works with the elderly. These methods can be applied in widely differing individual cases and used selectively under certain conditions and times. More than in most therapies, however, REBT is oriented toward helping older people to achieve unconditional self-acceptance and high frustration tolerance. These philosophies are useful with almost any clients—but particularly with those who are likely to be less competent than they previously were and to have greater frustrations than they previously had.

A unique study by Faucher and Kiely (1997) tends to show that the REBT philosophy is especially useful in the treatment of elderly individuals. They studied thirty-two well-adapted and nondepressed male war veterans, aged from sixty-one to ninety-seven years (mean = 80.53 years old) and who were institutionalized on a permanent basis in a veterans hospital in Canada. They were institutionalized for poor health and/or a lack of physical autonomy. These individuals were studied to find the cognitive strategies that they most used to keep themselves undepressed and satisfied with their restrictive life. It was found that the strategies most used by these elderly men were self-determination, focalization on the positive, problem-solving thinking, relativization of one's demands, ideas of acceptance, cognitive realism, and altruistic thinking. These philosophies, which were spontaneously used by elderly hospitalized men to compensate for their restrictions and keep them relatively happy, are quite similar to the beliefs which REBT has found to be effective in treating older people who are plagued with anxietizing and depressing. If people in their older years can be prophylactically prevented from becoming demoralized, can be helped to be less disturbed when they are emotionally afflicted, and can in some instances spontaneously help themselves to devise philosophies to live happier lives, this would tend to show that there is a commonality among Rational *Beliefs* to replace the Irrational *Beliefs* that are frequent in older populations. This would indeed be a useful idea for considerably more research.

SELF-HELP SUGGESTIONS

- If you are older than sixty years, you may have some Irrational *Beliefs* (IBs) that make you especially prone to self-downing, anger, and low frustration tolerance. Some of these main IBs are described in this chapter. Look to see if you have any of them.
- You can Dispute your Irrational *Beliefs* if you have them by using some of the REBT cognitive, emotive, and behavioral techniques that are also mentioned in this chapter.
- In particular, you can use these methods to acquire several rational attitudes that have been found to be useful to a group of institutionalized elderly men who kept themselves from being depressed in spite of their distinctly restricted life. These philosophies included: (1) Determination to take care of themselves as much as they could. (2) Minimizing absolutistic demands for relative desires and preferences. (3) Resolving to do problem-solving thinking. (4) Accepting themselves and others in spite of their human failings. (5) Realistically accepting, though not liking, unfortunate events. (6) Getting involved with helping other people. No matter what your age, these sound like undepressing views!

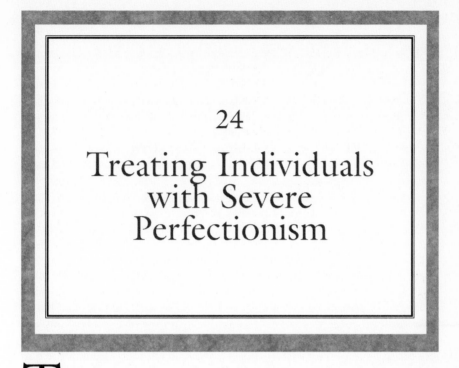

24

Treating Individuals with Severe Perfectionism

T he importance of perfectionism in helping people to become anxious, depressed, and otherwise emotionally disturbed was at least vaguely seen by the Stoic philosopher Epictetus two thousand years ago; and has been pointed out by pioneering cognitive-oriented therapists such as Alfred Adler for over a century. It was also noted by the non-Freudian psychoanalyst Karen Horney (1950) in her concept of the idealized image.

I was the first cognitive behavioral therapist to specifically include perfectionism as an irrational, self-defeating *Belief* in my original paper on Rational Emotive Behavior Therapy (REBT) in August 1956 (Ellis 1958). Thus, among twelve basic irrational ideas that I included in this paper, I listed "The idea that one should be thoroughly competent, adequate, intelligent, and achieving in all possible respects—instead of the idea that one should *do* rather than desperately try to do well and that one should accept oneself as a quite imperfect creature, who has general human limitations and specific fallibilities" (p. 41).

In my first book on REBT, *How to Live With a "Neurotic,"* published in

This chapter is partly adapted from "The Role of Irrational Beliefs in Perfectionism" in *Perfectionism*, ed. G. L. Flett and P. Hewitt (Washington, D.C.: American Psychological Association, 2001). Used with permission of Springer Publishing Company.

1957, I included among the main irrational ideas leading to disturbance, "A person should be thoroughly competent, adequate, talented, and intelligent in all possible respects; the main goal and purpose of life is achievement and success; incompetence in anything whatsoever is an indication that a person is inadequate or valueless" (p. 89). I also noted, "*Perfectionism* . . . excessive striving to be perfect will inevitably lead to disillusionment, heartache, and self-hatred" (p. 89).

In 1962, after practicing, lecturing, and writing on REBT for seven years, I included in my first book for the psychological profession, *Reason and Emotion in Psychotherapy*, these ideas among eleven main Irrational *Beliefs* that contribute to emotional disturbance: "2. The idea that one should be competent, achieving, and adequate in all possible respects if one is to consider oneself worthwhile. . . . 4. The idea that it is awful and catastrophic when things are not the way one would very much like them to be. . . . 11. The idea that there is invariably a right, precise, and perfect solution to human problems and that it is catastrophic if this perfect solution is not found" (Ellis 1962, pp. 69–88).

Obviously REBT has particularly stressed the irrationality and self-defeatism of perfectionism from its start. Scores of REBT articles and books have endlessly made this point, including many of my own publications and books by other leading REBTers. Following REBT's singling out perfectionism as an important irrational belief, a vast literature has been devoted in recent years to the findings and treatment of cognitive behavior therapy that has also frequently emphasized the treatment of perfectionism. Aaron Beck (1976) and David Burns (1999) particularly have emphasized its importance, and many other cognitive behaviorists have described its treatment (Flett, Hewitt, Blankstein, and Kolodin 1998; Lazarus, Lazarus, and Fay 1993).

Although I have been one of the main theorists and therapists to emphasize the importance of perfectionism in behavioral disturbance, I now see that I have never fully described what are the main Irrational *Beliefs* that lead to perfectionism and why they probably "naturally" exist and interfere with people's surrendering their strong perfectionistic tendencies. Let me now do so.

REBT's theory of rational and irrational human behavior follows the ancient notion that humans, in order to stay alive and well-functioning, have several basic desires, goals, and preferences that help them to do so. Thus they are commonly said to survive better and be more effective (1) when they have a sense of self-efficacy or mastery; (2) when they actually succeed in getting what they want and avoiding what they don't want; (3) when they get approval and minimal disapproval from other people whom they consider important; (4) when they are safe and sound, and not likely to be diseased, hurt, or killed. It is not that people *cannot* exist or *must be* completely miserable if they don't fulfill any or all of these desires and goals. Therefore, we had better not call them *needs* or *dire necessities*. But it is usually agreed that humans tend to be better off and live longer when they achieve these kinds of goals.

Assuming that people are more likely to survive and be glad they're alive if they satisfy their basic desires, they are likely to consider their mastery goals and rationally conclude, "If I have self-inefficacy and view myself as only being able to function ineptly, I actually will tend to function worse. Therefore, I will probably actually get less of what I want; I will get less approval from significant other people; and I will probably be more in danger of being harmed and killed by dangerous conditions."

Your *wish* or *desire* to have a sense of self-efficacy or power is therefore a rational, self-helping *Belief*, as many studies by Albert Bandura and his colleagues have shown. However, you may *also* have an irrational, self-defeating *Belief* about achievement, such as, "Because I *desire* to perform well, I *absolutely must* do so, else I am a worthless, hopelessly endangered person!" To go one step farther, your Irrational *Belief* about self-efficacy may be, "Because I desire to achieve, I *absolutely must* have a *guarantee* that I will do so perfectly!" If performing well is good, isn't performing *perfectly* well much better?

Your *wish* to reach your important goals outstandingly or even perfectly sounds reasonable. But your escalating this desire to a demand, and especially to a *perfectionistic* demand, is quite another matter! Listen to this: "I *absolutely must*, under all conditions and at all times, *perfectly achieve* my goals!" Or else? Or else you will tend to conclude that you'll *never* get what you want; that you'll be *totally* unworthy of approval and love by significant others; that you will be in *continual danger* of harm and annihilation. Quite a series of "horrors" you've predicted for yourself!

You can easily have rational, self-helping *desires* for success and even for perfect success. For example, you can wish for a top grade on a test or to have your mate love you *completely*. That would be nice. But necessary?

Again, you can have even strong desires for some people's approval. It would be great if they always—yes, always—favored you and gave you everything you wanted. But if you *absolutely need* others' approval, and especially if you need their undying, perfect approval, watch it!

So your having self-efficacy, competence, lovability, and safety tend to aid your living. Not always, of course, for your "perfect" performances may turn off some important people and encourage them to balk you. Why, then, should you self-sabotagingly escalate your desires to unrealistic, perfectionistic, demands?

The usual answer psychologists give to this paradox is that you and many other people may be born and reared to be perfectionistic. First, for evolutionary, survival reasons, you wish *and* demand. Second, your parents and teachers reinforce your wishing and demanding. Third, you practice both wishing and demanding and thus train yourself to habitually think and feel these ways—usually for the rest of your life.

These are probably all reasons why both rational preferring and irrational demanding are both so common among millions of people and lead to distinct benefits and disbenefits. For some sixty years of doing psychotherapy with thousands of clients, I have also figured out some specific reasons why humans are often perfectionistic demanders, when they would probably get better results if they were only preferrers and unimperative goal seekers. Let me present these as hypotheses that can be empirically tested.

1. People can easily distinguish their weak and moderate desires from their demands, but frequently have great difficulty distinguishing their strong, forceful wishes from insistences. When they have a weak desire to succeed at an important task, to gain social approval, or to be safe from harm, they rarely think that they *absolutely must* achieve these goals. But when they strongly desire to do these things, they frequently insist that they *have to* do them. *Why* they have weak or strong desires to achieve depends on many factors, both biological and environmental. But my theory says that once, for any reason, they have *powerful* wishes—what Wolcott Gibbs, a *New Yorker* writer, called "a whim of iron"—they frequently think, and especially *feel* that they *must* attain them.

2. A mild or moderate preference to perform well or win others' approval implies the legitimacy of alternative behaviors. Thus: "I moderately like to win this tennis match but if I lose it's no big deal and I can probably go on to win the next one." "I mildly prefer to have Mary like me, *but* if she doesn't I can survive and probably induce Jane, who has good traits too, to prefer me." If you *mildly* want something, and don't get it, there is a good chance that you can get something almost equally desirable instead.

A strong preference, however, often leaves few alternative choices of equal valence. Thus: "I *greatly* want to win this tennis match, and thereby become champion, so if I lose this match I will lose the championship—which I also *strongly* want to win—and may never gain it at *all*. Therefore, I *must* win this match to get what I *really* want." "I greatly want to have Mary love me, because she is a *special* person with whom I could be *notably* happy. Therefore, if Mary doesn't love me, and I could win Jane's love instead, that is a poor alternative and it will not really satisfy me. Consequently, I *absolutely must* get Mary to love me."

Strong preferences leave little room for alternative choices—or, at least *equally* satisfying ones. They lead you to imply that because alternatives hardly exist, you *must* have your strong preferences fulfilled. By their very *strength*, they prejudice you against alternative choices and make your particular choice seem mandatory instead of preferential.

3. Strong desires encourage you, simply because of their strength, to focus, sometimes almost obsessively-compulsively, on *one* choice or a *special* choice, and to ignore or disparage alternate choices. Thus, if you *mildly* want to win a tennis match, you are free to think of many other things, such as the pleasure your opponent will have if he or she wins, or the fact that people will dislike you if you win. So you consider, again, alternate goals to winning the match and may even deliberately lose it. Or you may decide to play golf instead of tennis.

If, however, you *strongly* desire to win the tennis match—as well as, perhaps, win the championship along with it—you will tend to focus, focus, focus on the gains to be achieved by winning and the "horrible" consequences of losing; and your (obsessive-compulsive) focus will discourage alternate thoughts and selectively prejudice you against considering such alternatives. Strong desires, in other words, frequently lead to focused thinking and to prejudiced overgeneralization. Not always, of course; but significantly more frequently than mild or moderate desires. If so, the prejudiced overgeneralizations that strong desires encourage lead to the belief that because some goal is *highly* preferable it is also *necessary*. Overfocusing on its desirability encourages your seeing it as a dire necessity.

Suppose my hypothesis is sustained about your strong desires more often leading to demanding and musturbating than your weak desires, what has all this got to do with perfectionizing? My theory goes one step farther and says that if you believe, "I would *like* to perform perfectly well," you will act rationally about striving for outstanding performances. But if you believe, "I *absolutely must* perform perfectly well," you will often anxietize yourself about the realistic possibility of your *not* being perfect—especially since you always are a *fallible* person. Your anxietizing about your performing will often then interfere with your succeeding; and your additional demand, "I must not anxietize! I must not panic!" will likely create even more anxietizing. So your demanding rather than preferring perfection won't aid your goals. To insist that you *must* perfectly achieve your desire seems "logical" because it is motivating. Paradoxically, it illogically tends to create malfunctioning.

My theory says that your having strong rather than weak desires, first, makes you more likely to think that these desires *absolutely must* be fulfilled; and, second, makes you more likely to think that they must be *perfectly* fulfilled. Because if their successful fulfillment is beneficial to you and if perfect fulfillment is even more beneficial, as it may well be, it seems to be "logical" for you to jump from "I *absolutely must* fulfill my strong desires because they are so strong." Actually, this is a non sequitur. It also may seem "logical" for you to think and feel, "I *absolutely must* fulfill my strong desires *perfectly* because they are so strong." This, again, is actually a non sequitur.

I am theorizing, then, that strong rather than weak desires tend to be profound prejudices; that is, they are cognitive-emotional biases. They often encourage people to think, "Because I *strongly* want success, approval, or safety, and it would be beneficial for me to have them, I *absolutely must* have them." This is a grandiose and perfectionistic idea itself, because you and I obviously don't run the universe. So whatever we desire, no matter how strongly we crave it, our *preference* obviously doesn't *have to* be fulfilled.

Humans are, however, prone to grandiosity. They often demand that their strong desires absolutely must be fulfilled. They tend to think wish-fulfillingly, as Freud observed. More to the point, they often think and feel wish-demandingly. "Because I *strongly* want it so, I *should* achieve it!" Once they escalate their powerful wishes to dire necessities, they frequently take them one step further: "Because my important desires are sacred and *absolutely must* be fulfilled, they must be thoroughly, completely, and perfectly fulfilled!" Then they really have emotional and behavioral problems!

Let me consider one more important point. I noted in the first edition of *Reason and Emotion in Psychotherapy* that people who anxietize, and particularly those who panic, frequently strongly create anxietizing about their anxietizing. They thus produce secondary disturbing about their original disturbing. Why is this so common among humans? According to REBT theory, they are forcibly thinking, "I must not anxietize! It's terrible to create anxietizing! I'm an inadequate person for panicking!"

For a number of years, Steven Reiss and his coworkers (Reiss and McNally 1985) have theorized that some individuals have unusual sensitivity to their own feelings of anxiety, as I theorized in 1962. They have done many studies of this secondary-symptom anxietizing, which they call anxiety sensitivity, and have confirmed some of my and other clinicians' observations about it. Reiss's theory of anxiety sensitivity overlaps with my theory of strong desiring in that it implies that some people who anxietize themselves about their anxietizing find their feeling so uncomfortable that they awfulize about them and thus panic themselves. Their desire for relief from anxietizing is so intense that they *demand* they not do it, and thereby increase it.

What, we may ask, makes anxiety-sensitive people so *demanding* about their anxietizing? My theory answers this question as follows: (1) Anxietizing, and particularly panicking, is very *uncomfortable*. It feels bad, disrupts competence, may lead to social disapproval, and often brings on physical symptoms—such as shortness of breath and rapid heartbeat—which make you, a person afflicted with LFT, think you are in real physical danger, even that you are dying. (2) Because it is *so* uncomfortable you *strongly* wish that it not exist—disappear—and that all its disadvantages disappear with it. (3) Because you *strongly* desire it to vanish, you insist and demand "I must not anxietize! I must not panic!" (4) Then, perversely enough, you worry about your worrying, panic about your panicking. (5) Consequently, you increase your uncomfortable symptoms, especially your physical symptoms of suffocating and heart pounding. (6) You then panic even more! (7) Your vicious cycle continues. (8) Finally, because your panicking brings on *great* discomfort, you may frequently conclude, "I must never panic at *all*! I must *perfectly* never panic!" Moral: by being *acutely* aware of the discomfort of your panicking, you may demand that you *perfectly* must *never* panic; and you may increase the likelihood of your panicking.

My explanation of anxietizing about anxietizing and panicking about panicking nicely fits into my theory about strong desiring and its relationship to demanding and perfectionizing. However, beware! This explanatory power of my theory is interesting but may have little support from empirical findings. Many psychoanalytic theories brilliantly fit together and support their desired postulates; but they appear to be little connected with hard-headed facts.

So far in this chapter I have considered individualistic demanding for achievement, approval, and safety, but of course these exist in couples and families. Take couples therapy, which I have done extensively along REBT lines for years. Are husbands, wives, and other partners as demanding and as perfectionistic about their mates as they are about themselves? Frequently, yes; and with frightful musts about their relationship.

John, a thirty-six-year-old accountant, gave himself a perfectionistic hard time about his work and made himself exceptionally anxious if it wasn't wholly accurate. He excused his perfectionism in this respect by saying that of course it had to be perfectly accurate, since his job was accounting and that meant accuracy. But John was also perfectionistic about his dress, his tennis game, and several other aspects of his life. Because, however, he worked mightily to keep his accounting, his appearance, and his tennis game in order, he succeeded fairly well in doing so and was only temporarily anxious when things got a bit beyond his control. His compulsive striving kept things pretty much together.

John, however, was equally perfectionistic about his wife, Sally, and his two accounting partners. They, too, had to—yes, had to—perform well, dress well, and even play tennis well. And they often didn't, those laggards! John, of course, couldn't control others, as he strove for his own perfection. So he was frequently more enraged against his "careless" wife and partners than he was anxious about his own performances.

I saw John for therapy because his wife and his partners insisted that he go—or else! He was set for a double divorce. I had a rough time at first, showing him the folly of his performance-oriented perfectionism, as he was willing to strive mightily to achieve it, and to suffer only occasionally panic attacks when he didn't. I found it easier to show him that his demands on others simply wouldn't work. He had little control over them and they were going to continue to be just as abominably unperfectionistic as they chose. They *shouldn't* be that way—but they were.

After several sessions of REBT, John was able to *prefer* without *demanding* perfect behavior from Sally and his partners and therefore feel keenly disappointed but not enraged when they made accounting, tennis, or other errors. He lived with their imperfections, and no one divorced him. He only slightly gave up his own perfectionistic demands on himself, continued to perform well in most ways, but was decidedly more anxious than he need have been.

John's wife, Sally, who I also saw for a few sessions, was nondemanding of herself for the most part, but *couldn't stand* the obsessive-compulsiveness of John and their twelve-year-old daughter, Electra. They were both carved from the same perfectionistic family block (as was John's father and sister) and had to do many things absolutely perfectly. Sally couldn't take their frantically pushing themselves to achieve (which was bad enough) and their insistence that she, too, be faultlessly on the ball (which was impossible!). Though outwardly easy-going, she kept inwardly demanding, "They *must not* be that scrupulous! They *have to be* more tolerant! I can't bear their intolerance!"

I showed Sally—and she was much easier to work with than was John—that her intolerance of John's and Electra's intolerance simply was not working. Her rage was exceptionally self-upsetting, was not going to change John or Electra, and might lead to her divorcing John (not so bad), also lead to her divorcing Electra (not so good!), and create her own psychosomatic troubles (still worse!).

Sally saw the light and soon gave up her intolerance of John's and Electra's intolerance. She still *wanted* them to but didn't *insist* that they be more reasonable, and worked with me to change her own insistence that they be less perfectionistic. So John improved in his demands on Sally (and on his partners), and Sally distinctly improved in her perfectionistic demands on John and on Electra. John kept some of his perfectionistic commands on himself but did not let them interfere too seriously with his family and business relationships.

One reason why John kept his insistence that he *must* perform outstandingly was that he was fixated on the kind of competitiveness that I described about perfectionists in the original edition of *Reason and Emotion in Psychotherapy* in 1962. I said at the time:

> The individual who *must* succeed in an outstanding way is not merely challenging himself and testing his own powers (which may well be beneficial); but he is invariably comparing himself to and fighting to best *others*. He thereby becomes other- rather than self-directed and sets himself essentially impossible tasks (since no matter how outstandingly good he may be in a given field, it is most likely that there will be others who are still better). (Ellis 1962, pp. 63–64)

After practicing REBT for almost sixty years, and after studying the results obtained in scores of studies of Irrational *Beliefs*, I find this hypothesis more tenable than ever. Hypercompetitiveness is a common trait of "normal" musturbators—especially of perfectionists. They mainly have unhealthy conditional self-acceptance (CSA) instead of healthy *un*conditional self-acceptance (USA). Their condition for being a "good person" is notable achievement; and to be a "better person" than others requires perfect achievement.

Actually, to strive desperately to best others, and thereby to gain "better" worth as a person, is an undemocratic, fascistlike philosophy. Fascists like Hitler and Mussolini not only rated themselves to be better in some traits, such as physical prowess or blondeness, but self-evaluated as being superior *people*. Their *essence* is supposedly outstandingly good. This grandiose view is diametrically opposed to the concept of unconditional self-acceptance (USA), which means fully accepting and respecting oneself whether or not one is achieving.

Perfectionists, then, tend to be highly conditional self-acceptors who base their worth as persons on competitively besting others—and who, in the process, often lose out on discovering what they personally want to do and who tend to fascistically denigrate others.

How are perfectionists affected by stressful conditions? More so, I would say, than are nonperfectionists. First, they may demand that stress be minimal—or perfectly nonexistent. Second, they may insist that they get perfect solutions to practical problems that create stress—such as how to have a perfect job interview, how to get a perfect job, and how to deal with bosses or employees perfectly well. Third, when stressful conditions occur—such as business difficulties—they may demand that they have perfect solutions for them. They not only prefer these great solutions, but demand that they be easily and quickly available—which they normally are not. Therefore, under conditions that are equally stressful to others perfectionists "find" more stress, less satisfactory solutions, and more prolonged difficulties than do nonperfectionists. Their perfectionism opposes realistic and probabilistic expectations about the number and degree of stressors that should exist and often results in their making a hassle into a holocaust.

About the stressors of their lives, they have the usual Irrational *Beliefs* of disturbed people, but hold them more vigorously and rigidly. Thus, they tend to believe that stressful situations *absolutely must not* exist; that it is utterly awful and horrible (as bad as it could be) when they do; that they *completely can't stand them* (can't enjoy life *at all* because of them); that they are *quite powerless* to improve them; and that they rightly should damn themselves for not removing or coping beautifully with stressors.

According to REBT theory, practically all disturbed people *at times* hold these self-defeating beliefs. But perfectionists seem to hold them more frequently and insistently—and cling to them as *fixed ideas*. Consequently, they often require long-term treatment; and, if REBT is used with them, they frequently require a number of cognitive, emotive, and behavioral methods before they will surrender these beliefs. Why? A single method of disputing and acting against their Irrational *Beliefs* doesn't seem convincing enough. So a therapist's use of several techniques may finally work better.

By the same token, if perfectionists who react badly to stressful conditions are placed in cognitive-behavioral group therapy, where several group members, in addition to the therapist, actively try to help them give up their rigid beliefs and behaviors, I have often found this to work better than if they are in individual therapy with only a single therapist to counter their perfectionism. Again, the same issue seems to be that the perfectionists more than the nonperfectionists have (1) a stronger desire or preference to do well, (2) a stronger and more rigid demand that they do so, (3) a stronger insistence that they do perfectly well, (4) a long-term habit of perfectionistic thinking, feeling, and behaving that resists short-term change. For all these reasons, they frequently are difficult customers (DC's) who can use intensive, prolonged therapy.

My hypothesis, then, is that perfectionists are more rigid and persistent in their Irrational *Beliefs* than what I call the "nice neurotics." Many—not all—of them have severe personality disorders. They have *idées fixe* (fixed ideas), as Pierre Janet said a century ago of many severely disturbed people. Let us honestly admit this as we try to help them. If I am correct, therapists had better use many of the REBT cognitive and behavioral methods described in other chapters of this book and consider the powerful techniques described in the chapters on dealing with severe personality disorders—particularly those recommended in chapter 28, "Treating Individuals With Obsessive-Compulsive Disorders (OCD)." OCD and extreme perfectionism often hang together—and can be hanged together with REBT and CBT.

SELF-HELP SUGGESTIONS

- By all means keep your healthy *desires or preferences* to perform well and even perfectly well—for they will often motivate you, keep you goal-oriented, and help you to get the things you want in life. Raising your preferences for perfectionism to drastic demands will tend to create anxietizing, depressing, and low frustration tolerance and will often get you much less of what you really want.

- You may well have both innate and socially acquired tendencies to strive perfectionistically, to practically kill yourself to reach the top, and to seriously upset yourself if you are somewhat less than perfect. But if you meet the Buddha—who, of course, is perfect—on the road, kill him! Otherwise, you will insidiously compare yourself to him (or her)—and be quite unenlightened!

- If you are extremely perfectionistic, consider the possibility that you have a generous touch of Obsessive-Compulsive Disorder (OCD). If so, run, don't walk, for professional help!

- Perfectionism may encourage you, of course, to perfectionistically rid yourself of every single vestige of this mode of self-distressing! You thereby deny the healthy aspects of trying to do very well and create for yourself a doubly perfectionistic bind!

25

Treating Individuals with Morbid Jealousy

Having dealt elsewhere with the general etiology and treatment of jealousy, I shall limit myself in this chapter to the rational emotive behavioral treatment of morbid jealousy. What I have called rational or healthy amative heartburn consists of concern about the loss of a loved person or displeasure over a real or imagined attachment that he or she has with someone else. As Ewald Bohm points out, this feeling "can be directed toward the love-object, toward the rival, or toward both" (1961, p. 567).

Rational Emotive Behavior Therapy (REBT) assumes that nonmorbid or rational jealousy consists of one's caring for a sex-love partner and strongly *wanting* or *preferring* him or her to refrain from becoming too emotionally involved with others. This often leads to mating problems, but the concern and annoyance it produces is not too disruptive of the relationship or of the jealous partner's own life.

Irrational or morbid jealousy, however, tends to be accompanied by feelings of severe insecurity, hostility, self-pity, and depression, and frequently is fatal to good love relationships (Ellis 2000b). According to REBT theory, it

This chapter is partly adapted from "The Treatment of Morbid Jealousy: A Rational Emotive Behavior Therapy Approach," *Journal of Cognitive Psychotherapy* 10 (1996): 23–33. Used with permission of Springer Publishing Company.

largely consists of *demanding* or *commanding* that because one cares for a partner, she or her absolutely *must* not, under any conditions, become emotionally involved with others and thereby deprive one of interest, love, or sex.

CAUSES OF IRRATIONAL OR MORBID JEALOUSY

Extreme Ego-Insecurity: Irrationally jealous individuals often rate themselves as "good" or "worthy" or "acceptable" only when they are strongly loved by their beloved. They thereby jeopardize their feelings of self-acceptance when they are not loved as much as they *must* be—and they then make themselves insensately jealous (Klein 1984).

Serious Hostility: People who demand that others *always* treat them considerately and fairly, and who make themselves hostile when these others do not act as well as they *must*, frequently work themselves into rages against their love rivals and in some instances become obsessed with harming or killing them (Ellis and Gullo 1972; Ellis and Tafrate 1997).

Extreme Low Frustration Tolerance: While actual or possible frustration of love and sex desires leads people to feel rational jealousy, the whining attitude that they must *not* be frustrated, and that they can't stand it if they are, constitutes low frustration tolerance (LFT) which, I hypothesize, is significantly correlated with strong feelings of irrational jealousy (Ellis 1957/1975; Ellis and Becker 1983; Ellis and Harper 1997).

Dire Love Need and Dependency: People who have a dire need (rather than a strong desire) for their partner's attention and love and who make their happy existence utterly *dependent* on reciprocation tend to be much more jealous than nondependent lovers.

Obsessive-Compulsive Attachments: Some people are obsessive-compulsive disturbed and may become addicted to many things, including love. Such individuals sometimes are intensely jealous of their mates and can act quite self-defeatingly in this respect.

Projection: Jealousy often stems from a lover's desire for new or additional partners. Consequently he or she assumes that the mate is equally interested in others, greatly fears that a mate has such interests, and paranoically "finds" them.

Misdiagnosing a Partner's Unloving or Provocative Behavior: When a partner seems to lose interest or to act unlovingly, many lovers (rightly or wrongly) conclude that he or she is quite interested in someone else and become irrationally jealous. When partners are seen to be unusually interested in another person, jealousy frequently escalates and sometimes becomes enormous.

Childhood Traumas and Conditioning: Both psychoanalysts and behaviorists hold that morbid jealousy stems from traumatic childhood experiences, especially with other family members, and that early incidents involving separation anxiety, sibling rivalry, or other dangerous conditions created present-day obsessive-compulsive jealousy. This theory may have some validity but is still a superficial explanation of jealous disturbances. For even when jealousy-producing events occur in early life, analysts and behaviorists fail to show what cognitive and emotional predispositions people *bring* to these events that *make* them think and feel them to be so "traumatic." Psychoanalytic and conditioning explanations for morbid jealousy omit the deep philosophies that more directly and importantly "cause" early and present-day self-defeating feelings of morbid jealousy.

RATIONAL EMOTIVE BEHAVIORAL TREATMENT OF MORBID JEALOUSY

REBT, as noted above, assumes that morbid jealousy tends to occur when people transmute their desires and preferences for love into absolutist, all-pervasive musts and demands. When they believe, "I'd very much *prefer* my mate to care for me, but he or she doesn't *have* to, and it would be highly frustrating but *not* horrible if I lose him or her," they will be *concerned* but hardly *panicked* about being rejected. But if they dogmatically believe, "My mate *must not* under *any* conditions leave me! I couldn't *stand* such a horror! That would make me an inadequate, unlovable person!" they will make themselves exceptionally anxious, insecure, self-downing, and dependent—and often inordinately jealous.

In addition to having feelings of inadequacy if they lose their partners, jealous people frequently have intense feelings of hostility and low frustration tolerance. Their hostility largely stems from the philosophy, "My mate *must* love only me and *never* deprive me of affection, and if I am depressed from lack of love he or she is a *rotten person* for making me needlessly suffer!" Their low frustration tolerance (LFT) accompanies the irrational philosophy, "Because I *must* not be deprived of sex and love, and because I *can't stand* the discomfort of this deprivation, my life is *awful*, and I can't be happy *at all*!"

REBT includes a number of cognitive, emotive, and behavioral methods that therapists can use to help their clients to discover, clarify, and change their absolutist musts and perfectionist demands, to change them to realistic and rational preferences, and thereby to undo their feelings and acts of morbid jealousy. Some REBT antijealousy techniques follow.

COGNITIVE TECHNIQUES

Disputing Irrational Beliefs: Help your clients to discover their jealousy-creating irrational beliefs and to actively dispute them. Some of their basic unrealistic and illogical ideas are (1) "I *must* be greatly loved, at practically all times, by the partner I have chosen to love." (2) "When my love is not returned (as it *must* be!), it is *catastrophic* and my whole life is *awful*!" (3) "I *can't stand* my beloved not loving me as much as I love him or her!" (4) "Because I haven't induced my partner to love me as well as I *should*, I am an unlovable, inadequate person!" (5) "Because my mate doesn't love me as much as he or she *should*, I'll *never* find anyone who truly will love me!" (6) "The only way I can accept myself and get the love that I absolutely *need* is to have a guarantee that my partner will love me, and only me, forever!"

Once you and your clients discover their basic Irrational *Beliefs* that lead to their morbid feelings of jealousy, you can show them how to scientifically dispute and surrender these rigidly held ideas. Thus, you teach them to ask themselves, "*Why* must I be totally loved?" "*Where is the evidence* that it is absolutely awful when I am not?" "Prove that I *can't stand* my beloved not loving me." "Do I really become an unlovable, inadequate person when I am not totally loved?" "Is it true that I'll *never* find anyone who will truly love me just because my present mate doesn't love me enough?" "Why can't I accept myself and be reasonably happy even if I have no guarantee that my partner will love me forever?" "If I strongly believe that I must always be totally loved, will that belief bring me good or bad results?"

By showing your clients how to actively dispute their irrational beliefs about love, you will often help them to surrender these beliefs and replace them with realistic, self-helping ideas.

Using Rational Coping Statements: By answering their own disputing questions, clients will usually wind up with what REBT calls effective new philosophies. You can help them make these new philosophies into rational coping statements, which they can then write down, carry around with them, and say to themselves several times each day until their morbid jealousy wanes. Thus, they can tell themselves these kinds of coping, anti-jealousy self-statements: "I want my partner to be more loving and absorbed in me, but she doesn't *have to* be!" "I can be a quite happy person even if my mate loves others besides me!" "My partner's love for someone else means something about her and her tastes, but it doesn't necessarily mean anything about *me*." "I'll never *like* my mate's being interested in other people, but I can definitely *stand* it and view it as only an *inconvenience* instead of a *horror*."

Reframing: As a therapist, you can help your morbidly jealous clients to see the *good* sides, and not only the *bad* sides, of their partners' interest in others. Thus, if Mary is horrified about John's fond feelings for his ex-wife, or by his great attachment to his mother, she can be helped to see that (1) This shows that John is truly able to love. (2) This gives her more leeway to also love other people. (3) She can use the time John devotes to other people to do more things on her own. (4) Her distaste for and frustration about John's behavior gives *her* the *challenge* of working on her own feelings of grandiosity and low frustration tolerance, thereby helping herself grow emotionally.

Cost-Benefit Ratio: Morbid jealousy often stems from your clients' deifying their beloved and dogmatically insisting that he or she is the *only* person they could ever love and be happy with. To disrupt this kind of obsessive deification, you can help them make a list of the flaws and disadvantages of their beloved and a list of the assets and advantages of other potential partners. They can then refer and think about these lists several times each day until they see alternative, nonobsessive ways of viewing their beloved and other possible mates.

Morbidly jealous people usually obsess about the worst things that could happen—such as their partner leaving them for another mate—and the "horrors" that would then ensue. Using REBT, you can encourage them to imagine this worst possible situation and then write out a long list of things they could do to ward off depression and make themselves reasonably happy if this "terrible" situation actually occurred. Instead of obsessing about "horrors," they would then think about alternative solutions to their "awful" love problems.

Clients can be shown how to make a list of the great disadvantages of morbid feelings of jealousy and to go over this list every day to motivate themselves to keep working to change these feelings.

Cognitive Distraction: When clients morbidly obsess about the "terrors" of not being sufficiently loved by their partners, you can show them how to use cognitive distraction methods to divert themselves to less terrifying thoughts. Thus, they can focus on Edmund Jacobson's progressive relaxation technique, on yoga, on meditation, on pleasurable thoughts, on work, on entertainment, and on various other diverting things. Most cognitive distraction techniques are palliative and short-lasting, because inordinately jealous people tend to use them for a while and then return to their morbid love obsessions. But if you can encourage them to acquire an absorbing vital interest, or long-term devotion to some project or cause, they may actually cure themselves of obsessive jealousy. The problem here is that they may become obsessive-compulsive about this new cause! Even that, however, may be a gain, because morbid jealousy is almost always destructive while other kinds of obsessions (e.g., about fostering world peace) may be constructive.

Positive Imagery: Positive imagery or visualization may be used to help combat morbid jealousy, but also has its limitations. Thus people who obsess about the "horrors" of losing their beloved may be shown how to visualize themselves winning out over all other rivals and inducing their partner exclusively and greatly to love them. This kind of positive imagery will often help calm their fears but may also reinforce their Irrational *Beliefs* that they *must* gain their partner's undying love and that they *are* worthless individuals if they don't. So positive imagery and positive thinking about love are to be used with caution!

Positive Ideals: There are several philosophic ideals which therapists can help people acquire to uproot their feelings of morbid jealousy. Thus clients can adopt the ideals of freedom and democracy, and realize that by tolerating their mate's other love involvements they are giving this partner one of the greatest gifts one person can give another person—the freedom to be himself or herself without needless criticism and restraint (Ellis 1958/1965). Again, clients can adopt the philosophy of caring *so much* for their mate that they actually *want* him or her to enjoy other sex-love relations. Morbidly jealous people can also try to feel a form of universal love for all people—including their beloved—rather than monolithic, possessive love for only one partner.

EMOTIVE TECHNIQUES

Rational Emotive Imagery: To use rational emotive imagery (REI) with your morbidly jealous clients, you can use this REBT adaptation of Maultsby's (1971) original work in this area. Have clients imagine the worst thing that could happen—e.g., their mate is secretly having an affair with another partner—and let them experience very jealous feelings (e.g., anxiety and rage) as they visualize this happening. Then tell them to change their intense feelings so that they *only* feel healthy negative feelings (e.g., feel sorry and disappointed) instead of unhealthy emotions like panicking and raging. When they do so, ask them *how* they changed their feelings—and see that they did so by changing to a rational set of *Beliefs* (e.g., "I deplore my man's infidelity but he or she is *not* a rotten person for acting this way"). Encourage your clients to do REI at least once a day for a month until they train themselves to automatically feel healthy instead of unhealthy negative feelings when they think about an actual or potential "horrible" situation.

Unconditional Self-Acceptance and Other-Acceptance: No matter how foolishly or morbidly jealous clients act, show them that you unconditionally accept them *with* their self-sabotaging behavior and also show them that they can always accept *themselves* no matter how crazy their *behavior* is. Model and instruct them in the REBT principles described in chapter 5— that they cannot be globally ratable as persons, that they are never subhuman nor damnable, and that their partners, too, may easily betray them and do the wrong things but are never rotten, wicked *people*.

Role-Playing: Play the role of your client's unfaithful partner and show the client how to think, feel, and act when he or she is very jealous. Doing role reversal, you play the client and rigidly hold on to his or her irrational, jealousy-provoking ideas, and have the client talk you out of these ideas. When the client enacts his or her role of the jealous person, stop the role-playing and help him or her zero in on the Irrational *Beliefs* creating the jealousy and let the client, right then and there, forcefully dispute those *Beliefs*.

Forceful Coping Statements: Work out with your clients very forceful, vigorous coping statements and have them, as homework, say these *strongly* to themselves many times. For example, "I can definitely stand my partner's being interested in someone else, though I'll never, never like it!" "If my mate is unfaithful, it shows something about *him* or *her*, but it never shows my worthlessness. Not at all!" "Even if I helped drive my mate into someone else's arms, I may have acted stupidly, but I'm NEVER a rotten, stupid *person*!"

Humor: Because jealous people lose their sense of humor and highly exaggerate the horror of what their partners are supposedly doing, you can sometimes humorously rip up their grim ideas and help them place these in a humorous perspective. REBT often employs rational humorous songs in this regard such as this antijealousy song:

LOVE ME, LOVE ME, ONLY ME!

(Tune: "Yankee Doodle")

Love me, love me, only me
Or I will die without you!
O, make your love a guarantee,
So I can never doubt you!
Love me, love me totally—really, really try, dear!
But if you demand love, too,
I'll hate you till I die, dear!
Love me, love me all the time,
Thoroughly and wholly!
My life turns into slushy slime
Unless you love me solely!
Love me with great tenderness,
With no ifs or buts, dear.
If you love me somewhat less,
I'll hate your goddamned guts, dear!

(Lyrics by Albert Ellis; copyright by Albert Ellis Institute.)

BEHAVIORAL TECHNIQUES

Fixed Role Playing: George Kelly's (1955) technique of fixed role playing can be used by having your jealous client for a week adopt the role of an individual whose mate is provocative but who only acts sanely and with healthy negative feelings. The client, by acting this way for a week, may train himself or herself to dislike but not to be frantic about possible infidelity.

Reinforcement Methods: You can show clients how to reinforce themselves with some pleasant activity (such as reading or swimming) only after they have refrained from jealously plaguing their mates. They may also penalize themselves with something unpleasant (such as talking to a boring person or burning hundred-dollar bills) every time they act insanely jealous.

Courting Fearful Situations: You can encourage your clients to court fearful situations where they can actively bring on jealous reactions and work at feeling healthfully displeased instead of unhealthfully angry about their partner's provocative behavior. Thus they can watch their partners intimately talking to or dancing closely with attractive people. Or for a while they may practice open dating with their partners while working at changing their jealous feelings.

SELF-HELP SUGGESTIONS

- If you tend to be afflicted with morbid jealousy, see whether it basically stems from your somewhat rigid devotion to totally monogamous relationships and your musturbatory demand that your amative love partner must be equally devoted.
- If so, retain your strong *preferences* for amative and sexual exclusivity but work against making them into rigid demands.
- Morbid jealousy usually means that you are insecure about your partner and yourself and that you are demanding guarantees of security and exclusive faithfulness. It usually consists of ego-anxietizing, in the course of which you convince yourself, "I *must* win the complete and exclusive love of the person I care for, or I'm an inadequate person." Or it may also be created by your discomfort, your anxietizing, and your thinking, "Because it would be so nice and wonderful if my beloved loved me, she or he *must not* deprive me of this bliss and it's *awful* and I can't stand it if this does not occur!"
- Both these profound Irrational *Beliefs* can make you morbidly jealous. You can strongly Dispute them by using the cognitive, emotive, and behavioral methods described in this chapter.

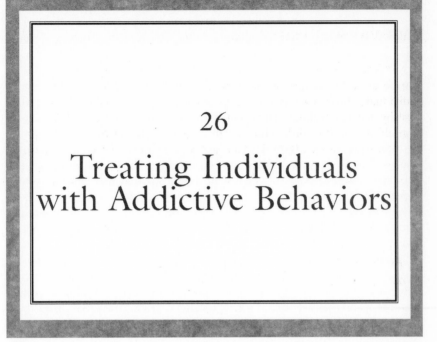

26

Treating Individuals with Addictive Behaviors

I have been working with various kinds of addicts since 1943. My first major interest and specialization was in sex, love, and relationship therapy, so I saw a good many addicts—both straight and gay—in those areas. But sex and love addicts also frequently compulsively drink, drug, smoke, overeat, and make themselves overly dependent on people and substances. So I soon started treating clients with multiple addictions—and what are now called dual diagnoses.

I began to suspect, soon after I started doing Rational Emotive Behavior Therapy (REBT) in 1955, that a large percentage of my severely addicted clients were not merely, as I originally thought, "nice neurotics," but that I could more accurately treat them as having severe personality disorders (PDs).

Not all addicts, of course, are this disturbed. As Michael Abrams, Lydia Dengelegi, and I say in our book, *The Art and Science of Rational Eating* (1992), eating addicts, when they are not bulimic or anorectic, may be no more disturbed than nonaddicts. Many of them have normal biological tendencies to get back to their "set points" when they diet too rigorously. Similarly, many smokers and sex "addicts" have powerful addictive urges in

---

This chapter is partly adapted from A. Ellis, "Addictive Behaviors and Personality Disorders," *Social Policy* (winter 1998): 25–30. Used with permission.

which they carelessly and harmfully indulge, but are still, at worst, afflicted with neurotic low frustration tolerance.

However, some of the most compulsive addicts I have seen are rigidly "stuck" because the appetitive centers in their brain have, for one reason or another, gone awry—so that they oversatiate themselves with alcohol, sweets, chocolate, or other substances mainly because of their physiological handicaps, and not only because of their psychological problems. Still other addicts, such as some gamblers and potheads, seem to be mainly neurotic, and indulge in childish low frustration tolerance (LFT). Because they *like* some substance or activity very much, they insist that they *absolutely must* indulge in it, even when they "know" how harmful their indulgence is to themselves and their loved ones. Addiction, then, comes in many shapes and sizes, and has multiple "causes," several of which tend to overlap and interact with each other.

What about the most serious addicts, such as the inevitable drinkers who go back to bingeing in spite of several hospitalizations, smokers who won't stop even when they have emphysema, and sex offenders who keep molesting children when they are still on parole for their last offense? What drives these "hopeless" addicts to their extreme destructiveness? Why are they so resistant to help from friends, relatives, therapists, and improved environments?

REASONS FOR INVETERATE ADDICTIONS

Many—perhaps the great majority—of inveterate addicts I have treated suffer from some kind of severe personality disorder (PD). I find them very often to be, in DSM IV terms, paranoid, schizoid, antisocial, borderline, avoidant, dependent, and/or obsessive-compulsive. When they are not quite diagnosable in these regular PD categories, and would often be labeled "neurotic," I still often find them to be prone to endogenous anxiety, panic, depression, and rage. Endogenous? Yes, I think that they frequently have an innate, biological tendency to overreact *easily* and/or underreact to the stresses and strains of everyday living.

Many of these individuals with severe PDs come from households where their close relatives, too, were innately highly disturbable. Therefore, their childhood and later years involved *more* stressors than the rest of us tend to experience. So the interaction between their innate disturbability *plus* their poor environment contribute significantly to making them even *more* upsettable than they otherwise would have been. But my long experience with thousands of clients leads me to believe that people who are biologically easily disturbable will often think, feel, and act self-defeatingly no matter how favorable are their early and later environments.

Practically all humans are both born and reared with strong tendencies to neuroticize themselves according to the ABCs of Rational Emotive Behavior Therapy (REBT) and cognitive behavior therapy (CBT). Unfortunate Activating Events or Adversities (As) occur in their lives, and then they adopt and invent dysfunctional or Irrational *Beliefs* (IBs) about these As. As I keep showing in this book, their core IBs, which are both conscious and unconscious (or implicit) are: (1) "I *absolutely must* perform well and be lovable or I am a pretty *worthless* person!" (2) "Other people *absolutely must* treat me kindly and fairly or they are no damned good!" (3) "Conditions under which I live *absolutely must* be comfortable and not too frustrating or else my existence is *intolerable* and horrible!" When people learn—*and* invent—these IBs, as all of them at times do, they create neurotic Consequences (Cs) that take the form of self-defeating thoughts (e.g., obsessive thoughts) destructive feelings (e.g., panic and depression), and dysfunctional behaviors (e.g., severe inhibitions and compulsions).

Almost all people with severe PDs start off with several main elements of disturbance: First, their strong biological tendencies to think, feel, and behave destructively, especially in complex social relationships. Second, the poor life Consequences (Cs) that they therefore create and are inflicted with because of their biological and social handicaps. Third, the interactions among their poor Adversities (As), dysfunctional Beliefs (Bs), and self-defeating Consequences (Cs).

THE NATURE OF PERSONALITY DISORDERS

If I am correct—as, of course, I may not be—people with severe PDs are usually (not always) biologically handicapped at the start, or at least quite early in their lives. They have distinct cognitive deficits or deficiencies (e.g., attention deficit disorder and focusing problems), emotional deficits (e.g., under- or overresponsiveness), and behavioral deficits (e.g., avoidant or compulsive proclivities). Like children who are born mentally deficient or with physical anomalies (e.g., cardiac or respiratory defects), they are distinctly handicapped.

Because of their innate—and environmentally exacerbated—deficiencies, they have unusual difficulties at *all* the ABCs of human disturbance. At point A (Adversity), they have more unfortunate experiences than non-handicapped children (e.g., have more disturbed parents and siblings and negative reactions from other children and adults who criticize and/or overprotect them because of their peculiarities). At point B (Belief System) they think crookedly about their unusual As (because of their innate and acquired cognitive-emotive deficiencies) and therefore end up with what we call severe personality disorders

(PDs) (e.g., schizoid personality or obsessive-compulsive disorder, OCD). Note that they are handicapped, innately and environmentally, at A, B, and C!

Like just about all of us humans, individuals with severe PDs are *also* neurotic or self-defeating. They therefore take their *desires* and *preferences* for success, approval, justice, and comfort and make them into grandiose demands—into absolutistic *musts*, *shoulds*, and *oughts*. As I have hypothesized for forty years, neurosis is practically the human condition, because humans are both innate and socially taught *must*urbators.

Whenever unfortunate Adversities (As) occur—or they *make* them occur—in their lives, addicts with personality disorders often *demand* that they must not exist, foolishly panic, depress, and enrage themselves about these As, and then (ironically) are least effectual at improving them. To make things worse, when they use their grandiose musts (and other cognitive distortions that go with them) to create neurotic Consequences (Cs) such as panic and depression, then they often command, "I *must* not be undepressed!" They thereby make themselves panicked about their panic, depressed about their depression, and so on. As I often humorously, but still seriously, tell my clients and audiences, they are nutty about their nuttiness—and thereby circularly neurotic.

Addiction Plus Personality Disorder

The REBT Theory says that when people are "normal neurotics," and do not have personality disordering, addiction has several ideological causes at B, people's Belief Systems. Thus, they have two main forms of low frustration tolerance (LFT): *Primary LFT*: "I like this harmful substance (alcohol, coke, cigarettes) or this activity (gambling, watching TV) very much and therefore I *absolutely must* have it, no matter what its disadvantages are! I *can't stand* being deprived! It's *awful* to stop indulging in it!" *Secondary LFT*: "I utterly hate discomfort and pain that result from my neurotic feelings (e.g., panic, depression), and I *absolutely must not* experience them! I have to stop blaming myself for the failures and rejections that go with them! So I *must* indulge in some substance or activity that is immediately gratifying, that distracts me from my pain, and that temporarily makes me feel good!"

Neurotic addiction, then, largely (not completely) stems from horrifying oneself about Adversities (As) in one's life *and* from awfulizing and having I-can't-stand-it-itis *about* one's cognitive-emotional-behavioral disturbance (Cs). These neuroses themselves mainly stem from grandiose *demands* (rather than *preferences*) that one perform well, be lovable, be treated fairly, and live comfortably. When such demands lead to disturbances—which they usually do—neurotics also have dysfunctional insistence that they must not feel disturbed. Addictive substances and activities temporarily allay both primary and secondary neuroses. So many (but hardly all) neurotics then *demand* (become *addicted to*) the distraction and relief from pain that their addictions temporarily produce.

People with severe PDs, if I am correct, are more prone to addiction than are "nice neurotics" for the following reasons: (1) They have more Adversities (As) and disturbed Consequences (Cs) than the rest of us neurotics. (2) They are therefore more frustrated than non-PDs. (3) Because of their greater and often overwhelming frustrations, many of them develop unusual degrees of LFT. (4) Because of their greater failures and rejections, many of them also develop neurotic self-damnation about their deficits, handicaps, and failings. (5) Some of them, for biological reasons, may be more prone than neurotics to *demand* that they must not be frustrated and must perform well. They may be *more* prone to demanding than neurotics. (6) For both biological and environmental reasons, persons with PDs often feel so disturbed that they are compulsively driven to alcohol, coke, food, gambling, and other addictions to temporarily allay their disordered thoughts, feelings, and actions. (7) Some of them, for biosocial reasons, are particularly afflicted with obsessive-compulsive disorders (OCD) and/or have neurological anomalies that interfere with normal appetite- and desire-controlling brain centers and that decrease their ability to stop their compulsive indulgences.

To make matters still worse, if all that I have just stated is even partially true, individuals with the dual diagnosis of addiction and PD will tend to addict themselves more often then neurotics, have more severe addictions (such as to barbiturates and heroin), and be more resistant to giving up their addictions. Their resistance to change results, again, from several factors, including:

- Their strong biological tendencies to have many thinking, feeling, and behavioral deficits.
- Their long history of being severely disturbed.
- Their history of poor social relationships, including with helpers and therapists.
- Their innate and acquired LFT that interferes with the very hard work that therapy, especially antiaddiction therapy, almost always requires.
- Their friendships and partnerships with other addicts.
- Their neurotic damning of themselves for their personality disorders, their foolish addictions, and their other failings and social rejections.
- Their deep-seated feelings of worthlessness and hopelessness that many PDs often have, and that may be an intrinsic, biologically based aspect of their having a severe personality disorder.

For reasons such as these, therapists had better recognize the important differences between "nice neurotic" addicts and those with severe personality disorders and have at their disposal special techniques of treating the latter. The special techniques used in REBT to treat addictive individuals, and especially those with personality disordering, are the many cognitive, emotive, and behavioral methods described throughout this book. They notably include your strongly teaching addicts to have unconditional self-accepting (USA), unconditional other-accepting (UOA), and, practically always, high frustration tolerance. They significantly overlap with the REBT and CBT methods described in the next three chapters of this book.

SELF-HELP SUGGESTIONS

- If you think that you have addicted yourself to some harmful substance, such as alcohol, drugs, or overeating, or to some destructive behavior, such as gambling, there is an excellent chance that you have low frustration tolerance, and devoutly believe that you absolutely must get what you desire and *have to* avoid restrictions on your immediate gratifying. Fully recognize your LFT—and fight it with the cognitive, emotive, and behavioral methods described in this book.
- Also look for your severe self-downing or lack of unconditional self-accepting (USA). This may occur on a primary level and cause you to distract yourself with strong addictions. Or it may occur secondarily—that is, you may put yourself down so severely for being harmfully (and stupidly) addicted that you feel incompetent to deal with your addictive behavior and may distinctly make it worse.
- You may well afflict yourself with neurotic addiction—which is hard enough to overcome. But if no amount of working to use REBT and CBT seems to help, suspect that you are both addictive and personality disordering. If you suspect this, get professional consultation to confirm it, and use the methods of REBT that have been most useful with individuals with personality disordering—especially the methods described in the next three chapters of this book.
- Whether or not you have neurotic or personality disordering addictive behavior, consider, with professional supervision, medication that may help you with your addiction itself and/or with any serious personality disordering that may accompany it.
- Self-help materials that may specifically help you to deal with addictive behaviors especially include books like A. Thomas Horvath (1999), *Sex, Drugs, Gambling, and Chocolate: Workbook for Overcoming Addiction*; Bill Knaus (2000), *Smart Recovery: A Sensible Primer* ; Philip Tate (1997), *Alcohol: How to Give It Up and Be Glad You Did*, and my own book with Emmett Velten (1992), *When AA Doesn't Work for You: Rational Steps for Quitting Alcohol.*

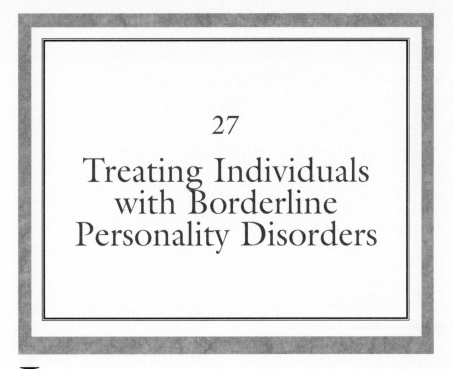

27
Treating Individuals with Borderline Personality Disorders

I have worked with thousands of people with personality disorders for the last fifty years, first as a psychoanalyst and later as a practitioner of Rational Emotive Behavior Therapy (REBT), and I have naturally given much thought to how these disorders originate and what are some of the best methods to help people alleviate or cope with this serious problem. After much thinking and experimenting, I have come up with some hypotheses that seem original to me but that may merely be restatements of other clinicians' ideas. In any event, I shall try to state them clearly in the hope that they may be clinically and experimentally tested.

HOW DO PERSONALITY DISORDERS ORIGINATE?

My first hypothesis is hardly startling but follows REBT theory: All "emotional" disturbances tend to have strong cognitive, emotive, and behavioral elements, and this is particularly true of the individuals with severe personality disorders, including those with borderline personality behaviors.

This chapter is partly adapted from "Treatment of Borderline Personality Disorder with Rational Emotive Behavior Therapy," in *Personality and Psychopathology,* ed. C. R. Cloninger (Washington, D.C.: American Psychiatric Press, 2000), pp. 475–96. Used with permission.

People with these conditions usually show severe dysfunction in their thinking, feeling, and behaving, so-called neurotics show less dysfunction, and so-called psychotics often show more severe dysfunction in these three areas.

People with personality disorders almost always have cognitive, emotive, and behavioral organic deficits for various reasons, including hereditary predispositions. They (and most properly diagnosed psychotics) have anomalies of their brain and central nervous system (as well as, often, other physiological defects), that significantly contribute, along with other environmental factors, to their personality disorders.

As I have pointed out (Ellis 1994) and as many other psychologists have shown, thought, feeling, and action always take place in environmental contexts and backgrounds, so that people and their situations interactively influence and affect each other. Humans have goals and purposes. In various environments, and especially in their social relationships, they construct thoughts, feelings, and behaviors that either actualize or defeat themselves, thereby creating conditions of "mental health" and "emotional disturbance."

There are many personality disorders, such as narcissism, borderline personality disorder (BPD), obsessive-compulsive disorder (OCD), schizoid personality, histrionic personality disorder, narcissistic personality disorder, avoidant personality disorder, and dependent personality disorder. They vary in intensity, often accompany each other, and often go along with other severe neurotic disorders, such as neurotic depression, panic states, and self-hatred.

Because personality disorders are so varied and complex, I shall mainly limit myself in this chapter to discussing individuals with borderline personality, a quite complex and varied entity that is often accompanied by serious neurotic disturbances and sometimes includes psychotic episodes. The main characteristics of the borderline personality include a pattern of unstable relationships, self-damaging impulsiveness, affective instability, intense inappropriate anger, recurrent suicidal threats, marked and persistent identity disturbance, chronic feelings of emptiness or boredom, and frantic efforts to avoid real or imagined abandonment (American Psychiatric Association 1987).

HOW DO PEOPLE WITH BPD GET THAT WAY?

We can start almost anywhere to examine the main causes of the problems of BPD, but let me arbitrarily start with organic deficits, which I hypothesize that individuals with borderline personality disorder (BPD) partly inherit. They seem to be born with innate tendencies that interact with their experiences to produce several deficiencies. Thus, cognitively they often exhibit (probably from childhood onward) attention deficit disorders, rigid ways of thinking, inability to organize well, impulsive thinking, forgetfulness, inconsistent images of others, inability to maintain a sense of time as an ongoing process, learning disability, perceptual disability, proneness to be double-bound, a tendency to exaggerate the significance of things, rigidity, demand-ingness, severe self-downing, purposelessness, impairment in recalling and recognition, and deficient semantic encoding. Neurotic individuals may have all these cognitive organic deficiencies too, but they usually have them less intensively, cope with them better, and exhibit them largely under stressful environmental conditions, whereas individuals with BPD tend to have them more endogenously and more severely (Linehan 1993; Cloninger 2000).

Individuals with borderline personalities, I again hypothesize, have *innate* emotional difficulties and deficiencies. Thus they are frequently dys-thymic, depressive, easily enraged, overexcitable, high-strung, easily pan-icked, and histrionic (Cloninger 2000). Behaviorally, individuals with BPD, again, are often born with distinct tendencies to be hyperactive, hypervigi-lant, impulsive, obstreperous, interruptive, excessively restless, temper ridden, and antisocial, and they often are alienated, addictive, overdepen-dent, inattentive, and purposeless (Cloninger 2000). Again, neurotic indi-viduals may at times and to some degree have the same emotional and behavioral traits, but persons with BPD tend to have them more intensely, severely, frequently, consistently, and endogenously.

Let us assume, for the moment, that people with BPD have some serious cognitive, emotional, and behavioral deficiencies. How will they neurotically react to them? First of all, they will on some levels, according to REBT theory, tend to observe or sense these deficits and put themselves down for having them. They will often note that they have poor intellectual functioning, demand that they *must* not act inadequately, berate themselves for acting that way, and easily feel like *inadequate people*—which individuals with BPD often tend to feel anyway, and which will then be significantly exacerbated.

If, as I theorize, individuals with borderline personality disordering have emotional deficiencies, they will often tend to be jealous and hostile toward less dysfunctional people, will insist that these individuals *must* not have greater advantages than they themselves have, and will often show, as DSM-III-R notes, "intense anger or lack of control of anger, e.g., frequent dis-plays of temper, constant anger, recurrent physical fights" (American Psy-chiatric Association 1987, p. 347).

If individuals with BPD, as I again theorize, often have innate behav-ioral problems, such as hyperactivity and temper tantrums, they will tend to create or exacerbate their natural low frustration tolerance (LFT) by demanding, "I must not be as handicapped by and looked down upon for these handicaps, as I indubitably am!" So they will easily have and aggravate, as DSM-III-R observes, "marked and persistent identity disturbance" and "frantic efforts to avoid real or imagined abandonment" (p. 347).

If I am right about this, and if people with cognitive, emotional, and behavioral deficiencies very often tend to severely down themselves, hate other people, and hate the world, why should people with BPD, who may well have all three of these deficiencies, not come up with similar—or worse—hatred of themselves and of others? Biologically, they may be *more* prone to hating themselves, others, and the world than are the rest of us, the neurotic population. But even if they are not directly so, their other specific cognitive, emotive, and behavioral handicaps would, interacting with their general disturbing tendencies, tend to produce these grim results.

To make matters still worse, if individuals with BPD are, first, innately handicapped in important ways; if they easily act neurotically about these handicaps; and if they then directly and indirectly produce their borderline conditions, their conditions themselves are quite cognitively, emotionally, and behaviorally handicapping—which, unless they are exceptionally stupid or defensive, they could hardly fail to observe. If and when they do observe their borderline characteristics and the real handicaps they bear in our society, they will often *once again* tend to neurotically demand, (1) "I must do better than I am actually doing!" (2) "Other people *absolutely must not* treat me unfairly for my handicaps!" and (3) "The conditions under which I live must not be so handicapping! It's *awful and I can't stand it* when they are!" If they think in these ways, individuals with borderline personality disorder (BPD) will make themselves more disturbed—and more borderline!

Moreover, they will usually then tend to take their hatred of themselves, of others, and of their handicaps into their therapy, upset themselves about it and about their therapists, and again make their condition and their potential for improvement much worse. As Benjamin (1996), Linehan (1993), and other authorities indicate, their extreme social difficulties will often include interpersonal problems with their often quite devoted therapists.

I am proposing, then, that individuals with BPD (as well as many other individuals with serious personality disordering) have several levels of disturbances all of which interact with and affect each other, and which had better be considered together if we are to understand the main causes and effects of BPD. Let me make a summary list of these levels.

Level 1: Individuals with BPD usually have cognitive, emotional, and behavioral deficits, some of which they are probably genetically predisposed to have. Some of their borderline behaving may directly stem from these deficiencies and some of their individual and social inadequacies most probably do.

Level 2: Individuals with BPD (like neurotic individuals) also have innate and acquired tendencies to *demand* that they must succeed in work, love, and play and to denigrate themselves when they fail; and they have innate and acquired tendencies to insist that they *must* not be very frustrated or handicapped and to have LFT, anger, and self-pity when they are seriously balked. They therefore tend to be at least as and probably more self-defeating than are individuals without personality disordering.

Level 3: Because of their innate cognitive, emotive, and behavioral impairments, and because of self-downing and LFT about these impairments, individuals with BPD became even more psychobiologically impaired and dysfunctional. Their self-deprecating and discomfort intolerance about their impairment then tends to make them still more impaired, still more disturbed about their dysfunctions, and then still more impaired. A vicious cycle ensues, in the course of which impairment encourages disturbance, disturbance promotes more impairment, and greater impairment encourages more disturbance.

This vicious circle can be partially alleviated if individuals with BPD are helped to minimize their self-denigrating and their LFT. But their original cognitive, emotional, and behavioral deficits—which often present them with tendencies to hold on to musturbatory, rigid demands that lead to self-downing and intolerance of frustration—block them from alleviating their dysfunctioning and often seriously exacerbate it. They may also be biologically prone to bringing on secondary neurotic symptoms by demanding that they *absolutely must* be anxious and depressed about (1) their original cognitive, emotional, and behavioral deficits; (2) their dysfunctional nonacceptance of these deficits; (3) their severe symptoms; and (4) their unusual difficulty in achieving self-improvement, both within or outside of therapy.

The vicious cycle already mentioned can also be partly or largely alleviated if it is possible to make up for the original biosocial deficits of persons with BPD. But these deficits are usually so varied and profound that our present medications and remedial teachings are often helpful but only partially effective. Nothing indicates that they will be truly curative in the near future.

If my descriptions are reasonably accurate, I think we had better face the reality that patients with borderline personality disordering are not hopelessly and totally incurable, but are still so biologically, psychologically, and socially handicapped that we can rarely help them achieve what may be called a "real" cure. Sometimes we can help them minimize their disturbing themselves about their borderline condition, but even that may be limited, because they often rigidly cling to self-deprecating and to their low tolerating of discomfort, and therefore have to work harder than other self-disturbing people to give them up. The catch-22 is that they rarely work hard at anything consistently because of their basic cognitive, emotional, and behavioral deficits (e.g., attentional deficit disorder and focusing deficits) and because their LFT and short-range hedonism interferes with sustained discipline.

GUIDELINES FOR TREATING CLIENTS WITH BPD

What, therapeutically, shall we do? Shall we expect very limited gains? Work mainly on clients' disturbing themselves about their borderline condition?

Train them to partially overcome or compensate for their basic cognitive, emotional, and behavioral deficits? Probably all of the above, depending on our own skills and patience as therapists and on clients' determination to improve, to do very hard and persistent therapeutic work, and to relate to anyone, including their therapist. What follows are some suggested guidelines for therapists who have the guts to work persistently with people with BPD.

Try for real improvement but expect limited gains with most of them. Even normal neurotic clients rarely improve as much as we would like them to do, and clients with BPD are much more disturbed and usually more resistant to changing. Fully accept this reality and don't discourage yourself when you encounter it. Have abundant patience and fortitude!

Work on yourself to acquire unconditional acceptance for your clients with BPD. This is what Carl Rogers called unconditional positive regard. Deplore and even hate their annoying, often hostile and antisocial traits, but accept *them* with their poor behavior. Often (unlike Rogers) confront them with their obnoxious and self-defeating thoughts, feelings, and actions, but do so supportively, protectively, and utterly nondamningly. Forgive the sinner but not necessarily the sin.

Teach your clients specifically how to unconditionally accept themselves. REBT's teaching emphasis has two main paths—a less elegant and a more elegant solution to this important human problem.

Less elegantly, you can teach your clients the existential, humanistic philosophy that they can accept themselves unconditionally *whether or not* they perform or relate well—simply because they are alive, simply because they *choose* to do so. All self-acceptance is really a choice and is definitional. When we gain what is usually called self-esteem, we wrongly *decide* to accept ourselves as "good" or "deserving" individuals on condition that we perform well and are lovable. This won't really work: Even when we meet these conditions today, we may well not meet them tomorrow, so we are always anxious and overconcerned about our performances.

When we decide to accept ourselves *unconditionally* with all our faults and failings, our sense of self or identity is still chosen and still definitional. But this time our defining ourselves as "good" or "worthy" is more practical and useful. For we will safely accept ourselves—as long as we are alive—and presumably will only have to worry about our identity when we are dead!

This solution to the problem of self-worth is somewhat inelegant, however, because it is not falsifiable. Thus you can firmly say, "I fully accept myself as a worthwhile person because I am alive and human" and other people can object, "But I think that, because you are alive and human, you are no good and worthless. In fact, all humans are worthless and only deserve to die!"

Which of you, then, is right—you or your detractors? I say that neither of you can substantiate or falsify your view of human worth, because both views are definitional and tautological. Yours will probably *work better*—if your goal is to keep yourself and the human race alive, healthy, and happy. But it is still quite definitional.

REBT has therefore proposed for more than three decades a more elegant solution to the problem of human worth that you can teach to your borderline (and other) clients. They can choose to rate or evaluate *only* their thoughts, feelings, and behaviors and *not* fall into the dangerous error of rating or measuring their self, their essence, their being, or their totality. Thus they can say, "Because I choose to stay alive and be healthy and reasonably happy, many of my *acts* and *traits* are 'bad,' 'harmful,' or 'against my purpose,' but I am too complex, *too much of an ongoing process*, to give any rating, good or bad, to my *self* or *being*." (See, again, chapter 5 of this book.)

This more elegant solution to self-acceptance is, I have found, difficult for most clients to achieve. Why? I hypothesize that self-rating has, through the course of human evolution, some distinct advantages, is biologically predisposed, and is hard to surrender. But even clients with BPD can minimize it, if they are unconditionally accepted by their therapists and actively taught how to accept themselves.

Show clients how LFT is self-defeating and how to ameliorate it. Clients with BPD, for reasons already mentioned, usually have both innate and acquired abysmal LFT. Their LFT includes the irrational, dysfunctional *Beliefs*, "Conditions *absolutely must not* be as hard as they are! It's *awful* and I *can't stand* it!" But these beliefs can be clearly revealed and forcefully Disputed. As noted previously, LFT itself will stop clients from thinking and working hard to overcome their LFT! But you, as a therapist, can persist in teaching them that LFT is self-defeating and amenable to improvement. Don't give up and give into your own LFT in this respect!

Many of the dysfunctional cognitions accompanying BPD can often be successfully reduced with the usual methods of REBT and cognitive-behavioral therapy. Complete cure in this regard is unlikely, but significant improvement can often be achieved (Beck, Freeman, and Associates 1990; Ellis 2002; Linehan 1993).

The original and partially biological thinking, feeling, and behavioral deficits of BPD mentioned earlier in this chapter are not easy to improve, but can often be ameliorated. You, as a therapist, can try to help your clients with BPD in this respect, or you can refer them to other suitable professionals: neuropsychologists, rehabilitation counselors, and teachers. As both Benjamin (1996) and Linehan (1993) indicate, skill training, which may partially compensate for their deficits, is almost mandatory with many clients with BPD.

At times it pays to be clever at unraveling, revealing, and disputing some of the thinking of the client with BPD. Such clients often think in what may be called "perverse" or "intentionally self-defeating" ways, underneath which may be found a method to their madness. At one and the same time they may attempt suicide to control others and induce them to surrender to their own overweening need for attention and support. But they may also try to kill themselves, as one of my own clients attempted, because she wanted to convince me how really sick she was and that I was wrong in trying to show her that she could live and have a happy existence.

Several techniques may work to make clients' Disputing effective, including the dialectical or oppositional persuasive techniques of Marcia Linehan (1993), the use of the client as a consultant method of Benjamin (1996), or the paradoxical and metaphorical method that Hayes (Hayes, Strosahl, and Wilson 1999) used with agoraphobic patients (but that can also sometimes be used with BPD). Because borderline clients are often fiendishly clever in holding on to their disturbances, the therapist who is equally clever at Disputing sometimes wins out. Although clever and well-calculated therapist ripostes sometimes win the game, sticking to the strategy of regular cognitive-behavior therapy is probably more effective in the long run.

Because clients with BPD are often so unpredictable and unique, cognitive-behavior therapy seems to be the best general choice. REBT includes a large number of cognitive, emotive, and behavioral methods, so that when the usual ones do not seem to be effective, I try some of the less usual ones and sometimes find that they work well. Thus, although I teach my clients that rage is almost always self-destructive, I induced one of my clients to give up all thoughts of killing herself because her archrival for her lover's affection would certainly live and be deliriously happy. So I encouraged my client, at least temporarily, to keep and vent her rage against her rival and thereby motivate herself to live and work for her own happiness.

Psychopharmacological treatment sometimes works well but often does not. I frequently recommend that my clients experimentally try antidepressants or other medications, and if they don't work and/or find taking them has bad side effects, they can always return to psychotherapy by itself. My helping them to increase their frustration tolerance and decrease their medication phobias frequently serves to help them try proper medication and to put up with some of its side effects. Conversely, being on an antidepressant and/or a tranquilizer sometimes helps them think better and benefit more from REBT. But, being tricky, they also may use psychopharmacological treatment as an excuse not to work hard to change their thinking, feeling, and acting.

Experience has taught me to abandon psychoanalysis for BPD, except for some of its relationship aspects, and heavily use cognitive-behavior therapy instead. Other cognitive-behavior therapists, and I think therapists in general, have found cognitive-behavioral methods quite useful with clients with BPD. As for psychoanalysis, I now feel that it is exceptionally wasteful for most neurotic individuals and fairly iatrogenic for most clients with BPD. Heinz Kohut's methods are basically Rogerian and probably less harmful than other psychoanalytic techniques. Otto Kernberg and William Masterson are more confrontative, but their interpretations are too sidetracking for my prejudiced tastes!

CASE PRESENTATION

Rona was a woman of twenty-five when I began treating her for what she called severe depression. She worked as a bookkeeper in a small office because she was afraid of human contacts. She considered herself "horribly ugly," although she was quite attractive. She strongly felt that she was a basket case; she was on one side of the human race and every other person was on the other side—the good side. She had no social relationships and was sure that she couldn't make any because of her extreme shyness, need for love, and self-rejecting. She had made suicide attempts at the ages of sixteen and twenty-one but was saved by her parents each time and rushed to the hospital. She was briefly hospitalized each time, refused to take medication after leaving the hospital, and went back to living with her critical parents. Rona hated them but couldn't set herself free. She felt they abandoned her and was determined to never risk abandonment again. She also felt continually bored and empty and spent her leisure hours sleeping or looking at television, although she was quite intelligent and had achieved an MBA degree with honors. Typically, Rona made no friends in college and none at work. Her one relationship, just before she came to see me, was a brief one with John, who was quite attracted to her, who pushed her for dates, but who was soon turned off by her intermittent hostility and dire need to be constantly assured that he really, really loved her and would never abandon her.

Rona came to see me when she was severely depressed after John had broken off with her. I could see quickly, from her history, her unstable emotionality, her complete focus on herself, and her phobic and panicked reactions, that she was hardly a nice neurotic and that she would most probably be a "DC" (or difficult customer).

I was right. She alternatively was very seductive and very hostile to me. She knew about REBT but was very skeptical of it because of her nine years of previous psychoanalytic therapy, which she considered "deep" but "highly ineffective." She threatened to stop seeing me from the first session onward and, during the three years that I saw her, she quit twice for a month at a time. She at first identified me with her hated supercritical father, but later became overattached to and overdependent on me. She was very resentful when I went out of town for a few days for talks, workshops, and conferences and would insist on phone sessions at the hotels where I was staying.

Following REBT principles, I fully accepted Rona with her difficultness and tried to teach her, over and over again, how to unconditionally accept herself, accept her critical parents, and accept her borderline, quite handicapping condition. I honestly and firmly kept showing her that she was probably innately disturbed—as were both her parents—and that she often behaved hostilely and had better—not *must*—change her hostility for her own sake.

Although Rona strongly objected to the REBT philosophy of fully accepting herself and others, I persistently showed her that the results she was getting from her self-hatred, withdrawal, and hostility weren't worth it and that only something like unconditional self-acceptance (USA) would bring better results. My efforts finally prevailed and within six months of therapy she started to "get it" and to become a devotee of undamning acceptance. She joined one of my therapy groups and consistently came to my regular Friday Night Workshop, where I demonstrate REBT with volunteers who have sessions of public therapy. She also attended a record number of four-hour-long public workshops that are given every other week at the Albert Ellis Institute in New York City. At the group and workshop sessions she vigorously kept convincing other participants of the value of unconditionally accepting themselves and others.

I had greater difficulty helping Rona reduce her abysmal LFT, but I was finally able to convince her that demanding immediate gratification at the expense of later pain wasn't worth it. No matter how uncomfortable she felt, she began to go through difficult dates, to make and keep friendships with somewhat unreliable people, to work in a larger office, to force herself to overcome her public speaking phobia, to accept my absences from her group therapy sessions when I was out of town, to stop smoking, and do other uncomfortable things for her later satisfaction.

I, her therapy group, and her workshop groups helped Rona acquire several skills in which she was deficient. In the course of this skill training, she became quite assertive, began to listen more attentively to others, learned how to actively break the ice and meet new people, became adept at job interviewing, and took courses that led to her becoming a CPA. At the same time, her innate and acquired tendencies to be unfocused, to think impulsively, to exaggerate the significance of things, to be emotionally labile, and to be purposeless clearly improved and interfered less with her social and work behavior.

I still see Rona for occasional therapy sessions and as a visitor at some of my Friday Night Workshops; and I hear about her from several of her friends and relatives whom she keeps sending to me for therapy. By all visible standards she is now only moderately neurotic—like most of the human race. But as a trained clinician, I can still see some of the remnants of her BPD showing through her outward demeanor. She now makes herself angry and depressed on relatively few occasions, but when she does, she becomes quite discombobulated, stutters and stammers, and for several days is disorganized and distraught. She has good social relationships but never becomes too deeply involved with anyone. She displays little overt hostility, but underneath she is very jealous of successful people and somewhat paranoid about being exploited by her friends. She is a successful CPA but sometimes feels that her life is meaningless and purposeless and that she is not truly integrated into the human race.

Rona, although vastly improved, is not quite whole. I have said for many years that REBT can help people overcome their neurosis about their psychosis and about BPD; and by working very hard to fully accept herself and to acquire higher frustration tolerance, Rona has used it to become much less neurotic. But I don't fool myself into believing that she or any of the other individuals with psychosis and BPD I have considerably helped with REBT for many decades have been truly cured. Nor have I seen any other therapists' clients with borderline and psychotic disorders who, even after many years of treatment, are now truly healthy. Some are significantly and even magnificently improved, but all still have underlying psychotic or personality disorders.

Being something of an optimist as well as a realist, I think that both the arts of psychotherapy and of psychopharmacology are in their infancy stages and that someday they will combine to help individuals with BPD do more than they do today—perhaps even cure them of their borderline states, and leave them, like the rest of the human race, only neurotic. Meanwhile, working with clients with BPD is damned difficult, but it can also be quite challenging and rewarding, for clients as well as for therapists.

SELF-HELP SUGGESTIONS

- If you think you have borderline personality disorder or something like it, get confirmation from a reputable psychiatrist and follow, at least experimentally, his or her suggestions to try psychotropic medication.
- With or without medication, you can probably help yourself with possible borderline personality disordering by conferring with an REBT or CBT practitioner and with suitable self-help materials.
- For the reasons explained in this chapter, if you suffer from borderline personality disordering you will probably have to work very hard, using several of REBT's cognitive, emotive, and behavioral methods, to alleviate your symptoms. You may never completely cure yourself, but you may make considerable improvement.
- While "neurotic" individuals may benefit greatly from using REBT techniques, if you suffer from borderline personality disordering you had better particularly use REBT's three main methods, as shown in this book and in *Feeling Better, Getting Better, and Staying Better* (Ellis 2001). These are: (1) Achieving unconditional self-accepting (USA). (2) Achieving unconditional other-accepting (UOA). (3) Achieving high frustration tolerance (HFT).
- Individuals with borderline personality disordering especially tend to denigrate themselves and anxietize and depress themselves *about* their mul-

tiple handicaps. If you have BPD or other severe personality disordering, acknowledge your handicaps but vigorously fight against any of your tendencies to damn yourself for having them.

28

Treating Individuals with Obsessive-Compulsive Disorders (OCDs)

I frankly used to be wrong about obsessive-compulsive disorder (OCD), because I considered it to be an extreme neurotic anxiety disorder, largely caused by afflicted people's unrealistic and illogical demands for certainty. I mistakenly thought that because they strongly thought and felt, "I *absolutely must* be safe under all *conditions at all times*!" OCD sufferers kept compulsively locking their homes many times or checking their pilot lights to *make sure* that nothing "terrible" happened to them. Also, because they demanded *absolute certainty* that they be clean and lovable, they washed their hands twenty times after defecating or kept calling their love partners to make sure that they were approved.

I still think that the need for certainty drives some people into nauseatingly repetitive, useless, and self-defeating rituals, countings, obsessions, and other common aspects of OCD. Probably *all* of us humans have *some* of these foolish tendencies; and our *dire need* for certainty, safety, and approval may well drive us to act on them—especially when, for example, we are passionately in love with someone and have doubts about our feelings for him or her being strongly reciprocated. This kind of obsessive-compulsive behavior is somewhat "normal"— and often temporary. Once we are no longer madly in love, we may give it up.

This chapter is partly adapted from "Rational Emotive Behavior Therapy Approaches to Obsessive Compulsive Disorder (OCD)," *Journal of Rational-Emotive and Cognitive-Behavior Therapy* 12 (1994): 121–41. Used with permission.

Real OCD is different. It takes many forms and guises—and seems to be rarely about one thing. It usually begins in childhood or adolescence and lasts a lifetime. But it may also accompany serious neurological disorders, including Huntington's disease, Sydenham's chorea, Pick's disease, Postencephalic Parkinsonism, and Tourette's syndrome.

Recent neuroimaging studies tend to show that dysfunction of the frontal lobes of the brain and the frontal-caudate circuit are associated with idiopathic OCD. Successful treatment of OCD with clomipramine (Anafranil), fluoxetine (Prozac), and other serotonic agents tends to show that deficiencies in the neurotransmitter serotonin are often involved with OCD.

The need for certainty, which I previously mentioned, may well be a factor in creating OCD, but it is not clear whether biological deficiencies create this "need" and/or they block obsessive-compulsive individuals from interrupting and giving up this "need" when they see that it is doing them little good. Quite likely, both!

OCD people, including practically all that I have seen over the years, also frequently have other related personality disorders. Thus, they often have severe panic states and serious depressive disorders. They also may be addicted to alcohol, drugs, nicotine, overeating, or gambling. Some of these afflictions may be reactions to the difficulties that ensue from their obsessive-compulsive behavior; but some of them may go with their biological handicaps.

The REBT theory of causation of severe personality disorders, including OCD, holds that afflicted individuals usually have cognitive, emotive, and behavioral deficits; and that they then have Irrational *Beliefs* or cognitive distortions about having these deficits and the difficulties of living that accompany them. Thus, cognitively, OCDers probably have more aspects of learning disability and focusing (or overfocusing) handicaps than what I call "nice, normal neurotics." Emotively, they tend to be overactive. Behaviorally, they are prone to disorganization, procrastination, and compulsivity. Such deficits, again, can partly be reactions to their OCD. But it is highly likely that they are also, at least in part, biological deficiencies.

Cognitive distortions, or what I have often called Irrational *Beliefs* (IBs), seem to be the human condition. All "neurotics" have them *fairly* frequently, and virtually all humans make themselves somewhat neurotic. OCDers, like other people with personality disorders, and like psychotics, not only have the usual kinds of IBs, but they may (for biological reasons, again) hold them more rigidly and strongly, than "nice, normal neurotics" do.

Moreover, because neurotic cognitive distortions are about life's adversities and handicaps (e.g., "I hate failing and *therefore* I must not fail!"), and because OCD itself *is* a handicap, obsessive-compulsive personalities usually make themselves neurotic about their personality disorder and their neurosis consequently aggravates their OCD and their other life problems.

The sequence often goes somewhat as follows:

1. The person with OCD is usually born and reared with several cognitive, emotive, and behavioral deficits, including the strong tendency to overfocus on a particular problem and to compulsively perform ritualistic and/or other habits (such as compulsively checking, handwashing, and locking doors). He or she also has great difficulty in stopping the obsessive-compulsive behavior, no matter how foolish and destructive it is acknowledged to be.

2. OCDers, because of their somewhat bizarre behavior, engender many more frustrations and criticisms than the rest of us "nice neurotics" do. They therefore *easily* develop great low frustration tolerance (LFT) by Irrationally *Believing*, "I *absolutely should not, must not* be so severely frustrated by my OCD and the disadvantages to which it leads. *Such great* frustration and *such severe* handicaps *must not* afflict me!" It's *awful* [completely bad] when they do. I *can't stand* it and will *never* be able to conquer it. How horrible!"

3. At the same time, because of social disapproval of their dysfunctional behavior, and of *themselves* for having it, OCDers frequently put themselves down, depress themselves, and make themselves anxious about other failures and disapproval. This self-denigration and feelings of worthlessness stem from Irrational *Beliefs* (IBs) such as, "I *must* not be disapproved and severely put down! I'm *no good* for bringing on this disapproval! If I can't function better than I do function, I'm a *worthless person!*"

4. OCDers often then construct secondary disturbances about their cognitive distortions and about the poor emotional and behavioral results which accompany such Irrational *Beliefs*. Thus, they may think, "I *must not* be anxious about my OCD! I must not *demand* that I be free of OCD! I must not have low frustration tolerance about my OCD!" In this manner OCDers can easily create self-downing about their self-downing and LFT about their LFT—all related to their OCD.

5. In addition, OCDers can have *regular* self-denigration and *regular* LFT about other aspects of their lives. Thus, they can put themselves down for *any* failures or inability to achieve their ideal goals; and they can define as "unbearable" any hassles, mild or serious. Their tendency to castigate *themselves* for their "poor" *performances* and their tendency to make "utter horrors" out of normal hassles may, once again, be partly innate. I suspect this but have no hard evidence to back it up. An alternative hypothesis is that they have *so many* and *so profound* difficulties and failures because of their OCD that they *easily* develop self-downing and LFT when non-OCD-related problems are *added* to their OCD-related difficulties.

6. OCDers, then, frequently have ego anxiety and depression (self-downing) and discomfort anxiety and depression (LFT) about (a) their OCD difficulties, about (b) their other regular life problems, and about (c) their self-downing and their LFT that often—probably, usually!—accompany their OCD and their non-OCD difficulties. Quite a series of interrelated disorders and neuroses!

GENERAL CBT AND REBT METHODS OF TREATMENT

The treatment of OCD itself has been fairly intensively studied by a number of practitioners of Behavior Therapy (BT) and Cognitive Behavior Therapy (CBT). Nearly all of these BT and CBT practitioners emphasize *in vivo* desensitization or exposure and activity-oriented homework assignments designed to significantly cut down, if not entirely eliminate, the interminable ruminations and wasteful compulsions to which victims of OCD are subjected. Because REBT has always favored *in vivo* desensitization and activity homework assignments, I have used these methods with OCDers for more than forty years and find that they usually work—*if* my clients consistently and steadily effect them.

But, of course, OCDers often don't do this steady work. They find it most difficult to cut down their incessant checking, ritualizing, and ruminating; and when they finally do so, they easily fall back to their former pernicious habits. Moreover, when they give up or minimize one set of compulsions they frequently begin to establish a set of different ones. They then often convince themselves that they *can't* change and *can't* stay free of obsession and compulsions; and then, because of these convictions, they "really" can't.

Nonetheless, even before the advent of medications like Anafranil and Prozac, I have had some startling successes. Thus, a man of forty years, who all his life got out of bed at least fifteen times every night to make absolutely sure that the "dangerous" pilot light in his kitchen was extinguished, cut down his checking compulsion to no more than one or two checkings a night, and maintained that schedule for the next five years. A woman who took from one to four hours to shower every morning—and who couldn't hold any regular jobs because of the time she consumed showering—cut down her time in the shower to at most fifteen minutes a day and began to hold a regular nine-to-five job.

So OCDers can change with the persistent use of REBT and CBT methods. But often they don't—or they make very limited gains. Why? For a number of reasons, including the fact that some clients with severe OCD seem to be so basically disorganized and so obsessed with repetitive behaviors that they find it almost impossible to follow the cognitive, emotive, and behavioral methods of REBT (and of other forms of therapy) and therefore fail to do so. So not only are they DCs (difficult customers) for therapy; many of them are VDCs (*very* difficult customers)!

A number of OCDers, however, not only can significantly improve but some of them work hard and actually do cut down their obsessive-compulsiveness. With these clients, the use of regular REBT and CBT methods can be quite helpful, especially when combined with proper medication.

Regular REBT and CBT procedures have been quite adequately presented by several authorities in this field, including Foa and Wilson (1991), Greist (1992), and Steketee (1993).

Let me summarize these techniques as follows, as particularly described by Foa and Wilson (1991) and as combined with some methods of regular REBT.

1. Show OCDers that their anxietizing and panicking include: (a) Negative, continual obsessions, thoughts, images, and/or impulses. (b) Severe feelings of anxiety, panic, disgust, and/or shame. (c) Compulsions that exist in their own right or are attempts to relieve the OCDers' anxiety and panic—compulsions may include repetitious thoughts, images, urges, and/or actions. (d) Temporary relief from anxiety and panic when an OCDer constructs and follows compulsive rituals to interrupt and halt his or her anxiety.

2. Show OCDers that they can reduce their afflictions by working with a therapist, and/or with self-help procedures, but that this work usually has to be consistent, persistent, and forceful. They'd better strongly *commit* themselves to reducing their OCD.

3. Have OCDers explore and check to see which symptoms they have and how severely they have them. Thus, they can determine how often and how strongly they check and repeat, wash and clean, compulsively hoard, compulsively order, engage in thinking rituals, and obsessively worry.

4. Show them that when they desperately resist having a thought or a ritual—and demand that they *absolutely must* not have it—they make themselves obsess more about it and frequently repeat it more compulsively.

5. Show them that mild or brief obsessions and compulsions—like looking three times to "make sure" that one has her or his keys before leaving home—are innocuous and tolerable but that severe and prolonged rituals are destructive and had better be minimized or stopped.

6. Teach them that severe OCD may well have a strong biological or innate tendency that is difficult to change and may never be completely overcome. Show them that OCDers like themselves may well have innate tendencies to denigrate themselves for their foolish behaviors and to have low frustration tolerance about life's difficulties and about their OCD.

7. Encourage them to make a list of situations that frequently and intensively help them to feel anxiety, panic, or the impulse to act impulsively and undertake repeated rituals.

8. If they have repetitious thoughts, feelings, or urges that lead to serious anxiety and panic, let them list these and how distressful they are.

9. They can also make a list of the "horrible" consequences they fear will result if they stop their compulsions and their rituals and how much they believe these "horrors" will actually occur.

10. They can list their worst compulsions and how much time they spend in indulging in them each day.

11. You, as a therapist, can help them to be strongly determined to minimize their obsessions and compulsions.

12. Show them that the anxieties that underlie their OCD behaviors are irrational—that is, unrealistic, illogical, and self-defeating. Show them how to Dispute their Irrational *Beliefs* (IBs) that spark these anxieties.

13. Show them that reducing their anxieties by OCD rituals will only work temporarily and in the long run exacerbate them; and that they can use much better cognitive, emotive, and behavioral ways of reducing them.

14. Particularly show them that they can see their obsessions and compulsions as "bad," "handicapping," and "undesirable" but never put *themselves* down for having them and never think that their OCD behaviors are so bad that they absolutely *must* not exist. Teach them to *undesperately* work to reduce their obsessions. Persuade them to accept their OCD manifestations as *only* undesirable and not *horrible*.

15. Show them how to schedule their obsessions and compulsions only at certain specified and limited times—e.g., at 7 P.M. for fifteen minutes—and to think and do other things at other times.

16. Convince them—and help them convince themselves—that they can practically always keep postponing indulging in their obsessions and compulsions—and can increasingly keep postponing their indulgence in them.

17. Teach them how to use distraction methods—such as Jacobson's (1938) progressive relaxation technique, yoga, meditation, breathing, and biofeedback methods—to interrupt and postpone their OCD behaviors. They can also use other behaviors—such as exercise, writing, and playing music—to interrupt their obsessions and compulsions.

18. Show OCDers how to make a loop tape of their obsessive thoughts and compulsive urges and to desensitize themselves to them and to their "horrors" by listening to the tape a half hour more every day.

19. Instruct your OCD clients how to change some aspects of their rituals—to change their specific thoughts or actions, or the number of repetitions, or the exact times they ritualize.

SPECIAL REBT METHODS OF TREATMENT

It is often best to assume, as I noted previously, that OCDers have a strong biological tendency to think and act in the ways that they do, that they will make smaller gains than most other clients, and that they will have to work harder than these others to achieve improvement. Consequently, they frequently put themselves down for having severe OCD, and *Believe*—at point B in the ABCs of REBT—"I *absolutely must not* be so handicapped! Because I am more handicapped than I *must not* be, I am an *inadequate person* and probably *don't deserve* to do better than I have done in the past and am still badly doing!"

Using REBT, you, as a therapist, can show your OCD clients that they frequently have OCD as their primary symptom, but they also may well have self-denigration as a secondary symptom. Thus, Activating event$_1$ (A$_1$) is a "dangerous" situation. Irrational *Belief*$_1$ (IB$_1$) is "I must check this danger twenty times!" and the Consequence$_1$ (C$_1$) is their OCD symptom. Then Activating event$_2$ (A$_2$) is their OCD, Irrational *Belief*$_2$ (IB$_2$) is a self-downing *Belief* such as those mentioned in the previous paragraph, and Consequence$_2$ (C$_2$) is their feelings of inadequacy or worthlessness.

After helping your clients to fully acknowledge their self-deprecation (C$_2$), you unconditionally accept them *with* their OCD and *with* their feelings of worthlessness and then you use a variety of REBT cognitive, emotive, and behavioral methods to help them Dispute (D) their anxietizing, depressing, and self-hating *about* their having OCD and *about* their having a most difficult time ameliorating it.

In addition, for reasons explained in the beginning of this chapter, OCDers frequently have low frustration tolerance (LFT) or discomfort neurosis about their affliction. Thus they may *Believe* (at point B), "I *shouldn't* be so afflicted! It's too unfair! And I *must* not have to work so hard to reduce my OCD! It's *awful* that so much work is required!"

Using REBT, try to show OCDers that they probably do have these secondary symptoms of self-downing and LFT about their handicaps. Once they acknowledge either or both these secondary disturbances, they are helped to overcome them: First, by acquiring unconditional self-acceptance (USA). This method is an REBT specialty that is used with practically all seriously disturbed individuals, a large percentage of whom often make themselves feel worthless for having deficiencies and therefore had better alleviate this secondary neurosis about their primary emotional problems.

These seriously disturbed individuals, moreover, frequently have self-downing as a primary issue—because they denigrate themselves for other "deficiencies" and "inadequacies." Thus a large number of OCDers are perfectionistic and demand that they *absolutely must* do many things, including their rituals, counting, and checking, exactly and perfectly right; and their "natural" or "biological" tendency may be perfectionistic.

In any event, the achieving of USA is a prime REBT recipe for helping OCDers on both the primary and secondary level of disturbance. To this end, as previously noted, unconditionally accept them, in manner as well as word. But also specifically teach them that they do not *need* your approval in order to fully accept themselves.

Instead, clients afflicted with OCD are taught the two main REBT solutions to achieving unconditional self-acceptance (USA) that I have previously described in other chapters of this book: (1) The practical, if somewhat inelegant, solution: That they can choose to fully accept themselves, *whether or not* they perform well and *whether or not* they are approved by significant others, simply because they are alive and human, simply because they choose to do so. (2) REBT's more 'elegant' solution to this problem of human intrinsic worth. Thus, you encourage your OCD clients to stubbornly refuse to rate, evaluate, or measure their *self*, their *being*, their *essence*, or their *personhood* at all. They rate *only* the "goodness" of their thoughts, feelings, and behaviors, but not the "goodness" or "badness" of their *self*.

REBT offers both these "elegant" and "inelegant" concepts of self-worth to all its clients, including—especially—OCDers. It does its best to help all handicapped individuals—actually, the human race!—to unconditionally accept themselves *whatever* they think, feel, or do. Not, again, to accept as "good" their "foolish," "rotten," or "immoral" behaviors, but to fully accept *themselves*, the doers of these "vile" deeds.

This includes teaching OCDers to accept themselves unconditionally with their (frequently) abysmal LFT. Because they have more than their share of frustrations, often from childhood onwards, OCDers frequently have considerable LFT. They therefore may not push themselves to control their OCD, to work at using REBT methods, or even to strive for USA. No matter. If you use REBT, you still unconditionally accept them and try to persuade them to have USA for themselves. I and other REBT practitioners hardly always succeed in this endeavor. But, damn it, we try!

While doing so, we usually try to help OCDers ameliorate and raise their LFT. For unless they persist in curbing their obsessive-compulsive tendencies and acts, they will *temporarily* feel good about indulging in them—and a little later probably feel much worse. In the long run, indulgence in OCD behaviors will frustrate and hinder them more—and thereby often encourage them to have *lower* frustration tolerance!

Therapists, however, had better unmask and persuade OCDers to ameliorate their LFT with caution, because it is not easy to define exactly what it is, how it arises, and what can effectively be done to reduce it. Let me give a fascinating example.

Mary, a forty-year-old attorney, had OCD in the form of continually checking on her pension if she retired from her firm at the age of forty-five, fifty, or fifty-five, and spent hours doing so, even though she knew that her rumination didn't affect the amount of her pension one whit and that it was a complete waste of time. She also procrastinated on her briefs for her court presentations because, first, she was afraid to do an imperfect case and, second, she hated some of the nervous activity involved in getting her briefs together. She agreed that she had LFT about cutting down the time she spent obsessing and that she also had LFT about buckling down, doing her briefs, and getting them out of the way before she and her partners tried a case. So I kept after her to work on her LFT by convincing herself that the immediate "gratification" she received from indulging in her obsessive checking on the amount of her pension and that the relief she felt when putting off finishing her briefs until the last minute weren't worth the short-term gains she received and were irrational and self-defeating. She "intellec-tually" agreed with me, but still refused to work to ameliorate her LFT.

After weeks of this kind of "resistance," Mary and I figured out that she was really very depressed and lacking in energy and that was why it was "easier" to indulge in her checking obsessions, to procrastinate on her briefs—and to indulge in other forms of "LFT," such as eating too much, not exercising, and smoking. We were both treating her as if she were a "normal neurotic" instead of a severe endogenous depressive and a biologically inclined OCDer. She felt—and somewhat rightly—that I was blaming her LFT behavior and also blaming *her* for having it. She finally admitted that I was only doing the former (that is, I *was* trying to get her to assume respon-sibility for her indulgences, but that I was *not* blaming her as a person).

We both agreed, however, that OCDers like Mary who are also severely depressed—and have panic states as well—are not really as self-indulgent as the rest of us "nice neurotics" may be. She, like many other OCDers, had several "good" or "legitimate" reasons for her "goofing off." Thus: (1) She had innate and very strong OCD tendencies. (2) She was often naturally and innately depressing. (3) When in a state of panic—which she also was prone to experience—she was "naturally" sidetracked from working to reduce her so-called LFT. (4) She had more frustrations, because of her disturbances, than the great majority of other people—and therefore *was* "unfairly" put upon. (5) She may well have been born with strong biological tendencies to avoid frustrations, even sensible ones like those involved in exercising. (6) Like a majority of OCDers, she also was a strong self-damner; and by casti-gating herself for her handicaps she tended to exacerbate them, sidetrack herself from working against them, and waste time and energy that could have been much better spent in trying to ameliorate these handicaps.

Working with this client, and several others somewhat like her, showed me how unfair life really *is* to OCDers and how I (and other therapists) can also be unfair to them by giving them *too much* responsibility for their hand-icaps and ignoring their *natural* resistance to improving themselves. With this particular client, Mary, I showed her how natural and expectable was her resistance to change, and I simultaneously induced her to give herself unconditional self-acceptance (USA) even if she *had been* "goofing" neu-rotically, instead of as a more direct result of her innate handicaps. When she started to feel USA, Mary worked harder than ever to overcome her resis-tance to change and did to some degree alleviate it.

REBT, then, tries to fully acknowledge the unusual difficulties of OCDers to stop their obsessive-compulsive behavior and to resist defaming themselves for engaging in it. It emphasizes showing them that they often have a biologically based personality disorder and that they may also act neu-rotically about this disorder—including indulging in serious self-downing and low frustration tolerance. It tries to help them to stop damning themselves for *anything*, including their "terrible" disturbances *about* their disturbances. As this treatment process proceeds, it also uses the regular REBT and CBT methods previously described to help clients reduce and minimize, but rarely entirely eliminate, their OCD behaviors.

OTHER SPECIAL REBT TREATMENTS OF OCD

In addition to the general and specific REBT methods of treating individuals afflicted with OCD, I consistently use a number of common REBT methods to help OCDers cope with their personality disorder and with their neurosis about this disorder. These methods have been described in detail in a number of my writings and in the first part of this book.

Let me briefly describe some of these methods as I often use them with clients afflicted with OCD. First, some REBT cognitive methods:

REBT Cognitive Methods

Disputing Irrational Beliefs (IBs). OCD clients are helped to see that they have IBs on two levels. Thus, they often first believe dogmatic, *absolutist musts*, such as "I *must* check my door (or wash my hands, or add up the value of my securities) at least twenty times, else it's *awful* and I *can't stand* the pain of not checking and the disasters that will then ensue if I stop checking!" Second, when clients suffer the Consequences of these *musts*, *awfulizing*, and *I-can't-stand-it-itis*, they then produce secondary symptoms of self-downing such as, "I must not indulge in my compulsive checking and suffer from doing so. I'm an *inadequate person* for indulging so stupidly!" And they also often produce secondary symptoms of LFT, especially, "I must not have such a hard life! It's terrible that I do!"

REBT practitioners show OCDers how to actively keep Disputing their musts, their awfulizing, their I-can't-stand-it-itis, and their self-deprecation: (1) *Realistic Disputing*: "Is it actually true that I *must* check my door twenty times and that great disasters will occur if I don't?" (2) *Logical Disputing*: "Because it is painful to suffer from my OCD, do I *have to* quickly stop it and remove my pain?" (3) *Pragmatic Disputing*: "What results will I get if I keep endlessly checking and if I despise myself for continuing to check?"

Cost-benefit Analysis. REBT encourages OCDers to make a long list of the real disadvantages of their obsessive-compulsive behaviors and to think about them and sink them into their heads and hearts until they remain fully conscious of them. They are also encouraged to use cost-benefit analysis about the hazards of downing themselves and awfulizing about their indulging in OCD behaviors.

Rational Coping Statements. By using Disputing of their IBs and thinking about their primary and secondary symptoms, OCDers are taught how to rehearse them several times a day. These can be realistic or empirical self-statements, such as, "I can cut down my rituals, even though it's hard for me to do so" and "If I keep washing my hands twenty times after I urinate, they won't be much cleaner than if I wash them once." And they can be philosophical coping statements, such as "If I fail to lock the car door fifteen times and my car actually is stolen, the world won't come to an end and I can still lead an enjoyable life."

Teaching Others REBT. Clients are often encouraged to use REBT with their friends and relatives and, by showing them how to use it, to better help themselves.

Modeling. OCDers are urged to model themselves after people they know or others that they read or hear about who (1) have coped well with serious emotional and/or physical problems, and who (2) have not downed themselves or whined about having such problems.

Cognitive Homework. Clients are persuaded to do regular homework on their ABCDs of REBT, including using the REBT Self-Help Form that the Albert Ellis Institute (Dryden, Walker, and Ellis 1996) publishes (see p. 135).

Psychoeducational Materials. OCDers agree on homework assignments of reading or listening to REBT psychoeducational materials, such as *A Guide to Rational Living, How to Stubbornly Refuse to Make Yourself Miserable About Anything—Yes, Anything!, How to Control Your Anxiety Before It Controls You*, and *How to Make Yourself Happy and Remarkably Less Disturbable*. Because OCD overlaps with and includes other compulsive behavior, such as addiction to alcohol, drugs, nicotine, and gambling, they are encouraged to use REBT materials on addiction, such as *When AA Doesn't Work for You: Rational Steps to Quitting Alcohol* and *The Art and Science of Rational Eating*. To help them achieve unconditional self-acceptance (USA) they are motivated by REBT practitioners to use materials describing USA and how to achieve it, such as the handout in chapter 5 of this book.

REBT holds that severely disturbed individuals, such as OCDers, hold their irrational *Beliefs* (IBs) strongly and powerfully and that therefore they had better forcefully, vigorously, and emotively Dispute and act against them. Some popular REBT emotive-evocative methods that often work with OCDers are these:

Relationship Procedures. Like Carl Rogers (1961), REBT practitioners go out of their way to give all their clients, especially OCDers, unconditional acceptance. But instead of encouraging these clients to accept themselves because their therapist fully accepts them—which leads to highly *conditional* self-acceptance (CSA)—they teach self-downing OCDers to achieve *unconditional self-acceptance (USA), as noted previously in this chapter.

Forceful Coping Statements. I often help my OCD clients to use forceful coping statements. Doing this, they can tell themselves vigorously and powerfully, sometimes aloud and sometimes in front of a mirror or in the presence of their friends and intimates, "I NEVER have to carry out my compulsive rituals. I DEFINITELY CAN limit them and *can* keep them to a minimum!" "I will *only, only* allow myself to obsess about money [or about someone I care for] twenty minutes a day. No more, no more!" "My OCD behaviors are stupid and wasteful. But they NEVER, NEVER make me a *stupid person*! No, *never*!"

Rational Emotive Imagery. Maxie Maultsby Jr., a rational psychiatrist who studied with me in 1968, created Rational Emotive Imagery (REI). The REBT version that I use is often especially useful when taught to OCDers. To perform REI, they close their eyes and imagine one of the worst things that could happen to them. For example, their being compulsively hooked on checking or performing a foolish ritual, and getting more and more compulsive about performing it. Or they can imagine their *not* checking or performing a ritual and consequently some "disaster" occurring. While imagining this "terrible" Activating event, they let themselves feel panicking, depressing, and/or self-hating. Then, still focusing on this grim image, they work at making themselves feel, instead, healthily or appropriately sorry, disappointed, or frustrated (which they can do, of course, by changing their Irrational to Rational *Beliefs*). They practice doing this (which generally only takes a few minutes) once a day for twenty or thirty consecutive days, until they begin to regularly and automatically feel healthily sorry and disappointed instead of self-defeatingly panicking and depressing. (See chapter 11.) Simultaneously, they can use other REBT methods to reduce their OCD behaviors.

Shame-Attacking Exercises. Because OCDers quite frequently and vehemently condemn themselves for their inept and foolish behavior, I find it useful to persuade them to do shame-attacking exercises, which I first created in the 1960s. They think of some activity that they would feel ashamed or embarrassed to do in public, and they deliberately do it, while strongly convincing themselves that, no matter how they are disapproved of by others for doing it, they are not shameful, ridiculous, or rotten *people*. Thus, I often have my OCD clients reveal their "silly" obsessions and compulsions to some of their friends, or perhaps to strangers, to prove that they do not have to put themselves down if people look askance at them. And I sometimes persuade my OCD clients to force themselves to refrain from one of their compulsive acts (such as repetitive handwashing), to let themselves feel anxious and ashamed for *not* performing it, and then work at feeling only sorry and disappointed rather than horrified at their "careless" or "dirty" avoidances. Later, they can even feel happy that they were able to refrain and to remain "dirty."

Forceful Disputing. I often encourage my OCD clients to state one of their Irrational *Beliefs*—e.g., "I *absolutely must* count to one hundred before

I eat breakfast or else I'll choke on my food!"—and vigorously Dispute it on a cassette tape. Then they let their friends, relatives, or members of their therapy group listen to see if their Disputing is really sufficiently forceful and vigorous. If not, they keep making new Disputational tapes until they succeed in doing them more strongly. (See chapter 11.)

Role-playing. REBT uses role-playing with OCD (and other) clients to help them, for example, get practice in revealing their obsessive-compulsive behaviors to others in doing this kind of shame-attacking exercise. But in REBT, if the client makes himself or herself anxious or depressed while engaged in role-playing with a friend (or a therapist), the role-playing is halted and the client and the friend explore what the client is thinking to create these disturbed feelings and what he or she can think, instead, to minimize them.

Reverse Role-playing. With my OCD clients I sometimes play *their* role, hold stoutly to some of their dysfunctional *Beliefs*, and give them practice in talking me (playing them) out of these *Beliefs*. They then learn how to do better Disputing of their own firmly held IBs.

REBT Behavioral Techniques. REBT behavioral methods of treating people with OCD overlap significantly with the general CBT and general REBT methods described above. REBT, however, is often *more* behavioral than regular CBT, in that it stresses *in vivo* desensitization and it often recommends penalties for failure to do homework assignments in addition to reinforcements for doing them. Specifically some behavioral REBT methods for use with OCDers include these:

In Vivo Desensitization. I often encourage my OCD clients, sometimes in their early sessions, to actually do harmless actions that they are afraid to do. Such as: (1) Force themselves to reduce their obsessive-compulsive rituals, checking, handwashing, etc., no matter how uncomfortable they at first feel when reducing it. (2) Force themselves *un*comfortably to do other actions that they are anxious or panicked about doing—e.g., riding in cars and planes, making public speeches, or going for difficult job interviews. (3) Cut down drastically the amount of time they spend on strong obsessions. (4) Spend a minimum amount of time every day nonobsessively Disputing their absolutist shoulds and musts, their awfulizing, their I-can't-stand-it-itis, and their self-downing.

Remaining in "Bad" Situations. When OCDers see themselves as being in "bad" situations—such as a poor marriage, working for an angry boss, or having very critical friends—I often persuade them to *temporarily* stay in those uncomfortable situations until they minimize their anxietizing, depressing, and raging about them. *Then* they can decide whether it is worth their while to remain in these "horrible" conditions.

Use of Reinforcements. OCDers, like severe addicts, usually won't reduce their obsessions and compulsions when they are reinforced for doing so. They suffer so much (at least temporarily) from stopping their OCD behav-

386   Overcoming Destructive Beliefs, Feelings, and Behaviors

iors and feel so greatly relieved after indulging in them that reinforcements like eating good food, enjoying entertainment, or engaging in other plea-sures *after* curbing their rituals and obsessions won't work. However, if the reinforcers they use are things they *very strongly* desire, reinforcement will sometimes be effective. Thus I saw Jill, a twenty-eight-year-old graduate student, who agreed to allow herself to register for her next term at school only *after* she had cut down her handwashing to no more than twice each time she went to the bathroom. And Harry, a forty-two-year-old investment banker, tried several reinforcers that did not help him reduce his obsessive-compulsive putting everything in his office in perfect order before he started to work every day. But when he forced himself to make dates with Joanne, with whom he was madly in love, only *after* he cut his office-ordering time to no more than seven (lucky number!) minutes every day, he was able to keep his compulsive ordering under control.

Use of Penalties. As again with addicts, I have found that if OCD clients will make sure that they enact what they consider (and not what I consider) a stiff penalty every time they fail to cut down their OCD behaviors, they will sometimes—but hardly always!—minimize them. Sid, one of my clients, said that he absolutely could not stop putting reams of toilet paper on every toilet seat that he used when away from home. He insisted that only in that way could he ward off all venereal diseases, including AIDS. When he agreed to burn a hundred-dollar bill (one of REBT's favorite penalties) every time he used more than a few sheets of toilet paper, and when his wife, who was helping monitor him, actually burned a hundred-dollar bill on three dif-ferent occasions, he began to considerably moderate his compulsive use of "protective" toilet paper. As this case shows, the use of truly aversive penal-ties sometimes—but not always!—works.

SELF-HELP SUGGESTIONS

- Suspect that you may have some degree of obsessive-compulsive disorder if you keep constantly ruminating about some past or present happening—particularly a "dreadful" happening, even if you try hard to think about it much less, and if you have great difficulty not obsessing about it.
- Suspect that you may have a harmful compulsion—such as drinking, smoking, overeating, gambling, and child molesting, and particularly one that jeopardizes your health, productivity, and general happiness—and, again, a compulsive behavior that you find it almost impossible to stop, even though you very much want to do so.
- Keep working to stop your obsessive-compulsiveness, and fully realize how self-defeating it is, but never blame *your self*, your *being*, your totality

for indulging in it. Yes, you may well be *responsible* for your destructive OCD, but you are never a worm or a no-goodnik for being responsible. Go over this differentiation many times until you clearly see it.

- Use some of the main methods described in this chapter, possibly including medication, such as Antabuse for compulsive drinking or Anafranil for other forms of OCD. Strongly show yourself several specific harms of your OCD and give yourself some stiff additional penalties— with friends or relatives to monitor you for avoiding them—that make your indulgence far from worth it.
- You will require some unusually high frustration tolerance (HFT) to reduce or stop your OCD behaviors. Work like hell to get it by convincing yourself that you don't have to indulge, that it's not *awful* to resist your compulsiveness, that your life will be much harder if you keep giving in to it, and that you even have a choice of harmless or beneficial compulsions that you can substantiate for the harmful ones that you "must" have.

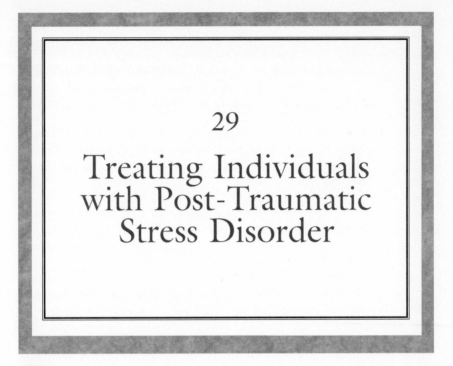

29

Treating Individuals with Post-Traumatic Stress Disorder

Post-traumatic stress disorder (PTSD) is a highly complex and often highly individualized syndrome which, recent theory and research has shown, fits quite well with the theory and practice of Rational Emotive Behavior Therapy (REBT). For REBT, as this chapter will show, particularly stresses the creation of PTSD by its victims' dysfunctional or Irrational *Beliefs* (IBs), by their frequently avoiding and numbing themselves to the severe pain of their traumatic experiences, and by their requiring some form of exposure to overcome their disorder. Many authorities on and researchers of PTSD also stress these factors.

As a number of writers have noted, PTSD can misleadingly be viewed as a relatively simple disorder, but actually had better be seen in a complex systems, constructivist, holistic, and connectionist light (Resick and Schnicke 1992). In an excellent review of PTSD Theory, Williams (1992, p. 362) points out that "schemas both shape and are shaped by . . . traumatic life experiences." This complex evolutionary model provides a basis for systematic assessment of impact of trauma as well as treatment planning. Williams

This chapter is partly adapted from "Post-Traumatic Stress Disorder (PTSD): A Rational-Emotive Behavioral Theory," *Journal of Rational-Emotive and Cognitive-Behavior Therapy* 12 (1994): 3–25. Used with permission.

also agrees with E. Jantsch, who observed that people recreate and shape the outer world according to the self-organizing dynamics of their inner visions and plans. In other words, their beliefs, expectations, and self schema (re)structure how they relate to the world. This systems-oriented view of PTSD is highly consonant with REBT.

The REBT Theory of post-traumatic stress disorder (PTSD) has been presented by Robert Moore (1992) and Warren and Zgourides (1991); and the present chapter is an attempt to expand on this theory and specifically relate it to Rational Emotive Behavior Therapy practice. This theory holds that neurotic conditions—but not necessarily personality disorders and psychotic conditions—are partly instigated or "caused" by people's demandingness, by their raising their strong preferences for success, approval, justice, and comfort to absolutist demands and musts, and consequently upsetting themselves when these demands are not fulfilled.

As Moore and Warren and Zgourides indicate, people who experience unusual and severe traumas—such as rape, incest, serious accidents, war, and torture—do not always suffer from PTSD and have flashbacks, recurrent nightmares, avoidance of thoughts, feelings, and situations associated with the trauma, and persistent symptoms of increased arousal. Often, though hardly always, traumatized individuals are afflicted with PTSD. As would be expected by REBT Theory, and as a number of other investigators have shown, PTSD sufferers often have one or more irrational or dysfunctional *Beliefs* about their experiences. Thus they believe that they *should be* invulnerable to and not overact to traumatic events; that a "just world" *must* exist; that life *has to* be meaningful and comprehensible; and that they *should* act well in practically all situations in order to accept themselves as "good" persons (Foa, Zinberg, and Rothbaum 1992; Resick and Schnicke 1992).

These irrational and self-defeating demands, as REBT theorizes, are often experienced on two levels, primary and secondary. On the primary level a victim of rape may insist that this very unfair act *absolutely should not* have occurred (especially if she were raped during a date with a friend or lover); that she *should have* somehow prevented it; that therefore the world is a *horrible* place; and that she, as one who did not do as she supposedly *should have* done, is an inadequate person. Her dysfunctional thoughts about her being raped, as well as the traumatic incident itself, will combine to make her feel appropriately concerned and fearful as well as inappropriately devastated and self-downing. If, REBT says, she did not insist that bad things like rape absolutely *must* not happen and that she *should* have prevented it, she would indeed still be traumatized and feel very bad about being raped, but she would not tend to feel so devastated and would possibly not create secondary symptoms about her primary ones.

On a secondary level, PTSD victims often create symptom stress, or disturbances about their disturbances, especially when they are very upset about the original Activating experience or Adversity (A), such as rape or incest (Walen, DiGiuseppe, and Dryden 1992). This REBT theory of secondary disturbance or symptom stress, which I described in *Reason and Emotion in Psychotherapy* in 1962, has been noted by other clinicians and researchers to be a common symptom of PTSD victims.

THE CASE OF SYLVIA

Let me give an actual case. Sylvia, a twenty-five-year-old teacher, was sexually molested by one of her drunken uncles when she was thirteen, but managed to escape from his caresses and never be alone with him again. She was wary of males, especially those who drank; and she only dated safe, somewhat passive males, and had sex with them only when she had gone with them for many months. Her appropriate fear of aggressive, alcoholic males worked quite well. But at the age of twenty-two, she sexually put off a steady boyfriend for six months until he made himself very angry at her because she never permitted anything but light petting. Late one night, after such petting, he insisted on having violent intercourse with her against her will, and painfully bruised her while forcing himself on her.

As might be expected, Sylvia was shocked at her boyfriend's brutal attack, refused to speak to him again, stopped all dating, and vowed to be abstinent for the rest of her life. She became enraged when her female friends dated steadily and got engaged, and she broke off with several of them who didn't agree with her that men are beasts. She even raged against her mother when she continued to have enjoyable sex with Sylvia's father.

After thinking obsessively about the details of her date rape for several months after it occurred, and vividly picturing the horror of it, Sylvia found these thoughts too painful to bear. So she pushed them out of her mind, and only thought about them when she was in a hypnogogic state just prior to falling asleep. But she had frequent nightmares and flashbacks, in the course of which her uncle, her last boyfriend, and some of the other men she had put off sexually, were tying her up and forcing her to have painful intercourse. When she woke from these nightmares, she panicked, could not sleep the rest of the night, and was terrified that she would have a similar nightmare the next night. That is exactly what often happened: her horror of having repeated nightmares increased her having them.

After a year and a half of seeing a psychiatrist who used psychoanalytic therapy and put her on several different kinds of antidepressive and antianxiety medications, Sylvia felt just as much post-traumatic shock disorder (PTSD) as ever, was sure that her panic and her nightmares would never go away, and developed suicidal thoughts. She said that she would never, for religious reasons, actually kill herself but she often thought of doing so and was afraid that some day she might.

I listened to Sylvia's story for the first few sessions, empathized with her shocking experiences, tried to show her that her severe reactions to them were expectable and fairly common, and that her PTSD didn't mean—as she often felt it did—that she was "completely crazy" and would one of these days end up in a mental hospital. I showed her that her imagining prolonged hospitalization was "normal" but that few sex victims with PTSD had psychotic breakdowns and were hospitalized.

This kind of educational explanation of PTSD and its consequences is often used in REBT and is also widely used by other cognitive behavior therapists who treat PTSD victims (Foa, Zinberg, and Rothbaum 1992; Resick and Schnicke 1992).

My accepting Sylvia and her panicking as expectable and "normal" reassured her somewhat and enabled her to discuss the REBT theory and practice regarding PTSD. Thus I explained to her the ABCs of REBT. At point A (Activating event or Adversity) she was sexually abused, first by her uncle, then by her last boyfriend. Because these experiences were highly obnoxious, immoral, and unfair As, she told herself at point B (her *Belief* System) self-helping or Rational *Beliefs*, including, "This is shockingly unjust! How unfortunate that I am being subjected to this abuse! I hate what's happened to me and I hope it never occurs again! Let me see what I can do to stay away from males like this and prevent any kind of sexual assault or rape from happening to me in the future!"

These *Beliefs* of Sylvia were rational or healthy because they acknowledged her traumatic history, led to her feeling very concerned about further violations, and encouraged her to stay away from dangerous sex situations. At point C (Consequence) she therefore felt strong (and healthy) shock, fear, vigilance, and determination to protect herself from future violations.

If Sylvia had only had these rational *Beliefs* (RBs) and healthy negative feelings, REBT hypothesizes, she would probably *not* suffer from PTSD and also not suffer from panic *about* her panicking. Those severe symptoms usually stem from dysfunctional or Irrational *Beliefs* (IBs)—which in REBT we look for, and which in Sylvia's case I probed for and actually found her to hold. People's IBs, as I have noted since the 1950s, usually consist of absolutist demands, commands, shoulds, and musts on themselves and others, and on external conditions; and lead to accompanying awfulizing, I-can't-stand-it-itis, damning of themselves and others, and overgeneralizing.

In Sylvia's case she had all three of the major demands that lead to the disturbed reactions of PTSD:

1. "I, Sylvia, *absolutely must* not allow males to sexually molest or rape me, and if I don't stop them, as I *definitely must*, I'm a *weak and inadequate*

person." With this self-defeating demand, Sylvia made herself feel guilty and self-downing about her sex abuse, and to blame herself for "causing" it.

2. "Men, especially those I trust and care for, *absolutely must not* treat me unfairly and force me to have sex that I don't want. If they do, they are completely rotten *individuals* and show that virtually all men are bad and that I *must not* trust or get very involved with any of them!" These musturbatory IBs led Sylvia to panic about sex and love relationships, to avoid them, and anger herself at women, including her mother, who engaged in them.

3. "Unfair and untrustworthy conditions *absolutely must not* exist! It's *completely awful* when they do, and I *can't stand* them. The world's a *rotten place*, and always will be! What's the use of living in such a horrible place?" These Irrational *Beliefs* (IBs) drove Sylvia to make herself depressing and suicidal.

To make matters much worse, Sylvia had dysfunctional *Beliefs about* her self-downing, panicking, avoiding, and depressing—as many PTSD victims do. Thus she told herself that she *absolutely should not* panic and that if she drove herself crazy and ended up in the mental hospital, that would prove that she was a *weak and rotten person*. She also strongly believed that she *couldn't stand* her panicking, that it made her life totally *unbearable*, and that she *must* completely stop it. Her dogmatic secondary demands, as I explained to her, made her primary symptoms much worse. Thus her strong *Belief*, "I *must not* have another single nightmare! I'll die if they continue!" only served to paradoxically enhance panic and produce more nightmares. Many people, like Sylvia, wrongly believe, "If I tell myself, 'I *must not* think of traumatic events!' that will push them out of my mind." Sometimes this temporarily works; but later the thoughts return and consequently they obsess more about them. So Sylvia's *Belief* that she *absolutely must not* have another nightmare made her worry about having one every time she went to bed; and this worry helped her to have recurring nightmares.

I therefore first helped Sylvia change her absolutist demand that she *should not* panic, and that she couldn't stand it if she continued to obsess about the details of her traumatic sex abuse and kept depressing herself about them, I showed her how to question and challenge at point D (Disputing) her dysfunctional *Belief* about her PTSD symptoms and to change them to functional preferences instead of insistent commands. Thus, she started to convince herself, "I hate my nightmares and intrusive thoughts, but I *can* stand having them!"

As Sylvia began to do this, she not only reduced her panicking about her panicking, but, as frequently happens with individuals who lessen their panic about their panic, her original PTSD symptoms of self-deprecating, raging against almost all males, and recurring nightmares somewhat abated.

This is what often happens in the case of agoraphobia and other panic states. When panicking, people horrify themselves about feeling panic and insist, "I *must not* panic! I *must not* feel this terrible panic!" Then they often distinctly panic more. But they can change these demands to preferences, such as, "I don't like my panicking and I will do my best to eliminate it. But it's *only* uncomfortable, not *unbearable*, and I won't die of it. I'm okay and I am not a weakling even if I still severely panic." They then often panic much less.

Sylvia used these kinds of coping statements about her horror of her PTSD symptoms and within a few weeks her secondary symptoms, especially her panicking about having nightmares, were greatly reduced. Shortly after that her primary symptom, the nightmares themselves, became infrequent. As REBT theory hypothesizes, once she stopped terrorizing herself about the nightmares, she stopped bringing on most of them.

On a primary level, however, Sylvia still downed herself for not having been able to stop her sex abusers; still was phobic about all sex-interested men; and still was angry at women, including her mother, who related well to men and had sex with them. She still depressed herself and had suicidal thoughts. I therefore used, over the next year of weekly sessions, a number of REBT's cognitive, emotive, and behavioral methods with her.

Cognitively, I showed her how to actively Dispute (at point D) her Irrational *Beliefs* (IBs) that she *absolutely should* have handled her abusers better, that *all* males often sexually abused women, that women who trust and relate to men are invariably stupid and despicable, and that bad Activating events or Adversities must never even exist, and when they do exist make this world so rotten that she could experience no pleasure and might as well consider killing herself. She gradually challenged these dysfunctional *Beliefs* and changed them into preferences, such as "I handled my uncle and my boyfriend as well as I could. But even if I could have done better, I didn't *have to* do so. When I handle shocking events very imperfectly, that never makes me a weak, stupid person."

The irrational *Belief* that Sylvia had most trouble changing was her deep conviction that men were not to be trusted at all and that women who related to them were despicable. However, after she succeeded in unconditionally accepting herself with her imperfect and sometimes foolish behavior—which was the main theme we continually worked on—she was able to accept other women whom she thought behaved stupidly with men. She even accepted her mother for having sex with her father and for relating well to the uncle who had sexually abused Sylvia. Finally, after more than a year of REBT, she was able to see her alcoholic uncle and her abusing boyfrend as having disturbances and to forgive *them* but not their *deeds*. She was then able to have some dates with men in her church group who seemed to be quite ethical and harmless.

Cognitively, I also used several other REBT methods with Sylvia. Thus, I had her reframe her abusive sex experiences and realize that her boyfriend acted wrongly and immorally but that he may have mistakenly thought that having forceful sex with her would be good for her. I employed modeling, and helped her see that many women, and a few of whom she personally knew, suffered similar traumatic experiences, were shocked for a while but then recovered, and were able to have enjoyable sex and love relationships. I had her record our sessions and listen to each one several times until she saw how strongly she held her musts and how they led to her feeling devastated. I encouraged her to use her REBT teachings with others, to show them how they often needlessly upset themselves and how they could talk to themselves and act against their dysfunctioning.

I showed Sylvia how to use REBT's cost-benefit analysis. When she avoided and hated all men and many women, I had her write down a list of fifteen disadvantages of this kind of avoidant behavior and to reconsider it. When we started using exposure methods, I also encouraged her to list and to make herself conscious of the drawbacks of blocking out her traumatic experiences.

Emotively, I encouraged Sylvia to use several forceful evocative methods that are often included in the REBT armamentarium. Employing Rational Emotive Imagery, she would imagine some of the worst things that might happen to her—such as a man gaining her trust and then proving to be highly untrustworthy—let herself feel angry at herself for being taken in by him, and then work on changing her feeling to the healthy one of disappointment with her gullibility, but not self-deprecating. She also did some of the famous shame-attacking exercises of REBT and deliberately forced herself to disclose her sex traumas and her panicking to some people to whom she was ashamed to reveal her "weaknesses."

Emotively, I used the basic principles of REBT to unconditionally accept Sylvia with her weaknesses, her self-hatred, and her rage at men— including, at first, her anger at me. I showed her, by my manner and tone as well as my words, that I could easily accept *her*, though I was not enthusiastic about some of the things *she did*. In fact, I was determined to help her change her self- and social-defeating behaviors for her own sake and not mainly to please me or other people.

As is the rule, however, in REBT, I not only *gave* Sylvia unconditional other-acceptance (UOA), but I also actively tried to *teach* her how to fully accept herself. As usual, I gave her the choice of two viable solutions for unconditional self-acceptance (USA): (1) She could choose to decide to accept herself *whether or not* she performed well and *whether or not* significant people approved of her simply—yes *simply*—because she was human and alive, *simply* because she was a *person*. (2) She could choose, even more elegantly, not to rate her being, her essence, or her totality *at all*, but only evaluate her *thoughts, feelings*, and *behaviors*. That is, not her *self*, as "good" when she fulfilled her main goals and purposes and as "bad" when she sabotaged them. Sylvia sometimes took the first of these choices of unconditionally accepting herself and sometimes took the second. As noted above, she finally did largely stop condemning herself for her undesirable behaviors; and then she was much better able to give up her raging at others.

Behaviorally, Sylvia was encouraged to use several of REBT's activity-oriented methods. She tried *in vivo* desensitization, and forced herself to do several things she was deathly afraid to do since she was date raped. First she double-dated with some of her woman friends, and then she went on several dates by herself. As she kept seeing that nothing terrible happened on these occasions, she became much less fearful of dating, and shortly before therapy ended she started going steady with one of her churchgoing males and later became engaged to him.

REBT has always favored exposure for panicking individuals and many trauma victims, as do many practitioners of CBT (Resick and Schnicke 1992). So after seeing Sylvia for several weeks I began to suggest that she try to remember all the details of the incidents when her uncle molested her and when her boyfriend raped her. I had her write out these details, make some tape recordings of them, and tell them at times to me and to her best womanfriend. The more she exposed herself to the details of her traumas, the less fearful of thinking about them she became and her nightmares appreciably decreased. She also realized, in recounting the details of the two assaults on her, that she had really not been responsible for either of them and that, out of her guilt about her possible complicity, she actually had imagined herself being more culpable than she had actually been.

Sylvia was also taught assertion training, so she could let her dates know, right from the start, how she felt about having quick sex, and why she was cautious about sex relationships. She became much more assertive in this respect.

I had twenty-five sessions of REBT with Sylvia, spread over a period of a little more than a year, and have seen her briefly several times since then at my regular Friday Night Workshops at the Albert Ellis Institute in New York, which she attends from time to time. Since ending her therapy sessions, she has married her fiancé and is having regular sex relations with him that she enjoys. She rarely has nightmares of any kind, has stopped hating men except those she finds quite aggressive, and is no longer angry when her women friends have intimate relations with males. She is very thankful and enthusiastic about her REBT sessions and has referred a number of other people, especially women who have been abused, to the Institute's psychological clinic.

The REBT theory of PTSD holds that almost all people who experience serious traumas such as rape, physical abuse, terrorism, continued incest, and harrowing war experiences suffer severe stress and shock from these experiences, especially when they are unexpected, unfair, and senseless. They normally view such violent depredations as traumatic and they tend to horrify themselves about them. If they are unusually hardy and toughminded they are shocked for a while, then assure themselves that their traumatic experiences are past and that similar ones will probably not happen again. So they adjust reasonably well, develop rational fear about the future, and only occasionally remember and feel terrified about their past traumas. But when confronted with memories that bring back vivid images of the traumatic events they may again be shocked and may sometimes develop PTSD.

People who are more vulnerable—because of their innate tendencies and social learning—are more likely to keep remembering their traumas and to panic about their reoccurrence. Even though there may be little likelihood of this happening, they keep repanicking themselves by insisting that traumatic events *absolutely must* not happen again, fail to get such a guarantee, and keep upsetting themselves. They sometimes have flashbacks and nightmares, and develop and persist in overprotective, avoidant behavior— e.g., refusing to see violent movies, or refraining (as did Sylvia) from "dangerous" sex and love involvements. These victims are afflicted with a moderate form of PTSD.

People who are still more vulnerable and/or experience unusually painful or prolonged traumas often believe that they cannot bear to remember or in any way think about the traumatic events they were afflicted with, numb themselves to such memories and thoughts, sometimes completely repress them, and then have flashbacks, nightmares, and recurrent fears that some dire events will soon occur again. Such victims of traumas may be, but not necessarily are, more disturbed than PTSD victims who are quite conscious of their traumas, and one of their problems is their repression and their defensive refusal to think about what happened to them. So they had better be helped during therapy to expose themselves to some of the details of their victimization, in order to fully face them and work through the "horror" of remembering them.

Most practitioners of REBT and of cognitive behavior therapy (CBT) recognize that PTSD victims partly create their severe distress by holding dysfunctional or Irrational *Beliefs* (IBs), and that to alleviate their overwhelming fears they had better be treated with cognitive restructuring plus exposure. Almost all these CBT therapists, however, seem to follow a cognitive processing theory of dysfunctional beliefs, for which they offer some degree of empirical support, but which largely ignores the musturbatory philosophies that REBT hypothesizes underlie the kinds of cognitive processing they have emphasized.

Resick and Schnicke (1992) have devised cognitive processing therapy (CPT) in the course of which an information processing formulation of PTSD is presented to sexual assault survivors for twelve weekly group sessions and compared to a comparison sample who wait for group therapy for at least twelve weeks. CPT clients are given ABC sheets as homework, so that they can see the connection between self-statements and emotion. As Resick and Schnicke (1992, p. 751) state, during their third and fourth sessions, "the clients were asked to write an account of the rape. Rather than a dry, factual version, all of the sensory details, emotions, and thoughts they could remember were solicited. They were also encouraged to experience their emotions fully while writing and reading over the account. Beginning with the fifth session, CPT clients were taught to identify and challenge irrational beliefs."

As can be seen, Resick and Schnicke's cognitive processing therapy includes many of the elements of REBT that I describe above in the case of Sylvia. They do remarkably well with this form of CPT, and report that when three- and six-month follow-up studies are done, compared to the control group "CPT subjects improved significantly from pre- to post-treatment on both PTSD and depression measures and maintained their improvement for six months" (Resick and Schnicke 1992, p. 748). They are to be congratulated on devising this effective procedure for treating PTSD victims.

As may be expected, I like Resick and Schnicke's procedure and its results. But in examining the cognitive processing theory that they hold to explain their results, and several other related cognitive-behavioral theories of PTSD that they cite in their paper, I note that they ignore the underlying irrational and dysfunctional musts that REBT hypothesizes. Let me therefore briefly analyze their cognitive processing theory to see if it would be improved by being combined with REBT's theory of absolutist shoulds, oughts, and musts.

REBT constructivist theory holds that underlying the cognitive processing of PTSD victims that Resick and Schnicke point out there are "deeper" cognitive structures, especially absolutist musts: (1) "I *must* perform well!" (2) "Other people *must* treat me fairly!" (3) "Conditions must be favorable for me!" These "deep" core cognitive philosophies, I contend, almost always, overtly or tacitly, lie beneath the distorted beliefs that several proponents of cognitive information processing place at the center of the negative attributions and "automatic" thoughts that are involved in PTSD victims. To explore whether my REBT theory possibly better explains the main points made by information processing theorists who treat PTSD, let me review several suggestions they have made to see if they may be more incisively explained by REBT theory.

Chemtob, Roitblat, Hamada, Carlson, and Twentyman (1988) hold that in PTSD activation of a threat-arousal node potentiates threat expectancy, the belief that a threatening event *will* occur. They propose that in PTSD the threat schema is always at least weakly potentiated. If this is true, as it well may be, REBT theory would suggest that PTSD rape victims often have a strong underlying belief that rape (or other trauma) is *so* bad that it *absolutely must not* occur again, and that it would be *utterly horrible* if it did. This powerful *demand* that trauma *must* never again occur largely *potentiates* the threat of possible future traumas and leads to the antiempirical "automatic" belief that they *will* probably occur.

Absolutist musts are in themselves so unconditional and so overgeneralized—e.g., "Really bad things must *never* under *any* conditions occur!"—that they naturally lead to other antiempirical overgeneralizations—e.g., "Because these really bad things that *must* not occur actually *have* occurred, they will *always*, under *all kinds of conditions*, easily occur again!" As Kevin FitzMaurice, Alfred Korzybski, and others have shown, overgeneralized assumptions commonly lead to further self-defeating thinking.

McCann, Sakheim and Abrahamson (1988) show that five major areas of functioning or themes are affected and disrupted by victimization: safety, trust, power, esteem, and intimacy, each of which are further divided into two loci: schemata related to the self and schemata related to others. This seems accurate, and is subsumed under the REBT theory of emotional disturbance described in the beginning of the present chapter. REBT assumes that PTSD victims often have musturbatory *Beliefs* that insist that they *always* have safety, trust, power, esteem, and intimacy. It therefore uses a number of cognitive, emotive, and behavioral methods, as do Resick and Schnicke, to forcefully and dramatically dispute these imperatives.

Resick and Schnicke, following the lead of Foa, Zinberg, and Rothbaum (1992), use systematic exposure in their cognitive processing therapy "to encourage the expression of affect" and to elicit "all of the emotions and their related beliefs." REBT, as I show above, uses exposure, *in vivo* desensitization, and sometimes implosive desensitization to help phobic and panicked individuals to face and do what they are afraid to face and do. Why? Because exposure not only elicits PTSD victim's emotions and their related beliefs but also may actively contradict their musts. Thus, these victims frequently seem to believe, "Because my trauma was so severe, I *must not* remember and think about it, but *must* numb myself to it and sweep it out of my mind!" And: "Because I panic when I think of my being raped, and because I *must not* experience such a horrible feeling, therefore I *must not* risk any situation, such as dating or having sex, that would lead me to feeling panicked!" When encouraged by their therapists to expose themselves to their feelings about being raped, PTSD rape victims can ameliorate these musts and see that they can deal with the panic (and panic about panic) that they create. So they can more easily deal with their panic than can non-exposed victims.

Resick and Schnicke (1992) are to be congratulated on devising and testing their cognitive processing therapy (CPT) for PTSD symptoms in rape victims. From their report it seems to work well for both panicking and depressing clients. Their and other cognitive-behavior therapists' explanations, in terms of information processing theory, however, appear to be accurate but perhaps superficial. The "causal" dysfunctional attributions, inferences, and ascriptions that they find and treat in PTSD rape victims may well exist; but there is a good possibility that, on a "deeper" cognitive level, they are underlain by, and partly created by, these victims strongly believing absolutist, unconditional shoulds, oughts, and musts that clearly go beyond their realistic preferences. To best help PTSD sufferers, REBT accepts the cognitive processing theories of Resick and Schnicke and other practitioners of CBT. But it also goes beyond them to cognitively, emotively, and behaviorally reveal and Dispute PTSD victims' core musturbatory philosophies.

Self-Help Suggestions

- If you are prone to post-traumatic stress disorder (PTSD) and to panicking on a number of occasions, suspect that you may possibly have a biological and a social learning tendency to make yourself panicky rather than anxietizing when traumatic events occur in your life. If you think you have this tendency, consult reputable mental health professionals, including psychiatrists, to check it out. With their consultation, you may agree to have psychotherapy and perhaps suitable psychotropic medications.
- As this chapter describes, your possible PTSD may well partly result not only from encountering unusual traumatic events, but also by your insistence that they are *so* bad, unexpected, and incomprehensible that they absolutely should not have afflicted you.
- You may also have—as many people with PTSD do—unreasonable demands on yourself: that you definitely should not have allowed the traumatic events to occur and are therefore distinctly to blame for them.
- In addition—as is also frequent in victims of PTSD—you may insist that you *should not* and *must not* be as panicking about your traumas as you actually feel. If you then panic about your panic, you may be almost incapable to reducing it and getting on with your life.
- Your possible self-downing about your panicking and your convincing yourself that it is *too* horrible to bear and to deal with, may considerably exacerbate and prolong it.
- One main reason for PTSD is that people who suffer traumatic shock awfulize so much about it that they sometimes suppress or repress it and, by not facing it and working it through, keep feelings about it going almost forever and likely to break out again. Therefore, if you suffer from it, you can use imaginal exposure, and sometimes risk-taking with some real exposure, to desensitize yourself to your shock. This may help you considerably.
- If you use several REBT cognitive, emotive, and behavioral methods described in this chapter and other chapters of this book, you may help yourself considerably even when you suffer from serious PTSD symptoms.

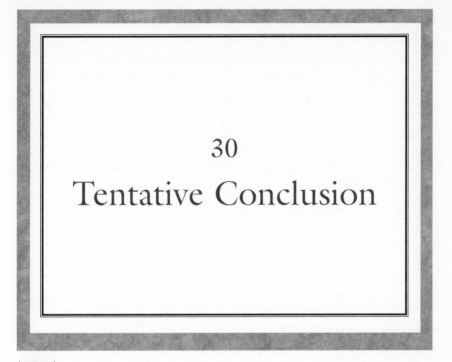

30
Tentative Conclusion

The foregoing chapters bring Rational Emotive Behavior Therapy (REBT) up to date for the twenty-first century. Not forever! REBT and CBT, as noted in chapter 17, are likely to have a busy and productive future. They are already in integrative forms of psychotherapy and will continue to be integrated with other therapeutic systems. Their theories and practices will change and develop just as individuals and their societies keep changing. No kind of therapy is written in stone—and even stone is subject to change! No final word on REBT is likely to be proclaimed and established. At least, let us hope not!

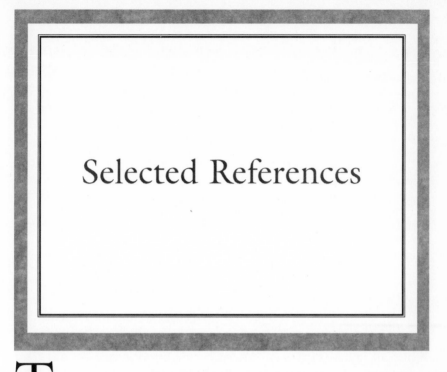

Selected References

The original articles that are adapted for this book included hundreds of references, which would have cluttered up the book if they were completely cited in it. Therefore, only the most important references are cited in the text and only some of the most relevant of these are included in the following list of references.

Alder, A. 1964. *Social Interest: A Challenge to Mankind.* New York: Capricorn.

Alberti, R., and R. Emmons. 1970/1975. *Your Perfect Right.* 7th ed. Atascadero, Calif.: Impact Publishers.

Alford, B. A., and A. D. Beck. 1997. *The Integrative Power of Cognitive Therapy.* New York: Guilford.

American Psychiatric Association. 1987. *Diagnostic and Statistical Manual of Mental Disorders.* 4th ed. Washington, D.C.: American Psychiatric Association.

Araoz, D. L. 1983. *Hypnosis and Sex Therapy.* New York: Brunner/Mazel.

Bandura, A. 1997. *Self-Efficacy: The Exercise of Control.* New York: Freeman.

Bargh, J. A., and T. L. Chartrand. 1999. "The Unbearable Automaticity of Being." *American Psychologist* 54: 462–79.

Barlow, D. H., and N. G. Craske 1994. *Mastery of Your Anxiety and Panic.* Albany, N.Y.: Graywind Publishers.

Baucom, D. H., and N. Epstein 1990. *Cognitive-Behavioral Marital Therapy.* New York: Brunner/Mazel.

403

Beck, A. T. 1967. *Depression.* New York: Hoeber-Harper.

———. 1976. *Cognitive Therapy and the Emotional Disorders.* New York: International Universities Press.

———. 1988. *Love Is Not Enough.* New York: Harper and Row.

Beck, A. T., A. J. Rush, B. F. Shaw, and G. Emery. 1979. *Cognitive Therapy of Depression.* New York: Guilford.

Beck, J. S. 1995. *Cognitive Therapy: Basics and Beyond.* New York: Guilford.

Benjamin, L. S. 1996. *Interpersonal Diagnosis and Treatment of Personality Disorders.* New York: Guilford.

Bernard, M. E., and A. Ellis. 1998. "Albert Ellis at Eighty-Five: Professional Reflections." *Journal of Rational-Emotive and Cognitive-Behavior Therapy* 16: 151–81.

Bernard, M. E., and M. R. Joyce. 1984. *Rational-Emotive Therapy with Children and Adolescents.* New York: Wiley.

Beutler, L. G. 1991. "Have All Won and Must Have Prizes: Revisiting Luborsky et al.'s Verdict." *Journal of Counseling and Clinical Psychology* 59: 226–32.

Bohm, E. 1961. "Jealousy." In A. Ellis and A. Abarbanel, *Encyclopedia of Sexual Behavior*, vol. 1, pp. 567–74. New York: Hawthorn Books.

Bone, H. 1968. "Two Proposed Alternatives to Psychoanalytic Interpreting." In *Use of Interpretation in Treatment*, edited by Ed. E. Hammer, pp. 169–96. New York: Grune and Stratton.

Border, M. 1995a. *Overcoming Your Anger in the Shortest Possible Period of Time.* Cassette recording. New York: Albert Ellis Institute.

———. 1995b. *Overcoming Your Anxiety in the Shortest Possible Period of Time.* Cassette recording. New York: Albert Ellis Institute.

Bourland, D. D., Jr., and P. D. Johnston, eds. 1991. *To Be or Not: An E-Prime Anthology.* San Francisco: International Society for General Semantics.

Burns, D. D. 1999. *Feeling Good: The New Mood Therapy.* New York: Morrow, Williams & Co.

Chentob, C., et al. 1988. "A Cognitive Action Theory of Post-Traumatic Stress Disorder." *Journal of Anxiety Disorders* 2: 253–75.

Clark, D. A. 1997. "Twenty Years of Cognitive Assessment: Current Status and Future Directions." *Journal of Consulting and Clinical Psychology* 65: 996–1000.

Cloninger, C. R., ed. *Personality and Psychopathology.* Washington, D.C.: American Psychiatric Association.

Dryden, W., R. DiGiuseppe, and M. Neenan. 2002. *A Primer on Rational-Emotive Therapy*, rev. ed. Champaign, Ill.: Research Press.

Dryden, W. 1999a. *How to Accept Yourself.* London: Sheldon Press.

———. 1999b. *Rational-Emotive Behavior Therapy: A Training Manual.* New York: Springer.

Dryden, W., J. Walker, and A. Ellis. 1996. *REBT Self-Help Form.* New York: Albert Ellis Institute.

Ellis, A. 1950. "An Introduction to the Scientific Principles of Psychoanalysis." *Genetic Psychology Monographs* 41: 147–212.

———. 1955a. *New Approaches to Psychotherapy Techniques.* Brandon, Vt.: Journal of Clinical Psychology Monograph Supplement.

———. 1955b. "Psychotherapy Techniques for Use with Psychotics." *American Journal of Psychotherapy* 9: 452–76.

———. 1956. "An Operational Reformulation of Some of the Basic Principles of Psychoanalysis." In H. Feigl and M. Scriven, *The Foundation of Science and the Concept of Psychology and Psychoanalysis*, pp. 131–54. Minneapolis: University of Minnesota Press.

———. 1957/1975. *How to Live with a Neurotic: At Home and at Work*. New York: Crown. Hollywood, Calif.: Wilshire Books.

———. 1958. "Rational Psychotherapy." *Journal of General Psychology* 59: 35–49. Reprinted. New York: Albert Ellis Institute.

———. 1958/1965. *Sex Without Guilt*. North Hollywood, Calif.: Wilshire Books.

———. 1962. *Reason and Emotion in Psychotherapy*. Secaucus, N.J.: Citadel.

———. 1963/1979. *The Intelligent Woman's Guide to Dating and Mating*. Secaucus, N.J.: Lyle Stuart.

———. 1972. "Helping People Get Better Rather Than Merely Feel Better." *Rational Living* 7, no. 2: 2–9.

———. 1972/1991. *Psychotherapy and the Value of a Human Being*. New York: Albert Ellis Institute.

———. (Speaker). 1973a. *How to Stubbornly Refuse to Be Ashamed of Anything*. Cassette recording. New York: Albert Ellis Institute.

———. 1973b. *Humanistic Psychotherapy: The Rational-Emotive Approach*. New York: McGraw-Hill.

———. 1975. "The Rational Approach to Sex Therapy." *Counseling Psychologist* 5, no. 1: 14–22.

———. 1976a. "The Biological Basis of Human Irrationality." *Journal of Individual Psychology* 32: 145–68. Reprinted. New York: Albert Ellis Institute.

———. 1976b. *Sex and the Liberated Man*. Secaucus, N.J.: Lyle Stuart.

———. 1979. "Discomfort Anxiety: A New Cognitive Behavioral Construct, Part 1." *Rational Living* 14, no. 2: 3–8.

———. 1980. "Discomfort Anxiety: A New Cognitive Behavioral Construct, Part 2." *Rational Living* 15, no. 1: 25–30.

———. 1985. *Overcoming Resistance: Rational-Emotive Therapy with Difficult Clients*. New York: Springer.

———. 1986. "Anxiety About Anxiety." In *Case Studies in Hypnotherapy*, edited by E. T. Dowd and J. M. Healy, pp. 3–11. New York: Guilford.

———. 1988. *How to Stubbornly Refuse to Make Yourself Miserable about Anything—Yes, Anything!* New York: Kensington Publishers.

———. 1994. *Reason and Emotion in Psychotherapy*. Revised and updated. New York: Kensington Publishers.

———. 1996. *Better, Deeper, and More Enduring Brief Therapy*. New York: Brunner/Mazel.

———. 1997. "The Uniquely Human Science of Treatment Development: Commentary on 'Science and Treatment Development: Lessons from the History Behavior Therapy.' " *Behavior Therapy* 28: 559–61.

———. 1999. *How to Make Yourself Happy and Remarkably Less Disturbable*. Atascadero, Calif.: Impact Publishers.

————. 2000a. "Can Rational Emotive Behavior Therapy be Effectively Used with People Who Have Devout Beliefs in God and Religion?" *Professional Psychology* 31: 29–33.

————. 2000b. *How to Control Your Anxiety Before It Controls You.* New York: Citadel Press.

————. 2000c. "Rational Emotive Imagery: RET Version." In *The RET Source Book for Practitioners,* edited by M. E. Bernard and J. L. Wolfe, pp. II, 8–II, 10. New York: Albert Ellis Institute.

————. 2001. *Feeling Better, Getting Better, Staying Better.* Atascadero, Calif.: Impact Publishers.

————. 2002. *Overcoming Resistance.* 2d ed. New York: Springer.

————. (in press). "Rational and Irrational Aspects of Transference." *Journal of Clinical Psychology.*

Ellis, A., M. Abrams, and L. Dengelegl. 1992. *The Art and Science of Rational Eating.* Fort Lee, N.J.: Barricade Books.

Ellis, A., and I. Becker. 1982. *A Guide to Personal Happiness.* North Hollywood, Calif.: Melvin Powers.

Ellis, A., and M. E. Bernard, eds. 1983. *Rational-Emotive Approaches to Problems of Childhood.* New York: Plenum.

Ellis, A., and S. Blau, eds. 1998. *The Albert Ellis Reader.* New York: Kensington Publishers.

Ellis, A., and T. Crawford. 2000. *Making Intimate Connections: Seven Guidelines for Great Relationships and Better Communication.* Atascadero, Calif.: Impact Publishers.

Ellis, A., and W. Dryden. 1997. *The Practice of Rational Emotive Behavior Therapy.* New York: Springer.

Ellis, A., J. Gordon, M. Neenan, and S. Palmer. 1998. *Stress Counseling.* New York: Springer.

Ellis, A., and J. Gullo. 1972. *Murder and Assassination.* New York: Lyle Stuart.

Ellis, A., and R. A. Harper. 1961. *A Guide to Successful Marriage.* North Hollywood, Calif.: Wilshire Books.

————. 1961/1997. *A Guide to Rational Living.* Rev. ed. North Hollywood, Calif.: Melvin Powers/Wilshire Books.

————. 1975. *A New Guide to Rational Living.* North Hollywood, Calif.: Melvin Powers/Wilshire Books.

Ellis, A., and W. Knaus. 1977. *Overcoming Procrastination.* New York: New American Library.

Ellis, A., and A. Lange. 1994. *How to Keep People From Pushing Your Buttons.* New York: Kensington Publications.

Ellis, A., and C. MacLaren. 1998. *Rational Emotive Behavior Therapy: A Therapist's Guide.* Atascadero, Calif.: Impact Publishers.

Ellis, A., J. L. Sichel, R. J. Yeager, D. J. DiMattia, and R. A. DiGiuseppe. 1989. *Rational-Emotive Couples Therapy.* Needham, Mass.: Allyn & Bacon.

Ellis, A., and R. C. Tafrate. 1997. *How to Control Your Anger Before It Controls You.* New York: Kensington Publishers.

Ellis, A., and E. Velten. 1992. *When AA Doesn't Work for You: Rational Steps for Quitting Alcohol.* Fort Lee, N.J.: Barricade Books.

Ellis, A., and E. Velten. 1998. *Optimal Again: Getting Over Getting Older.* Chicago: Open Court.

Ellis, A., and J. Wilde. 2001. *Casebook of Rational Emotive Behavior Therapy.* Columbus, Ohio: Merrill.

Ellis, A., and R. Yeager. 1989. *Why Some Therapies Don't Work: The Dangers of Transpersonal Psychology.* Amherst, N.Y.: Prometheus Books.

Engels, G. I., N. Garnefski, and R. F. W. Diekstra. 1993. "Efficacy of Rational-Emotive Therapy: A Quantitative Analysis." *Journal of Consulting and Clinical Psychology* 61: 1083–1090.

Faucher, A., and P. Kiely. 1955. "Viellecse: Strategies cognitives et processes de devil." In *Le devil comme processus de guerison,* edited by D. L. Bassett, pp. 42–50. Montreal: Publications MNH.

FitzMaurice, K. E. 1997. *Attitude Is All You Need.* Omaha, Nebr.: Palm Tree Publishers.

———. 2000. *Planet Earth: Insane Asylum for the Universe.* Omaha, Nebr.: Palm Tree Publishers.

Flett, G. L., P. L. Hewitt, K. R. Blankstein, M. Solnik, and M. Van Brunschot. 1996. "Perfectionism, Social Problem-Solving Ability, and Psychological Distress." *Journal of Rational-Emotive and Cognitive-Behavioral Therapy* 14: 245–75.

Foa, E. B., and R. Wilson. 1991. *Stop Obsessing: How to Overcome Your Obsessions and Compulsions.* New York: Bantam.

Foa, E. B., Z. Zinberg, and B. O. Rothbaum. 1992. "Uncontrollability and Unpredictability in Post-Traumatic Stress Disorder: An Animal Model." *Psychological Bulletin* 112: 218–38.

Frank, J. D., and J. B. Frank. 1991. *Persuasion and Healing.* Baltimore, Md.: Johns Hopkins University Press.

Frankl, V. 1959. *Man's Search for Meaning.* New York: Pocket Books.

Freier, P. 1972. *Pedagogy of the Oppressed.* New York: Harder and Harder.

Freud, S. 1965. *Standard Edition of the Complete Works of Sigmund Freud.* New York: Basic Books.

Fried, R. 1999. *Breathe Well, Be Well.* New York: Wiley.

Gergen, K. J. 1995. "Postmodernism as Humanism." *Humanistic Psychologist* 23: 71–82.

Glasser, W. 1965. *Reality Therapy.* New York: Harper & Row.

———. 1998. *Choice Theory.* New York: Harper Collins.

———. 2000. *Reality Therapy in Action.* New York: Harper Collins.

Glass, C. R., and D. B. Arnkoff. 1997. "Questionnaire Methods of Cognitive Self-Statement Assessment." *Journal of Consulting and Clinical Psychology* 65: 921–27.

Golden, W. L., E. T. Dowd, and F. Friedberg. 1987. *Hypnotherapy: A Modern Approach.* New York: Pergamon.

Goldfried, M. R. 1995. *From Cognitive-Behavior to Psychotherapy Integration.* New York: Springer.

Gollwitzer, P. M. 1999. "Implementation Intentions: Strong Effects of Simple Plans." *American Psychologist* 56: 493–503.

Gordon, S. 1980. *The New You.* Lafayette, N.Y.: Ed. U Press.

Greist, J. H. 1993. *Obsessive Compulsive Disorder.* Madison, Wis.: Dean Foundation for Health and Education.

Guidano, V. F. 1991. *The Self in Process*. New York: Guilford.

Guterman, J. T. 1994. "A Social Constructivist Position for Mental Health Counseling." *Journal of Mental Health Counseling* 16: 226–44.

Haas, J. R. 1994. "The Nature of Acceptance." In S. C. Hayes et al., *Acceptance and Change*, pp. 33–35. Reno, Nev.: Context Press.

Hajzler, D. and M. E. Bernard. 1991. "A Review of Rational-Emotive Outcome Studies." *School Psychology Quarterly* 6, no. 1: 27–49.

Hartman, R. S. 1967. *The Measurement of Value*. Carbondale: University of Southern Illinois Press.

Hauck, P. A. 1991. *Overcoming the Rating Game: Beyond Self-Love—Beyond Self-Esteem*. Louisville, Ky.: Westminster/John Knox.

Hayes, S. C. 1994. "Context and the Type of Psychological Acceptance." In S. E. Hayes et al., *Acceptance and Change*, pp. 13–32. Reno, Nev.: Context Press.

Hayes, S. C., N. S. Jacobson, V. M. Follette, and M. J. Dougher. 1994. *Acceptance and Change: Content and Context in Psychotherapy*. Reno, Nev.: Contact Press.

Hayes, S. C., K. Strosahl, and K. G. Wilson. 1999. *Acceptance and Commitment Therapy*. New York: Guilford.

Heidegger, M. 1962. *Being and Time*. New York: Harper & Row.

Held, B. S. 1995. *Back to Reality: A Critique of Postmodern Theory in Psychotherapy*. New York: Norton.

Hoellen, B. 1998. "Hypnoverfahren im Rahmender REBT" (Hypnosis in the REBT Framework). In *Klinische hypnose* (Clinical Hypnosis), edited by J. Laux and H. J. Schubert, pp. 73–80. Pfaffenweiler, Germany: Centaurus-Verlag.

Hollon, S. D., and A. T. Beck. 1994. "Cognitive and Cognitive-Behavioral Therapies." In *Handbook of Psychotherapy and Behavior Change*, edited by A. E. Bergin and S. L. Garfield, pp. 428–66. New York: Wiley.

Horney, K. 1950. *Neurosis and Human Growth*. New York: Norton.

Horvath, A. T. 1999. *Sex, Drugs, Gambling, and Chocolate*. Atascadero, Calif.: Impact Publishers.

Huber, C. H., and L. G. Baruth. 1989. *Rational-Emotive Family Therapy: A Systems Perspective*. New York: Springer.

Ivey, A. E., and D. Goncalves. 1988. "Developmental Therapy." *Journal of Counseling and Development* 66: 406–13.

Ivey, A. E., M. Ivey, and L. Simek-Morgan. 1997. *Counseling and Psychotherapy: A Multicultural Perspective*. Boston: Allyn & Bacon.

Jacobson, E. 1938. *You Must Relax*. New York: McGraw-Hill.

Jacobson, N. S. 1992. "Behavioral Couple Therapy: A New Beginning." *Behavior Therapy* 23: 491–506.

Johnson, W. 1946. *People in Quandaries*. New York: Harper & Row.

Kelly, G. 1955. *The Psychology of Personal Constructs*. New York: Norton.

Klein, M. 1984. *Envy and Gratitude and Other Works*. New York: Free Press.

Kirsch, I. 1999. *How Expectations Shape Experience*. Washington, D.C.: American Psychological Association.

Knaus, W. 1974. *Rational Emotive Education*. New York: Albert Ellis Institute.

Knaus, W. 2000. *Smart Recovery: A Sensible Primer*. 4th ed. Mentor, Ohio: SMART Recovery.

Korzybski, A. 1951. "The Role of Language in Perceptual Processes." In *Perception: An Approach to Personality*, edited by R. R. Blake and G. V. Ramsey, pp. 170–205. New York: Ronald.

Korzybski, A. 1933/1990. *Science and Sanity*. Concord, Calif.: International Society for General Semantics.

Kurtz, P. 1986. *The Transcendental Temptation*. Amherst, N.Y.: Prometheus Books.

Kwee, M. G. T., and A. Ellis. 1997. "Can Multimodal and Rational Emotive Behavior Therapy Be Reconciled?" *Journal of Rational-Emotive and Cognitive-Behavior Therapy* 15, no. 2: 95–132.

Kwee, M., and A. Ellis. 1998. "The Interface Between Rational Emotive Behavior Therapy (REBT) and Zen." *Journal of Rational-Emotive and Cognitive-Behavior Therapy* 16: 5–44.

Langer, E. J., and M. Moldovenu. 2000. "The Construct of Mindfulness." *Journal of Social Issues* 56, no. 1: 1–9.

Lazarus, A. A. 1997. *Brief but Comprehensive Therapy: The Multimodal Way*. New York: Springer.

Lazarus, A. A., C. Lazarus, and A. Fay. 1993. *Don't Believe It for a Minute: Forty Toxic Ideas that Are Driving You Crazy*. San Luis Obispo, Calif.: Impact Publishers.

Leiblum, S. R., and R. C. Rosen, eds. 1998. *Principles and Practice of Sex Therapy*. 3d ed. New York: Guilford.

Lewinsohn, P. 1974. "A Behavioral Approach to Depression." In *The Psychology of Depression: Contemporary Theory and Research*, edited by R. J. Friedman and M. M. Katz, pp. 3–22. Washington, D.C.: Wiley.

Linehan, M. 1992. *Cognitive Behavioral Treatment of Borderline Personality Disorder*. New York: Guilford.

Lyons, L. C., and P. J. Woods. 1991. "The Efficacy of Rational-Emotive Therapy: A Quantitative Review of the Outcome Research. *Clinical Psychology Review* 11: 357–69.

Mahoney, M. J. 1991. *Human Change Processes*. New York: Basic Books.

———. 1974. *Cognition and Behavior Modification*. Cambridge, Mass.: Ballinger.

Marlatt, G. A., and J. R. Gordon, eds. 1989. *Relapse Prevention*. New York: Guilford.

Martin, J., and J. Sugerman. 2000. "Between the Modern and the Postmodern: The Possibility of Self and Progressive Understanding in Psychology." *American Psychologist* 55: 397–406.

Maultsby, M. C., Jr. 1971. "Rational Emotive Imagery." *Rational Living* 6, no. 1: 24–27.

McCann, I. L., and L. H. Pearlman. 1990. *Psychological Trauma and the Adult Survivor*. New York: Brunner/Mazel.

McGovern, T. E., and M. S. Silverman. 1984. "A Review of Outcome Studies of Rational-Emotive Therapy from 1977 to 1982." *Journal of Rational-Emotive and Cognitive-Behavior Therapy* 2, no. 1: 7–18.

McMullin, R. E. 2000. *The New Handbook of Cognitive Therapy*. New York: Norton.

Meichenbaum, D. 1977. *Cognitive-Behavior Modification*. New York: Plenum.

———. 1992. "Evolution of Cognitive Behavior Therapy: Origins, Tenets, and Clinical Examples." In *The Evolution of Psychotherapy: The Second Conference*, J. K. Zeig, pp. 114–28. New York: Brunner/Mazel.

Mills, D. 1993. *Overcoming Self-Esteem*. New York: Albert Ellis Institute.

Moore, R. 1993. "Traumatic Incident Reduction." In *Innovations in Rational-Emotive Therapy*, edited by W. Dryden and L. Hill, pp. 126–59. Newbury Park, Calif.: Sage.

Nielsen, S. L., W. B. Johnson, and A. Ellis. 2001. *Counseling and Psychotherapy with Religious Persons: A Rational Emotive Behavior Approach*. Mahway, N.J.: Erlbaum.

Norcross, J. C., J. W. Santrock, L. F. Campbell, T. P. Smith, R. Sommer, and E. L. Zuckerman. 2000. *Authoritative Guide to Self-Help Resources in Mental*. New York: Guilford.

Palmer, S., and P. Laungani. 1999. *Counseling in a Multicultural Society*. London: Sage Publications.

Peele, S. 1989. *The Meaning of Addiction*. Lexington, Mass.: Lexington Books.

Perls, F. 1969. *Gestalt Therapy Verbatim*. New York: Delta.

Piatelli-Palmarini, M. 1994. *Inevitable Illusions: How Mistakes of Reason Rule Our Minds*. New York: Wiley.

Reiss, S., and R. J. McNally. 1985. "Expectancy Model of Fear." In *Theoretical Issues in Behavior Therapy*, edited by S. Reiss and R. R. Bootzin. New York: Academic Press.

Resick, P. A., and M. F. Schicke. 1992. "Cognitive Processing Therapy for Sexual Assault Victims." *Journal of Consulting and Clinical Psychology* 60: 748–56.

Rigazio-DiGilio, S. A., A. E. Ivey, and D. C. Locke. 1997. "Continuing the Post-Modern Dialogue: Enhancing and Contextualizing Multiple Voices." *Journal of Mental Health Counseling* 19: 233–55.

Rogers, C. R. 1961. *On Becoming a Person*. Boston: Houghton-Mifflin.

Rorty, R. 1991. *Objectivism, Relativism, and Truth*. Cambridge: Cambridge University Press.

Russell, B. 1950. *The Conquest of Happiness*. New York: New American Library.

———. 1965. *The Basic Writings of Bertrand Russell*. New York: Simon & Schuster.

Sampson, E. E. 1989. "The Challenge of Social Change in Psychology. Globalization and Psychology's Theory of the Person." *American Psychologist* 44: 914–21.

Schutz, W. 1967. *Joy*. New York: Grove.

Scoggin, F., J. Bynum, G. Stephens, and S. Calhoun. 1990. "Efficacy of Self-Administered Treatment Programs: Meta-Analytic Review." *Professional Psychology* 21: 42–47.

Seligman, M. E. P. 1991. *Learned Optimism*. New York: Knopf.

Seligman, M. E. P., with K. Revich, L. Jaycox, and Jane Gillham. 1995. *The Optimistic Child*. New York: Houghton Mifflin.

Seligman, M. E. P., and M. Cziksentmihali. 2000. "Positive Psychology: An Introduction." *American Psychologist* 55: 5–14.

Silverman, M. S., M. McCarthy, and T. McGovern. 1992. "A Review of Outcome Studies of Rational-Emotive Therapy from 1982–1989." *Journal of Rational-Emotive and Cognitive-Behavior Therapy* 1, no. 3: 111–86.

Skinner, B. F. 1971. *Beyond Freedom and Dignity*. New York: Knopf.

Smith, M. D. 1994. Humanistic Psychology. In *Encyclopedia of psychology*, edited by R. Corsini, pp. 176–80.

Stanton, H. E. 1989. "Hypnosis and Rational-Emotive Therapy: A De-Stressing Combination." *International Journal of Clinical and Experimental Hypnosis* 37: 95–99.

Steketee, G. S. 1993. *Treatment of Obsessive Compulsive Disorder*. New York: Guilford.

Tate, P. 1997. *Alcohol: How to Give It Up and Be Glad You Did*. 2d ed. Tucson, Ariz.: See Sharp Press.

Thorne, F. C. 1950. *Principles of Personality Counseling*. Brandon, Vt.: Journal of Clinical Psychology Press.

Tillich, P. 1953. *The Courage to Be*. Cambridge: Harvard University Press.

Tosi, D. J., and M. A. Murphy. 1995. *The Effect of Cognitive Experiential Therapy on Selected Psychobiological and Behavioral Disorders*. Columbus, Ohio: Authors.

Vernon, A. 1989. *Thinking, Feeling, Behaving: An Emotional Education Curriculum for Children*. Champaign, Ill.: Research Press.

Vernon, A. 1999. *The Passport Program*. Champaign, Ill.: Research Press.

Walen, S., R. DiGiuseppe, and W. Dryden. 1992. *A Practitioner's Guide to Rational-Emotive Therapy*. New York: Oxford University Press.

Warren, R., and G. D. Zgourides. 1991. *Anxiety Disorders: A Rational-Emotive Approach*. Des Moines, Iowa: Allyn & Bacon.

Watson, J. B. 1919. *Psychology from the Standpoint of a Behaviorist*. Philadelphia: Lippincott.

Williams, M. B. 1992. "A Systems View of Psychological Traumas." *Journal of Contemporary Psychotherapy* 22: 89–105.

Wolfe, J. L. 1992. *What to Do When He Has a Headache*. New York: Hyperion.

———. (Speaker). 1980. *Woman—Assert Yourself*. Cassette recording. New York: Albert Ellis Institute.

Wolfe, J. L., and H. Maimark. 1991. "Psychological Messages and Social Context. Strategies for Increasing RET's Effectiveness with Women." In *Using Rational-Emotive Therapy Effectively*, edited by M. Bernard. New York: Plenum.

Wolpe, J. 1997. "From Psychoanalytic to Behavioral Methods in Anxiety Disorders." In *The Evolution of Psychotherapy: The Third Conference*, edited by J. Zeig, pp. 107–19. New York: Brunner/Mazel.

Wolpe, J. 1990. *The Practice of Behavior Therapy*. 4th ed. Needham Heights, Mass.: Allyn and Bacon.

Yalom, I. D. 1995. *The Theory and Practice of Group Psychotherapy*. New York: Basic Books.

Yankura, J., and W. Dryden. 1990. *Doing RET: Albert Ellis in Action*. New York: Springer.

Yankura, J., and W. Dryden. 1994. *Albert Ellis*. Thousand Oaks, Calif.: Sage.

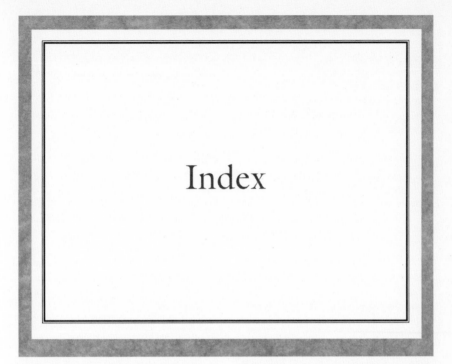

Index

About the Author

Albert Ellis, Ph.D., is the author of more than sixty-five books on psychotherapy, relationship therapy, and self-help books, including *Reason and Emotion in Psychotherapy, A Guide to Rational Living, Rational Emotive Behavior Therapy: A Therapist's Guide, How to Control Your Anxiety Before It Controls You, The Albert Ellis Reader, and How to Make Yourself Happy and Remarkably Less Disturbable.*

Dr. Ellis has been rated by psychologists and counselors in the United States as one of the most influential psychologists (Carl Rogers came first and Sigmund Freud third) and by Canadian psychologists as number one in importance. He has revolutionized psychotherapy since 1955, when he created Rational Emotive Behavior Therapy (REBT), the first of the now popular cognitive behavior therapies.

Dr. Ellis is president of the Albert Ellis Institute in New York City, where he sees a large number of individual and group therapy clients, leads its psychotherapy training program, conducts research activities, and gives numerous talks and workshops every year, including his regular Friday night workshop where he conducts demonstration interviews with people in public. He is also a widely traveled speaker who gives many professional and public workshops throughout the world.